James Connolly
Socialist
Nationalist &
Internationalist

'By situating James Connolly as part of the international workers' movement, McNulty sheds new light on the development of his thought. Far from a narrow nationalist, Connolly emerges as a devoted working-class activist, trade unionist and internationalist socialist grappling seriously with the strategic debates and challenges of his time. This book breaks new ground in assessing his contributions and arming those who seek to continue Connolly's struggle for socialist change today.'
– *Paul Murphy, People Before Profit TD.*

'James Connolly has long been considered an uncomplicated if heroic plaster-saint in the Irish pantheon. That Connolly was an indefatigable tribune for the urban working class is beyond doubt, but Liam McNulty shows that he was much more than that. Connolly was a profound Marxist thinker, perhaps the greatest of his era who came from a genuinely proletarian background, a theorist who grappled with the question of rural class-consciousness, and a transnational activist who absorbed and melded multiple political currents. Connolly was a careful strategist but an audacious activist, always prepared to strike too soon rather than miss the opportunity. McNulty's carefully researched and eloquently written book is a vital contribution to our understanding of this most extraordinary man.'
– *Marc Mulholland, Professor of Modern History at St Catherine's College, Oxford.*

'This book takes Connolly off the statue's plinth and depicts the dynamic Marxist revolutionary class fighter that he was and as importantly explains the location of his politics at the heart of the ebb and flow of the global socialist debates and movements of his time.'
– *John McDonnell MP*

Liam McNulty

James Connolly
Socialist
Nationalist &
Internationalist

MERLIN PRESS

First published in 2022 by
The Merlin Press Ltd
Central Books Building
50 Freshwater Road
Dagenham
RM8 1RX

www.merlinpress.co.uk

ISBN 978-0-85036-783-6

A CIP catalogue record for this book is available at the British Library

Printed in the UK by Imprint Digital, Exeter

Contents

Acknowledgements 7

Abbreviations 8

Introduction 11

Chapter 1: A socialist apprenticeship 21

Chapter 2: The Irish Socialist Republican Party (ISRP) 53

Chapter 3: Connolly and the Second International 97

Chapter 4: Connolly in America 137

Chapter 5: Connolly returns to Ireland 186

Chapter 6: The Dublin Lockout 234

Chapter 7: War and the International 275

Chapter 8: The road to the Easter Rising 301

Conclusion: Between the Second and the Third Internationals? 347

Notes 357

Index 399

For Elen and Carys

Acknowledgements

I have incurred many debts and obligations in the writing of this book. My first thanks goes to Elen for her constant love, support and encouragement. Thanks also to my family, including my parents, my sister Anna and my aunt Geraldine for their support over many years. Particular thanks to my uncle Billy for introducing me to the works of James Connolly in the first place.

I also would like to put on record my thanks to my comrades for creating a critical, creative and collective intellectual tradition which informed the arguments in this book, directly and indirectly. Particular thanks to Sean Matgamna for comments and suggestions on early versions of this draft and continued dialogue on Connolly, Paul Hampton for help with the structure of the book and information on the Second International, Martin Thomas and Cathy Nugent for publishing early articles on Connolly, and Bruce Robinson and Edward McWilliams for valuable discussions on key arguments. Thank you to Ed Maltby for translation of German sources and Jill Mountford for references on Sylvia Pankhurst. I am obliged also to Janine Booth for suggesting I contact Merlin Press about publishing this book.

I wish to give particular thanks to Anthony Zurbrugg at Merlin for being a patient, supportive and attentive editor and for believing in the project in its earliest stages. The book is much improved for all his input. Thanks also to Adrian Howe for his careful copy-editing.

Finally, this book would not have been possible without the labour of library and archive staff in the UK, in Ireland and the vendors of caffeinated drinks in the north London area. Thank you to my former colleagues at the London Library, the staff at the Cambridge University Library and British Library, and to Gerry Kavanagh and the team at the National Library of Ireland.

It should go without saying that all errors in the text are mine alone.

Abbreviations

ASS Adult Suffrage Society
AIU Advocates for Industrial Unionism
AFL American Federation of Labor
ASLEF Associated Society of Locomotive Engineers and Firemen
BPA Belfast Protestant Association
BSP British Socialist Party
CGT *Confédération Générale du Travail* (General Confederation of Labor)
CNT *Confederación Nacional del Trabajo* (National Confederation of Labour)
CPGB Communist Party of Great Britain
CPI Communist Party of Ireland
CPUSA Communist Party USA
CWC Clyde Workers' Committee
DF Democratic Federation
DORA Defence of the Realm Act 1914
DMP Dublin Metropolitan Police
DTC Dublin Trades Council
ELFS East London Federation of Suffragettes
FSI *Federazione Socialista Italiana del Nord America* (Italian Socialist Federation)
GPO General Post Office
ICA Irish Citizen Army
ILP Independent Labour Party
ILP(I) Independent Labour Party of Ireland
INL Irish National League
IOO Independent Orange Order
IPP Irish Parliamentary Party
IRA Irish Republican Army
IRB Irish Republican Brotherhood
ISRP Irish Socialist Republican Party
ISEL Industrial Syndicalist Education League

ISF Irish Socialist Federation
ISR *International Socialist Review*
ITUC Irish Trades Union Congress
ITWGU Irish Transport and General Workers' Union
ITWU Irish Textile Workers' Union
IWFL Irish Women's Franchise League
IWGB Industrial Workers of Great Britain
IWL Irish Worker League
IWW Industrial Workers of the World
IWWU Irish Women Workers' Union
KPD *Kommunistische Partei Deutschlands* (Communist Party of Germany)
LRC Labour Representation Committee
NSFU National Sailors' and Firemen's Union
NUDL National Union of Dock Labourers
NUR National Union of Railwaymen
PLP Parliamentary Labour Party
POF *Parti Ouvrier Français* (French Workers' Party)
RIC Royal Irish Constabulary
RSDLP *Rossiyskaya sotsial-demokraticheskaya rabochaya partiya* (Russian
    Social Democratic and Labour Party)
RWG Revolutionary Workers' Groups
SDF Social Democratic Federation
SDP Social Democratic Party [American]
SLNA Syndicalist League of North America
SLP Socialist Labor Party [American]
SLP Socialist Labour Party
SPA Socialist Party of America
SPD *Sozialdemokratische Partei Deutschlands* (German Social Democratic
    Party)
SPGB Socialist Party of Great Britain
SPI Socialist Party of Ireland
STLA Socialist Trades and Labor Alliance
TOSI Textiles Operatives Society of Ireland
TUC Trades Union Congress
UIL United Ireland League
UILA United Irish League of America
USI *Unione Sindacale Italiana* (Italian Syndicalist Union)
UUC Ulster Unionist Council
UVF Ulster Volunteer Force

WFM Western Federation of Miners
WPSU Women's Social and Political Union
WSF Women's Suffrage Federation

Introduction

Work on this book began in late 2015, as Ireland geared up to commemorate the centenary of the Easter Rising. The book was finished in 2021, as the island marked one hundred years since partition – a tragic eventuality that Connolly correctly predicted would lead to a 'carnival of reaction' on both sides of the border, North and South.[1] The years between beginning and finishing this book have been marked by the United Kingdom's vote to leave the European Union, sparking a constitutional crisis of a scale not seen in Britain since the Third Home Rule crisis 1912-14. The fallout from Brexit, moreover, has significantly destabilised the post-Belfast Agreement peace settlement in the North of Ireland. Amid calls for a 'border poll' for Irish reunification, the socialist and labour movements in Ireland have begun to tentatively discuss the shape of a post-unification Irish state, and Connolly's name and ideas have been to the fore in the debate.

If James Connolly was alive today he would see a more confident, socially liberal society, owing in large part to the brave struggles over many years of the feminist and women's movement for reproductive rights and against the power of the Church. It is also, in many ways, a more cosmopolitan society, with twenty-six counties politically (and increasingly economically) independent from Britain, though enmeshed to an unprecedented degree in the world market and subject to its pressures.

Yet Ireland remains a stubbornly unequal society, with low trade union density and a severe housing crisis.[2] It has consistently had some of the lowest corporate tax rates of any developed economy and its economic model has been plausibly described as a 'tax haven'.[3] Moreover, the prolonged 'lockdowns' of 2020-21, and unprecedented peacetime economic interventions by governments have cast into doubt many old certainties about the 'normal' limits of politics in an era of neoliberalism. If the fiscal weapons of the state can be mobilised in the service of drastic public health measures, what are the implications for citizens' expectations for action in solving the interlinked crises of poverty, inequality and looming ecological collapse?

Suddenly, what would only recently have struck many as the outmoded

optimism of James Connolly, whose whole political life was motivated by
the possibility of a revolutionary socialist alternative to capitalism, looks
both prophetic and contemporary. Connolly's voice, silenced by a British
bullet in 1916, is now heard again, amidst a renewed interest in Irish history
throughout the so-called 'decade of centenaries', and at a time when bold
political alternatives are sorely needed.

So much has been written on James Connolly that it has almost become
a cliché to note how difficult it is to justify adding to the bibliography.
Nevertheless, I do, perhaps out of hubris or a misplaced confidence, think
that the present work contributes something new.

For a long time, due largely to his murder by the British government as
a leader of the 1916 Easter Rising, James Connolly had been subsumed into
the pantheon of Irish nationalist heroes. Such was the myth that developed
around Connolly that he was subject, in the words of an early biographer,
to the 'partisan claims on his corpse' by all manner of mutually hostile and
contradictory political movements.[4] By this process Connolly's socialist
commitment was placed in the shadow, and a bloodless Connolly emerged,
acceptable to nationalists, republicans, Labourites, Catholics alike, or to
anyone else who wished to add a touch of socialistic sparkle to their political
rhetoric. Connolly's thought was safely assimilated into a populist Irish
nationalism or even the social teachings of the Catholic Church. The process
is a familiar one. As the Russian revolutionary Vladimir Lenin wrote of the
treatment of Karl Marx:

> During the lifetime of great revolutionaries, the oppressing classes constantly
> hounded them, received their theories with the most savage malice, the most
> furious hatred, and the most unscrupulous campaigns of lies and slander.
> After their deaths, attempts are made to convert them into harmless icons,
> to canonize them … robbing the revolutionary theory of its substance,
> blunting its revolutionary edge, and vulgarizing it.[5]

Thus, it is by such tendentious claims on Connolly's legacy that we have
the paradox – often commented on – that such a conservative a state as
the Republic of Ireland would name its principal railway station after a
revolutionary Marxist.

This bourgeois appropriation of Connolly was despite the fact that the
latter was, as his contemporary Arthur McManus put it, 'a man whose whole
life was unquestionably devoted very definitely to work in, and on behalf of,
the revolutionary working class movement [and] whose activities had been
so essentially working class, as to have him recognised in many lands as a

great revolutionary leader of working class struggle.'[6] Since the 1960s, with the publication of C. Desmond Greaves's biography of Connolly in 1961 and the 50th anniversary of the Easter Rising in 1966, Connolly's socialism has been more widely recognised. As Peter Graham, a Trotskyist involved in the armed left-republican group Saor Éire recalled, following the half-centenary of the Rising:

> The writings of James Connolly, which prior to then had been read little, and then only by the older 'hands', began to be read more widely. The younger generation found through his writings that he was not quite as the Christian Brothers in school taught – 'only the 7th leader of 1916'. They found in his writings Connolly the revolutionary, the worker, the union organiser and Marxist.[7]

Yet, those coming to Connolly via the route of the Greaves biography experienced him heavily filtered through the 'Marxist-Leninist' ideological requirements of the Communist Party of Great Britain (CPGB) and its front for Irish workers in Britain, the Connolly Association.[8] Moreover, as the 'Troubles' erupted in the North in the late 1960s, Connolly primarily became an artefact in contemporary arguments about the inter-relation between socialism and nationalism. This was a subject which gained obvious importance on the British and Irish left as the Provisional IRA launched its armed campaign in the early 1970s. Nuance and texture suffered, however, as Connolly's legacy became a battleground in polarised arguments on the left in the 1970s and 1980s.[9] Today, in the context of renewed speculation about Irish reunification, political forces in Ireland continue to lay claim to the legacy of James Connolly, with varying degrees of plausibility.

Time enough has passed for a more measured consideration of Connolly, which is nevertheless at the same time alive to his continuing political relevance. This book takes it largely as read that Connolly was, above all, a socialist. In particular, he was a revolutionary Marxist with a lifelong commitment to the cause of the working class. Not only that: since the 1980s, further studies, both scholarly and polemical, have appeared which interrogate in more depth Connolly's relationship to the international socialist movement of his day, the Second International (1889-1914).[10] The existence of the International bounded Connolly's own period of political activity almost exactly, and it is a vital framing for any understanding of Connolly's political activity. The present work also seeks build on these insights and explain his political development with reference to his engagement in the debates, arguments and controversies of that movement.

Next, a word on the methodology and approach of this book. All too often, the history of the Second International has been written in the manner of old-fashioned labour history, as a top-down view focused on formal institutions such as international congresses and prominent theorists or political leaders like Karl Kautsky, Rosa Luxemburg or Eduard Bernstein.[11] Moreover, the emphasis has been on prominent national parties, such as the *Sozialdemokratische Partei Deutschlands* (German Social Democratic Party; SPD).[12] Where a comparative approach has been taken, it nevertheless still assumes national parties as the primary unit of analysis.[13] This is understandable, given that the Second International was 'a loose association of autonomous working-class parties', whose 'arena of action was first and foremost the nation-state'.[14] National political activities, such as parliamentary elections, were to the fore of the International's focus. Nevertheless, much of the International's wider activity can be described as 'transnational' in character, and this book attempts to maintain a 'transnational' perspective on James Connolly and his political activity and thinking. A transnational approach to history is concerned with 'the characteristics, development and effects of ideas, people, social movements, cultures, goods, commodities, systems, structures and institutions which move and extend beyond national boundaries'.[15] While a transnational approach does not deny that nation states are important, it does not assume that all phenomena are necessarily or primarily 'national' in character, or that events, processes or social movements develop within separate walled-off national cultures or states. Applied to labour movement history in particular, one group of historians has defined the approach in the following terms:

> In relativizing and historicizing the nation state, transnational labor history directs attention towards examining workers' movements from a global perspective, stressing the role of transnational processes and interconnections in shaping labor history and the importance of comparative analysis.[16]

The circulation of the socialist press, the translation of key works, the debates within the International, the emigration or exile of working-class activists – all of these activities crossed borders and cut through national lines and cannot be bounded within an understanding of the international socialist movement as purely the sum of separate national parts.

A transnational approach to James Connolly is particularly apposite because it is suggested by the facts of Connolly's life itself. Connolly's world was, increasingly, a global one. Between 1880s, when Connolly entered the socialist movement, and 1914, when he was reaching political maturity, industrial capitalism became increasingly global. Competition between nation states and their empires for new markets and sources of cheap labour intensified. The half-century before the First World War was characterised by

> [the] free mass migration of people, ideas and cultures across the globe technological revolutions in transport and communication (especially the steamship and the telegraph), the spread of industrialisation and urbanisation and the mushrooming of rivalries and conflicts of the 'new imperialism'.[17]

On the basis of this early form of globalisation, working-class activists a century ago were increasingly inter-connected. One writer has usefully coined the concept of 'proletarian globe-hopping' to understand the era of free-trade globalisation and the transnational radical world. This involved 'a multitude of workers, including radicals and labour leaders, searching the globe for work, opportunities, encounters, experiences, lessons and escape from poverty, oppression and persecution'.[18] Connolly, alongside contemporaries such as the syndicalist Tom Mann, was a prime example of a 'proletarian globe-hopper'. Two wonderful maps in Emmet O'Connor's chapter on Larkin and Connolly in the landmark *Atlas of the Irish Revolution* show the extent of Connolly's travels, from Scotland to Ireland and back in the 1880s, to Ireland again in the 1890s, including four cross-Atlantic voyages on the steamboat, and substantial journeys across the United States of America.[19] At each step of the journey, Connolly took political ideas from one political culture, applied them to another, and developed his own thinking through a creative fusion of different political traditions.

The present work draws on this approach and that of more recent accounts, which stress that 'the Second International is best understood as a movement, not a rigid and fixed entity'.[20] Closely related to the 'transnational' approach, a 'new labour history' developed in the 1990s has shifted the emphasis away from a traditional focus on the formal institutions of the labour movement. Instead, it has given attention to the role of migration and exile, and the importance of newspapers, pamphlets and ephemera in the transmission and reception of political ideas, and the everyday experiences and struggles of working-class militants. 'A vibrant socialist press and the international travels and exchanges of militants,' writes one such account, 'nurtured an organic internationalism ... .' Out of these activities arose what Constance Bantman, the historian of cross-channel anarchist networks between France and Britain, has termed an 'informal internationalism'. This notion captures the idea that internationalism in the late nineteenth and early twentieth century was not merely the preserve of the formal Congresses of the Second International or electorally oriented political parties. An internationalist sensibility was spread through more informal contact between activists, in political clubs, through correspondence, by the exchange of political literature, and through the symbolic performance of internationalism through commemorations of key moments of working-class history.[21] Connolly maintained a voluminous cross-Atlantic correspondence with friends and comrades, in which key debates and developments in the international labour and socialist movements were discussed. As for the role of commemoration in creating an internationalist political culture, the Paris Commune of 1871 possessed a unique fascination for late-nineteenth-century socialist activists, and the annual Commune commemoration was a staple event in Connolly's political calendar in Edinburgh and in Dublin.[22]

By approaching the international movement in this way, through a transnational lens and 'from below', it becomes clear that in the era of the Second International some of the fixed boundaries between political tendencies that appear so rigid in retrospect were actually much more in flux at the time. Connolly is a perfect vantage point from which to study, for example, the relationship between 'political' socialists, syndicalists and industrial unionists, straddling the boundaries between them as he did. Beginning life as an orthodox Social-Democrat, Connolly became influenced by Daniel De Leon's Socialist Labor Party (SLP) in the US, with its distinctive blend of electoralism and industrial unionism. From there, he worked with revolutionary industrial unionists and syndicalists, including anarcho-syndicalists, in the Industrial Workers of the World (IWW). Returning to Ireland, Connolly applied his experience in the trans-Atlantic syndicalist milieu with the exigencies of Irish conditions, developing his own particular fusion of industrial unionism, labour representation and working-class republicanism. Connolly, therefore, is viewed in the context of a febrile revolutionary left within the International, some elements of which only later cohered, temporarily, into Bolshevism after the Russian Revolution of 1917 and the foundation of the Communist International in 1919.

This approach to the Second International applies also to its intellectual history. All too often, it is assumed that the key debates at the top – issues of controversy at International Congresses or debates sparked by major theoretical interventions – were mechanically and automatically translated down to the level of the rank-and-file activist, as if by osmosis. There is little need, therefore, to concretely spell out the transmission mechanisms

– be they particular translations, newspaper reports, pamphlets or local discussions. Rather than assume Connolly was necessarily aware of particular contemporary debates and arguments within the International, specific care is taken so far as possible to trace the mediations and connections between the formal institutional or theoretical pronouncements and particular national and local movements on the ground. Often this mediation of international to local took place through reports of international news and debates in national party newspapers. Of crucial importance, too, was the work of translation and popularisation undertaken by socialist printing companies, such as the Charles H. Kerr Company or De Leon's New York Labor News Company. Connolly read the works of both of these publishing companies, and his own pamphlets were published by them in turn. He worked alongside hundreds and thousands of popularisers and agitators, many of whom now sadly forgotten, whose activity was key in creating a socialist world-view within the working class for the first time. Thus, the written word, and especially the pamphlet and socialist newspaper, is granted important status in this book.

All that being said, just as transnational history does not deny but seeks to relativise the nation state, this work does not in the slightest deny the importance of more formal political structures to Connolly's life or the important distinctions between political tendencies. Connolly was, after all, the founder of no fewer than three socialist political parties and the unquestioned leader of another. Moreover, towards the end of his life he was the general secretary of one of the largest trade unions in Ireland, the Irish Transport and General Workers Movement (ITGWU). This book seeks, then, to integrate elements of a more traditional political biography with a transnational account of the international socialist movement in which Connolly operated.

Finally, I believe the best way that Connolly can be understood is to understand him as part of, and in dialogue with, an international and transnational socialist movement. My first engagement with his writings came through the loan (only recently returned) of a hardback copy of *Labour in Irish History* from my uncle, a socialist and trade unionist. After this, I acquired a copy of the second volume of the misleadingly titled *Collected Works,* compiled by the Communist Party of Ireland (CPI) in the 1980s from the earlier volumes edited by Desmond Ryan for the ITGWU in the late 1940s and early 1950s. The coverage of Connolly's literary corpus in the Ryan volumes was deliberately partial, suiting the political requirements of ITGWU general secretary William O'Brien, who had just split the Irish labour movement with support of Fianna Fáil and the Catholic Church.

Connolly's Marxist syndicalism, with its attacks on trade union officials, was downplayed, along with his articles on British workers' solidarity with the Dublin Lock-Out and Connolly's trenchant criticisms of the Church.[23] Thus, from flicking through the *Collected Works* (sic), it became very difficult to form a fixed or coherent understanding of James Connolly, to trace the chronological development of his thought, to distinguish the constant ideas from the fleeting, or to perceive continuities or ruptures in his views. It was obvious, even so, that Connolly was not a speculative philosopher, considering issues from the safe distance of the academy. He was a working-class socialist activist, always in the thick of the struggle. With the exception of some of his more considered historical works, Connolly's writings are mostly short and sharp articles, often interventions directed to particular debates or issues of controversy in the labour movement. He was, arguably then, what Antonio Gramsci, the Italian communist, described as 'a nonsystematic thinker, with a personality in whom theoretical and practical activity are indissolubly intertwined, and with an intellect that is therefore in continuous creation and perpetual movement'.[24] Connolly's articles were only one side of a dialogue with a wider national and international socialist movement. At best, the objects of the dialogue were preserved as a negative image as on film; at worst, they remained obscure and little-known. Either way, our understanding of Connolly without this vital context is stunted.

I have sought, to the best of my abilities, to restore some of this context by attempting to place Connolly consistently in the socialist movement of his times, and to trace the reciprocal influence that each exerts on the other. That has necessitated a foray into the historiographies of various and national labour movements, debates and controversies. I pretend no expertise in all, or indeed any, of them, and I am sure that my efforts will upset and frustrate specialists of all stripes. Nevertheless, it was necessary to make the attempt so as to better form a rounded understanding of this remarkable hero of working-class socialism.

It should also be clear from the above that Connolly's thought developed throughout the course of his political lifetime, in keeping with changes in the world and the socialist movement around him. The key problem is to determine, in each succeeding stage, which elements remained constant, which left only a trace, which were synthesised with newer ideas, and which were completely jettisoned, as Connolly accumulated political experience throughout his life. This book, then, takes the opposite approach to that of one of Connolly's very earliest biographers, the socialist W.P. Ryan. In a sense, wrote Ryan, Connolly's basic ideas were all 'explicit or implicit in the programme and teaching of 1896', and 'there was no evolution in

Connolly's teaching,' only additional 'emphasis, illustration, elucidation, not further discoveries'.[25] While intended as hagiography, conferring on Connolly almost superhuman powers of foresight, Ryan's thesis, in fact, does a disservice to the creativity and ingenuity of Connolly's thought. It is hoped that this book, in tracing Connolly's thought since his earliest days, and the manifold influences which conditioned it, can provide a more dynamic view.

The shape of the book follows a loosely chronological and biographical structure. As the book develops through time, each chapter focuses on particular important themes in Connolly's politics or the international socialist movement and assumes license to depart from the chronology if the argument requires it.

The first chapter outlines Connolly's formation as a socialist in the context of the late-Victorian 'socialist revival' in Great Britain. The British socialist movement of the time was shaped to a remarkable extent by European exiles from events such as the Paris Commune of 1871 and by the political thought of revolutionaries such as Karl Marx and Friedrich Engels. As well as this, it was the era of 'New Unionism', the beginnings of labour representation and of the first attempts to relate Marxism to a mass working-class movement.

The second chapter seeks to explain how Connolly applied the tools of his socialist apprenticeship in Edinburgh to Ireland, with the formation of the ISRP in 1896. In particular, it reconstructs Connolly's early views on the national question against the backdrop of the Second International and the *fin de siècle* neo-romanticism of the Victorian British socialist movement.

The third chapter develops the analysis of Connolly and the ISRP, situating it in global debates over the nature of imperialism at the dawn of the twentieth century and arguments about how socialists should confront the 'land question', i.e. the stubborn persistence of mass peasant populations in the context of the uneven development of industrialisation. It describes the ISRP's attendance at the 1900 Congress of the Second International, and its growing embrace of De Leonism as a dissident transnational tendency in the United States and Britain within the International.

The discussion of De Leonism leads naturally in chapter four to Connolly's time in the United States, where he spent almost a decade in America's multi-ethnic labour movement. It was here that Connolly got a taste of mass trade union work in the industrial unionist IWW, worked alongside exiles from Italy, Ireland and other European countries, published his first widely circulated pamphlet *Socialism Made Easy* for the Charles H. Kerr Company and grew in confidence and stature as an organiser and propagandist.

The fifth chapter relates Connolly's return to Ireland, against the backdrop of the 'Great Unrest' labour militancy of 1910-1914, the rise of the radical women's suffrage movement in Great Britain and Ireland, and the Third Home Rule Crisis. It will be seen how Connolly was involved in and mediated between the radical political movements which grew out of all three of these crises of Edwardian Britain.

The thread of the 'Great Unrest' are picked up again in chapter six, which recounts its highpoint – the Dublin Lock Out of 1913. Transnational themes are again emphasised, from global syndicalism to the transnational transmission of strike tactics from Europe to America and back again.

Both the 'Great Unrest' and the seemingly inevitable civil war in Ireland as a consequence of Unionist opposition to Home Rule were cut short suddenly by the outbreak of the First World War, which is the subject of chapter 7. The impact of the war on Connolly is examined, with particular emphasis on the collapse of the Second International. Connolly is placed in the context of revolutionary anti-war socialists and his involvement in radical networks between Ireland and Britain is explored.

Finally, this account of Connolly and the First World War leads inevitably to the Easter Rising in chapter eight. Connolly's involvement in the Rising is explained, in part, by his incorrigible revolutionism in the face of the seeming collapse of the international socialist movement.

Chapter 1

A socialist apprenticeship

James Connolly, Ireland's foremost socialist revolutionary, was born in poverty in the Edinburgh slum of Cowgate in 1868 to Irish parents from County Monaghan.[26] His father, John Connolly, was a refuse carter for the Edinburgh Corporation and his mother, Mary (née McGinn), a domestic servant. Cowgate was part of Edinburgh's 'Little Ireland' ghetto, home largely to working-class Irish Catholic immigrants, housed in single-room dwellings. The area was described by one contemporary in 1880, as it would have been to a twelve-year-old Connolly, as 'the most densely people and poorest district in the metropolis, the most picturesque and squalid'.[27]

The squalor of Connolly's early life only illuminates the magnitude of his later achievements. His formal schooling at St Patrick's School, mere yards from his birthplace, came to an end in 1879, when Connolly was aged eleven. Too poor to continue into secondary education, the young James entered the workforce as a 'printer's devil' for the *Edinburgh Evening News* to supplement the family income. The job involved cleaning the ink from the print rollers and Connolly would later draw on this early experience of the printing process as the editor, printer and compositor of his very own socialist publications. Dismissed from his job at the paper when a visiting factory inspector noticed he was underage, Connolly worked for two years morning to night in a bakery. Then, his health failing, he found work for a further year in a small mosaic factory before finally deciding to follow his older brother John into the British Army.

Connolly was understandably reticent about his time in the Army and little is really known. More recent biographers have established the basic facts. Under a false name and age, Connolly joined the 1st Battalion of the King's Liverpool Regiment, aged fourteen. The battalion was shipped to Cork on 30 July 1882, and this was the first time Connolly set foot in Ireland. By 1886, Connolly was stationed in Beggars Bush in Dublin. Around this time he met his future wife, Lillie Reynolds, a domestic servant from a Protestant background born in County Wicklow in 1867. James and

Lillie met by chance, when both of them missed the same tram in Dublin in 1886; they would remain together for the rest of Connolly's life. By 1888, the couple had decided to marry. In February of the following year, with only months left to run on his military service, Connolly decided to abscond from the Army. Though the exact reasons are unknown, it seems likely that the battalion was soon to be shipped to Aldershot in preparation for an overseas posting, possibly in India. A decade later, Connolly recalled with distaste the culture of the Army, writing in the *Workers' Republic* that 'the moral atmosphere of a barrack room is of the most revolting character' and the 'Army is a veritable moral cesspool corrupting all within its bounds ...'.[28]

Few would have guessed he was writing from personal experience. Soon afterwards, with his father ill in Edinburgh, Connolly moved back to Scotland, with Lillie to follow afterwards. He arrived in Perth, and soon moved to the more industrialised city of Dundee.

Making socialists

In April 1889, while living in Dundee, James Connolly joined the socialist movement, beginning what would be a lifetime commitment. He was inspired to do so by John Leslie, a veteran socialist nine years Connolly's senior, and from a similar second generation Irish working-class upbringing in Edinburgh. Leslie recalled:

> I noticed the young man as a very interested and constant attendant at the open air meetings. Once when a very sustained and virulent personal attack was being made upon me and when I was almost succumbing to it, Connolly sprung upon the stool and to say the least of it, retrieved the situation. I never forgot it. The following week, he joined our organisation and it is needless to say what an acquisition he was ...[29]

The organisation which Connolly joined was the Socialist League. It had been formed in January 1885 by some of the leading lights of British socialism, William Morris, Eleanor Marx, Edward Aveling and Ernest Belfort Bax, '[advocating] the principles of Revolutionary International Socialism'.[30] By the time Connolly joined, the League was home to a diverse mix of tendencies, including Marxists, Anarchists and Christian Socialists. It is necessary to first provide some background to the socialist movement that Connolly stepped into, so that its formative and lasting influence on the young activist can be understood.

Though British socialism has its roots in earlier traditions, most notably the utopian socialist followers of Robert Owen and the more radical wing of the Chartist movement of the 1830s and 1840s, the roots of what considered itself to be a Marxist movement in Britain can be traced to the formation of the Democratic Federation (DF) in 1881. The DF was founded by Henry Myers Hyndman, a journalist from a well-off Conservative background, who has been described as a 'public moralist' who 'moved freely among the "conventionally educated, comfortably situation, professionally successful, intellectually inclined men" who governed Victorian Britain'.[31] In 1881, Hyndman wrote a manifesto *England For All,* which combined an uncredited summary of Karl Marx's economics with a range of radical liberal or 'municipal socialist' demands such as the eight-hour day and free compulsory education. Overall, it was a moral critique of the upper classes for failing to instigate reform, and one which owed more 'to Mazzini and Mill than to Marx'.[32]

In the prior two decades, writes historian E.P. Thompson, 'no consistent Socialist propaganda – not even of a dozen or twenty members – had existed in Britain'. What did exist were aged survivors of the Owenites and, scattered in London and other major cities, 'refugees from the terror in Russia, from the [Paris] Commune [of 1871], from the persecutions of the Austrian police, and – after 1878 – from Bismarck's Anti-Socialist laws in Germany'.[33] Britain's first modern working-class movement, the Chartists, withered away after the failure to win their wide-ranging democratic demands in 1848. Much of the movement was absorbed into the radical wing of the Liberal Party, but some true followers of the radical republican and socialist ideas of Bronterre O'Brien, George Julian Harney and Ernest Jones survived, providing 'a link between the old Chartism and the new Socialism'. From these varying sources, there was, in the late 1870s,

> a small but active group in contact with the working-class Radical Clubs of East London, which advocated universal manhood suffrage and the fullest democratic rights: republicanism: the nationalization of the land: solidarity with the democratic movements abroad: and which had hazy ideas of Socialist theory, drawn both from Owenite and from European sources.[34]

Hyndman's primary achievement in founding the DF was, as Thompson has written, in 'bringing together in a single organization the various elements, proletarian and middle-class, moving towards Socialism in 1881'.[35] *England for All* would serve as the manifesto of the organisation, and Hyndman distributed copies of the pamphlet at its founding conference. Friedrich Engels, who had a consistently low opinion of Hyndman, described the DF as 'some 20-30 little societies which, under various names (always the same people), have been persistently trying to look important for the past twenty years at least and always with the same lack of success.[36] The DF was comprised, in the main, of 'popular liberals estranged from Gladstone' over his policy of coercion in Ireland and the government's imperialist policy in Egypt, secularists, and the semi-socialist followers of the old Chartist Bronterre O'Brien.[37] Soon, most of the radicals peeled off, as the DF conducted vigorous agitation against the Liberals, and developed in an increasingly socialist direction. Before long, Hyndman gathered around him a band of enthusiastic supporters, including the socialist Eton schoolmaster J.L. Joynes, Henry Hyde Champion (who resigned his military commission over his disgust at the bombardment of Alexandria in 1882), the Austrian exile Andreas Scheu, and veterans of London's radical and socialist clubs, such as the brothers Charles and James Murray. Though many of its initial supports were drawn from educated bourgeois circles, it soon began to recruit talented working-class activists – among them, John Burns, Tom Mann and Harry Quelch – who would become mainstays of the socialist and trade union movement for decades to come.

In 1883, the DF adopted an explicitly socialist manifesto, *Socialism Made Plain,* and the following year renamed itself the Social Democratic Federation (SDF). The SDF has a poor historical reputation, much of it derived from Engels's hostile opinion of Hyndman and his organisation.

Almost as soon as it was founded, the SDF suffered from splits and divisions. In December 1884, several members of the SDF's leading council, including Morris, Eleanor Marx, Aveling, Belfort Bax and Scheu split away to form the Socialist League. The immediate triggers were Hyndman's authoritarian leadership style and his domination of the party newspaper *Justice,* which Hyndman owned personally and thus controlled editorially. However, many in the League, particularly Morris, were more sceptical than the SDF of agitating for 'palliatives' (reform) and standing candidates for election, viewing these activities as distractions from the main work of a socialist organisation: educating the working class in socialist ideas through political propaganda. Upon splitting from the SDF, Morris penned the following manifesto, expressing the view that the task of socialists was to make propaganda to educate the working-class pending some future crisis of the system:

> Our view is that such a body in the present state of things has no function but to educate the people in the principles of socialism, and to organise such as it can get hold of to take their due places, when the crisis shall come which will

force action on us. We believe that to hold out as baits hopes of amelioration of the condition of the workers, to be wrung out of the necessities of the rival factions of our privileged rulers, is delusive and mischievous. For carrying out our aims of education and organisation no overshadowing and indispensable leader is required, but only a band of instructed men, each of whom can learn to fulfil, as occasion requires it, the simple functions of the leader of a party of principle.[38]

The Socialist League put a supreme emphasis on this educational function, criticising the SDF for 'opportunist' attempts to run parliamentary candidates. Many in the League thought themselves vindicated after the SDF's 'Tory Gold' scandal in 1885. Champion arranged finance from the Tories to fund SDF candidates in Hampstead and Kensington against the Liberal Party, with a view to splitting the vote in the 1885 general election. The SDF candidates attracted derisory votes, and the organisation suffered severe reputational damage in working-class and radical circles when the source of the funding was revealed.[39]

Despite these differences, however, both the League and its parent body shared a basic propagandist approach, viewing their goal as 'making socialists' through political education. It was this form of socialist activity that brought many workers, including the young Connolly, into the movement. Through their impressively energetic efforts, from the East End of London to the coalfields of Northumbria and the docklands of Glasgow, the League and the SDF educated a whole generation of workers in basic socialist ideas. As Stephen Yeo has argued, 'the sheer scale of activity needs stressing' to a modern reader. In its intensity, socialist propaganda in the 1880s and 1890s resembled a religious 'crusade', going beyond mere economic concerns towards nothing more than a moral and cultural transformation, at a societal level and in individual ways of living.[40] By selling the *Commonweal* and *Justice* (and, later, the *Clarion*) at demonstrations, by producing pamphlets, organising meetings and conducting literally thousands of speeches on street corners or from soapboxes, bit by bit, socialists brought their ideas to the public and made a discernible impression on political debate. Indeed, the late-Victorian socialist movement created a powerful well of ideas and imagery, still drawn upon by socialists today, including – perhaps questionably – by its more statist, bureaucratic and reformist successors in the modern Labour Party. Thus, while Marx's ideas were largely obscure in his adopted country of England in 1880, a decade later commentators were able to remark that: 'It is felt by every student and every statesman, even by every one who reads the newspapers, that Socialism is "in the air".'[41] Or as a critic put it in 1891, albeit with some grudging respect:

> in 1883 a socialist movement seemed to break out spontaneously in England, the air hummed for a season with a multifarious social agitation, and we soon had a fairly complete equipment of Socialist organisations – social democrat, anarchist, and dilettante – which have ever since kept up a busy movement with newspapers, lectures, debates, speeches and demonstrations in the streets.[42]

At the time when Connolly joined the Socialist League, its newspaper *Commonweal* was advertising 'Meetings every Sunday in the Trades Hall, opposite Tay Bridge Station'.[43] It is through activities such as these Connolly soon learned the rudiments of socialism. His knowledge of the fundamentals was on display in an exchange of letters in the local press in 1891. A letter appeared in the 3 October edition of the *Dundee Weekly News* noting that 'socialism appears to be the paramount idea of a good few of your correspondents'. In the writer's view, however, 'the pure meaning of socialism is so obscure' the correspondent 'would like to ascertain what the Socialists really want'.[44] The letter provoked substantial debate in the pages of the paper, and two weeks later a 23-year-old James Connolly wrote in that:

> The meaning of Socialism is not in the least obscure, and it is only the misrepresentations of our enemies which make it so. Common property in the means of production and distribution – i.e., the land and instruments of labour – is Socialism as accepted by all schools of Socialistic thought. The industries of the country to be held and managed by the workers, and production and distribution of all goods to be arranged to supply the wants of all, instead of, as at present, to make a profit for a few – all classes of labour to be equally rewarded.[45]

The spread of socialist propaganda in Britain did not go unnoticed by the authorities. When Connolly joined the League in Dundee, the socialists in the city were in the midst of a great free speech fight about the right to hold public meetings. Since the mid-1880s, a pattern of harassment and intimidation of socialists by police and magistrates began to form. Several arrests of London SDF members for 'obstruction' were made in 1885, and in 1887 Glasgow members of the Socialist League noted 'the inordinate regard for the public convenience in the way of keeping vacant pieces of ground and spacious street corners free for the passage of hypothetical vehicles, which our presence invariably excites in the mind of the local policeman'.[46]

In Dundee, the growing following for the open-air meetings organised by the SDF in Barrack Park and High Street did not go unnoticed by the authorities either. In March 1889, 'the magistrates issued proclamations forbidding public meetings in certain districts without their sanction. The districts, needless to say, were those where the socialist meetings were customarily held.' In response, the SDF held a rally of 20,000 people in Albert Square, just outside the proscribed area, and marched to High Street where the speakers were promptly arrested. An indignation meeting went ahead in response but was not interfered with. Next, on 1 April, several meetings were held with speakers from Edinburgh and Glasgow including Leslie and Bruce Glasier, the future Fabian but then a prominent member of the Socialist League. The day culminated in a huge protest meeting in Barrack Park. In the face of pressure, the magistrates backed down.[47]

The Scottish Socialist Federation (SSF) and 'New Unionism'

Though the split between the SDF and the League in London was replicated in Scotland, the socialists there managed to establish a greater working relationship. Both organisations did joint work in support of striking miners in Lanarkshire 1887 and increasingly held joint meetings. In December 1888, moves were made to end the divisions in Scotland as a whole, and though there were no immediate results, the Edinburgh groups continued to co-operate closely. This paved the way to the fusion of the Edinburgh branches of the Socialist League and the SDF in October 1889 to form a single propagandist body, the Scottish Socialist Federation (SSF).

Connolly moved to Edinburgh in 1890 to work as a carter for the Edinburgh Corporation, and continued his involvement in the socialist movement as a member of the SSF. Edinburgh, with its large professional middle class, small industrial base, and preponderance of skilled trades, was in many senses an unpromising area for socialist advance. Connolly himself wrote in an early piece of journalism that the population was

largely composed of snobs, flunkeys, mashers, lawyers, students, middle-class pensioners and dividend hunters. Even the working-class portion of the population seemed to have imbibed the snobbish would-be respectable spirit of their 'betters', and look with aversion upon every movement running counter to conventional ideas.[48]

This did not stop the SSF from trying to introduce socialist ideas to the Edinburgh public. Bernard Ransom, in his study of Connolly and the

Scottish socialist movement, describes the SSF routines in late 1889 and early 1890:

> In addition to the Sunday evening public meeting, S.S.F. weekly routine consisted of a French class on Sunday afternoons, an economic study class on Tuesday evenings and a branch business meeting every Friday.[49]

It was becoming clear, towards the end of the 1880s, that the old propagandist mode of organising, effective in producing individual recruits to the cause, was not sufficient to create a mass working-class socialist movement. Thus, one-time national secretary of the Socialist League John Lincoln Mahon complained in 1889 that 'there is no Socialist Party, but only a propaganda'. The SSF's single-minded focus on educational activity would be challenged by two key developments: the rise of 'New Unionism' amongst unskilled workers and, secondly, moves to establish independent 'labour' representation in Parliament.

Before the late 1880s, trade unionism in Britain was largely the preserve of skilled male workers. The Trades Union Congress (TUC) founded in 1868 was dominated, as its name would suggest by *trades* – carpenters, bricklayers, printers, bookbinders, engineers and shoemakers – while 'unskilled' agricultural labourers, transport and gas workers were largely thwarted in their attempts to organise by illiteracy and the casual nature of their employment.[50] All of this would change in the late 1880s, with the onset of 'New Unionism'. As Henry Pelling explains:

> The 'new unionism' appeared to differ from the old both in tactics and in organization. Catering largely for unskilled and poorly paid workers, the new unions tended to have low entrance fees and subscriptions, and depended not on benefits but on aggressive strike tactics to win concessions from their employers. Furthermore, they were willing to recruit workers without distinction of the type of employment, as was indicated by the word 'general' which was often to be found in their titles.[51]

In 1888, an important harbinger of things to come was the strike of the match women at the Bryant and May factory in London's East End. The strike was sparked when the women refused to sign a statement disavowing an article published by the Fabian socialist Annie Besant on 23 June describing the long hours, poverty wages and dangerous working conditions at the factory in Bow. When one alleged ringleader of the refusal to sign the company's statement was sacked, it prompted a walkout of women in the whole factory. Socialists, including Besant, supported the strike, which won all of its demands by 18 July, and saw widespread support from across the movement.

The Bryant and May strike 'was the small spark that ignited the blaze of revolt and the wildfire spread of trade unionism among the unskilled'.[52] In March 1889, a young SDF member, Will Thorne, began to organise a union among his fellow workers in the Beckton Gas Works in East Ham, with assistance from Eleanor Marx. Within four months, he had won a cut in the working day from 12 hours to 8. This stunning victory inspired the dockers, led by Ben Tillet. On 12 August, the dockers struck for an increase to six pence per hour, eight pence for overtime and a minimum employment period of four hours. The mass meetings and processions by the workers made a strong impression on those who thought unskilled workers were incapable of organising. Aided by funds donated by the Australian labour movement, the strike lasted five weeks before the employers conceded the demands for overtime pay and six pence per hour – the 'full round orb of the docker's tanner' as John Burns described it.[53]

'The autumn and winter of 1889-90', writes Pelling, 'saw the spreading of the unionist enthusiasm through the industrial areas of England, Wales, and Scotland.'[54] By the time of the 1890 TUC, the 'New Unions' boasted impressive memberships. Thorne's Gasworkers' and General Labourers' Union claimed 60,000 members, while Tillett's Dock Wharf, Riverside and General Workers' Union had 56,000. Elsewhere, the National Union of Dock Labourers (NUDL), which was founded in Glasgow but had its stronghold in Liverpool, had 50,000 and the National Amalgamated Union of Labour in Tyneside a further 40,000.[55] Gas workers everywhere sought the eight-hour day, casual railway workers were recruited to the General Railway Workers Union and there was a revival in agricultural labourers' unions. Though these were some of the main new unions, 'there was hardly a single occupational group, from laundresses and waiters to post office sorters, which was not brought into the movement'.[56] The impact was immediate:

> Such bodies, claiming to speak for masses of hitherto unorganised workers, were a new and, to some, disturbing phenomenon in the previously staid world of the TUC. The old balance of forces there was disrupted; a challenge to the cautious Lib-Lab leadership was left no longer to a few faithful propagandists who could be treated with a ridicule and tolerance.[57]

What increased the alarm was that many of the leaders of the 'New Unions' were convinced socialists. Thorne, as has been noted, was a member of the SDF. His close association with Eleanor Marx, who sat on the Gasworkers' Executive, brought him into direct contact with Engels. Tom Mann, President of the dockers' union, too, had been an SDF member, though he moved later to the Independent Labour Party (ILP). Other leading 'New Unionists' who joined the latter organisation included James Sexton of NUDL and Tillett himself. Though the 'equivalence of New Unionist activism to socialist or even Independent Labour sympathies was not absolute,' as David Howell has argued, 'it was sufficiently common to lend its own edge to New Unionists' frequent advocacy of the legislative eight hour day'.[58]

Connolly, too, was caught up in the new movement. Following his move to Scotland, Lillie moved to London and the couple made plans to reunite and marry in Perth. At one stage, it looked like Lillie would be delayed in London for a week before making the trip north of the border. A concerned Connolly wrote her:

If we get married next week I shall be unable to go to Dundee as I promised, as my fellow-workmen on the job are preparing for a strike at the end of this month, for a reduction of their hours of labour. As my brother and I are ringleaders in the matter it is necessary we should be on the ground. If we were not we should be looked upon as black-legs, which the Lord forbid.[59]

Echoing the exciting developments in east London, the organisation of semi and unskilled workers made progress in Scotland throughout the 1880s, including on the Leith waterfront. Contrasting Leith to Edinburgh – at the time the former was still a separate municipal burgh – Connolly wrote: 'Leith on the other hand is pre-eminently an industrial centre. The overwhelming majority of its population belong to the disinherited class ... reasonably expected to develop socialistic sentiments much more readily than the Modern Athens.'[60]

In May 1889, dockers in Leith began to organise a branch of NUDL, reaching one thousand members by August. In June, the local branch of the National Amalgamated Sailors and Firemen's union paralysed the waterfront, as seamen and firemen struck for increased pay. June 1889 also saw local gas workers resolve to form a trade union. A strike on the Leith waterfront also provided the dramatic backdrop to what is probably Connolly's first known piece of fiction writing, 'The Agitator's Wife', a short story which he wrote in 1894. The story, which was published in a short-lived Christian socialist journal, was long believed to be a play and was only discovered in 2018.[61]

In late 1889, the Edinburgh socialists discussed 'the blessings and otherwise of trades unionism, and the wisdom of directing our energies more in the way of unionism'.[62] Though socialism is today associated closely with the labour movement, this was not so obvious in 1889. Though many of the 'New Unionists' were members of socialist organisations such as the SDF, the socialist groups as a whole did not have a coherent strategy to intervene in the new movement. Worse, the SDF leadership was diffident, even hostile. Tom Mann later recalled that while 'Hyndman's ability to state the case [for socialisms] comprehensively, logically, and argumentatively … was of very great value indeed', he was convinced the SDF leader's 'bourgeois mentality made it impossible for him to estimate the worth of industrial organisation correctly. For many years he attached no importance whatever to the trade-union movement, and his influence told disastrously on others.'[63] Thus, the SDF paper *Justice,* commented remarkably that the dock strike was 'a lowering of the flag, a departure from active propaganda, and a waste of energy'.[64]

This position was not just a personal quirk of Hyndman's, however, but reflected the deterministic form of Marxism that was prevalent in Britain the 1880s. Only a fraction of Marx's writings were available in English but one text, *Wage-Labour and Capital* (1849), had a wide impact. In 1886, J. L. Joynes published the first English translation of the pamphlet. As one historian has noted, 'the importance of this work of the first generation of British marxists can hardly be over-estimated; it was the main source-book of marxist political economy' and its 'directness and brevity made it comprehensible to the average working class SDF member'.[65] *Wage Labour and Capital,* however, was one of Marx's earliest works on political economy. It was 'still partly based on a faulty theory of wages, taken wholesale from' classical political economist David Ricardo which implied 'a tendency for wages to decline towards the physiological living wage and stay there'.[66] Thus, it depicted a model of capitalist development in which 'the more productive capital grows, the more it extends the division of labour and the application of machinery; the more the division of labour and the application of machinery extend, the more does competition extend among the workers, the more do their wages shrink together'.[67] Nowhere is attention paid to the possibility of trade union action in increasing wages. This was for partly understandable reasons given its time, when trade unions were the preserve of a very small proportion of the skilled male working class. Nevertheless, an uncritical absorption of early works such as *Wage Labour and Capital* tended to stamp on British Marxism a rather didactic, sectarian and deterministic character. These ideas co-existed with non-Marxist socialist ideas too, which further downplayed the importance of trade unions in the eyes of socialists. The SDF held to a variant of the 'Iron Law of Wages', an idea popular in the pre-Marxist German socialism influenced by Ferdinand Lassalle. This held that all increases in wages will be cancelled out by an increase in prices; trade union action to increase wages is, therefore, pointless. The idea can also be found in Joynes's highly popular 1885 work *The Socialist Catechism*, and despite being savaged by Marx decades before, it was still present in writings by leading SDF theoreticians Ernest Belfort Bax and Harry Quelch in the early twentieth century.

Engels, however, saw much more potential in the new movement. Writing to the old German socialist, Adolph Sorge, in New Jersey, Engels reported in December 1889:

Here in England one can see that it is impossible simply to drill a theory in an abstract dogmatic way into a great nation, even if one has the best of theories …The movement has now got going at last and I believe for good. But it is not directly Socialist, and those English who have understood our theory best remain outside it: Hyndman because he is incurably jealous and intriguing, Bax because he is only a bookworm. Formally the movement is at the moment a trade union movement, but utterly different from that of the old trade unions, the skilled labourers, the aristocracy of labour.[68]

A group of socialists gathered around Engels, including Eleanor Marx, advocated and practiced a more active orientation towards the new movement. As Engels explained to Sorge:

The people are throwing themselves into the job in quite a different way, are leading far more colossal masses into the fight, are shaking society much more deeply, are putting forward much more far-reaching demands: eight-hour day, general federation of all organisations, complete solidarity. Thanks to Tussy [Eleanor Marx] women's branches have been formed for the first time – in the Gas Workers and General Labourers' Union. Moreover, the people only regard their immediate demands themselves as provisional, although they themselves do not know as yet what final aim they are working for. But this dim idea is strongly enough rooted to make them choose only openly declared Socialists as their leaders. Like everyone else they will have to learn by their own experiences and the consequences of their own mistakes. But as, unlike the old trade unions, they greet every suggestion of an identity of interest between capital and labour with scorn and ridicule this will not take very long.[69]

These debates were also happening in Scotland. 'Perhaps the cardinal concern of the S.S.F. membership in the years 1889-90,' writes Ransom, 'was definition of its attitude to the emergent "new unionism".'[70] Some, influenced by Morris and the Socialist League, saw it as a distraction from socialist propaganda work. The only strike worth having, they argued, was a political general strike to overthrow capitalism and inaugurate the new society. At a meeting in Leith in November 1890 on the Eight Hours issue, the SSF speaker, Frederick Hamilton, referred to 'all the efforts of Trade Unionists [tending] to court defeat and disaster for their Unions …'. In his pessimistic opinion, any possibilities created by union organisation would be negated by the employment of scab labour.[71]

Others in the SSF, however, threw themselves in to the new labour movement. On 4 May 1890, the Federation sponsored the only 'Labour Day' demonstration to be held in Scotland, with SSF speakers sharing a platform with Ayrshire miners' leader James Keir Hardie and supporting his call for the eight-hour day. The Federation also threw itself in to a strike of workers at the *Scottish Leader* newspaper, supporting the union's call for a boycott. When it came to supporting a widespread strike on the Scottish railways in January and February 1891, the emphasis was very much still on abstract revolutionary propaganda. Counterposed to the workers' own action, the SSF issued a 'Manifesto to Scotch Railway Workers' which advocated 'a UNION among ALL workers' to match the class unity of the employers: 'One general strike would be sufficient … [and] … bring the holders of capital … to their senses, and to their knees at the same time.' Nevertheless, one participant in the socialist movement of this time remembers that the agitation around the rail strike brought members of the Trades Council into a closer relationship with local socialist activists: '*Then* they stood on and spoke from the same platforms; *then* the Trades Councillors heard more Socialism preached in an hour than they possibly had heard in all their life before.'[72]

As the early 1890s progressed, the successes of the 'new unions' were, Pelling writes, 'soon followed by defeats, and much of the ground that they took in the first flush of their progress was lost within a year or two'.[73] Those that survived, such as Tillett's Dockers, became more exclusive bodies, dropping their 'general' aspirations. By 1896, Tillett's union had shrunk to 10,000, while Thorne's Gasworkers had fallen below 30,000. 'Such declines reflected the operation of the trade cycle to a consideration extent.

The unions had recruited well in conditions of labour scarcity, but then contracted as the depression bit.'[74]

In Edinburgh, many of the new unions similarly succumbed to the trade depression in the early 1890s. This included Connolly's brother John's union, the Associated Carters' Society of Scotland, which collapsed. Around this time, many unskilled workers, labouring for long hours with low pay, subject to seasonal unemployment and the whims of the trade cycle, began to look for alternative means of bettering their situation. If trade union action was unable to offer the hope of a better life in the present, then the endless routine of abstract socialist propaganda held out only the prospect of change in the indeterminate future. Many workers looked towards political action to improve their condition – especially the demand for the eight-hour working day.

Labour representation

The idea of independent labour representation had been in the air for some time; Scotland in particular was precocious in this regard. From the mid-1880s, miners in the west of Scotland began to agitate for reforms including mine nationalisation and the eight-hour day. Keir Hardie initially looked towards the Liberals for support but, under the influence of socialist miners' official Robert Smillie, was won to the view that independent working-class representation in parliament was what was needed. A turning point came for Hardie in 1887, when a miners' strike in Lanarkshire was broken by the police. Then, in June, a vote on the eight-hour day for miners was lost in the House of Commons when Liberal-Labour MPs refused to speak in favour of it. Hardie drew the conclusion that Smillie was correct and stood as an Independent Labour candidate in the Mid-Lanark by-election of April 1888. Though his vote of 617 was disappointing, Hardie 'attempted to convert the coalition that had supported him into a more durable organisation', resulting in the formation of the Scottish Labour Party that same year.[75] Hardie and two other Independent Labour candidates were elected in the 1892 general election, and the ILP itself was founded in Bradford in January 1893.

The 1892 general election was also something of a watershed in Edinburgh. SSF members played a leading role in the moves of the Trades Council to return a labour candidate for the Edinburgh Central seat. This paved the way for the creation of a branch of the Scottish ILP in Edinburgh in November 1892, anticipating the formation of the national ILP by two months. The founding meeting was held in the Trades Hall. Connolly, by now aged 24 but growing in stature in the movement, took the chair and 'after insisting upon the necessity for an ILP, called George Carson, Organiser, Glasgow, to address the meeting'. Carson recalled the growing success of the Scottish Labour Party in the west of Scotland and 'urged those present to form themselves into a branch of the party without delay'.[76] John Leslie moved the motion to found the new branch, and was elected secretary. He was joined on its executive by several other SSF members, including John Connolly. From February 1893, the leading ILP committee would meet in James Connolly's house, on 6 Lothian Street, in Edinburgh's Old Town.[77]

As Ransom has pointed out, the Edinburgh ILP was peculiar in the extent to which it relied on the Marxists of the Federation for both its leadership and its activist base.[78] This was a function of the relative weakness of trade unionism in Scotland, which generated an appetite for working-class political representation but without the trade union resources to sustain the resulting party organisation.[79] Elsewhere, the politics of the ILP was not so clear-cut, mixing Radical Liberal and Christian Socialist themes; many Marxists viewed it with a combination of hostility and disdain. The situation in Glasgow was more typical, where the 'SDF activists were vehement and unrestrained in their attacks upon non-marxist labour organisations'.[80] This was a view shared also by the SDF leadership in London, not least by Hyndman and Harry Quelch, who in *Justice* dismissed the idea that 'the S.D.F. should give up political work altogether in favour of a nebulous Independent Labour Party'.[81]

It should not be supposed that Connolly's adherence to the ILP was evidence of a waning commitment to Marxism. As one biographer argues, Connolly 'was already emphasising the centrality of a Marxist understanding, but equally, he was committed to the search for a broadly-based mobilisation for immediate objectives'.[82] Rather, Connolly's position was much more a rejection of the sectarianism of the SDF than the loss of any revolutionary perspective.

For similar reasons, Engels also welcomed the formation of the ILP, finding in it a potential route to a mass socialist movement, freed from the sectarianism of the SDF and the Fabians. Writing to Sorge in January 1893, Engels noted that the SDF and the Fabians 'have not been able, with their sectarian attitudes, to absorb the mass pressure for socialism in the provinces'. The 'pressure has now become so great, especially in the industrial districts of the north,' he reported, 'that the new Party came out already at this first Congress stronger than the S.D.F. or the Fabians, if not stronger than both put together'.[83] In March, he updated Sorge that the ILP 'so far is the most genuine expression of the present movement'. It has 'all sorts of funny people among the leaders', Engels wrote, optimistically predicting that 'the masses are behind them and will either teach them manners or throw them overboard'.[84]

The new ideas propagated by the SSF comrades, of socialist politics and independent labour representation, began to have an effect on the local labour movement. In April 1891, the skilled trades represented on the Edinburgh Trades Council received an invitation from the SSF to participate in agitation for the eight-hour day. A record in the local press states that 'a communication from the city Socialistic body, urging the Council to hold a demonstration on 3rd May, in favour of an eight hour day, was read and received with laughter'.[85] By 1893, however, the Trades Council itself organised a joint May Day demonstration for the eight-hour day, with the involvement of the ILP and the SSF. The socialist presence on the Demonstration Committee secured the following internationalist resolution at the demonstration: 'That this meeting of the working classes of Edinburgh – in common with their brethren throughout the world – views with alarm the increasing congestion of the labour market of the world.' According to the local *Leith Burghs Pilot* newspaper, 'Mr. John Leslie, labourer' was chairman, and 'Mr. James Connolly, unskilled labourer, seconded the resolution ...'.[86]

Unfortunately, as a result of speaking from the platform on the demonstration, Connolly's brother John was dismissed from his job in a case of victimisation. Despite protests from the ILP and the Trades Council, it was clear by July that John was not going to be reinstated and would have to seek work elsewhere. In his place, Connolly became the SSF secretary, and soon afterwards was elected to the position of secretary of the Edinburgh Central division of the ILP. In the summer of 1893, John Leslie warned that the rapidly growth of the ILP, with its very loose political programme, would become a magnet for 'place hunters' and 'glib politicians'. He proposed moves to improve the 'unity and discipline' of the party but resigned when his position was defeated.[87] Connolly was elected to replace him, taking up yet another administrative position, as the Secretary of the Edinburgh ILP District Council, a city-wide body with authority to co-ordinate the work of the local branches. It was in this role that Connolly proved adept as a party manager and drafted the manifesto for the municipal elections in November 1893. It called for:

[the] municipalisation of the liquor trade, taxation of unlet houses, erection of special low rent workmen's dwellings, abolition of the contract system in public utilities in favour of direct employment of labour by the corporation,

municipalisation of the domestic fuel trade, a mandatory eight-hour day with pension rights for all municipal employees, institution of evening meetings of the Town Council, and 'unbending opposition to every effort to spend public monies in honouring royal or aristocratic idlers'.[88]

By the autumn of 1893, then, Connolly combined the roles of secretary to the SSF, the ILP District Council and the ILP Central Division Branch. His 'prime contribution to the movement at this time was still an administrative one', but this would soon change. On 1 September, Connolly gave his first public lecture at the Moulders Hall for the ILP. It was an uneventful debut, as attendance was poor and the meeting dispersed after a 'brief address' and some questions.[89] In February 1894, however, Connolly began his career as a socialist propagandist in earnest. At a public ILP meeting held in the Temperance Hall in High Street, the advertised lecturer, Leo Melliet, did not appear. Connolly saved the day, stepping in to deliver a speech in favour of a key plank of the local ILP's municipal policy, the taxation of empty properties. In mid-April, a campaign of open-air propaganda was decided upon, and Connolly, growing in both confidence and ability, was prominent on the roster of speakers. He delivered the initial public address to 'a good and appreciative audience' on 17 April and spoke again on 1 May, alongside fellow joint ILP-SSF member Frederick Hamilton. A week later, Connolly gave a solo performance, speaking 'for more than an hour to a very attentive audience'. In June, one ILP speaker was prevented from delivering his address by continued heckling, and Connolly stepped in once again and was more than a match for the heckler. Connolly, too, was 'subjected to the same interruption, but after a few exchanges between our comrade and the Liberal, the latter became quiet'.[90]

The following month, Connolly, a local division secretary, had cause to cross swords with the Keir Hardie, who had by this point been an MP for two years. Connolly wrote to Hardie for help in finding a suitable candidate for the Edinburgh Central constituency. Hardie recommended Councillor Beevor, president of the Halifax Trades Council, and Beevor was well-received at a public meeting in Edinburgh on 14 May. When Beevor's candidacy fell through, William Small, a miners' agent from Blantyre, was approached to stand in. Nevertheless, in a sign of his growing confidence and stature, Connolly complained that Hardie had announced the candidacy in advance in his *Labour Leader* newspaper. Presenting the Edinburgh workers with a fait accompli, Connolly reproved, smacked of the 'cliquism of the Liberal caucus', and he suggested a more democratic process in which the ILP should act in conjunction with the Trades Council in promoting the return of a good Socialist and Independent Labour candidate, who must be the free choice of a large number of the electors who can be induced to sign a requisition asking him to stand before we even announce him as our adopted candidate.[91]

Throughout the summer months, the open-air meetings continued, and Connolly carried the burden of public speaking. His prestige in the ILP was at its highest, and in July he was elected president of the branch. But suddenly, on 7 August, it was minuted that 'James Connolly gave in his resignation as a member of the I.L.P. and also as secretary of the Central Division Parliamentary Election Committee, because of the non-attendance of members at meetings, and especially the slowness and laxity in getting the Requisition Sheets filled up'.[92]

Clearly, Connolly expected his own commitment to the cause to be replicated by others, and was frustrated by the organisational laxity of the ILP and the low benchmark it had for membership activity. Yet there were also deeper reasons. The Edinburgh Marxists were propping up the local ILP, providing much of its leadership and administrative support and almost all of its public speakers. By April 1894, the SSF was even the local ILP's landlord, providing it with rented meeting space. This came at a cost to the SSF's own functioning. As happened elsewhere with the ILP, the demands of electoral activity and the goal 'making socialists', though formally complementary, came into tension in practice.[93] In Edinburgh, the bias of the ILP's activity towards parliamentary and municipal elections undoubtedly detracted energy from the SSF's main goal of promoting socialist propaganda. As Yeo has argued, this tension only deepened after the ILP's poor showing in the 1895 general elections. Before this, 'during the mass conversion, "making socialists", religion-of-socialism phase', it was less clear what impact electoral activity would have on propaganda work. Many predicted that greater education of the public in socialist ideas would translate seamlessly into electoral victories. As it soon became clear that this was not the case, the ILP in particular drew the conclusion that sustained electoral challenges required money, pushing them into a relationship first with sympathetic business patrons and then towards a 'Labour Alliance' with the trade unions, combined with tactical electoral pacts with the Liberals. This, of course, had a moderating impact on its politics: 'the exigencies of electoral politics in a recalcitrant climate led to a large and cautious machine being constructed, careful not to offend for fear of losing the stake it was painfully acquiring in machine politics.'[94]

Greater rapprochement between the SSF and the wider SDF was a trend which only accelerated the drive away from more broad-based efforts to promote labour representation. Connolly's brother John began sending reports of Edinburgh SSF activity to the SDF newspaper *Justice* in February 1893; Connolly continued these upon taking over as secretary in July. Glasgow SDF stalwart William Nairn went so far as to openly suggest a fusion on 15 July, writing that 'our comrades of the S.S.F. ... are all Social Democrats, I understand ... I think the relationship between our Edinburgh comrades and S.D.F. men should be somewhat closer than a mere exchange of speakers can give'.[95] The following summer, a Conference of Scottish Socialists was held in Dundee, bringing together the SSF and several branches of the SDF to discuss joint activity. Melliet was elected to the Chair, and Connolly was present as part of the Edinburgh delegation. A fund was established to pay an organiser for the purposes of strengthening existing branches and setting up new ones. A proposal was also heard for the establishment of joint SSF/SDF rambling clubs to promote socialism in agricultural areas, and it was agreed to organise women's ancillary groups and to convene a further conference, to take place in March 1895 in Edinburgh.[96]

During the summer of 1894, the SSF also stepped up its propaganda operation in Edinburgh, adding a new regular propaganda meeting in the suburb of Stockbridge to its existing sites on the Meadows and in Leith. The new meeting was opened by Katherine St John Conway, a founder of the ILP and the only woman elected to its National Administrative Council in 1893. The SSF also extended its reach with a meeting in Loanhead on 11 August, bringing the organisation's ideas to the miners of the Lothian coalfield for the first time.[97] Connolly himself addressed 'a large audience of miners' at Loanhead, taking part in a 'spirited debate ... fought out with coolness, skill, and great humour' between the SSF and Bernard Donoghue, described by the *Clarion* as a 'leading Irish Nationalist'. The paper reported that Donoghue 'conceded the wisdom and justice of the Socialist demands, and the debate turned on "Independent Political Action" v. "Liberal Labour Alliance"' and fifteen people enrolled in the SSF.[98]

This debate, whether Irish-background workers should back independent working-class representation or support the Liberal Party is one that we shall return to shortly. First, a word on another key element of the socialist movement Connolly had immersed himself in: internationalism.

Internationalism

As an active member of the SSF, Connolly was not merely a member of a local, or even national, organisation. The SSF considered itself to be part of the international army of socialism, which sought to put into practice Karl Marx's famous imperative, 'Workers of the world, unite!'

Socialism in Britain, from its very inception, was influenced and enriched by international events and by activists from beyond its shores, many arriving as political exiles seeking asylum from repression on the European continent. A sense of the cosmopolitan interests and internationalist character of the socialist movement in the 1880s and 1890s is provided by Jim Connell, the author of the socialist anthem 'The Red Flag', another socialist Irishman, and a contemporary of Connolly's. Asked many years later about his 'inspiration', Connell noted that the song was first published in the Christmas number of *Justice* in 1889, the year of the London Dock Strike when 'H. H. Champion, Tom Mann and John Burns aroused the whole of England by the work they did and the victory they won'. Yet, for Connell, this upsurge of local class struggle was only one part of the picture, and a relatively minor one at that. 'Much occurred, however, before that to elevate me,' he wrote:

> Not many years previously the Irish Land League aroused the Democracy of all countries ... About the same time the Russian Nihilists, the parents of the Bolsheviks, won the applause of all lovers of liberty and admirers of heroism ... It was my privilege to know Stepniak, himself one of the greatest of the Terrorists ... There happened also, in 1887, the hanging of the Chicago anarchists ... The widow of one of them, Mrs. Parsons ... made a lecturing tour in this country soon afterwards [and] I heard her tell a large audience that when she contemplated the service rendered to humanity she was glad her husband died as she did ... The reader may now understand how the souls of all true Socialists were elevated, and how I got into the mood which enabled me to write 'The Red Flag'.[99]

As Connell's testimony suggests, a sense of internationalism was inspired by speaking tours, providing activists in the British Isles with direct contact with socialist and anarchist activists from overseas. Not that socialists from outside Britain were merely 'external factors'; political exiles played a central role in sustaining British socialism between the defeat of Chartism in the late 1840s to its renaissance in the 1880s. Exiled activists were instrumental in maintaining journals, promoting advanced causes and organising radical clubs, several of which formed the basis for the Democratic Federation and, therefore, the SDF.

London was, unsurprisingly, a centre for socialist and anarchist exiles.[100] Scotland, too, had its share of political exiles and the Scottish socialist movement drew widely on international speakers to inspire its own ranks and bolster interest in its message. In Glasgow, Bruce Glasier of the Socialist League, who later became a leader of the ILP, recalls his mother 'becoming accustomed to entertaining Socialist agitators whom her son invited home with him, often without forewarning her of his intention'.[101] He gives the examples of Prince Kropotkin and Stepniak, both anarchist exiles from Russia who were based in Britain, as well as Danish-born socialist Lawrence Gronlund and the progressive American political economist Henry George, whose ideas found a wide reception in Britain.

Two more guests who sat around Mrs Bruce Glasier's kitchen table were Andreas Scheu and Léo Melliet, key figures in the leadership of the Edinburgh SSF who made a vital contribution to the socialist movement in Connolly's day. It was, in part, due to their 'cosmopolitan leadership' that the Edinburgh socialist movement avoided the 'catechistic narrowness' which typified British socialism elsewhere, 'despite its preponderant presbyterian membership and identical didactic Marxist ideology'.[102]

Scheu was a veteran of the Austrian socialist movement and had escaped from persecution in Vienna in 1874. 'A tall, impressive man with a black beard,' Scheu was a founder of the SDF and, with Morris, a leader of the Socialist League.[103] He was described by one contemporary as an 'able and zealous open-air orator' and a 'personality who impressed himself upon all who came in contact with him chiefly through his vigorous utterance and the obvious sincerity of all he said.'[104] As we have seen, Scheu's influence attempted to steer the SSF, with some success, towards a less sectarian position regarding the ILP.

Another mainstay of the SSF and an early influence on Connolly was Léo Melliet. Melliet was a veteran of the Paris Commune, the revolutionary workers' government that took power in Paris in the wake of France's defeat to Prussia in the Franco-Prussian War. A comrade described him as 'squat in stature, with the typical suave and polite manner of the Frenchman'. Melliet 'would begin his speech … much quieter than our friend Scheu, but by and by he was almost certain to work himself up to a very considerable heat and, fresh from the gory experiences of the Commune, he would emphatically insist … that without the shedding of blood, there could be no salvation.'[105] As one of the leaders of the revolutionary Committee of Public Safety which ran Paris between late March and May 1871, Melliet was a prominent target for the bloody wave of repression which was visited upon the city by the French Army after the fall of the Commune. After fleeing Paris, Melliet was sentenced to death in absentia by a hastily assembled Court Martial in Versailles.[106] He arrived first in Brussels and then to Scotland, taking up a post as a French professor at the University of Edinburgh until 1895, and throwing himself into the socialist movement. He would eventually return to France following his election as a deputy to the National Assembly in 1898, representing Lot-et-Garonne.[107]

Unsurprisingly, Melliet was a regular speaker at Paris Commune commemoration meetings in Britain. He was principal speaker at an SDF commemoration meeting, held in Salford Town Hall in March 1894. Connolly himself attended the 1895 Paris Commune commemoration in Edinburgh and would have heard Melliet speak. An excerpt from Melliet's Salford speech perhaps gives us a rough idea of what Connolly would have heard the following year:

> The Commune was the first affirmation in fact of the desire and the will of the people to choose their leaders among themselves and not among the class who had led them till now. It was a revolution itself not to apply to the rulers of the day in order to obtain reforms from them … Those who lost their lives in the service of the Commune had suffered, but they had conquered. If their life could not be a victory their death was a victory … In France at present there were only two systems, the capitalistic which was the system of the present and the past, and the socialistic system, which was that of the future.[108]

For socialist militants of this period, in the words of the French historian Georges Haupt, the Commune 'became an idea, a profession of faith, and a confirmation of a historical future, of the inevitable victory of the proletarian revolution'.[109] Paris Commune commemorations were a performance of working-class internationalism, connecting participants symbolically with the wider socialist movement and its place in history. Importantly, the young socialist movement 'no longer needed to feed solely on the memory of the revolutions of 1789 and 1848'. It now had 'a revolution in working-class garb'.[110] Connolly celebrated it in exactly these terms in 1899, writing that 'the Commune, if it had been successful, would have inaugurated the reign of real freedom the world over – it would have meant the emancipation of the working class… Long live the Commune!'[111] It was for this reason that Paris Commune meetings would become a regular fixture on the calendar of Connolly's Irish Socialist Republic Party (ISRP).

This internationalism took a more fixed institutional form with the formation of the Second International in July 1889, just three months after Connolly himself first joined the socialist movement. On Bastille Day, 14 July 1889, the centenary of the great French Revolution, 391 delegate representatives and many more observers from twenty-four countries gathered in Paris. Their task was to found an international socialist movement, the Socialist International.

The International is commonly referred to as the Second International, as it followed on from the International Working Men's Association, or 'First International' – Marx's attempt in 1864 to unite radicals across national boundaries. The First International brought together an eclectic mix of socialists, anarchists, trade unionists, and various other radicals, including Irish and Italian republicans. It 'had ceased to be an effective or coherent body at its Congress at The Hague in 1872', when a major breach took place between the followers of Karl Marx and the adherents of the Russian anarchist Mikhail Bakunin.[112] It also suffered from state repression in the wake of the Paris Commune. Though the International, formally, had little to do with the Commune, it provided the French government with a useful enemy – a shadowy network of dangerous revolutionaries – and thus 'on the eve of its extinction, the International was endowed with a legendary power it had lacked in its lifetime, and acquired a largely spurious tradition of heroic international revolutionary action'.[113]

From the mid-1870s, workers in Europe increasingly formed their own political parties. This was a consequence of expanded public education, suffrage rights and popular conscription in this decade, which 'sped up the "nationalization" and "politicization" of Europe's rural and urban populations'.[114] The German SPD was formed in 1875 and it soon became the largest socialist party in the world, after the repressive Anti-Socialist Laws of 1878 were allowed to lapse in 1890. In 1877, the Workingmen's Party in the United States, which was founded a year earlier by mostly foreign-born exiles, met at Newark, New Jersey and changed its name to the Socialistic Labor Party (SLP). The *Parti Ouvrier Français* (French Workers' Party: POF) followed in 1882-3. Russian exiles formed the Emancipation of Labour Group in Switzerland in 1883, which had links to the revolutionary underground in the Russian Empire, where political repression made it impossible to organise openly. Parties in Belgium (1885) and Austria and Sweden (1889) followed.

This growth in socialist political organisation prompted more calls for international links to be formally reconstituted, leading to two separate international conferences in Paris in July 1889. One conference, organised by the French 'Possibilists' and supported by British trade unions, met in the rue de Lancry, while the Marxists met in the Salle Petrelle. Present from Britain were William Morris and Eleanor Marx, representing the Socialist League. (Hyndman, despite his Marxism, attended the 'Possibilist' conference). It was the Marxist conference, 'genuinely and widely representative of organized Socialist parties from all over Europe as well as from the USA' which became recognised as the founding conference of the new International.[115] Its most important achievement was its very fact of meeting, as the French socialist Édouard Vaillant said at its opening plenary. 'A Second International had come into being; the isolation of the 1870s had been broken and the smaller Socialist parties felt that they had the support of a more powerful international movement behind them.'[116]

The first recorded mention of Connolly's views on international questions comes from July 1893, when the SSF and the ILP discussed the forthcoming Congress of the Second International, to be held in Zurich. Haldane Smith was elected as a delegate, and was given a free mandate except on one point: 'That our delegate to the International Workers Congress vote against any such proposal to allow Anarchists as such to take part in its deliberations.'[117] The image of the bomb-throwing anarchist captured the imagination of *fin de siècle* Europe. The Russian Tsar, Alexander II, was blown up by members of the underground revolutionary organisation Narodnaya Volya in 1881, and anarchists would kill several other heads of state in the 1890s and early 1900s, including the Presidents of France and the United States and the King of Italy. In France, there were 11 bomb explosions in Paris between 1892 and 1894 and 'the French Socialist parties were quick to see how embarrassing to them this sort of anarchism could be'. After an anarchist set off a bomb in the French Chamber of Deputies, Marxist leader Jules Guesde – who had recently been elected to the Chamber himself – condemned it as 'the act of a lunatic'.[118] Anarchists were largely excluded from the parties of the Second International, and thus 'many of those who had quarrelled with their own parties or been expelled for anarchist leanings inevitably tried to gain a hearing at international Socialist congresses and to find there the support they lacked at home'. This had been an issue at the 1891 Brussels Congress. Connolly, as SSF secretary, gave a clear line against the anarchists in his 'Scottish Notes' for *Justice,* and wrote:

> that at a time when the class-conscious workers of the world are dressing their ranks for the coming grapple with the forces of privilege it would be scarcely less than idiotic, were they to admit to their councils men whose whole philosophy of life is but an exaggerated form of that Individualism we are in revolt against.[119]

'A disturber of the political peace'

The success and energy of its propaganda activities throughout the summer of 1894 generated enthusiasm in the SSF to run a candidate of its own in the elections to the Edinburgh Corporation in November that year. There was one obvious choice: James Connolly was nominated to run for the SSF in the St. Giles ward and his candidacy was announced publicly on 22 October. Connolly was to be an explicitly socialist candidate, not merely a 'labour' one. John Leslie was quick to point out the error when the local press mistakenly reported that Connolly represented the ILP; he stood, rather, 'as an avowed Social Democrat, and was run by the Edinburgh Branch of the Scottish Socialist Federation'.[120] A report the *Clarion* described how, without the aid of canvassers, the socialists 'having merely laid their Socialistic views before the electors, will register their position on the poll the progress made by the masses in Edinburgh towards a realisation of the meaning of Social Democracy'.[121]

The contest in St. Giles ward was a four-cornered fight. The Liberal candidate, defending a seemingly unassailable majority, was a merchant and future Director of the Bank of Scotland, Mitchell Mitchell-Thomson. Connolly threw his hat in the ring, as did an Independent candidate, James Gardiner, a successful farmer who described himself as 'a Catholic and an Irishman'. The Liberals dismissed the socialists as 'a few noisy fanatics', while Gardiner denounced Connolly airily as 'a young man who, without any business experience, sought to enter the Council in order to ventilate extravagant ideas repugnant to all right-thinking citizens'. Then, a surprise Unionist candidate entered the fray, Duncan McLaren, an ironmonger.[122] Connolly, writing under the pseudonym 'R. Ascal' in his 'Plain Talk' column in the *Labour Chronicle,* asked: 'Why did the Tories not oppose Mr. Mitchell before Mr. Connolly entered into the field?' Answering his own question: 'Because they knew Mr. Mitchell was as great a Tory as any one they could bring forward.'[123] In other words, the Unionist candidate was a spoiler, designed to strengthen Mitchell 'by an appearance of Tory opposition'.[124]

It seems likely, however, that the Unionists were emboldened by the prospect of the Liberal vote splitting three ways. In reply, Connolly (or, rather, 'R. Ascal'), wrote that 'the Liberals and Tories are not two parties but rather two sections of the one party – the party of property'. Against them, Connolly based his manifesto on the earlier ILP municipal programme he had drafted a year earlier. Before an audience of 200 at the Free Tron Hall on 22 October, Connolly explained that 'as Social Democrats they had no sympathy with the cant about non-political candidates'. He made a speech emphasising housing issues, and 'denounced one-roomed houses, advocated the taxation of unlet property, and the acquisition of more open spaces'.[125]

On 24 October, the nomination for the St. Giles ward was held in the same venue. The *Edinburgh Evening News* reported that, before it started, 'a number of "Socialists" had evidently got together, and passed the time singing of the "Red Flag of Liberty" and the "Social Revolution"'. Nominations were given for the four candidates, with McLaren receiving a 'mixed reception' and Gardiner 'loud applause' but several interruptions 'and returned to his seat amid ironical laughter.' When Connolly rose to speak he 'got a loud cheer on stepping forward'. He was there, Connolly said, as 'the nominee of an organisation largely recruited from the working classes [and] was standing as a Social Democrat. (Cheers and hisses).' Connolly added: 'Unlike the other Councillors, he himself, his wife, and children would benefit from every social reform that took place. If the working classes wanted properly represented, they should send one of their own class to the Council.'[126]

This last remark provoked an editorial rebuke from the *Edinburgh Evening News* the next day. Reporting on the nomination meeting, the editor wrote, without concealing his class hatred, that:

Mr Connolly stated pretty plainly that the working classes could not be properly represented except by one of their own number. Against this doctrine we must raise a protest. While we admit that it may be advantageous to have a sprinkling of representatives from the working classes in Council or Parliament, it is absurd to suppose that a man must have an unwashed face and corduroy clothes in order to have common sense and humane feelings towards the labouring class ... It is to be hoped that the electors of St Giles at the proper time will stamp out the spurious doctrine of equality, which places on one level the ignorant and educated.[127]

The following day, the paper stepped up its attacks on Connolly, accusing him of attempting to 'pack' the nomination meeting by encouraging his supporters to attend 'and by voice and vote ensure the Socialist candidate a full and fair hearing'.[128] To this churlish complaint, Daniel Currie of the SSF replied:

You seem to object to the Socialists rallying round their comrade, and you call it unfair. It would be unfair if they didn't. You say that such rallying is a direct attempt to bias the electors in Mr Connolly's favour. Is not every election address, every election meeting, every unfair or hostile newspaper report a direct attempt to bias the electors either one way or the other?[129]

The newspaper's complaint was, of course, absurd, and accusations that the contest was biased towards Connolly ring hollow in light of the facts. Connolly was forced to address the electorate where he could, given that unsympathetic proprietors largely denied access to local halls.[130] On 26 October, he addressed an audience of 60 in an open-air meeting in Chambers Street, and later 'spoke to the electorate at street corners on … Jeffrey Street (Canongate), the Grassmarket, Guthrie Street and on Hunter Square.[131] At one point, Connolly even made use of the rally of a rival candidate. When Colonel Forbes Mackay, one of the candidates for the George Square ward, held a meeting in Messrs Miller & Richards type foundry, he received a note stating that Connolly, who was in the audience, wished to address the meeting. The Colonel replied that it was his meeting and he had asked the employer for leave to address the men, 'but he was willing to allow Mr Connolly five minutes'. The press reported:

> Mr Connolly then addressed the audience, observing that it did not lie with Mr Mackay to limit him to time, nor with the employer to say who the men were to hear, to which the Colonel replied, 'Here is a grateful man'. Mr Connolly monopolised nearly the whole of the time, and in concluding Colonel Mackay said he did not know what the electors of George Square had to do with St Giles. Mr Connolly replied that many of the electors though they worked in George Square voted in St Giles.[132]

The editor of the *Edinburgh Evening News,* continuing his criticisms of the Socialist candidate, accused him of 'a burglarious raid on the valuable time of the Unionist candidate for George Square', adding that 'before Mr Connolly enters public life he should take private lessons in etiquette and politeness'.[133]

Another barrier to success for the SSF was, according to Greaves, 'the peculiar stumbling block that many of its supports were not on the voters' roll'. This was because the 'publication of a new electoral list was the signal for every debt-collector's tout to make a beeline for the slums' and thus the 'most precious preferred to sacrifice their rights as householders and as citizens for the sake of a room and a chair'.[134]

The final barrier was the attitude of the Irish nationalists. The Home Rule question was a vexed one in Scottish politics and the source of much danger to attempts to establish Independent Labour and socialist politics. The Irish population in Scotland, predominantly employed in coal and iron, was concentrated in the industrial areas of the West – Lanarkshire, Renfrewshire, Glasgow – but with substantial communities too in Edinburgh and Dundee. Indeed, in a letter to Lillie in 1889, Connolly himself claimed that 'Dundee has, as proportion to its population a stronger Irish population than any other town in Great Britain' and that you can 'hear at once all the twangs of every district in Scotland and the brogue of every county in Ireland' in its street.[135]

Politically, the Irish National League (INL), founded in Ireland in 1882 by Charles Stewart Parnell, exercised great influence over the Irish population in Scotland. The INL's advice was to vote Liberal until Ireland had been granted Home Rule. Keir Hardie and other pioneers of Independent Labour representation found themselves accused of splitting the Liberal vote and letting the Unionists in. During Hardie's 1888 Mid-Lanark contest, one Irish journal was typical: 'We cannot afford much as we would like to serve the interests of the workmen ... We want to settle Home Rule first.'[136] This became all the more pressing after the 1892 general election. Within a year of being elected, Gladstone introduced a Second Home Rule Bill. It passed in the House of Commons only to be rejected in the Lords but Irish hopes remained high and the INL was motivated to demonstrate its strength at the polls at every opportunity.

The appearance in the Edinburgh municipal elections, therefore, of both an Irish Catholic-background Socialist candidate and an Independent posed somewhat of a problem for the Irish nationalists. The W. E. Gladstone branch of the INL held a meeting at the Moulders Hall on 28 October and declared that though Gardiner and 'Mr Connolly might deny it if they liked ... they were serving the Unionist interest by their candidature; their action would assist in the return of a Tory more than anything else'.[137]

Behind the scenes, the Irish nationalists resorted to more underhand tactics. In the *Labour Chronicle*, 'R. Ascal' reported that among Irish voters, Connolly had been vilified as 'a Freethinker, who wanted to overthrow the church', while the Tories denounced him as an 'Irish Papist who wanted to introduce the Scarlet Woman'.[138] Connolly, according to Greaves, responded by appealing to Irish workers to reject 'the crew of hucksters who have seized the National League'.[139] He appealed to Irish workers to identify with the interests of the working class as a whole, and break from cross-class Irish nationalist politics and support for the Liberal government. 'Perhaps,' Connolly wrote of the Irish electorate in Edinburgh, 'they will learn how foolish it is to denounce tyranny in Ireland, and then vote for tyrants and the instruments of tyrants at their own door.'[140]

In the end, Connolly came third. The Liberal candidate was elected with 1055, while McLaren the Unionist received 497, Connolly 263 and Gardiner, last, just 54.[141] In the *Labour Chronicle*, 'R. Ascal' provided a comprehensive report of the elections. The final outcome, he wrote, was that 'all the old gang are returned to office, and the municipal life of Edinburgh in the ensuing year will be marked by the same scrupulous regard to economy (in wages) and efficiency (in jobbery) to which we have been so well accustomed in the past'.

Though 'the Social Democrats were defeated', however, Connolly saw reason for optimism. Not only could the SSF be proud of its conduct in the campaign, as against 'all the mean and unscrupulous arts of the wirepullers' in the opposing camps, but 'last year the vote polled in George Square Ward for the I.L.P. candidate was only one-thirteenth of the total poll, whereas in St Giles, the vote for the avowed Social Democrat reached one-seventh of the total poll. A great advance, truly.'

A letter to the *Edinburgh Evening News* concurred. 'Radical Collectivist', wrote in to ask 'if the working class electors who voted for Mr Connolly have no reason to be proud of the significant success of their candidates'. He continued:

> Here is a man practically unknown to the electorate; no influential names appear in his election address; no person of authority or influence graces his platform, and minus the glamour of the great historic names of Liberal or Tory; having no experience of Town Council or other similar work, which his principal opponent could lay claim to; and yet he actually polls one-sixth of the voters of the successful man! ... Add to the fact that the whole of the Edinburgh newspaper press was directed against him, and you will, I am sure, admit it as a splendid moral victory for the cause of Independent Labour and Socialism.[142]

The Socialist result would have been even higher, Connolly argued, 'had there been no Unionist, and had the advanced working-class voters been left free to choose be-tween the revolutionary Social-Democrat and the orthodox Liberal and defender of the rights of property...' As it was, he continued,

> hundreds of men, who would otherwise have voted Socialist, cast their votes reluctantly for Mr Mitchell as the candidate most likely to ensure the defeat of the Tory. They will now have twelve months in which to meditate on the difference between the Liberal Tweedledee and the Tory Tweedledum ...

During his election, Connolly had been at pains to stress he was a Socialist candidate, not merely an Independent Labour one. In his closing rally at the Free Tron Hall on 5 November, Connolly addressed the audience and 'hoped they would not vote for the working man alone, but for the Social Democrat as well'.[143] In the *Labour Chronicle,* Connolly further set out the justification for running as a socialist propaganda candidate. It did not mean

> the immediate realisation of even the programme of palliatives commonly set before the electors ... For some time to come the work of Socialists on all such bodies will not be so much to pass new laws as to infuse into their administration the spirit of the new life, to use all power to inaugurate the reign of justice, to convert our industrial system from a machine for making profit into an instrument for sustaining life, to transform our politics from the government of men into the wise and well-ordered administration of things ...
>
> Therefore, [Connolly continued] the election of a Socialist to any public body at present, is only valuable in so far as it is the return of a disturber of the political peace.

This did not merely mean exposing the wrongdoings of the capitalist parties but, more constructively:

> by constantly placing our doctrines and our efforts upon the same platform as the class interests of the workers, to create such a public feeling in our favour as shall enable us to bridge the gulf between the old order and the new, and lead the people from the dark Egypt of our industrial anarchy, into the Promised Land of industrial freedom.[144]

Finally, it was during his November 1894 municipal contest that Connolly was faced with the complications of the 'Irish Question' for the first time. Before this, Ireland barely figured in Connolly's political imagination. This was despite his own background as an Irish Catholic, him having spent most of his teenage years in Ireland while in the service of the British Army, and the national political controversy surrounding Gladstone's Second Home Rule Bill in 1893.

In April 1895, the system of Poor Law Guardians was replaced by Parish Councils elected on a new democratic franchise, and Connolly took the opportunity to run for a Parish Council position in St. Giles. Connolly called on workers to elect 'a sufficient number of Social Democrats to counteract the despotic tendencies of our Liberal and Tory taskmasters' and hoped that 'the Irish vote … may this time be cast with discrimination as to the real interests of the electors. There is no "Liberal" vote to "split" and the population of St. Giles should know by now the folly of handing over the care of its to those who have made them poor'.[145] It was sadly not to be. Connolly, though he 'fought a valiant fight', came bottom of the poll. This proved, the *Labour Chronicle* argued that 'where poverty and ignorance are rampant, there socialism meets her greatest foe'.[146]

Undeterred, Connolly continue his work as a socialist propagandist. He addressed an audience of 3,000 at the joint SSF/ILP May Day demonstration in Edinburgh, alongside principal speaker Bruce Glasier. In September, the SSF finally voted to become the Edinburgh branch of the wider SDF, and it made the most of its national connections to organise an impressive winter series of public meetings. The branch booked the Operetta House, with a capacity of 1,500, for a series of Sunday evening lecturers. Throughout October, large audiences heard from some key figures in British socialism, including Eleanor Marx, Edward Aveling and Harry Quelch, the editor of *Justice.*

In December, Connolly himself appeared at the Operetta House, along-side national SDF leader Henry Hyndman, to address an audience of between seven and eight hundred. According to the report in *Justice,* as a 'test of the substantial progress of Socialism in Edinburgh', the meeting 'left little to be desired'. It was 'the first time in its history [that] the Edinburgh Trades Council was officially represented at a Socialist meeting,' and alongside Hyndman, 'comrades Melliet and James Connolly made a capital show, as well as good speeches.'[147] The season's propaganda came to a close with return visits from Eleanor Marx and Aveling at the end of March 1896. The SDF in Edinburgh reported that 60 new members had joined, while 'many more had been converted to Socialism, and were intending to join'. To reinforce the theoretical education of the new converts, Connolly held a Sunday afternoon economics class in the Edinburgh SDF's Nicholson Street offices. At the classes, *Justice* reported, 'the gospel according to Marx is then and there expounded by Connolly and, needless to say, his exegesis is the authoritative one … free from dilution or adulteration'.[148]

While socialism in Edinburgh was making progress, the same could unfortunately not be said for Connolly's personal situation. His electoral efforts had cost him his job at the Edinburgh Corporation. As well as running the SDF's local headquarters, Connolly tried to make ends meet for himself and his young family by opening up a cobblers' shop. He placed the following advertisement in the *Labour Chronicle* in May and June 1895:

'Socialists support one another. CONNOLLY, 73 Buccleuch St. Repairs the worn-out understandings of the brethren at standard rates. Ladies boots 1/6. gents 2/6. He looks towards you.'[149]

Connolly's many talents, it seems, did not stretch to shoe repair. The shop failed and, almost destitute, Connolly considered emigration to Chile. As part of an effort to dissuade him, John Leslie placed an appeal in *Justice* to find Connolly work as a socialist propagandist, writing:

> ... he is the most able propagandist in every sense of the word that Scotland has turned out. And because of it, and for his intrepidity, he is today on the verge of destitution and out of work ... is there no comrade in Glasgow, Dundee, or anywhere else who could secure a situation for one of the best and most self-sacrificing men in the movement?[150]

A reply came, not from Glasgow or Dundee, but from the Dublin Socialist Club, who wanted to recruit Connolly as an organiser. Connolly's last public appearance in Edinburgh would be the May Day celebration at the Meadows on 3 May. Before he left Scotland, the Edinburgh SDF branch held a special meeting 'in token of the respect and esteem in which he was held and as a recognition of the splendid services he has rendered to the cause of Socialism in this city.' Connolly, they said, 'is one of those best propagandist speakers in the movement'. Though his loss would 'be severely felt', the Edinburgh comrades hoped he would 'continue the good work in the place to which he has gone.'[151]

Connolly, delighted with his new posting, set sail for Dublin in May 1896 with his wife Lillie, his three daughters, and his small library of books. Beyond his electoral skirmishes with the Irish nationalists, he had not much grappled with the Irish Question. 'His principal emphasis,' in his Edinburgh days noted Howell, 'was on the relationship between the Irish vote in Britain, and Socialist and Labour organisations', and he 'did not develop any cogent arguments about Socialists attitudes to the National Question as such.' This would soon change. Leaving Edinburgh an orthodox Social Democrat, Connolly would arrive in Ireland seeking to apply the skills of his Edinburgh Marxist apprenticeship to the complex problems of Britain's oldest colony.

Chapter 2

The Irish Socialist Republican Party (ISRP)

When Connolly departed Edinburgh in May 1896, he left a city with a growing labour movement, taking tentative steps towards independent labour representation in politics, and where a minority of workers were increasingly receptive to advanced social-democratic ideas. Arriving in Dublin, Connolly faced a very different set of challenges. Not only was the situation for the working class even worse than in Edinburgh, but Dublin also lacked the beginnings of a strong labour movement to point the way towards a better future. Moreover, the long and tragic history of Ireland's colonial relationship with Britain was the dominating issue in politics. In the last century, Ireland had seen four armed rebellions for independence (in 1798, 1803, 1848 and 1867), as well as a mass constitutional movement for Catholic Emancipation in the 1830s and an explosive movement of tenant farmers mobilised under Irish nationalist leadership against landlordism in the late 1870s. Connolly's challenge, against this backdrop, was to develop, apply and build a following for socialist ideas capable of addressing themselves to Irish conditions. As we shall see, his Edinburgh days left him some, rather undeveloped, tools to do this; putting them to use would require boundless energy and much ideological creativity.

Any discussion of Connolly's attempts to root revolutionary socialism in Ireland's soil must be prefaced with a recognition of the objective difficulties he faced. In many ways, the Ireland that Connolly experienced in the 1890s still lived in the shadow of the Great Famine of 1845-48, which had a profound effect on the social and economic structure of the island. Over a million people had died and a similar number emigrated in what Connolly rightly described as the 'blackest period of Ireland's history'.[152] Between 1841 and 1851 the population of Ireland declined from 8,175,000 to 6,552,000. This represented a decrease of 19.9 per cent overall but it was greatest in the rural districts, where the population declined by 24.2 per cent.[153] Amidst the deaths from hunger and disease, the Famine exacerbated a dramatic shift in the use of land from tillage to pasture. As small tenants were driven by hunger and eviction, great estates were converted into sheep and cattle-raising farms, oriented towards export markets in Britain. Thus, in the same period to 1851, the area of land under crops and pasture increased by 9 per cent and by 1903 represented 81 per cent of land in the whole country.[154] As Marx put it in a speech to an audience of German socialists in London in 1867, when this process was well under way:

> Over 1,100,000 people have been replaced by 9,600,000 sheep. This is a thing unheard of in Europe. The Russians replace evicted Poles with Russians, not with sheep. Only under the Mongols in China was there once a discussion whether towns should be destroyed to make room for sheep.[155]

Unlike in Britain, which underwent rapid urbanisation throughout the nineteenth century, the 'surplus' agricultural population in Ireland could not be absorbed in towns and cities. Irish cities, especially Dublin, were underdeveloped, which reflected the island's generally subservient colonial relationship with its larger neighbour. In Dublin at the turn of the twentieth century, for example, only a fifth of male workers were employed in manufacturing, with 45 per cent finding themselves in 'unskilled' categories such as general labourer, building worker or transport worker. 40 per cent of women in Dublin were domestic labourers, as indeed was Connolly's wife Lillie before she moved to Scotland.[156] Rural depopulation, rather than being the signal for urban industrial development, produced wide-scale emigration. The most common destinations were Britain, as in the case of Connolly's own parents, John and Mary, who settled in Scotland, and North America. Indeed, in the 1840s, Irish people comprised over half of all immigrants to the United States, and by 1900 more Irish lived in the US than in the whole of Ireland.[157]

Marxism, of course, locates the agent of revolutionary transformation in the urban working class, a product of industrial capitalist development. Ireland, as we shall see below, was an overwhelmingly rural country. As for the cities, when Connolly arrived in Dublin, the Irish working class was small and the labour movement undeveloped. Despite the creation of the Irish Trades Union Congress (ITUC) in 1894, the labour movement had largely been untouched by the wave of New Unionism in Britain. Delegates remained in British-based trade unions and insisted that the formation of the ITUC was about logistical convenience, rather than an act of political separatism. The ITUC was dominated by skilled workers, and cautious craft unions based in luxury goods industries. An estimated 20 per cent unemployment rate made it difficult for the unskilled to organise, and the hostility of the craft unions only added to their problems. It would be 1906, for example, before an unskilled worker would sit on the ITUC's Parliamentary Committee.[158] In Dublin itself, by 1901 only 17,775 men worked in manufacturing and, of these, 2,472 worked in 'food and drinks', mainly brewing. Most workers were unskilled general labourers, excluded from the tightly knit craft unions who saw their purpose as excluding new entrants to the labour market rather than organising all workers to better their conditions.[159]

The main exception to all this was Belfast, which by 1891 had outstripped Dublin in terms of population. Belfast was a rapidly industrialising city based on the linen and shipbuilding industries. Belfast was part of the 'industrial' triangle with Glasgow and Liverpool and was therefore structurally integrated into the British economy. The Belfast labour movement was segregated along sectarian lines, generally with Protestant workers taking up skilled positions in the shipbuilding industries, while Catholics dominated lower-skilled jobs in textiles, building and the docks. The Belfast labour movement reflected and reproduced this sectarian dynamic. Though strong and growing in many senses, the labour movement was periodically disrupted by extreme outbreaks of sectarianism, especially as the two Home Rule Bills in 1886 and 1892 led to a mass Unionist movement to resist self-government for the whole of Ireland. Connolly's form of socialist republicanism would always struggle to find a foothold in Belfast, and this was especially true of his first attempts to organise a socialist movement after 1896.

Socialist predecessors

It is, however, necessary to qualify this picture by recognising that a socialist movement *did* precede Connolly's arrival in Ireland. As Fintan Lane has commented in his authoritative history of early Irish socialism, 'Connolly was not the Patrick of Irish socialism as he has been consistently presented,' though he would blaze a trail for a new form of socialist republicanism, whose ideas outlasted its shorter-term organisational expression.[160]

As Connolly himself would recognise in his *Labour in Irish History,* the man with perhaps the greatest claim to being 'Ireland's first socialist' was William Thompson.[161] Thompson was born in Cork in 1775 to a wealth merchant family. A supporter of the French Revolution, Thompson was influenced by the French utopian socialists Charles Fourier and Henri Saint-Simon. His own research into political economy led him to conclude that capital 'is that portion of the product of labour which … is capable of being made the instrument of profit'. Thompson's discovery of the notion of 'surplus value' was acknowledged by Marx himself in *Capital* and led

Thompson to promote the establishment of agricultural colonies on similar lines to the utopian socialist Robert Owen. Unlike Owen, Connolly pointed out that Thompson

> believed that such colonies must be built by the labourers themselves, and not by the governing class. He taught that the wealth of the ruling class was derived from the plunder of labour, and he advocated, as a necessary preliminary to Socialism, the conquest of political representation on the basis of the adult suffrage of both sexes.[162]

Marx and Engels, themselves, took a great interest in Ireland. Both wrote extensively on Irish history and made activity on the 'Irish Question' one focus for the activities of the First International in the early 1870s.[163] In March 1867, the British crushed a poorly armed Fenian uprising in Ireland, prompting the International to take up campaigning on Irish issues in Britain itself. In September, two leading Fenians, Thomas Kelly and Timothy Deasy, escaped to America after their prison van was ambushed in Manchester and a British police sergeant killed. In response, the authorities arrested dozens from the Irish community in Manchester and put five men on trial for murder. Three men, William Allen, Michael O'Brien and Michael Larkin – 'the Manchester Martyrs' – were publicly hanged on 23 November. In the weeks leading up to the executions, the International launched a solidarity campaign and took up the cause of the Fenian prisoners. Already, on 2 November, Marx admitted that his views on Irish independence had shifted. 'I once believed the separation of Ireland from England to be impossible,' he wrote to Engels. 'I now regard it as inevitable, although federation may follow upon separation.'[164]

By 1869, Marx's view of Ireland's revolutionary potential had also shifted. Previously, Marx had thought the initiative for the overthrow of 'the Irish regime' would come from 'English working class ascendancy'. Now, he located revolutionary agency in Ireland itself: 'Deeper study has now convinced me of the opposite,' he wrote. 'The English working class will never accomplish anything before it has got rid of Ireland. The lever must be applied in Ireland. That is why the Irish question is so important for the social movement in general.' Building on this position, Marx argued that Irish workers were an increasingly important part of the working class in Britain itself. However:

> All industrial and commercial centres in England now have a working class split into two hostile camps, English proletarians and Irish proletarians. The

ordinary English worker hates the Irish worker as a competitor who forces down the standard of life. In relation to the Irish worker, he feels himself to be a member of the dominant nation and, therefore, makes himself a tool of his aristocrats and capitalists against Ireland, thus strengthening their domination over himself.

Thus, in Marx's view, 'national emancipation of Ireland' was, for the British working-class, 'not just a question of abstract justice or humanitarian sentiment, but the first condition of their own social emancipation.'[165]

Marx and Engels were strong and genuine supporters of the Irish cause. Yet their approach to the 'Irish Question' was very much still to see it through the prism of developments in the *British* labour movement, which occupied a crucial place in their hopes for the future.

But what of socialist activity in Ireland itself? Engels was largely pessimistic, writing in 1888 that a 'purely socialist movement cannot be expected in Ireland for a considerable time. People there want first of all to become peasants owning a plot of land ...'[166] However, he argued, 'this should not prevent us from seeking to help them to get rid of their landlords, that is, to pass from semi-feudal conditions to capitalist conditions'. William Morris of the Socialist League largely agreed. Morris visited Dublin in April 1886, just two months before Gladstone tried and failed to pass the first Home Rule Bill in the House of Commons. Home Rule dominated the political agenda in Ireland, and Morris wrote pessimistically in *Commonweal* on 8 May that:

> It is a matter of course that until the Irish get Home Rule they will listen to nothing else, and equally so that as soon as they get Home Rule they must deal at once with the land question. On the whole, I fear it seems likely that they will have to go through the dismal road of peasant-proprietorship before they get to anything like Socialism; and that road in a country so isolated and so peculiar as Ireland, may be a long one.[167]

The nascent First International presence in Ireland was largely broken by a campaign of clerical hostility. This intensified further after the Paris Commune in 1871, for which the International was widely (and inaccurately) held responsible. The campaign against the Commune in Ireland would cast a long shadow. George King, an activist in Morris's Socialist League, would write to a party comrade fourteen years later, in September 1885, of the problems facing socialists then attempting to organise in Dublin: 'The one fact that the average Dublin working man knows about the [Paris] commune is that during the struggle the Archbishop of Paris was shot.'[168]

Despite this, there *was* socialist activity in Ireland in the 1880s. In the early part of that decade, Irish socialism was represented by a handful of individuals under the political influence of the larger British-based movement. The SDF in Britain, we will remember, was founded in 1884. Its newspaper *Justice* could be found in shops in Derry and Dublin by July 1884, and by the end of a year a short-lived 'Democratic Association' was founded by a mix of socialists and advocates of land nationalisation. When the SDF split in December 1884, the breakaway Socialist League attempted to gain a foothold in Ireland and, by April 1886, it could count 17 members. These included Fritz Schumann, a leading member of the Danish Social Democratic Workers' Party. Another new member was Roman Ivanovitch Lipmann, a Russian of Jewish extraction who was a follower of the Russian Populist Pyotr Lavrov, at a time when Russian socialism had not yet separated into its Populist and Marxist wings.[169]

Organised socialism in Dublin was in a fissiparous state for much of the late 1880s. In September 1886, the French socialist Auguste Coulon formed an International Club to ensure 'the establishment of socialism on a firmer basis' and organised the March 1887 Paris Commune celebration in Dublin. Though Coulon would later become involved in anarchist circles in London, where he acted as an informer for Scotland Yard, the annual tradition of Paris Commune celebrations did much to cohere an audience around socialism in the city, despite a bewildering array of short-lived organisations.[170]

All of the organisations mentioned above were in the ideological orbit of the British SDF and its Socialist League off-shoot. However, in Limavady, County Derry, the Christian socialist Rev. J. Bruce Wallace was active in the late 1880s. In 1887, Wallace, 'a well-known figure in late nineteenth-century socialist circles in both England and the United States,' founded the *Brotherhood* magazine, which lasted in various guises until 1931.[171] Described by Connolly in *Labour in Irish History* as being 'long a hard and unselfish worker for the cause of Socialism in Ireland', Wallace was an advocate of land nationalisation and was most prominent in the promotion of co-operatives, which he viewed as 'the next stage in the evolution of the higher form of society'.[172] By 1892, however, Wallace had moved to London, complaining that in Limavady 'nobody followed our example', and that Belfast was 'not a bed of flowers but a hot-bed of religious bigotry and intolerance'.[173] In London he inaugurated a Brotherhood Church on the Southgate Road in Hackney (which in 1907 played host to the 7th Congress of the Russian Social Democratic and Labour Party) and later established a

Brotherhood Trust aiming 'to crush out wasteful, corrupting labour, and to eliminate rent, interest, and profits in order to increase the share distributed to the workers and to establish the new cooperative commonwealth.'[174]

Meanwhile, the reformist Fabian Society, was founded in Belfast in February 1891, and the following year in Dublin. It catered for those who were uncomfortable with the revolutionary politics of the Socialist League and the SDF. According to Lane, 'between 1892 and 1895 we see the rise of labour socialism in Ireland and the obscuration of revolutionary socialism'.[175] The immediate cause was the election of Keir Hardie as an Independent Labour MP to the House of Commons in the 1892 General Election. Within months, over forty ILP branches were established across Britain, with the first branch in Ireland being inaugurated in Belfast in September 1892. The ILP took advantage of the British TUC congress being held in Belfast in September 1893. On 6 September, Hardie moved a motion for independent political representation in Parliament which fell narrowly by 119 votes to 96. Three days later, thousands attended a TUC demonstration in Ormeau Park. The TUC demonstration was marred, however, by working-class loyalists who attacked the British socialists for their support for Home Rule. John Burns was heckled, and Will Thorne was injured in the resulting scuffles. Attempts to hold public propaganda meetings on the Custom House steps in the city centre were well received, but their success prompted violence from anti-socialist mobs until they had to be abandoned. The Belfast ILP itself quietly lapsed in 1897.[176]

The ILP did not set up in Dublin until 1894, and the party did little to co-ordinate its activity with the other branches in Belfast and Waterford.[177] William O'Brien would later comment about the ILP that: 'In carrying on propaganda they met with criticism of the body because it was a branch of a British organisation, and also the only literature they had for sale at propaganda meetings was all written from an English point of view and printed in England.'[178] This would soon change. When the ILP branch in Dublin collapsed in 1895, a Dublin Socialist Society was formed, open to socialists of all persuasion. Its Secretary, Adolphus Shields, and its Chair, the Christian socialist Robert Dorman, noticed an advert placed in *Justice* in December 1895. It advertised the talents of a young Edinburgh socialist organiser and propagandist. The two men replied to the advert and offered the man one pound a week to transfer to Dublin to act as an organiser for their new group.[179] Thus, James Connolly moved to Dublin in May 1896 and a new chapter in Irish socialism began.

Founding the ISRP

Shields and Dorman perhaps over-estimated the importance of Connolly's ILP membership when they hired him because he was most definitely a Marxist in the British SDF tradition.[180] According to future ISRP stalwart Thomas Lyng, no doubt with some exaggeration, Connolly confronted the leaders of the Dublin Socialist Society, 'pulverised them in debate, preached socialism unblushingly to them, shattered their little organisation, and from the fragments he founded a small Irish Socialist Republican Party'.[181]

The motion to found the ISRP was tabled on 29 May in the snug of Pierce Ryan's public house at 50 Thomas Street. It was moved by Dorman and seconded by Thomas Lyng. According to Connolly, writing in March 1903, 'six working men assisted at its birth. The founders were poor, like the remainder of their class, and had arrayed against them all those things that are supposed to be essential to success.' Lyng, who was elected party secretary at the meeting, has stated that there were eight present.[182] In any case, the party was starting from a low base, and it would remain a small organisation for the duration of its existence. Nevertheless, despite the taunt of one contemporary newspaper that the ISRP had more syllables than members, it soon 'grew into a party of tens of members rather than just the handful of original founders and became very distinctive on the Dublin political scene'.[183]

The ISRP very much conceived of itself as part of the international socialist movement. As such, the party adopted a programme in 1896 along orthodox Second International lines. Much like the SDF's 1883 programme *Socialism made easy*, the 1896 programme contained a number of 'minimum demands' such as nationalisation of banks and industry, graduated income tax, a shorter working week, free education and universal suffrage. It also contained the 'maximum' demand of socialism, declaring that the 'private ownership by a class of the land and instruments of production, distribution and exchange is opposed to [the democratic principle] of justice, and is the fundamental basis of all oppression, national, political and social'.[184]

In common with the other Second International parties, following the 1893 Zurich Congress resolution on political action, which excluded the anarchists, the ISRP proclaimed that socialism was to be attained through the 'conquest by the Social Democracy of political power in Parliament, and on all public bodies in Ireland'. Like the SDF, whose view was that socialists must 'use political institutions and forms to educate the people and to prepare, as far as possible, peacefully for the social revolution,' the ISRP manifesto states that political action 'is the readiest and most effective means whereby the revolutionary forces may be organised and disciplined to attain' the Irish Socialist Republic.[185]

This did not, however, necessitate a naïve believe in the neutrality of the capitalist state. Connolly would write in July 1899 that if the will of the majority for socialism is blocked by the ruling class then 'the party which represents the revolutionary idea is justified in taking steps to assume the powers of government, and in using the weapons of force to dislodge the usurping class or government'.[186]

Connolly distinguished his politics from the reformist state socialism of the Fabian type. This brand of politics, he argued in 1900, would

> emasculate the working class movement, by denying the philosophy of class struggle, weakening the belief of the workers in the political self-sufficiency of their own class, and by substituting the principle of municipal capitalism, and bureaucratic State control for the principle of revolutionary reconstruction involved in Social Democracy.[187]

Connolly's clear commitment to working-class self-emancipation and democracy was pronounced and anticipated his later embrace of revolutionary syndicalist ideas. In 1899, he polemicised against those who mistook moves towards state intervention by capitalists as in any way 'socialistic'.

> State ownership and control, is not necessarily Socialism: if it were, then the Army, the Navy, the Police, the Judges, the Gaolers, the Informers, and the Hangmen, all would all be Socialist functionaries, as they are State officials – but the ownership by the State of all the land and materials for labour, combined with the co-operative control by the workers of such land and materials, would be Socialism ... To the cry of the middle class reformers, 'make this or that the property of the government,' we reply, 'yes, in proportion as the workers are ready to make the government their property'.[188]

The party was publicly launched at the Custom House steps in Dublin on 7 June 1896 at an open-air meeting. Former ILP members Murtagh Lyng and Laurence Strange joined, as did George King and John O'Gorman who had led the Dublin Socialist League in the 1880s. Following an appeal to socialists abroad to join in solidarity, Eleanor Marx's partner Edward Aveling was amongst the first to sign up.[189]

As well as Connolly, the O'Brien brothers, Daniel, Thomas and William, would also provide some of the most active ISRP members. From Clonakilty in Country Cork, the O'Briens moved to Dublin as children. Daniel was a brilliant writer, and William, too young to join in 1896, was recruited by Tom Lyng in 1899. He would become one of the twentieth century's key labour movement figures, and Connolly's literary executor after 1916. Another set of brothers, the Lyngs, Murtagh and Tom, would also become ISRP stalwarts. Another leading party activist, Edward Stewart, had been a tailor but would become a warehouse assistant in a major tailoring establishment in Dublin. One of the few party members with organised labour movement connections, in September 1902 he was elected President of the Dublin Trades Council and moved sharply to the right. The two men responsible for bringing Connolly to Ireland did not last long in the newly established party. Dorman resigned on 17 June 1897 and Shields quickly returned to his Fabian roots, after joining the ISRP for only a short time.[190]

Following its launch, the ISRP soon began a programme of weekly public meetings and established small branches in Cork and Belfast, though it would always struggle to develop a base outside of Dublin. A Manchester expatriate branch in Pendleton lasted only a few weeks. The Cork branch was established when Con Lehane transformed Wolfe Tone Literary Society into a branch of the ISRP in January 1899. There was little initial activity but in 1901 the branch organised open air meetings attracting crowds of around 400.[191] As with its socialist predecessors, however, the ISRP suffered attacks from the clergy. When the Bishop of Cork warned publicly of the dangers of socialism, Lehane lost his job and moved to London at the end of 1901. He would later become a founder member of the Socialist Party of Great Britain (SPGB). Connolly, recounting the affair later to Matheson, appeared to have had little sympathy, referring to Lehane as a 'deserter'.[192]

The Belfast branch, too, did not last long. It was launched in the Typographical Hall in September 1898 by Ernest Milligan, the younger brother of the Irish republican Alice Milligan who edited the newspaper the *Shan Van Vocht*, to which Connolly himself would contribute articles. Unfortunately for the ISRP's ambitions to extend its reach, the branch had 'a fleeting and fitful existence, coming under pressure from the Orange Order and being viewed with distrust by the socialists already active in Belfast as too "pro-nationalist"'.[193]

The ISRP struggled to establish itself, undermined by its small membership numbers and a lack of the funds and resources required to maintain its office and publications. Connolly would write that the ISRP recognised 'no person as leader, the most prominent speaker or writer has no more sway in the organisation than the most silent worker' and the members 'transact all business at weekly meetings in which every member is invited to take part'.[194] In reality, the informality of these structures (the party never held an annual conference or formal regional meetings) reflected the low level of its membership and its concentration in Dublin. And though the party had no elected president, aspiring instead towards a collective leadership, 'Connolly', William O'Brien recalled, 'was, of course, the presiding genius of the whole business' as the party's leading theorist, writer and propagandist. O'Brien's older brothers joined the ISRP, and he remembers how they were drawn to the party by Connolly's erudition and his knowledge of socialism:

> I continued to listen to their talk and there was mention continually of somebody named Connolly. Connolly says so and so. Connolly does not agree with that. Connolly's point of view is this, and so on. Then when I had an opportunity I asked who was this Connolly. 'He is a very smart fellow,' I was told. 'Where does he come from?' 'From Edinburgh.' 'And what is he?' 'Just a labourer.' 'A labourer!' said I. 'How could a labourer know all these things?' 'He went to the National Library and he studied.' This was not very convincing to me. I could not understand how a labourer should be so important as all that … However, I had to accept what was stated.[195]

If the party struggled to build its membership, it was equally unsuccessful in the electoral field. Following the establishment of household suffrage for the municipalities and local governing bodies allowed for under the Local Government Act of 1898, introduced as part of the Tory attempts to 'kill Home Rule with kindness', the road was potentially open for Labour and socialist candidates to break through. In January 1899, the ISRP ran E.W. Stewart in North Dock Ward in Dublin. Stewart received 448 votes (12 per cent of the total) but it cannot have helped that the party's meagre resources confined its campaigning to open-air meetings, while the *Evening Telegraph* refused to publish its advertisements.

At the same time, the Dublin Trades Council had established the Labour Electoral Association at a special conference on 27 August 1898, to run labour movement candidates under the new Act. Connolly welcomed this as 'the most important step yet taken by organised workers in Ireland'. In the *Workers' Republic* Connolly made the orthodox Marxist distinction that 'the trade unionist wishes to limit the power of the master but still wishes to have masters [while] the socialist wishes to have done with masters'. However, showing a non-sectarian approach to the wider labour movement, Connolly was hopeful that the trade union candidate, 'if he be true to his class when elected, will find that every step he takes in the Council in furtherance of the interests of his class, must of necessity take the form of an application of socialist principles.[196]

However, tension between the socialists and the LEA was present from the outset. Stewart approached the LEA for backing in his North Dock Ward campaign and was refused. While the ISRP failed to break through, the LEA returned several members to Dublin Corporation. Unfortunately, though undoubtedly a step forward, the experience of the LEA representatives demonstrated all too clearly that organisational independence of the working class is not enough unless accompanied by a programme of political independence from all ruling-class parties.

The LEA representatives became a byword for incompetence and corruption, and Connolly wrote with disappointment in September 1899: 'No single important move in the interest of the worker was even mooted' and 'where the workers have looked for inspiration and leadership, they have received nothing but discouragement and disgust ...'[197] In 1900, the LEA was routed on the Dublin Corporation, prompting the ISRP to comment:

> We must remember that the municipal backwash of this year was the almost inevitable result of the disappointment felt by the public at the miserable intrigues and squalid squabbling with which the Labour Party in the Council had signalised their years in office.[198]

How are we to assess the ISRP then? 'The real significance of this little party', FSL Lyons argued, 'had nothing to do with its numerical strength.' It was important

> because it gave James Connolly a platform and allowed him in his speeches, and in the first of his newspapers, the *Workers' Republic,* to evolve his doctrines not from theory alone, or by observation from afar, but through direct experience of what it meant to be a poor man living in the slums.[199]

It would, in the end, be the party's ideas that proved more enduring than its organisational presence. What is most interesting about the ISRP, in retrospect, is that it represented Connolly's first attempts to work out his position on the interrelation of socialism and nationalism. In late nineteenth century Ireland, 'both Socialist and Labour groups faced the problem posed by the National Question's dominance of Irish politics'.[200] For Connolly, a thorough grasp of this question was an absolute necessity for the ISRP if it wished to establish itself among the Irish working class.

The National Question

As we have seen above, the ISRP's programme was, in many respects, an orthodox Social-Democratic one, similar in content and approach to the SDF. That is, however, in all respects but one: its militant advocacy of the right of Ireland to self-determination. Many British socialists, to Connolly's frustration, were content to limit themselves to calling for 'legislative independence' for 'colonies and dependencies'. Hyndman, for example, justified this view not on the principle the Irish had a right to self-determination as a people but on the more pragmatic grounds that 'separation would be injurious to both countries, as mutual understanding would be beneficial, that Irishmen should at length be granted fair play and self-government'.[201] The ISRP took a far more principled stance. In its 1896 programme, the party declared 'the subjection of one nation to another, as of Ireland to the authority of the British Crown, is a barrier to the free political and economic development of the subjected nation, and can only serve the interests of the exploiting classes of both nations'.[202] The party called, therefore, for an Irish Socialist Republic, and full separation from the British Empire. Connolly later recalled that the party was founded on his proposition that:

> ... the two currents of revolutionary thought in Ireland – the Socialist and the National – were not antagonistic, but complementary, and that the Irish Socialist was in reality the best Irish patriot, but that in order to convince the Irish people of that fact he must first of all learn to look inward upon Ireland for his justification, rest his arguments upon the facts of Irish history, and be the champion against the subjection of Ireland and all that it implies. That the Irish National question was at bottom an economic question, and that the economic struggle must first be able to function freely nationally before it could function internationally, and as Socialists were opposed to all oppression, so they should ever be foremost in the daily battle against all its manifestations, social and political.[203]

Connolly's particular innovation, conditioned by Ireland's experience of colonialism, was to position the socialist movement within the centuries-old struggle between Ireland and Britain. This perspective, Connolly recalls, 'aroused interest alike among Nationalists and Socialists' and inspired 'requests for enlightenment' from both sources, 'each side inquiring upon that part of the policy which seemed to touch most closely their own previous ideas of politics'.[204] From the Irish republicans, Alice Milligan, poet and editor of the monthly literary magazine the *Shan Van Vocht* requested an article from Connolly, which appeared as 'Can Irish Republicans be Politicians?' in November 1896. At the same time, Keir Hardie's newspaper the *Labour Leader* had given the ISRP an enthusiastic welcome, writing that the 'new movement, born on Irish soil and inaugurated by Irishmen, will appeal to the Irish people as nothing else has yet done, and the times we believe to be right for this development'.[205] Hardie, Connolly recalled, asked 'for a series of articles upon the relation of the Irish question to Socialism' for his paper.[206] Connolly's three articles duly appeared in successive issues of the *Labour Leader* in October 1896 under the title 'Ireland for the Irish'. These four articles, taken together, were published as the ISRP's first pamphlet, *Erin's Hope: the ends and means* in 1897. This pamphlet is of crucial importance as Connolly's first extended effort on the national question in Ireland and is worthy of some attention.

First, let us examine Connolly's influence in approaching the 'Irish Question'. When Connolly turned to write *Erin's Hope,* there were few intellectual raw materials available with which to elaborate a Marxist interpretation of Irish history. One source that Connolly could turn to, however, was a series of articles written by his early mentor, the Scottish socialist John Leslie. Leslie's articles appeared from March to May 1894 in the SDF newspaper *Justice* and were compiled into a pamphlet, *The Present Condition of the Irish Question.* The pamphlet, an attempt at a Marxist analysis of nineteenth century Irish political and social history was, it has been argued, 'perhaps the most crucial seminal influence on the young Connolly, Marx himself excepted'.[207]

The immediate stimulus for Leslie's pamphlet was a resolution passed by the Irish Trades Union Congress (ITUC) in 1894 supporting the idea of an Irish working-class party. Leslie's pamphlet aims to lay out a perspective for such a party, by way of a critical analysis of the land agitation of the late 1870s to mid-1880s. Speaking 'as an Irish wage-worker, and an unskilled one at that', Leslie wrote that mere political independence was insufficient; he did not believe the 'Alpha and the Omega of the Irish Question consists in the hoisting of the green and gold banner above the old Parliament House in Dublin'. Nor, he argued, 'were the interests of the Irish working-class' likely to be advanced by the Irish party any more than those of the British workers would be by the Tories or Liberals.[208]

Leslie argued that the misery and the hopes of the Irish people had long been exploited by political demagogues and channelled towards constitutional politics. Instead, Leslie turns to the ideas of the almost forgotten mid-nineteenth century figure James Fintan Lalor, who Leslie regarded as 'the man who first pointed out the class nature of the Irish movement'.[209]

Lalor had been involved in the Young Ireland. This was a political and cultural nationalist movement which, influenced by the 1848 revolutions in Europe, and in the context of the Famine of 1845-49, attempted a conspiratorial rebellion in Ireland in July 1848. Most Young Ireland leaders offered little in the way of social demands or reforms, focusing instead on political independence. Lalor, on the other hand, asserted that the English consequent was double-sided, political and social, and that 'the re-conquest of our liberties would be incomplete and worthless without the re-conquest of our lands'.[210] Lalor therefore tried to harness Irish national aspirations to the material conditions of life, rather than to a romantic cultural vision, or a desire for mere political independence. In Ireland at this time, that meant the conditions of the native peasantry, burdened by high rents, tormented by evictions and starved by famine.

Though Connolly later referred to Lalor as the 'Irish apostle of revolutionary socialism', the latter was, in effect, an agrarian populist who based his programme on the small-holding peasantry's hatred of the landlord class – described, simplistically, as an 'English garrison in Ireland'.[211] To be sure, Lalor advocated potentially socially revolutionary means, such as a mass refusal to pay rents. When he maintained, however, 'that the entire soil of a country belongs of right to the people of that country, and is the rightful property not of any one class, but of the nation at large', Lalor did not envisage an end to private property in land as such.[212] Rather, that the 'nation' would hold the land in trust, and real ownership would effectively be exercised by a new class of peasant proprietors. Lalor's object was, as he wrote, 'not to resume or restore an old constitution but to found a new nation and raise up a free people, and strong as well as free, and secure as well as strong, based on a peasantry rooted like rocks in the soil of the land.'[213]

Nevertheless, Lalor's idea that the 'Irish Question' had a social content, as well as a political one, was developed by Leslie and then by Connolly. In *Erin's Hope*, Connolly develops Leslie's argument that the real issue at stake was not whether Ireland should be politically independent from Britain, but the establishment of a new social system based on working-class rule. In this pamphlet Connolly set out a number of important historiographical themes, which would henceforth recur in his writings, including in a more developed form in his 1910 classic *Labour in Irish History*.

Building on Leslie, Connolly claims that the essence of the national question lies not simply in the struggle for political independence but in 'fundamentally different ideas upon the vital question of property in land'. It was a clash between the British 'system of feudalism and private ownership of land, as opposed to the Celtic system of clan or common ownership' which provided 'the pivot around which centred all the struggles and rebellions of which that history has been so prolific'.[214] Connolly argued that a form of 'primitive communism' had survived in Ireland much longer than in other European countries, and was only destroyed by the British when the clans were dispersed after the break-up of the Kilkenny confederation in 1649. In an attempt to make contemporary Marxist-inspired socialism acceptable to the Irish population of the late nineteenth-century, Connolly sought an authentically Irish antecedent. 'The Irish system,' he argued,

> was thus on a par with those conceptions of social rights and duties which we find the ruling classes to-day denouncing so fiercely as 'Socialistic'. It was apparently inspired by the democratic principle that property was intended to serve the people, and not by the principle so universally acted upon at present, viz., that the people have no other function in existing than to be the bondslaves of those who by force or by fraud have managed to possess themselves of property.[215]

Thus, these 'Celtic forefathers ... foreshadowed in the democratic organisation of the Irish clan the more perfect organisation of the free society of the future'.[216] This 'free society' was none other than an Irish Socialist Republic. National liberation, the undoing of the dual social and political effects of the conquest, was in effect the social revolution. 'The act of social emancipation,' wrote Connolly:

> requires the conversion of the land and instruments of production from private property into the public or common property of the entire nation. This necessitates a social system of the most absolute democracy, and in establishing that necessary social system the working class must grapple with every form of government which could interfere with the most unfettered control by the people of Ireland of all the resources of their country.[217]

In Connolly's historical narrative, the Irish bourgeoisie 'by virtue of their social position and education stepped to the front as Irish patriot leaders' from the 18th century onwards. However, 'while professedly ultra-nationalistic in its political aims,' the Irish bourgeoisie had accepted the 'alien social system' of the coloniser, along 'with its accompanying manifestations, the legal dispossession and economic dependence of the vast mass of the Irish people, as part of the natural order of society'.[218] As with Leslie, this view allowed Connolly to puncture the pretensions of the tepid Home Rulers, arguing that their focus on purely governmental forms was shallow and superficial. In view of the social character of the question, wrong were those politicians, British and Irish alike, 'who are to-day complacently trotting out the discredited abortion of Home Rule as a sovereign remedy for Ireland's misery'.[219]

In one sense, we can agree with Bernard Ransom that Connolly developed a 'Hibernicised' version of Marxism.[220] Connolly himself was explicit that 'in order to convince the Irish people' that 'the Irish Socialist was in reality the best Irish patriot', the former 'must first of all learn to look inward upon Ireland for his justification, rest his arguments upon the facts of Irish history, and be the champion against the subjection of Ireland and all that it implies'.[221] His own socialist historiography was an innovative attempt by Connolly, leader of an extremely marginalised socialist propaganda organisation, to place socialism full-square in the middle of the Irish nationalist revival movement. As Bill Anderson has argued: 'There is a breath-taking audacity in Connolly's political objectives.' Far from seeking 'to make an accommodation with the nationalists, to find a comfortable if sterile niche for socialism on the periphery of the nationalist movement,' Connolly 'intended rather to make a commitment to socialism the litmus test of patriotism'.[222] Indeed, modern socialism is seen, he wrote later, as the culmination of centuries of struggle between Ireland's communal inheritance and a 'feudal-capitalist system of which England was the exponent in Ireland'.[223]

The ISRP, then, can be seen as part of, and an intervention into, the new nationalist movement of the Gaelic Revival. Not only was Labour in Irish History accepted by Maunsel and Co., publishers of J.M. Synge and many other Gaelic Revival writers, but Connolly himself wrote in the foreword to the book that it 'may justly be looked upon as part of the literature of the Gaelic revival'.[224] Like the cultural revivalists, Connolly was, for his own purposes, reaching deep into Irish history, rooting his socialism in the Irish revolutionary tradition.

However, this 'Hibernicisation' should not be seen as an Irish particularism. It does no disservice to Connolly's originality to place his intervention in a wider context.

The Second International and fin de siècle socialism

Connolly's earliest comments on the national question come in the year 1896, when the Second International first recognised the right of nations to self-determination. At its London Congress that year, it passed the following resolution:

The Congress declares in favor of the full autonomy of all nationalities, and its sympathy with the workers of any country at present suffering under the yoke of military, national, or other despotisms; and calls upon the workers in all such countries to fall into line, side by side with the class-conscious workers of the world, to organise for the overthrow of international capitalism and the establishment of international social democracy.[225]

In 1909, Connolly would reflect on the ISRP's adoption of 'the watchword, Irish Socialist Republic', as its aim. In the introduction to the US edition of *Erin's Hope* Connolly wrote, appealing to the authority of the International:

This policy received its formal endorsement by the International Socialist movement when at the International Socialist Congress at Paris in 1900 the delegates of the I.S.R.P. were formally seated as the delegates of a nation separate from England.[226]

Within this broad principle of self-determination, however, a number of positions could be discerned throughout the life of the International to 1914. Lenin would be one of the most consistent advocates of the right of nations to self-determination, arguing that it was in essence a question of political democracy. National oppression was a barrier to working-class unity, both in the oppressor and oppressed nation. The Austro-Marxists, most notably Otto Bauer, argued on the other hand that in multi-national states such as the Austrian-Hungarian Empire, socialists should aspire to 'cultural-national autonomy' rather than separate national states as such. At the other extreme, the Polish-born socialist Rosa Luxemburg, though willing to defend elements of national autonomy – such as language rights and separate schooling – did not defend the right of nations, such as Poland, to self-determination. She argued that Poland was economically integrated into the Russian Empire, that therefore the bourgeoisie had no interest in separation, and that the working class had nothing to gain from an independent Poland.

As Paul Bew, Peter Gibson and Henry Patterson have argued, in some of Connolly's early writings he anticipates the classic view that Irish self-determination is a question of political democracy.[227] In an article in 1897 for Maud Gonne's Paris newspaper *L'Ireland Libre,* Connolly argues that if socialism means the common ownership of property, that requires 'the transference of the means of production from the hands of private owners to those of public bodies directly responsible to the entire community'. If Socialism seeks to 'strengthen popular action on all public bodies', then 'representative bodies in Ireland would express more directly the will of the Irish people than when those bodies reside in England', so therefore:

> An Irish Republic would then be the natural depository of popular power; the weapon of popular emancipation, the only power which would show in the full light of day all these class antagonisms and lines of economic demarcation now obscured by the mists of bourgeois patriotism.[228]

This echoed Lenin's comment that 'a wider, freer more open form of class struggle and class opposition vastly assists the proletariat in its struggle'.[229] Elsewhere, however, Connolly tends to a more 'Luxemburgist' position that national self-determination is unrealisable under capitalism in any meaningful form, and anticipated twentieth century debates on 'neo-colonialism' in formally politically independent former colonies. In January 1897, he wrote famously in the *Shan Van Vocht*, that:

> If you remove the English army to-morrow and hoist the green flag over Dublin Castle, unless you set about the organisation of the Socialist Republic your efforts would be in vain. England would still rule you. She would rule you through her capitalists, through her landlords, through her financiers, through the whole array of commercial and individualist institutions she has planted in this country and watered with the tears of our mothers and the blood of our martyrs. England would still rule you to your ruin, even while your lips offered hypocritical homage at the shrine of that Freedom whose cause you had betrayed. Nationalism without Socialism – without a reorganisation of society on the basis of a broader and more developed form of that common property which underlay the social structure of Ancient Erin – is only national recreancy.[230]

As Bew et al. argue,

> Connolly actually shared *all* these views. English rule was treated as a mere 'symbol' of 'foreign' (i.e. capitalist) property relations which colonialism had imposed on Ireland. The Irish national bourgeoise was equally implicated in these relations. Any political independence it achieved would be meaningless. The difference between Luxemburg and Connolly was simply that while this reasonably led Luxemburg to reject all national struggles as reactionary, it led Connolly to argue that they could only be 'properly' fought as socialist revolutions.[231]

Connolly developed *his own* views on Irish national self-determination from his own thinking. Though he followed debates in the International and was aware of some of Marx's own writings on Ireland which had been published in English, there is no evidence that he was aware of Lenin's and Luxemburg's arguments. Connolly's main contact with the Polish movement, where the debate over national self-determination was sharp, was through the Union of Polish Socialists Abroad. This group was linked to the Polish Socialist Party, a rival to Luxemburg's organisation (the Social Democracy of the Kingdom of Poland and Lithuania, SDKPiL) which, unlike the latter, advocated self-determination for Poland. Connolly wrote an article in 1898, 'Socyalizm w Irlandyi ('Socialism in Ireland') in *Swiatlo*, published in Polish by Joseph Kaniowski, which outlined the ISRP's general position on Irish history.[232] Where he mentions the Russian movement in the early period, he quoted Georgi Plekhanov in the *Workers' Republic* to the effect that 'International solidarity cannot exist where one nation is oppressed by another' and 'revolutionary and Social Democratic Russia protests indignantly against the suppression of the national independence of Poland'.[233]

Beyond this, Marxist thinking on nationalism was, in the 1890s, rather underdeveloped. The Second International's focus was on the advanced metropolitan countries. Those socialists who operated in contexts where national issues were of prime importance – the Austro-Marxists and the Social-Democrats in the Russian Empire – had not fully made their own theoretical innovations.

Rather, the sources of Connolly's own thinking on the national question must be located closer to home. Ironically, given his attempts to work out an approach to Irish nationalism, the immediate theoretical resources available to him were those derived from his apprenticeship in the British socialist movement. Leslie's pamphlet on the 'Irish Question' we have already mentioned; let us look more closely at the other potential sources of Connolly's early position on national liberation.

One particularly interesting aspect of *Erin's Hope* is its precocity. Written in 1896 and published the following year, it preceded many of the historical works of the Irish Revival that Connolly later drew upon to write *Labour in Irish History* (which though published in 1910 started to take form as a series of articles after September 1898).[234] For instance, Connolly is upfront in *Labour In Irish History* that, in addition to Karl Marx, a central framework for his historical work is the non-Marxist Irish nationalist historian Alice Stopford Green, whose 'great work *The Making of Ireland and Its Undoing*', wrote Connolly, was 'the only contribution to Irish history we know of which conforms to the methods of modern historical science'. It is from Stopford Green that Connolly finds reinforcement for his schema of the conquest and re-conquest, by which Irish history underwent a fundamental rupture in the Elizabethan era, and a supposedly foreign 'feudal-capitalist system' was adopted and urged 'upon the Gaelic Irish'. This system, it is said, quoting Stopford Green, was 'antagonistic to the immemorial law of Ireland', its Brehon Code, the juridical expression of Ireland's supposed communal social order.[235]

Peter Beresford Ellis has also argued that *Labour in Irish History* was influenced by the work of Patrick Joyce, whose *A Social History of Ancient Ireland* was published in two volumes in 1906. This may well be true. However, Joyce's section on the 'Five main Classes of People' admits the existence of 'Non-Free Classes', whose number include 'some being absolute slaves, some little removed from slavery, and others far above it'. This somewhat undermines Connolly's claims for an idealised 'Gaelic communism'. Indeed, Connolly himself later recognises the existence of slavery in ancient Ireland, though never reconciles this with his view of Irish history.[236]

But, as we have stressed, *Erin's Hope* was written before Joyce's book. Connolly is, in fact, clear about his sources. His argument regarding the Irish clan system as an instance of primitive communism is based, he writes, on 'recent scientific research by such eminent sociologists as Letourneau, Lewis Morgan, Sir Henry Maine, and others, [which] has amply demonstrated the fact that common ownership of land formed the basis of primitive society in almost every country'.[237] Connolly, therefore, is intervening in a much wider debate in European and North American circles on the stages of world historical development. As Raphael Samuel has argued, the 1860s and 1870s saw the establishment of 'pre-history' as a subject for academic debate. This was based on developments in the fields of archaeology, anthropology, philology and comparative jurisprudence. By the 1870s, moreover, 'the notion of primitive communism was one on which scholars of many different tendencies were converging'.[238]

Sir Henry Maine, whom Connolly cites, is best known for his connections to India. Maine served as a Legal Member of the Viceroy's Council in the 1860s and his writings shaped the way British colonial officials governed the country. Maine also had a scholarly interest in Ireland. In 1852, the British government agreed to fund a Commission 'to transcribe, translate, edit, and make available for publication the Brehon Law manuscripts'.[239] Maine took a keen interest in the project and was in touch with the translators. He delivered a series of lectures before the University of Oxford on the

Brehon Laws, which were published in 1875 as *Lectures on the Early History of Institutions*. In these lectures, Maine wrote that 'the collective ownership of the soil by groups of men either in fact united by blood relationship, or believing … that they are so united' was a global historical reality 'entitled to rank as an ascertained primitive phenomenon, universally characterising those communities of mankind between whose civilisation and ours there is any distinct connection ….'

Two years later, the progressive North American anthropologist Lewis Henry Morgan published his *Ancient Society*. Morgan developed a theory of cultural evolution which held, in essence, that human society developed through a number of stages driven primarily by changes in food production. Society progressed from hunting-and-gathering (a 'communism in living', with no surplus and no division of labour), to settled agriculture, to urban society (or 'civilisation'). *Ancient Society* caused excitement in socialist circles, as it appeared to independently confirm the materialist conception of history. Marx himself made extensive notes on Morgan's book. In Engels's view, 'Morgan in his own way had discovered afresh in America the materialistic conception of history discovered by Marx forty years ago, and in his comparison of barbarism and civilisation it had led him, in the main points, to the same conclusions as Marx.' *Ancient Society* gave, as Engels wrote to Kautsky, a 'factual basis we have hitherto lacked' for the existence of class struggle throughout human society.[240] Following Marx's death in 1883, Engels took up this analysis of Morgan's (unintentional) contribution to historical materialism and wrote his classic work *On the Origins of the Family, Private Property and the State* in 1884. Essentially a précis and a commentary on Morgan, Engels' book explicitly set out 'to present the results of Morgan's researches in the light of the conclusions [of the] materialistic examination of history, and thus to make clear their full significance'.[241]

Connolly might have been expected to reference Engels's work explicitly in *Erin's Hope* but *Origins* was not available in English until 1902, when the Charles H. Kerr company commissioned a translation from the original German for its popular 'Standard Socialist Series'.[242] From what we know of Connolly's own views on the subject, he too might have had serious problems with Engels extending the historical analysis into a critical dissection of modern family life.

Even if Connolly was not familiar with Engels' book, Morgan's book was known about, if not widely. Hyndman was a particular enthusiast, putting Morgan's work on a par with Marx's *Capital* in 1884 and the work of Charles Darwin four years later.[243] He did, however, express regret that a hostile review by Sir Henry Maine may be the main introduction to Morgan in English.[244] Moreover, Connolly's claim in *Erin's Hope* that the contemporary Ireland's 'Celtic forefathers … foreshadowed in the democratic organisation of the Irish clan the more perfect organisation of the free society of the future' bears a striking resemblance to the following claim by Morgan:

> Democracy in government, brotherhood in society, equality in rights and privileges and universal education, foreshadow the next higher plane of society to which experience, intelligence and knowledge are steadily tending. It will be a revival, in a higher form, of the liberty, equality and fraternity of the ancient gentes.[245]

Connolly also mentions the French anthropologist Charles Letourneau (1831-1902), who wrote widely on the evolution of property in 'primitive' society. Letourneau's books had been a feature of socialists' personal libraries since the mid-1880s. In 1884, the SDF recommended his *Sociology* as a 'useful work for students of Scientific Socialism'. In 1892, Letourneau's *Evolutionary of Property* was cited by H. W. Lee in *Justice* in 1892 as 'one of the most valuable and interesting contributions to the great question now looming up so portentously before the scared eyes of the capitalists' and was being advertised in the *Labour Leader* in 1897, the year Connolly wrote *Erin's Hope.*[246] In 1892, his book *Property: its Origins and Development* was added to the Contemporary Science series produced by Walter Scott Publishing Co., which published literature for a mass audience in affordable editions. It received positive reviews in the anarchist newspaper *Freedom* and was advertised in Robert Blatchford's *Clarion* as an 'ethnological account of the beginnings of property among animals, of its communistic stage among primitive races, and of its later individualistic developments, together with a brief sketch of its probable evolution in the future'.[247]

Maine's work in particular was received with 'considerably scholarly interest and acclaim.'[248] However, as J.W. Burrow has argued, Maine was less enamoured about the political uses to which his research was often put. Maine, 'whose political attitudes can be loosely described as a hard-headed Peelite elitism varied by a taste for Burkean rhetoric, was incensed to find himself hailed in the press as a "prophet of agrarian radicalism"'.[249] Indeed, John Stuart Mill, who Connolly also cites in *Erin's Hope*, 'used his review of [Maine's] *Village Communities* to preach a sermon on the mutability of concepts of property and the desirability of the redistribution of the land'.[250] As Burrow writes, this was not unnatural, for references to agricultural communes inexorably attached themselves, in the absence of explicit disclaimers, to that long tradition of nostalgic agrarian radicalism whose course Christopher Hill has traced in *The Norman Yoke*, and which was being given a fresh if relatively short-lived impetus in the 1870s by the agitation for land reform [by Henry George, among others].[251]

Hill's notion of the 'Norman Yoke' myth provides another suggestive lens through which to examine Connolly's early writings on Irish history. The Marxist historian Christopher Hill, writing of the myth of the 'Norman Yolk' has outlined the recurrence of such idealised pasts in early modern movements of agrarian radicalism, through to the Chartists and the early socialist movement. As Hill argued:

Theories of lost rights, of a primitive happy state, have existed in nearly all communities. The Fall of Man; the Golden Age; Arcadia; the Noble Savage – all these in their different ways express a belief that inequality and the exploitation of man by man have a historical origin, and a hope that the period of equality which survived in popular imagination may one day be restored.[252]

One of the most prevalent myths in agrarian radical movements in Britain was the idea of the 'Norman Yoke'. In the sixteen and seventeenth centuries, writes Hill, 'it was generally agreed that there had been a state of primitive communism which was also a Golden Age, and that both had ended when private property and political authority were introduced'.[253] Before 1066, the Anglo-Saxons had 'lived as free and equal citizens, governing themselves through representative institutions. The Norman Conquest deprived them of this liberty, and established the tyranny of an alien King and landlords.'[254] As Hill argues, though it was lacking as an accurate historical account, 'as a rudimentary class theory of politics, the myth had great historical significance'. It was

entirely secular, whereas most popular opposition theories before the seventeenth century had been religious. It united the Third Estate against Crown, Church and landlords, branding them as hereditary enemies of the people. It suggested that the ruling class is alien to the interests of the majority of the population. Even if they no longer speak French, whether or not they are of Norman descent, the upper classes are isolated from the life of the working population and oppose their interests. The people can conduct their own affairs better without their Norman rulers, whose wealth and privilege are an obstacle to equality. The nation is the people.'[255]

The similarities to Connolly's own arguments are clear. For Connolly, the Irish working class is the nation, and the bourgeoisie 'while professedly ultra-nationalistic in its political aims, had nevertheless so far compounded with the enemy as to accept the alien social system ...' The Irish people could conduct *their* own affairs without 'those whom we must remove in our onward march' to the Irish Socialist Republic.[256]

As Hill writes, the 'Norman Yoke' myth became less relevant for the urban working class created in 1820s as a consequence of the Industrial Revolution. However, it did not die and could be found in the arguments of the Chartist movement of the 1830s and 1840s. Following the decline of Chartism, 'the theory of the Norman Yoke persisted among advanced Radical working men, free-thinkers and land reformers. It was given a last lease of life by the revival of republicanism and the land reform agitation of the eighteen-seventies.'[257] Land reform was, of course, a prominent theme in Irish politics of the 1870s, with the Land League, and in Scotland. Henry George exercised a strong influence over many figures in the 'socialist revival' of the 1880s, bringing the connection right up to Connolly's day. Indeed, Hill points out that the 'Norman Yoke' myth was present in the works of Robert Blatchford of the Clarion movement. His *Britain for the British* argued that 'titles to land ownership must be based on the Norman Conquest, or on theft by enclosure of common land'.[258] It is significant, therefore, that the title of Connolly's articles in the *Labour Leader,* which comprised the largest part of *Erin's Hope* was 'Ireland for the Irish'. We know Connolly was aware of Blatchford's *Britain for the British* and indeed recommended it as a piece of political propaganda. Nellie Gordon, a mill worker and trade union activists with whom Connolly became acquainted in Belfast in 1912, remembered that he bought her Blatchford's book. When Gordon told Connolly that she enjoyed it, '[h]e said "I knew you would" as he had read it in his early days and it helped him to become convinced. Then he bought me *A Tale of Two Cities.*'[259]

The debate about 'primitive communism' in the late 19th century socialist movement is not limited to Britain. It also sits within a wider cultural phenomenon: *fin de siècle* resurgence Romanticism, sometimes referred to as neo-Romanticism. As Michael Löwy and Robert Sayre have convincingly argued, Romanticism is not simply a literary or artistic movement but a '*weltanschauung* or worldview, that is a collective mental structure'.[260] It thus embraces a much wider field of human culture than the arts, including political philosophy. At its root, Romanticism 'represents a critique of modernity, that is, of modern capitalist civilisation, in the name of value and ideals drawn from the past (the precapitalist, premodern past)'.[261] This critique is based, above all, on a sense of nostalgia, 'a sense that characterized by the painful and melancholic conviction that in modern reality something precious has been lost, at the level of both individuals and humanity at large; certain essential human values have been alienated'.[262] This sense of nostalgia, or a longing for the past, can be based on a highly idealised form of a real past, or on a mythological or legendary past. Either way, the Romantic vision, Löwy and Sayre, argue:

> selects a moment from the actual past in which the harmful characteristics of modernity did not yet exist and in which the human values that have been since stifled by modernity were still operative; that moment is then transformed into a utopia, shaped as the embodiment of Romantic aspirations. This is one way to explain the seeming paradox according to which the Romantic orientation towards the past can also involve looking ahead; the image of a dreamed-of future beyond the contemporary world is inscribed within the evocation of a precapitalist era.[263]

As this suggests, a Romantic worldview could be reactionary, even counter-revolutionary or fascistic, but can also be revolutionary and utopian. The latter form of Romanticism:

> goes beyond the types already mentioned to invest the nostalgia for a precapitalist past in the hope for a radically new future. Rejecting both the illusion of a pure and simple return to the organic communities of the past and the resigned acceptance of the bourgeois present or its amelioration by means of reforms, revolutionary or utopian Romanticism aspires … to the abolition of capitalism or to an egalitarian utopia in which certain features of values or earlier societies would reappear.[264]

Löwy and Sayre give examples of a Romantic standpoint that is 'oriented toward future accomplishments', highlighting in particular Percy Bysshe Shelley, William Morris and Walter Benjamin. For these figures, 'the recollection of the past serves as a weapon in the struggle for the future'.[265] It is argued here that Connolly could be added to his list, as his 'recollection' (or, rather, construction) of a mythic Irish Gaelic communism serves precisely as such a weapon in the struggle for an Irish Workers' Republic against the Home Rule bourgeoisie.

Indeed, the whole debate over primitive communism was a controversial one in post-independence Ireland, as more conservative figures sought to dispute Connolly's claim. Three years after the Easter Rising, Eoin MacNeill, Professor of Irish History at Universal College Dublin published a series of articles in the Catholic *Irish Review*, in which he sought to undermine the notion of communal ownership by the clan.[266] Tellingly, MacNeill took aim at Weston Joyce, and did not address the recently executed Connolly directly. Writing in 1937, however, the republican Aodh be Blacam was clear about the political import of the debate of Ireland's past: 'In the present time of controversy over socialism, the truth, established by MacNeill, that Gaelic Ireland was a State based on peasant proprietorship, has high importance, which need not be stressed here.'[267]

Connolly was not unique in mobilising history for this purpose. In fact, he drew from a large well of neo-Romanticism in the late nineteenth century. Common in the socialist movement of the British Isles in this period were themes of a lost and often communistic past. In David Howell's study of the ILP, he explores the intellectual basis of the party and notes that many of the principal spokespersons developed their ideas from self-education. Their reading 'blended social, economic and literary works characteristic of late Victorian Radicalism', with Thomas Carlyle, John Ruskin as 'typically formative influences'. As this suggests, a Romantic critique of capitalism was often a gateway to socialism, attracted by its critique of the alienation of the worker and the inhumanity of the factory system. Thus, Keir Hardie looked back to 'the romanticised world of the independent Scottish colliers' and spoke of a 'Golden Age' across Europe as a whole, which 'lasted from the beginning of the thirteenth to the middle of the fifteenth century [where] there were neither Millionaires nor Paupers in those days, but a rude abundance for all'.[268] Most typically, Blatchford's major work, *Merrie England,* one of the most popular texts of the late nineteenth-century 'socialist revival', contrasted the idealised rural idylls of the past with the contemporary reality of industrial Britain. And, of course, there was William Morris, whose medievalism, informed by his reading of Ruskin, inspired his political commitment and infused his socialism. Thus, in *News From Nowhere,* serialised in the Socialist League journal *Commonweal* in 1890, the protagonist William Guest wakes up in a near-future and post-revolutionary London. In contrast to the urban technological utopia of Edward Bellamy's *Looking Backward,* to which Morris's novel was a something of a response, *News from Nowhere* reflects Morris's aesthetic concerns. The factory system has been abandoned in favour of handicrafts, while labour is conducted in a non-alienated manner by means of voluntary co-operation; meanwhile, the balance between humans and nature has been restored, the state has dissolved, and relations between persons dealt with without recourse to the coercive institutions of the law. Its value as political propaganda is directly addressed in the text itself: 'Yes, surely!' concludes Guest at the end of novel; 'and if others can see it as I have seen it, then it may be called a vision rather than a dream.'[269]

It is surely no coincidence, then, that the first organisation that Connolly joined was the Socialist League, led by Morris, who was its outstanding theorist between 1885 and 1890. Nor is it a surprise that Connolly's own poetry was informed by a love of Shelley, whose Romantic invocation of nature was formed in the context of rapid industrialisation of the sort that Ireland had yet to experience. In John Leslie's 'The Irish Question', a text which also draws on Morris, and exercised a profound and formative influence on Connolly, Leslie argued that Ireland could skip industrialisation, proceeding straight to socialism. Leslie bolstered his argument with a pamphlet 'Economic Evolution' written by Robert Cunningham Graham, a wealthy adventurer who was converted to socialism by works of Hyndman and Morris in 1883, and who sat as a radical Liberal MP for North-West Lanarkshire from 1886 to 1892. If Leslie 'was able to place in the hands of every working man and woman in Ireland' a copy of this work, they would see the impact of industrialisation on Ireland:

If the Irish people wish to see their fair island turned into a pandemonium even worse than the landlord has been able to make it, let them call in the capitalist. If they wish to see whole districts of their towns and cities inhabited by the thief and the prostitute, let them call in the capitalist.[270]

We find a direct echo of these arguments in *Erin's Hope*, where Connolly argues:

Let the produce of Irish soil go first to feed the Irish people, and after a sufficient store has been retained to insure of that being accomplished, let the surplus be exchanged with other countries in return for those manufactured goods Ireland needs but does not herself produce.

Thus we will abolish at one stroke the dread of foreign competition and render perfectly needless any attempt to create an industrial hell in Ireland under the specious pretext of "developing our resources".[271]

All that is missing from Connolly's invocation of an 'industrial hell in Ireland' is a Blakean indictment of the 'dark satanic mills'.

It must be stressed that this strain of revolutionary Romanticism does not in the slightest qualify Connolly's own commitment to Marxism. It was not just the ethical or Christian socialist traditions of the ILP that drew on the notion of the 'Golden Age'; more orthodox Second International Marxism, too, found a future-oriented use for visions of the past. As Vincent Geoghan has argued, the 'principal theoreticians of the Second International', living as they did in the age of Darwin and of technological advancement, 'prided themselves on the scientific nature of their socialism'.[272] For Marx and Engels, 'scientific socialism' was elaborated in contrast to and in a struggle with 'utopian socialism'. In the *Communist Manifesto*, Marx and Engels poured scorn on 'Feudal Socialism' ('half lamentation, half lampoon; half an echo of the past, half menace of the future') and 'Petty-Bourgeois Socialism' ('both reactionary and Utopian'), while in the *Eighteen Brumaire of Louis Napoleon*, Marx wrote that: 'The social revolution of the nineteenth century cannot take its poetry from the past but only from the future. It cannot begin with itself before it has stripped away all superstition about the past ... [It] must let the dead bury their dead in order to arrive at its own content.'[273]

Nevertheless, while Second International Marxists strived to avoid the sins of utopianism, and largely steered clear of 'blueprints' for the socialist future, 'these thinkers found it quite impossible to do without a future orientation. In the complex world of the late nineteenth century, Marxists, like everybody else, felt the need for both long- and short-term speculation.' If utopian speculation about the future was precluded by the need to be 'scientific' then, argues Geoghan:

> recourse to history was one way out. It was possible to speculate about the future by talking about the past. Discussion of an ancient freedom could become the arena for anticipation of future freedom. Furthermore, one could give greater substance and plausibility to an imagine of the future by showing that such arrangements once obtained in the past. If a Golden Age had once existed, was not a Golden Future a real possibility?[274]

Thus, the 'discovery' in the 1870s of 'primitive communism' as a distinct stage in human history provided a 'scientifically' sound basis for the argument that capitalism was neither a natural nor eternal system. We have seen already how Marx and Engels greeted the publication of Morgan's *Ancient Society* as independent verification of the materialist conception of history. Between 1879 and 1882, Marx conducted extensive readings of the works of anthropologists, and made hundreds of thousands of pages of notes on topics as diverse as the Indian village culture, communal property in Latin America, kinship patterns in Ireland and among Native Americans, studies of Ancient Greece and Rome, and the impact of Dutch colonialism on the village economy of Indonesia (Java). Engels draws out the political import of this work most clearly in *The Origins of the Family, Private Property and the State* where he explicitly criticises contemporary capitalist values from the standpoint of the Iroquois gens, referring to the indigenous confederacy in north-east America:

> The power of this primitive community had to be broken, and it was broken. But it was broken by influences which from the very start appear as a degradation, a fall from the simple moral greatness of the old gentile society. The lowest interests – base greed, brutal appetites, sordid avarice, selfish robbery of the common wealth – inaugurate the new, civilized, class society.[275]

It was not only past societies that caught Marx's interest. Linked closely with the greater awareness of pre-capitalist societies 'was the extension of knowledge of the rural non-capitalist enmeshed in the capitalist world'.[276] As Kevin Anderson has argued, from the early 1870s, Marx himself focused increasingly 'on forms of resistance to capital outside Western Europe and North America' and a more multi-linear approach to history, in contrast to the emphasis of his main published works on advanced capitalist development, the *Communist Manifesto* (1848) and *Capital* (1867).[277]

Besides India, the main contemporary example Marx had in mind in his final decades was that of Russia, which offered to him 'rich evidence concerning rural communes ("archaic" yet evidently alive in a world of capitalist triumphs)', as well as 'direct revolutionary experience, all encompassed by the theory and practice of Russian revolutionary populism'.[278] In 1877, he was prompted to reply to a favourable review by the Populist leader Nikolai Mikhailovsky, who attributed to Marx the view that all societies are destined to follow the same development route to capitalism as England and Western Europe. In a draft reply to the article, Marx complained that Mikhailovsky

> insists on transforming my historical sketch of the genesis of capitalism in Western Europe into a historico-philosophical theory of the general course fatally imposed on all peoples, whatever the historical circumstances in which they find themselves placed.[279]

These points, Anderson argues, are applicable not only to Russia but 'the other contemporary non-Western, non-industrialized societies that [Marx] was studying in this period', such as India, Indonesia, Algeria and Latin America, though these 'through colonialism ... had all been impacted by capitalism more directly than Russia'.[280]

More concretely, Marx in fact developed a hypothetical sketch of what a non-capitalist course of development might look like for Russia. This very question was at the centre of revolutionary debates in Russia. The dominant Populist strand of opinion was that if the Tsarist autocracy could be overthrown, Russia's peasant communes could serve as a point of departure for socialism without first passing through a stage of industrial capitalist development. In 1881, in a letter to his Russian follower Vera Zassulich, and in his final publication, the preface to the second Russian edition of *Communist Manifesto* in 1882, co-signed by Marx and Engels, Marx speculated that a socialist revolution in Western Europe may allow Russia to skip capitalist development and directly appropriate the fruits of modern technological progress in alliance with more developed socialist states:

> Now the question is: can the Russian obshchina, though greatly undermined, yet a form of the primeval common ownership of land, pass directly to the higher form of communist common ownership? Or on the contrary, must it first pass through the same process of dissolution as constitutes the historical evolution of the West? The only answer to that possible today is this: If the Russian Revolution becomes the signal for a proletarian revolution in the West, so that both complement each other.[281]

In the end, the Russian commune dissolved, and capitalism developed before a revolution could occur in Western Europe. In 1883, the year Marx died, his followers in Russia, Georgi Plekhanov, Vera Zassulich and Pavel Axelrod formed the Emancipation of Labour Group and broke sharply from any residual Populism. In a series of pioneering works, *Socialism and the Political Struggle* (1883) and *Our Differences* (1884), Plekhanov accepted beyond doubt that the triumph of capitalism in Russia would be irreversible, dissolving the peasant commune, breaking down traditional rural social relations, and increasing the differentiation of the peasantry along class lines. On the other hand, they proclaimed a new road to socialism in Russia, not through the peasant commune but through capitalist development, and with it, the creation of an industrial working class. As a consequence, they drew the practical conclusion that the task of Russian socialists was the creation in Russia of a labour movement analogous to those in Western Europe.

The development of a workers' movement in Russia, through sporadic strikes in the 1890s, vindicated the Emancipation of Labour Group, proving that they based their political programme on the curve of Russian historical development. In 1894, recognising this, Engels attempted to give a balance sheet to the whole debate, writing that:

> The Russian commune has existed for hundreds of years without ever providing the impetus for the development of a higher form of common ownership out of itself; no more so than in the case of the German Mark system, the Celtic clans, the Indian and other communes with primitive, communistic institutions.[282]

There are similarities and crucial differences in Connolly's approach to Ireland. What is similar is that in places Connolly explicitly challenged the deterministic view that all societies must proceed through a set series of pre-conceived stages. In a key passage in *Erin's Hope*, Connolly gives an insight into his view of history which, though it has Ireland as its object, nevertheless has much wider significance:

> The ardent student of sociology, who believes that the progress of the human race through the various economic stages of communism, chattel slavery, feudalism and wage slavery, has been but a preparation for the higher ordered society of the future; that the most industrially advanced countries are but, albeit often unconsciously, developing the social conditions which, since the break-up of universal tribal communism, have been rendered historically necessary for the inauguration of a new and juster economic order, in which social, political and national antagonism will be unknown, will perhaps regard the Irish adherence to clan ownership at such a comparatively recent date as the 17th Century as evidence of retarded economical development, and therefore a real hindrance to progress. But the sympathetic student of history, who believes in the possibility of a people by political intuition anticipating the lessons afterwards revealed to them in the sad school of experience, will not be indisposed to join with the ardent Irish patriot in his lavish expressions of admiration for the sagacity of his Celtic forefathers, who foreshadowed in the democratic organisation of the Irish clan the more perfect organisation of the free society of the future.[283]

This fascinating and instructive passage points to the ingenuity of Connolly's early Marxism. Here, Connolly attempts to transcend the linear, stadial and deterministic Marxism that was common in the Marxist movement of his time, towards a much more multilinear and contingent approach to historical development. In his contrast between the 'ardent student of sociology' and the 'sympathetic student of history', Connolly's own affinity leans firmly towards the latter. This much is clear if one looks at Connolly's earlier article in the *Labour Leader* on which this section of his pamphlet is based. There, the viewpoint of the 'ardent student of sociology' was referred to as:

the strange theory that the progress of the human race has been in some strange manner pre-ordained to pass through the various stages of communism, chattel-slavery, feudalism, and wage-slavery as a preparation for the high ordered society of the future, who teach that since society has walked along certain lines it might not under altered circumstances have reached the same high goal along totally different lines ...[284]

However, the crucial difference between Marx's views on the Russian commune and Connolly's invocation of a primitive Gaelic communism is, of course, that the Russian commune still existed – for a time – while Marx was writing. As Howell has written, Connolly's case for Ireland 'involved no institutional inheritance – only a historical memory with a substantial accretion of myth'.[285] Connolly himself admits this when he writes that

[the] clans are now no more and could not be revived, even if it were desirable to do so, which is more than questionable, but the right of ownership still lives on, and should now be established in the modern Corporate embodiment of the life of the Irish nation – our public boards, municipality and independent Irish Congress when we are men enough to win one.[286]

Thus, Connolly's approach to Ireland's past perhaps most closely parallels that of the Peruvian Marxist José Carlos Mariátegui, writing in the 1920s. In building a socialist movement in Peru, Mariátegui used Incan communism as an analogy. Mariátegui was clear, however, that:

Modern communism is different from Inca communism ... The two communisms are products of different human experiences. They belong to different historical epochs. They were evolved by dissimilar civilizations ... It is therefore absurd to compare the forms and institutions of the two communisms. All that can be compared is their essential and material likeness, within the essential and material difference of time and space.[287]

Mariátegui's phrase is a good one. Connolly, too, argued for an 'essential and material likeness' between ancient Gaelic civilisation and modern socialism 'within the essential and material difference of time and space'. Connolly, as a Marxist, knew well that socialism was not a literal return to the Gaelic communism of the past; nor would it be brought into being by a mere cultural memory of the past. Socialism, for Connolly, 'is not the product of the brains of any man nor of any number of men' but would be 'the legitimate child of a long, drawn-out historical evolution, and its consummation will only be finally possible when that evolutionary process has attained to a suitable degree of development'. It is 'not a mere piece of speculative philosophy, primarily a scientific analysis of the past and present structure of society, a comprehensive *summing up of the facts of history'*.[288]

In this context, Connolly's historical analysis was intended to destroy the myths of Irish middle-class Catholic history, reveal the class lines within the national movement, and forge a proletarian worldview as a spur and a guide to action. However disputable as 'history', *Erin's Hope* and, later, *Labour in Irish History,* can be seen as 'living books', in the sense Antonio Gramsci understood Machiavelli's *The Prince*: 'not a systematic treatment, but a "living book", in which political ideology and political science are fused in the dramatic form of a "myth".'[289] Myths, as Joseph Mali, reminds us, are no less powerful for their lack of strict historical accuracy.[290]

The ISRP and the Republicans

With this analysis in tow, Connolly and the ISRP launched themselves into the political scene in Dublin. Connolly's period in the city coincided with the period of the Gaelic Revival, and the rediscovery (and re-invention) of Ireland's historical, literary and cultural past.

The Gaelic Revival was an intensely creative period of literary and political activity, lasting roughly from the late nineteenth century to the creation of the Irish Free State in 1922. The Gaelic League, founded in 1893 by Douglas Hyde to promote the use of the Irish language, was gathering a huge following. The Gaelic Athletic Association had been formed earlier, in 1884, to promote interest in Irish sports such as hurling in order to counter the influence of British soccer, cricket and rugby. At the same time, the young poet William Butler Yeats fuelled an Irish literary revival in high culture, geared at creating Irish forms of verse, stories and history. In 1892 Yeats founded the National Literary Society in Dublin and hoped for 'a school of Irish poetry – founded on Irish myth and history – a neo-romantic movement' which was steeped in Celtic mythology, then-fashionable Victorian medievalism and echoes of the earlier pre-Raphaelite movement.[291]

As with many nations in the throes of modernisation, the revival movement was often romantic and backward-looking, appealing to a mythical and idealised national past. The vision of Ireland promoted by the likes of Yeats was, in Liz Curtis's words, an 'ideal Ireland as imagined by a member of the Protestant ascendancy caste, influenced by Victorian romanticism' in which an idealised aristocracy ruled benevolently over the peasantry.[292]

Yet at the same time, the new cultural nationalism was forward-looking in that it wanted to construct a new sense of Irish nationality for twentieth century, based not on the British Empire but on values and a virile quality lacking in the then seemingly moribund Home Rule movement. As Joe Cleary has argued, the Revival is best understood as

a complex cultural moment in which a declining Ascendancy colonial elite, an emergent anti-colonial, constitutionally democratic, but socially conservative Irish middle-class bourgeois nationalism, and more radical republican and socialist versions of anti-colonial nationalism engaged in a protracted contest for dominance within the Irish national movement.[293]

Connolly and the ISRP, while warning that 'you cannot teach a starving man Gaelic', were not indifferent to the cultural Revival and were close to many of its moving spirits.[294] Fred Ryan, later to be a founding member of Yeats's Abbey Theatre, was close to the party and joined for a short time. As has already been mentioned, Connolly was on good terms with Alice Milligan of the *Shan Van Vocht* and her younger brother Ernest attempted to establish a Belfast branch of the ISRP. Moreover, the ISRP saw an opportunity to intervene into the political and cultural ferment in Dublin at the time.

In 1897, the ISRP was determined that celebrations of Queen Victoria's Diamond Jubilee would not go off without visible opposition. Connolly devised a plan to hold a demonstration, as he recalled over a decade later, to '[shatter] all the elaborate attempts of the British government to represent Ireland as loyal'. The ISRP issued a proclamation to the Irish working class to '[j]oin your voice with ours in protesting against the base assumption that we owe to this Empire any other debt than that of hatred of all its plundering institutions'.[295]

Then, on 3 April, Connolly joined with Maud Gonne, recently returned from an American lecture tour to promote the Irish nationalist cause, to organise the counter-demonstration to the Jubilee celebrations. Gonne recalled in her memoirs that:

Jubilee Day arrived. All the shops which relied on Unionist custom had decorations and electric lamps for night-display. James Connolly and other friends arranged our Jubilee display also I had obtained a window in the National Club in Parnell Square from which, on a huge screen, Pat O'Brien's photos of the Eviction scenes could be shown and the photos of the men who, during Victoria's reign, had been executed or who had died in prison.[296]

Connolly, with the help of workers at the Dublin Corporation, had arranged that the wires be cut to prevent the electric lamp displays in Unionist-owned shops, and Maud Gonne, working with the utmost secrecy, 'had been busy making black flags with suitable inscriptions in white, showing the numbers who had died of famine during Victoria's reign, the number of houses destroyed and the number of men jailed, etc'.[297] For the following day, Connolly 'had arranged for the making of a big coffin symbolic of the fate of the British Empire, and had obtained the services of a workers' band whose instruments were so old and battered that if they were broken by the police it would be no great loss'.[298] The ISRP marched in a procession with the black coffin, while the workers' brass band played a funeral dirge on their rickety instruments. This led to 'charges by mounted police and baton charges and people began to be carried off in ambulance'. Connolly, Gonne recalled,

was not a man to be easily stopped … [At O'Connell Bridge] the fighting was furious and, seeing the coffin in danger of being captured by the police, Connolly gave the order to throw it in the Liffey. The whole crowd shouted: 'Here goes the coffin of the British Empire. To hell with the British Empire!'[299]

Connolly was arrested for his troubles, but the city was in darkness, and none of the Jubilee electric lamp displays visible. By contrast, Gonne's lantern display of famine scenes and evictions had been a huge success. Later that night, as the crowd refused to disperse, a police baton-charge fatally injured an elderly woman, causing a riot during which shop windows displaying jubilee decorations were smashed up. In spite of this tragedy, the ISRP could count the day's events as a huge propaganda success for the small organisation. Despite the desperate wishes of the British government, the myth of 'loyal Dublin' had been smashed as thoroughly as the Jubilee window displays.

The Jubilee celebration was only the first instance of collaboration between Connolly and the Irish republicans. The following year was the centenary of the 1798 United Irishmen rebellion, the revolutionary bourgeois movement inspired by the French Revolution. Across the country, activists established '98 Clubs, which 'quickly became the fastest growing nationalist movement in the country', reaching 10,000 members by July 1897.[300] So successful were the republican-inspired commemoration committees that the constitutional nationalists and the Catholic Church felt the need to orchestrate a takeover, bringing the clubs under the control of their own rival 'United Ireland Centennial Association'. Provoking the anger of the ISRP, even the millionaire capitalist William Martin Murphy got involved in the commemorations. The ISRP formed its own 'Rank and File '98 Club', which held several meetings and attempted, unsuccessfully, to have the Centennial Association sponsor an anti-Jubilee demonstration. When this proposal was rejected, the Rank and File Club 'put down a motion at a convention of the Centennial Association that the body should be confined to those who approved the aims and methods of the men of 1798'.[301] The motion was rejected, and the Rank and File Club disaffiliated.

It is often assumed in retrospect that Home Ruler and Irish republican nationalism are wholly separate and parallel traditions, drawing on their own respective pantheons of dates and heroes. As the Home Ruler attempts to elbow into the 1798 commemorations, the latter had no compunction about co-opting the revolutionary and non-sectarian ideals of 1798 for its own moderate, nationalist and more explicitly Catholic aims and purposes. In the end, the priests, Home Rule politicians and members of the sectarian Catholic Ancient Order of Hibernians were able to ensure the participation of MPs on the platform at the centenary celebrations. At Westport, for example, William O'Brien MP, the leader of one of the Home Rule parties, the United Ireland League (UIL), addressed a centenary 'in which he spoke almost entirely about Gladstone and Parnell's legacy regarding the land question'. Meanwhile, the late Parnell's brother John chaired the '98 demonstration in Arklow and 'spoke merely about the contrasting attitudes of [Conservative politicians] Chamberlain and Balfour regarding the local government bill currently being debated in Westminster'. Even at the 'Wolfe Tone Day' event in Dublin on 15 August, organised by the IRB, 'the Irish Party was able to ensure that the main political speeches for the event were delivered by MPs, who consequently derived perhaps the biggest political benefit from the event'.[302]

The Rank and File Club's motion was an attempt to expose this process. As part of its intervention, the ISRP published its own set of five *'98 Readings,* announced by the party as 'a series of reprints of the most important literature, current in Ireland 100 years ago, including the chief official documents on the United Irishmen and their writings in prose and verse'. Developed from Connolly's extensive researches in the National Library, the *Readings* carried little critical introductory material, rather seeking to allow the United Irishmen 'to present in their own language the principles and ideas which animated them'. These includes Tone's own *An Argument on behalf of the Catholics of Ireland,* an account of the Belfast Commemoration of the French Revolution from Bastille Day 1791 and the address to the French National Convention in November 1792 by Edward Fitzgerald and Tom Paine. As Donal Nevin comments: 'The themes that recur throughout the *'98 Readings* were those that dominated Connolly's thinking and his actions: liberty, the rights of man, truth, fraternity, justice, resistance to oppression, democracy.'[303]

Then, in August 1898, the ISRP published the first issue of its newspaper, the *Workers' Republic.* Funded by a £50 loan from Keir Hardie, the *Workers' Republic* was Ireland's first Marxist newspaper, with the stated aim 'to unite the workers and to bury, in one common grave, the religious hatreds, the provincial jealousies and mutual distrusts upon which oppression has so long depended for security'.[304] In a blistering article, 'The Men We Honour', the ISRP intervened sharply into the 1798 commemoration movement. 'Apostles of Freedom', wrote Connolly, 'are ever idolised when dead, but crucified when living. Universally true as this statement is, it applies with more than usual point to the revolutionary hero in whose memory the Irish people will, on Monday, 15th August, lay the foundation stone of a great memorial.' Connolly continued, with the Home Rulers in his sights:

> the men who push forward most arrogantly to burn incense at the altar of his fame are drawn from the very class who, were he alive today, would hasten to repudiate him as a dangerous malcontent. … Our Home Rule leaders will find that the glory of Wolfe Tone's memory will serve, not to cover, but to accentuate the darkness of their shame.

Like the Home Rulers, Wolfe Tone was a bourgeois figure. However, unlike them, he represented the most advanced thinking of his day, at a time when the bourgeoise was revolutionary as a class. As Connolly argued:

Wolfe Tone was abreast of the revolutionary thought of his day, as are the Socialist Republicans of our day. He saw clearly, as we see, that a dominion as long rooted in any country as British dominion in Ireland can only be dislodged by a revolutionary impulse in line with the development of the entire epoch. Grasping this truth in all its fulness he broke with the so-called 'practical' men of the time, and wherever he could get a hearing he, by voice and pen, inculcated the republican principles of the French Revolution and counselled his countrymen to embark the national movement on the crest of that revolutionary wave.

It was in this sense, then, 'a grateful Irish people will carve the name of our precursor, Theobald Wolfe Tone, the man whose virtues we can only honour by imitation as the Socialist Republic will yet honour his principles by realisation'.[305]

It was not just the Home Rulers, however, that the ISRP came into sharp conflict with over the 1798 commemorations. As John Newsinger has argued, any claims that Connolly in this time wished to 'build Socialism in Ireland on a Fenian base' or that his writings in this period 'were an important precedent for Connolly's standpoint in 1916' must reckon with his view on the Irish republican movement of the late 1890s.[306] In July 1899, Connolly recalled:

The '98 Executive, organised in the commencement by professed believers in the physical force doctrine, started by proclaiming its adherence to the principle of national independence 'as understood by Wolfe Tone and the United Irishmen', and in less than twelve months from doing so, deliberately rejected a similar resolution and elected on its governing body men notorious for their Royalist proclivities. [This was, Connolly continued] an interesting corroboration of the truth of our statement that the advanced Nationalists of our day are utterly regardless of principle and only attach importance to methods – an instance of putting the cart before the horse, absolutely unique in its imbecility and unparalleled in the history of the world.[307]

It was not just the events surrounding the 1798 centenary which brought Connolly into conflict in the IRB. Around the same time, he entered into a bad-tempered and public spat with senior IRB man Fred Allan. At the time, Allan was treasurer of the Irish Journalists' Association. In the *Workers' Republic,* Connolly lambasted Allan for allowing a toast to the queen to be made at the association's annual dinner. In June 1899, Connolly heckled Allan at the Bodenstown Wolfe Tone memorial, prompting the latter to accuse Connolly of being a 'blackleg' for operating a newspaper while refusing to join the Dublin printers' union. Moreover, he defended his conduct, arguing that he refrained from making the toast personally in a 'silent protest'.[308] In reply, Connolly wrote in his paper that the 'nationalist principles (?) of Mr. Allan may be of secondary importance to the harmony of a dinner party, but the revolutionary principles of the working-class democracy are to them a matter of life and death'.[309]

More fundamentally, looking back in 1909 Connolly recalled the difference between the ISRP and what he called the 'remnants of the secret societies of a past generation'. The ISRP, Connolly wrote, 'completely revolutionised advanced politics in Ireland'.

When it was first initiated the word 'republic' was looked upon as a word to be only whispered among intimates … The thought of revolution was the exclusive possession of a few remnants of the secret societies of a past generation, and was never mentioned by them except with heads closely together and eyes fearfully glancing around; the Socialists broke through this ridiculous secrecy, and in hundreds of speeches in the most public places of the metropolis, as well as in scores of thousands of pieces of literature scattered through the country, announced their purpose to muster all the forces of labour for a revolutionary reconstruction of society and the incidental destruction of the British Empire.[310]

As early as November 1896 in the *Shan Van Vocht,* Connolly had criticised the Irish republican movement for eschewing political action in favour of a narrow conspiratorial approach. 'Up to the present every genuine Irish revolutionist has acted on this belief, that political action was impossible for republicans', he wrote:

Now I assert the contrary. A revolution can only succeed in any country when it has the moral sanction of the people. It is so, even in an independent country; it is doubly so in a country subject like Ireland, to the rule of another.

Connolly went on to note the Young Irelanders of 1848 and the Fenian rising of 1867 as examples of those times when minority action was out of step with the majority of the population. Connolly, instead, urged that a republican political party be formed 'to educate the people in sound national ideas by pledging every candidate to openly repudiate the authority of the Crown, and work for the realisation of republican principles'. This would ensure that 'when a majority of the Irish people had at the ballot boxes declared in favour of the revolutionary party', the revolutionist would know that he was 'not merely one of a numerically insignificant band of malcontents, but a citizen soldier [backed] by a majority of his fellow-countrymen'. Such an approach 'would make Irish republicanism no longer the "politics of despair", but the Science of Revolution'.[311]

Connolly's critique became only sharper in the wake of the republicans' failure to back the ISRP attempt to exclude William Martin Murphy and the Home Rulers from the 1798 commemorations. In the *Workers' Republic*, Connolly wrote:

Ireland occupies a position among the nations of the earth unique in a great variety of its aspects, but in no one particular is this singularity more marked than in the possession of what is known as a 'physical force party' – a party, that is to say, whose members are united upon no one point, and agree upon no single principle, except upon the use of physical force as the sole means of settling the dispute between the people of this country and the governing power of Great Britain.

Connolly's critique, in essence, was that between the Home Rulers and the republicans was more a disagreement on means than on ultimate ends. Both favoured a merely political independence from England – an idea which Connolly subjected to lengthy criticism in *Erin's Hope*. Whereas the Home Rulers seek their goal through constitutional politics, the republicans do so through the advocacy of 'physical force'. As Connolly wrote, the 'so-called physical force movement of today … bases its hopes upon the disgust of the people over the failure of the Home Rule movement'. However, as the people 'after having exhausted their constitutional efforts' turn 'in despair … to thoughts of physical force', Connolly wrote that 'their conception of what constitutes freedom was in no sense changed or revolutionised; they still believed in the political form of freedom which had been their ideal in their constitutional days'.

The Socialist Republican 'conception of the functions and use of physical force in a popular movement', by contrast, 'neither [exalts] it into a principle nor repudiate it as something to be thought of'. Crucially, 'the really important question is of the principles upon which is based the movement that may or may not need the use of force to realise its object'. The necessity of basing the movement on sound principles, Connolly argues, 'is the immense difference between the Socialist Republicans and our friends the physical force men'.

The latter, by stifling all discussions of principles, earn the passive and fleeting commendation of the unthinking multitude; the former, by insisting upon a thorough understanding of their basic principles, do not so readily attract the multitude, but do attract and hold the more thoughtful amongst them. It is the difference betwixt a mob in revolt and an army in preparation.[312]

For the 1902 US edition of *Erin's Hope*, Connolly went even further. The Irish working class, he wrote, was 'the only secure foundation on which a free nation can be reared' as it was 'the only class in Ireland which has no interest to serve in perpetuating either the political or social forms of oppression – the British connection or the capitalist system'. Moreover:

This task can only he safely entered upon by men and women who recognise that the first action of a revolutionary army must harmonise in principle with those likely to be its last, and that, therefore, no revolutionists can safely invite the co-operation of men or classes, whose ideals are not theirs, and whom, therefore, they may be compelled to fight at some future critical stage of the journey to freedom ... The freedom of the working class must be the work of the working class.[313]

This critique was a thoroughgoing one. Yet, in some senses Connolly did not go far enough, and underestimated the potential of the republican movement. In this period, Connolly's view that national liberation would be synonymous with socialism was based on an analysis that suggested an indigenous Irish capitalism was an impossibility.

In *Erin's Hope*, Connolly makes an underconsumptionist argument, writing that Ireland 'cannot create new markets. This world is only limited after all, and the nations of Europe are pushing their way into its remote corners so rapidly that in a few years' time, at most, the entire world will have been exhausted as a market for their wares.'[314] In particular, in an early article on the Land Question, he discounts the possibility of capitalist agriculture in Ireland, arguing that:

Every perfection of agricultural methods or machinery lowers prices; every fall in prices renders more unstable the position of the farmer, whether tenant or proprietor ... We are left no choice but socialism or universal bankruptcy.[315]

The argument that capital accumulation was impossible on the grounds that the ruin of small producers would destroy the domestic market was a common one in the late nineteenth century. It was the basis for the Narodnik theories of writers such as V.P. Voronstov who, like Leslie and early Connolly, 'hoped for a painless transition to socialist labour through state-led industrialisation,' and was further evidence of a form of 'economic romanticism'.[316]

Crucially, however, this dichotomous choice – socialism or bankruptcy – disarmed Connolly in understanding the true nature of the republican movement. As Henry Patterson has argued,

> [it] failed to anticipate the space which existed in Catholic Ireland for a nationalism that was not as obesely bourgeois as that of the Irish Parliamentary Party and yet in no sense socialist – a space which the revivified Sinn Féin organisation would fill in the aftermath of 1916 ... There would prove to be a space for a revolutionary nationalism with conservative social content.[317]

The advanced nationalist milieu of Irish republicans and Gaelic revivalists produced more than just a set of political or cultural ideas. In the hands of journalists such as D.P. Moran and Arthur Griffith, those ideas would constitute a more or less coherent programme for an independent capitalist Ireland to rival the assimilationist project of the Home Rule elite. Griffith, the son of a Dublin artisan recently returned from South Africa, founded the *United Irishman* journal in 1899. Through his journalism, he 'translated the evolutionary ideas of the revivalists into economic, social and political programmes for the generation of Ireland as a modern urban civilisation'. The revivalist energies were mobilised 'towards the construction of a distinctive and autonomous modern nation', which was envisaged less as a return to the traditions of the Irish-speaking peasantry and more a 'projected ascetic, sober and industrious urban middle-class nation, educated for Ireland's economic and social development rather than for the British civil service'.[318]

Inspired by the German protectionist economist Friedrich List, Griffith's vision was for an economically self-sufficient capitalist Ireland, with native industry nurtured behind strong tariff barriers. He viewed the labour movement as representative of a 'sectional' interest and promoted a strategy borrowed from the Hungarian nationalists, who had won a Dual Monarchy constitution from Austria in 1867. In a series of articles, published in 1904 as a popular pamphlet *The Resurrection of Hungary*, Griffith 'devised a policy of parliamentary withdrawal, the declaration of an Irish state, and passive resistance to the British state, using the existing powers and resources of Irish local government'.[319] Through his writings, Griffith inspired a following of writers, artisans, clerks and some workers to establish an overlapping array of separatist cultural and literary societies to promote his national vision. The main groups, *Cumman na nGaedhal* (formed in 1902), the National Council (1903) and the Dungannon Clubs (1905) merged between 1905 and 1906 to form *Sinn Féin* (Ourselves), based on Griffith's ethos of Irish self-reliance.[320]

Connolly was friendly with Griffith but thought his vision utopian. Viewing a capitalist Ireland as a naïve impossibility, Connolly was overly optimistic that the republicans would eventually be drawn to the socialist programme of the ISRP:

> Our honest and compromising nationalist friends may not choose to own up to the fact but they are nevertheless rapidly forced to adopt the line of action we have all along advocated as the only possible one for a revolutionary party which really means business.[321]

When Griffith backed Connolly's candidature in the 1903 local elections, Connolly wrote optimistically that: 'We have always maintained that every honest friend of freedom would sooner or later find themselves in accord with us. The support now spoken proves this.'[322] Yet, Griffith backed Connolly personally, with no intention of adopting the programme of the ISRP.

As one historian of the party has concluded, Connolly's belief that 'republicans could be won over to the cause of socialism because, unknown to themselves, the advanced nationalists held beliefs that could only be realised throughout the establishment of a socialist Ireland', in fact, 'massively underestimated the powerful hold that republican politics had over its adherents as well as the complex class nature of republican politics'.[323] Maud Gonne recalled in her memoirs that at the turn of the century 'Connolly was little known outside the labour movement'. She personally 'had absolute confidence in him, but the people with whom I was working hardly knew him and distrusted all Socialists'.[324] Therefore, despite Connolly's undoubted powers as a socialist propagandist, though individuals such as Alice Milligan, Gonne and P.T. Daly were attracted to the party, he was 'unable to convince a substantial number of advanced nationalists to join the ISRP'.[325]

Chapter 3

Connolly and the Second International

As the turn of the century approached, Connolly and the ISRP found themselves grappling with issues of international significance, including the nature of 'imperialism' and debates at the 1900 Paris Congress of the International.

The ISRP was proud of its internationalist character, viewing itself as part of what Connolly later called 'the Revolutionary Social-Democracy of the Continent of Europe'.[326] For a small and relatively isolated political organisation such as the ISRP, the sense of belonging to a much wider movement was a continuing source of inspiration and encouragement. Thus, when Wilhelm Liebknecht, the father of German Social-Democracy, died in August 1900, the Dublin ISRP passed a resolution treating him, appropriately, as a comrade of their own:

> Resolved that we place on record our profound grief at the death of our illustrious comrade, Wilhelm Liebknecht, whose untiring and brilliant advocacy of the peoples' cause, has made his name known and revered wherever the militant proletariat are battling for their rights.[327]

Another clear indication of the party's concern with international issues is the range of coverage in its newspaper, the *Workers' Republic*. Started in 1898 with a £50 loan from Keir Hardie, the *Workers' Republic* was Ireland's first Marxist newspaper. Its stated aim was, the paper declared, 'to unite the workers and to bury, in one common grave, the religious hatreds, the provincial jealousies and mutual distrusts upon which oppression has so long depended for security'.[328] The first issue was set by P.T. Daly, later secretary of the Dublin Trades Council and a left-wing Irish republican. An advertisement in the SDF's paper *Justice* announced it as a new journal, a 'Literary Champion of the Irish Democracy', advocating 'an Irish Republic, the Abolition of landlordism and Wage-Slavery, the Co-operative Organisation of Industry under Irish Representative Governing Bodies'.[329]

The paper could be purchased in several Irish and British cities, as it listed wholesalers in 'Dublin (Eason and Son), Cork, Drogheda, Limerick, Belfast, Liverpool, London, Glasgow, Dundee, Edinburgh, Manchester' in its pages. As early as October 1898, the paper could even be bought in the United States, from members of the American SLP.[330] This connection, as we shall see, would become of increasing importance to the ISRP and to Connolly personally.

Connolly saw the paper as integral to the success of the ISRP and stretched its meagre resources to produce it as regularly as possible. In 1903, Thomas Lyng recalled:

> Many of our members, after toiling for a capitalist during the day, had to spend the entire evening in [the] arduous work of a printing press and Mr Connolly had to be for years at one and the same the editor, compositor, assistant printer, principal writer, speaker, and organiser.[331]

Initially intended to be a weekly, the newspaper soon ran into difficulties. Some Belfast socialists mistrusted its republican content and failed to rally around when the paper's northern distributer was denounced by a Catholic bishop. When the *Workers' Republic* was reissued in May 1899, Connolly took over much of the editing and technical work himself and joked darkly that the first series was 'so weekly it almost died', whereas the second would only appear 'whenever it was strong enough to get out'.[332]

Reflecting the ISRP's connection to the wider Second International, the *Workers' Republic* carried worldwide news items and reprinted articles from the international socialist movement. From the USA, the paper reprinted articles from the *Workers' Call* in Chicago and the *San Francisco Examiner*. More than this, regular columns entitled 'World Siftings' and 'Continental Jottings' consisted of snippets from *La Petite Republique* in France, the Italian *Il Proletario*, the German SPD newspaper *Vorwaerts* and Hardie's *Labour Leader*. In order to piece these columns together and educate its membership, the ISRP subscribed to various foreign journals.

One particular highlight of the ISRP calendar was the annual Paris Commune commemoration, a tradition which Connolly had inherited from his days in Edinburgh, though it was also staple of the party's predecessors on the Dublin socialist scene. 'Celebrations of the Commune were popular,' writes historian of commemoration, Laura C. Forster, 'and often were the best attended meetings of the year ....' The 1899 ISRP celebration in particular made a hefty profit of 20 shillings.[333] One can see why, for:

a beautiful supply of eatables and refreshments of a less solid nature were provided all of which suffered a more ruthless dispersion than ever was inflicted on the Communards ... The instrumentalist music consisted of harp, violin, fife and clarionette. There were a very large number of songs rendered during the night (and part of the morning) ... the proceedings ended about 2.30 am Monday morning.[334]

One factor in the success of such celebrations was 'the Commune's symbolic draw, which helped Irish socialists to see beyond localised divisions and connected them to an international cohort of activists with some shared broad aims'.[335] The outbreak of the Second Boer War in October 1899 would provide Connolly and the ISRP with another opportunity to link their immediate struggle against the British Empire with wider issues in international debate in the socialist movement. To the fore were arguments about the very nature of imperialism itself and its connection to global capitalist development.

Connolly and the Boer War

The Second Boer War, fought from 11 October 1899 to 31 May 1902, between Britain and the Afrikaner republics of the South African Republic (Transvaal) and the Orange Free State, provided a renewed focus for ISRP activity in Dublin. It also offers an instructive insight into Connolly's developing views on issues of imperialism at the turn of the twentieth century.

The conflict had its origins in the tensions between the British Empire, which was attempting to consolidate its grip on the states of southern Africa, and the Boers, the white farmers originally settled by the Dutch East Indian Company in the seventeenth and eighteenth centuries. The immediate background to the war was the discovery of the Kimberley diamond fields in 1869-70 and the struggle for control of the Witwatersrand gold-mining complex in the Transvaal. The build-up of British troops in the region provoked the Boers to launch an offensive in October 1899, sparking the beginning of the conflict.

The Boer War was of both national and international significance for the ISRP. In an Irish context, the war was, as Roy Foster has argued, 'nearly as crucial an event for Irish Nationalism as the death of Parnell'.[336] In the days following the outbreak of the war, 'pro-Boer rallies and riots took place in nationalist towns throughout the country', as Irish nationalists formed the strongest pro-Boer movement in Europe.[337] The Boer cause sparked ballads and songs, and sports teams were named after Boer generals, many of whom were also offered the freedom of several Irish towns. Most tangibly, two Irish brigades even fought alongside the Boers. One brigade was led by IRB man John McBride, future husband of Maud Gonne, who died during the Easter Rising of 1916.

Quick to seize the initiative, the first protest against English policy in the Transvaal came from the ISRP on 27 August 1899. Then after the war actually broke out in October, Gonne and Griffith founded the Irish Transvaal Committee, and the ISRP pledged its support for the venture.

On 17 December, a protest meeting was organised under the auspices of the Committee against the visit to the city of Liberal Unionist Joseph Chamberlain. Chamberlain had just been awarded an honorary degree at Trinity College Dublin and the pro-Boer activists sought to use the occasion to build support for their cause. The venue for the protest, however, was occupied by the police, preventing the meeting from taking place. Never one to be discouraged, Connolly, along with Gonne and Griffith, rode into nearby Beresford Square in a horse-drawn carriage. Gonne recalled that the police stopped the carriage and ordered: 'Go Back. You can't pass, the meeting is banned.' Connolly urged the driver to continue and, as the driver hesitated, the police rushed forward and arrested him. At this point, Gonne recounted:

I understood then why Connolly had taken the box seat. While the driver was being hauled off he seized the reins, whipped up the horses, and at a furious gallop, scattering people and police, he drove right through the police cordon, the brake swaying wildly and rushing in through the broken cordon and breaking it on the opposite side.[338]

When the Connolly's cart broke the cordon, Griffith's *United Irishman* newspaper described 'the enthusiastic cheers of the people, who immediately fell in behind the brake and formed an impromptu procession' around Dublin city centre. With words that gain poignancy in light of the events of 1916, Gonne recalls that Connolly whispered to her: 'There are only two sentries at the gates of Dublin Castle. Shall I drive in and seize and the Castle?' She replied: 'There are soldiers inside. It will mean shooting and the people are unarmed,' and Connolly instead turned down Parliament Street and over Capel Street Bridge.[339] The police had been humiliated, and socialist and republican opposition to the Boer War and Chamberlain's visit expressed. In retaliation, however, the police smashed the press of the *Workers' Republic*, leaving the ISRP temporarily unable to produce its newspaper.

The war split the British socialist movement, with some, such as Robert Blatchford succumbing to what Connolly condemned as an 'unqualifiedly chauvinist [position, and] a brutal endorsement of every act of brigandage and murder in which the capitalists of England may involve their country'. Connolly summed up the British response in rather scathing terms. 'The English Socialists are apparently divided over the question of the war on the Transvaal,' he wrote in the *Workers' Republic*:

> one section of the Social Democratic Federation going strongly for the Boers and against the war; another also declaring against the war, but equally denouncing the Boers; and finally, one English Socialist leader, Mr Robert Blatchford, editor of *The Clarion* and author of *Merrie England*, coming out bluntly for the war and toasting the health of the Queen, and the success of the British arms.[340]

Connolly and his party formed a united front with the republicans in pro-Boer activity. Indeed, Connolly freely admitted that the ISRP 'would welcome the humiliation of the British arms in any one of the conflicts in which it is at present engaged, or with which it has been lately menaced'. Connolly, however, was careful to distinguish his opposition to the British side in the Boer War from the straightforward republican one. In opposing Britain, Connolly warned his readers, for example, not to 'make the mistake of lauding the Kaiser, either, as our so-called nationalist journals do'. The Kaiser of Germany, Britain's main rival in South Africa, Connolly wrote, 'has always proven himself to be a most determined enemy of the working class, and longs for the day when he may drown in blood their hopes for freedom'. He pointed out that the Kaiser had only recently 'introduced to his Parliament a bill which would have made it a penal offence to ask a workman to go on strike, had it not been defeated by the determined opposition of the Social Democrats' and, in an internationalist flourish added that: 'He is your enemy, as the English governing class is your enemy, as the Irish propertied class is your enemy, as all the classes who live upon your labour in all the nations of the world are your enemy.'[341]

Nevertheless, Connolly was clear in backing the Boers against the British. While acknowledging that 'it may be urged that our Irish nationality plays a large part in forming this conception of international politics', Connolly denied it and instead looked to the authority of the parties of the Second International to justify his position. Writing in the *Workers' Republic* on 4 November 1899, Connolly argued that 'all the journals of the party on the continent of Europe and in America, as far as we are aware, come out in this instance wholeheartedly on the side of the Transvaal and against what the organ of our Austrian comrades fittingly terms England's act of "blood-thirsty piracy"'.[342] He argued further that it was necessary for the socialist movement to find an independent working-class position, a 'common standpoint from which all questions of race or nationality shall be carefully excluded' in judging international conflicts, in which 'every question dealt with from the position of its effect upon the industrial development required to bring the Socialist movement to a head ...'.[343]

Connolly's concern with viewing the question in this way spoke to international debates on the very nature of imperialism sparked by the Boer War. 'Imperialism' as a term had hitherto had a very limited application, referring to the policies of Napoleon III of the Second French Empire. The term was 'given broader economic meaning when used to describe the new expansionist turn in American foreign policy, initiated in 1898 by the Spanish-American War' and by the Second Boer War, which prompted the English radical liberal J.A. Hobson to write his book 'associating imperialism with the emerging imperatives of capitalist competition'.[344] Thus, with both the Boer War and the Spanish-American war in mind, Connolly branded the war in the Transvaal 'a capitalist's war [and] one manifestation of the Class War. 'So,' he added, 'is the war in the Philippines.'[345]

In the Second International, Karl Kautsky, then its leading theorist, linked imperialism to new tendencies within the advanced capitalist metropole. In particular, the industrial development of Germany and the United States in competition with the British Empire generated a need for colony-grabbing to secure new fields of investment and for the export of capital.[346]

Connolly too saw war and imperialism as extensions of capitalist development. 'The influence which impels towards war today is the influence of capitalism,' Connolly argued in 1898. 'Every war now is a capitalist move for new markets and it is a move capitalism must make or perish.' Connolly's argument, however, was that capitalists' competition to create 'newer and more efficient wealth-producing machines' led to unemployment, such that 'the home market is now no longer able to dispose of their produce [and] they are driven to foreign markets'. Citing the example of China, Connolly argued that the great powers 'with swords in hand, threaten to set the armed millions of Europe in terrible and bloody conflict, in order to decide which shall have the right to force upon John Chinaman the goods which his European brother produces'.[347]

Nevertheless, Connolly, like the key Second International critics of imperialism, was clear in rooting imperialism in the contemporary development of capitalism and sought to draw strategic conclusions for the socialist movement. One may also detect the influence of Ernest Belford Bax who, as a leading member the Socialist League, pioneered an analysis of imperialism in the British socialist movement. Bax argued that

> the foreign policy of the great international Socialist party must be to break up these hideous race monopolies called empires, beginning in each case at home. Hence everything which makes for the disruption and disintegration of the empire to which he belongs must be welcomed by the Socialist as an ally. It is his duty to urge on any movement tending in any way to dislocate the commercial relations of the world, knowing that every shock the modern complex commercial system suffers weakens it and brings its destruction nearer.[348]

Setting out the ISRP's position 'on all questions of international policy', Connolly argued in very similar terms to Bax that:

> as colonial expansion and the conquest of new markets are necessary for the prolongation of the life of capitalism, the prevention of colonial expansion and the loss of markets to countries capitalistically developed, such as England, precipitates economic crises there, and so gives an impulse to revolutionary thought and helps to shorten the period required to develop backward countries and thus prepare the economic conditions needed for our triumph.

On this basis, Connolly stated,

> we hold that as England is the most capitalistically developed country in Europe, every fresh conquest of territory by her armies, every sphere of influence acquired in the interests of her commercialists, is a span added to the life of capitalist society; and that every market lost, every sphere of influence captured by the non-capitalist enemies of England, shortens the life of Capitalism by aiding the development of reactionary countries, and hurling back upon itself the socially conservative industrial population of England.

There is a crucial difference between Bax and Connolly, however. Bax, contra the *Communist Manifesto*, appears to view continued capitalist development as a hindrance to socialism, and raises the purely *negative* slogan of 'dislocat[ing] the commercial relations of the world' in order to provoke a terminal crisis. Connolly, on the other hand, argues on more orthodox grounds that:

> Scientific revolutionary Socialism teaches us that Socialism can only be realised when Capitalism has reached its zenith of development; that consequently the advance of nations industrially undeveloped into the capitalistic stage of industry is a thing highly to be desired, since such advance will breed a revolutionary proletariat in such countries and force forward here the political freedom necessary for the speedy success of the Socialist movement.

This, however, leads Connolly to the questionable conclusion that capitalist expansion of *already industrialised capitalist states* such as England should be opposed while further capitalist development of semi-feudal states such as Russia is progressive, *even* if this capitalist development is on the basis on colonial expansion, as it creates a 'revolutionary proletariat'.[349] Thus, Connolly argued,

> Drive the Russian out of Poland! By all means! Prevent his extension towards Europe! Certainly; but favour his extension and his acquisition of new markets in Asia (at the expense of England if need be) if you would see Capitalism hurry onward to its death.

Nevertheless, Connolly was making an admirable attempt to theorise his way through a novel problem. What Gary Johnson writes of the SDF is applicable to Connolly and the ISRP too. Socialists at the turn of the century 'should not be criticised severely for not having a mature and articulated theory of imperialism before the 1900s' because 'the development of imperialism as a systematic concept backed by a coherent theory only really emerged in the two decades after 1900'. Moreover, it was in this decade that 'the whole of the European Social Democratic movement was groping its way towards an adequate analysis of imperialism', and the main works of Kautsky, Luxemburg, Hilferding, Bukharin and Lenin did not appear until the period 1907-1916.[350]

The emphasis on economic developments in the advanced capitalist countries did mean, however, that accounts of how imperialism impacted on the countries it subjugated were, though suitably scathing, often more cursory. An exception here within the Second International was Rosa Luxemburg, and in particular her 1913 work *Accumulation of Capital,* which argued that capitalist development is predicated on its violent interaction with pre-capitalist societies. She therefore paid closer attention to the social structures of the colonised territories, and showed how imperialism violently despoiled non-capitalist economies in the process of incorporating them into international circuits of capital. Her treatment of the Boer War is a case in point. While Connolly characterised it straightforwardly as a war 'by a government of financiers upon a nation of farmers' and Kautsky a conflict 'to make the South African market free as a field for the investment of British capital', Luxemburg exceeded both in her concern for the super-exploited black majority population in South Africa. For Luxemburg, the Boer War *was* 'a blatant conflict between agricultural and political peasant economy on the one hand, and the demands and requirements of the accumulation of capital on the other', but not just that. The Boer economy, she charged, was built 'on the backs of the Negroes, compelling them to do slave-labour for them and corrupting and enervating them deliberately and systematically'. For Luxemburg, therefore, it was not simply a straight fight between British imperialism and the Boers, but a three-cornered conflict between the 'peasant economy' and 'great capitalist colonial policy' for the land and labour power of the native population. 'Both competitors had precisely the same aim,' she argued, 'to subject, expel or destroy the coloured peoples, to appropriate their land and press them into service by the abolition of their social organisations.'[351] Similar points were echoed by contemporary anarchists, with *Freedom* in Britain noting that the conflict concerned the form of capitalist management in mining areas. The Boers did not allow black workers to work in the gold mines, whereas Britain capital was seeking to exploit more African labour, anticipating that 'the value of the shares of the different South African companies would double and treble ....'[352]

As a group of socialist in Ireland, Connolly and the ISRP felt they had particular strategic reasons for emphasising British defeat. 'The British Army is getting its hands full in South Africa,' Connolly wrote. 'The defeated, demoralised, disheartened, subjugated, routed, dispersed, conquered, disarmed and humiliated Boers' were keeping the British tied up, so that 'not a single soldier can be spared from South Africa for a long time to come.' Elsewhere, he pointed in the *Workers' Republic* that there 'are at present but few soldiers in Ireland; the militia and the last of the reserves are about to be called out and sent to the front'. The implications were obvious. He suggested to his readers that 'it would be a safer, more judicious, and altogether more honourable course to stay in Ireland and fight their tyrants at home instead of risking life and losing honour by fighting for their tyrants abroad ...'.[353]

The Land Question

A second issue of international significance that occupied the ISRP in these years was a controversy over the position which should be taken by socialists towards the 'Land Question' and, more specifically, how socialists should approach the peasantry.

The foundational texts of Marxism provided only some basic principles, which needed to be further developed and applied to specific political contexts. The *Manifesto of the Communist Party,* written by Marx and Engels in 1848, contains only scattered references to the peasantry, but subsumed 'handicraftsmen and peasants' into the petit-bourgeoisie, or 'lower strata of the middle class', along with 'small tradespeople, shopkeepers, and retired tradesmen generally'. These would all 'sink gradually into the proletariat' due to 'competition with the large capitalists' and 'new methods of production'.[354] Regarding the property of the peasant, 'the development of industry has to a great extent already destroyed it, and is still destroying it daily'.[355]

In 1894, however, prompted by debates within the French and German parties, Engels wrote his most sustained intervention on the subject, *The Peasant Question in France and Germany.* Contrary to the predictions of their earlier work, Engels recognised that the peasantry had not yet disappeared, and consequently that it presented challenging strategic, political and electoral problems for socialist parties of the Second International. 'From Ireland to Sicily, from Andalusia to Russia, and Bulgaria,' he wrote, 'the peasant is a very essential factor of the population, production and political power. Only two regions of Western Europe form an exception,' Great Britain and Prussia east of the river Elbe.[356]

This led some on the reformist wing of the International, such as Georg von Vollmer, a Bavarian SPD leader, to call for a specific peasant programme, which would reconcile the SPD to the continued existence of smallholding in order to attract electoral support from the peasants. In 1894, as in 1848, Engels still saw the peasant as 'hopelessly doomed' and a 'future proletarian', in the manner of the *Manifesto*. It follows, then, that 'neither now, nor at any time in the future, can we promise the small-holding peasants to preserve their individual property and individual enterprise against the overwhelming power of capitalist production'. Yet, argued Engels, it is 'not our mission to hasten it by any interference on our part', and 'we shall not even think of forcibly expropriating the small peasants (regardless of whether with or without compensation), as we shall have to do in the case of the big landowners'.

Rather than simply pointing out the existence of objective economic forces, Engels outlined a perspective of bridging the transition between smallholding through offering inducements for the peasant to join large-scale co-operative farming. 'Our task relative to the small peasant consists,' he wrote,

> in the first place, in effecting a transition of his private enterprise and private possession to cooperative ones, not forcibly but by dint of example and the proffer of social assistance for this purpose.

This could include, for example, offering co-operatives further advantages such as the provision of credit at lower interest rates or advances in money or in kind 'for the establishment of large-scale production'. However, 'the main point is, and will be,' Engels concluded, 'to make the peasants understand that we can save, preserve their houses and fields for them only by transforming them into co-operative property operated co-operatively'.

Similar views to those of Engels were given a hearing in *The Agrarian Question* (1899) by Kautsky, which was a polemic against the Vollmer side of the argument in the German party, and 'set down the "official Marxist" position on that subject for the world socialist movement prior to World War I'.[357] It predicted, rather simplistically, that proletarianisation in the countryside would mirror processes in industry, and would take the form of, as one summary puts it, 'a specific deployment of labour – the introduction of stable centralised workforces, capable of exerting collective bargaining pressure for the kind of improvements industrial workers were now taking for granted'.[358]

As Paul Dillon has argued, 'although Connolly had little direct contact with the political and social struggles of the countryside,' nevertheless, 'his neglect of rural questions and their place in the revolutionary process has been overstated'.[359] Material can be found in Connolly's pamphlets addressing the question, and his newspaper articles addressed both contemporary and historical issues related to land and the peasantry.

Generally speaking, Connolly's views were similar to the Engels-Kautsky orthodoxy. The first work of Connolly's to deal at any length about the peasantry was *Erin's Hopes: the ends and means* in 1897, which was extensively covered in the previous chapter. In this work, Connolly makes two arguments against advocates of peasant proprietorship. The first is a moral argument. Regarding the establishment of individual ownership in land to 'make every man the owner of his farm, let every man live, if not under his own vine and fig tree, at least upon his own potato patch', wrote Connolly, 'I consider such an act to be, even if practicable, one of very questionable justice'. He continued:

> To make the land of a country the property of a class is to my mind equally iniquitous, whether that class number a few hundreds or a few thousands. The land of a country belongs of right to the people of that country, and not to any particular class, nor even to any single generation of the people.

The second argument was an economic one, citing the inability of smallholding to compete with the improvements of technology and efficiency in large-scale capitalist agriculture. In terms not out of place in Engels' contention that the 'small production is irretrievably going to rack and ruin', Connolly wrote that:

> The world is progressive, and peasant proprietary, which a hundred years ago might have been a boon, would now be powerless to save from ruin the agriculture of Ireland. The day of small farmers, as of small capitalists, is gone, and wherever they are still found they find it impossible to compete with the improved machinery and mammoth farms of America and Australia.[360]

So much for the economic basis of the issue. What, however, did Connolly think that the Irish socialists should *do* about the Land Question? In his article, 'Peasant Proprietorship and Socialism,' Connolly explicitly cites the cases of the French and German Social-Democrats, perhaps indicating an awareness of the arguments of the debate to which Engels had addressed himself. At one point, however, Connolly appears to suggest that the socialists have nothing to offer. His argument is starkly objectivist, more so than that of Engels: 'We do not need to fight peasant proprietary,' he argued, 'we only need to allow free scope for the development of capitalist enterprise in order to see the system of small farming crushed out by the competition of the great farms and scientific cultivation of America and Australia.' While the old system of landlordism 'is fast becoming an economic impossibility in Ireland,' the survival of 'peasant proprietary itself in nowise provides the small farmer with an outlet from the life of constant toil and hunger which is his lot today'.[361]

Yet, Connolly pulls back from this rather passive stance, and outlines some measures for the peasant in similar terms to Engels. Connolly envisages a society in which 'agriculture ceases to be a private enterprise, when a free nation organises the production of its own food stuffs as a public function, and intrusts [sic] the management of the function to the agricultural population, under popular boards of their own election ....'[362]

This was expressed in the programme of the ISRP in 1896 as a demand for 'agriculture to be administered as a public function, under boards of management elected by the agricultural population and responsible to them and to the nation at large'.[363]

Under a system of public land ownership, Connolly wrote in 1898, 'all the aids to agriculture which science supplies, but which are impossible to the poverty-stricken peasant, will be utilised by the national administrators and placed at the service of the cultivators of the soil'.[364] More specifically, the third point of the ISRP programme demanded the 'establishment at public expense of rural depots for the most improved agricultural machinery, to be lent out to the agricultural population at a rent covering cost and management alone'.[365]

Finally, Connolly approximates Engels' perspective of persuading the peasantry to give up their smallholdings through offering them an alternative. 'The same shrewd sense', argued Connolly,

> which has inspired the Irish farmers to appreciate the advantages of agricultural cooperation in dairies and banks, with only their little savings to finance the enterprise, will also lead them to appreciate the advantages which might be derived from cooperation on a national scale with the entire resources of the nation to equip it. And such cooperation applied to industry as well as land is the basic idea of the future socialist republic.[366]

The ISRP's demands were cited in a dispute that took place in the American socialist movement in 1899 between the SLP and the more moderate Social Democratic Party (SDP) – with the latter taking a position close to Vollmer's in Germany. Connolly intervened in the SLP side. In his article 'America and Ireland: farmers' demands', Connolly took up the cudgels for the De Leon and the SLP. First, Connolly laid out his view of the two parties. The SLP holds 'the position known in Europe as the Marxist position, from its being first definitely formulated by the founder of Modern Socialism – Karl Marx'. By contrast, Connolly told his readers, and this is where the agrarian programme was concerned:

> The Social Democratic Party, on the other hand, look to the fact that the small middle class, and especially the farmers, still wield an enormous voting power, and, looking to the present rather than to the future, they have embodied in their programme certain 'Farmers' Demands' – proposals for legislation to enable the petty farmers to bear up against the competition of

those mammoth farms for which the United States is so famous. The object being, of course, to win the votes of the farmers as a class.[367]

When the SDP cited the ISRP's agrarian programme in support of their own call for 'Farmer's Demands', Connolly replied that his party values 'our reputation as a straight Socialist Party too much to allow our name to be used as a cover for any kind of looseness in principles, tactics, or policy, even when it is used accompanied by flattery'. Connolly objected that the cases of America and Ireland were different. In America, the SPD was adopting demands to protect a more backward form of agriculture – small farmers – from a more progressive one: large-scale capitalist farming. In Ireland, on the other hand, 'Irish agriculturists are not threatened with absorption, but with extinction and enforced exile'. Thus, the ISRP's demands 'are demands which aim at preserving Agriculture in Ireland from being annihilated as a native industry by the competition of foreign agriculturists'. The ISRP's main demand was for the 'Establishment at public expense of rural depots for the most improved agricultural machinery, to be lent out to the agricultural population at a rent covering cost and management alone'. This, Connolly argued, was 'not a sectional demand, but is the outcome of a national exigency'.

Though the ISRP was an urban-based party, Connolly also made some limited efforts to understand and intervene in peasant struggle. In 1898, Connolly and Maud Gonne travelled to County Kerry, which was stricken by famine due to the failure of the potato crop, and experienced the issue of land hunger first-hand. The two printed a leaflet in Gonne's name, 'The Right to Life and the Rights of Property,' which called for peasants to take direct action to secure food supplies. It appealed to religious authorities, such as Pope Clement I and Cardinal Manning, in an attempt to 'counter those priests and others who might try to stop such direct action by appeals to religion ....' Gonne distributed it at a large meeting in Ballycastle, County Mayo. In April, Connolly travelled through Kerry speaking to priests, evicted tenants, tenant representatives, innkeepers and schoolteachers about living conditions among the smallholding peasantry of the west and the ruthlessness of landlords. He wrote up his experiences for Gonne's *L'Irlande Libre* and De Leon's *People* and addressed for the ISRP in Dublin on 1 May.[368]

Though theoretically correct, the ISRP's proposals for land national-isation did not find much grip in Ireland at the turn of the century. Connolly's optimism that the 'keen individualism of the Irish peasant' will find its expression in constant watchfulness over the common stock and supervision of each other's labour' overestimated the extent to which the Irish tenant wanted individual ownership of the land. As Michael Davitt, the leader of the Land League, reflected in 1902 about his own demands for land nationalisation,

> The plan was either disliked, or misunderstood, or the principle on which it rested – national, as against individual, lordship of the soil – did not appeal to the strong human desire or passion to hold the land as 'owner' which is so inherent in Celtic nature … [369]

Nevertheless, the difficulties with Connolly's position were shared with the orthodoxy of the Second International generally. Moreover, it is unfair to charge Connolly – as some biographers have done – with completely ignoring the issue; he did not.[370] The ISRP was a small urban-based organisation, and there were limits to what it could practically achieve in agitational terms beyond its numbers.

The 1900 Paris Congress

It had been four years since the Second International had held its last congress, in London in the summer of 1896. The fifth International Socialist Congress was scheduled for 23 to 27 September 1900 in Paris and, as William O'Brien recalled, the members of the ISRP were 'very anxious to emphasise that they were Socialists and International Socialists and it was arranged there would be delegates sent to this conference'.[371] As O'Brien's account suggests, the Congress provides solid evidence for the internationalist character of the ISRP. Three delegates were selected to go to Paris, and were expected to pay their own expenses, 'a kind of holiday as well as a representation'. The party decided to send Dan O'Brien, Mark Deering and E.W. Stewart. Strictly speaking, O'Brien and Deering represented the ISRP, while E.W. Stewart was a delegate of an affiliated organisation, the Cork-based Fintan Lalor Club, essentially a front for the ISRP.

The three men would have rubbed shoulders with the likes of Karl Kautsky, August Bebel and Rosa Luxemburg. R.M. Fox, in his early biography, gets carried away, and places Connolly himself at the centre of the action, either through lack of sources or by reproducing one of the many legends about the man.[372] Connolly, alas, was not in attendance. Indeed, it is a shame that financial considerations prevented Connolly from traveling to Paris, as it would have been a major opportunity to meet some of the leading figures in the international socialist movement.

The Congress is often cited as a success for the ISRP, as the party was able to assert its status as a separate and distinct Irish socialist organisation. The ISRP delegates represented socialists from an oppressed nation, and therefore claimed the right to separate representation from the British delegation to the International. As Connolly himself recorded in his introduction to the 1909 American edition of *Erin's Hope*:

> Socialists were opposed to all oppression, so they should ever be foremost in the daily battle against all its manifestations, social and political. As the embodiment of this teaching, the party adopted the watchword, Irish Socialist Republic, and by deduction therefrom, the aforementioned name of their organisation … This policy received its formal endorsement by the International Socialist movement when at the International Socialist Congress at Paris in 1900 the delegates of the I.S.R.P. were formally seated as the delegates of a nation separate from England.

However, in a volume of reminiscences published under the title *Forth the Banners Go*, William O'Brien goes further and advances the claim that Hyndman of the SDF challenged the Irish socialists' right to sit as a separate nation:

> When the conference opened the English Socialists, led by H.M. Hyndman, took the view that Great Britain and Ireland should sit together. The voting arrangement was two from each country – that would mean that the two votes would be shared between Britain and Ireland perhaps, or the British Socialists, being very much larger, would probably claim the whole two. However, that did not take place and the Irish delegation made it quite clear that unless they were admitted separately as a nation they would return home. That was written up by Connolly, who praised them for their patriotic vigour in doing that and we have the minute book of the Socialist Party, which records Connolly's views on it.[373]

This has been repeated by subsequent studies, such as David Howell's *A Lost Left*.[374] Howell only cites Ruth Dudley Edwards's biography which itself makes no mention of the alleged SDF challenge to the ISRP's delegates, and O'Brien's aforementioned reminiscences.[375] One other source making the claim is T.A. Jackson's *Solo Trumpet*. Jackson's work is a fine read, rich in detail about the turn of the century socialist movement but is often inaccurate. For instance, Jackson recounts a conversation between himself, Con Lehane and Connolly which has the latter, wrongly, placed in attendance at the Congress.[376]

The report back from the ISRP's delegates, both in the party's minute book and in its public press, tells a different story. The minute books contain no separate standalone report.[377] By 9 October, Tom Lyng was moved to table a motion that 'D O'Brien and E.W. Stewart furnish reports of [the Congress] by the next meeting – the former for the I.S.R.P., the latter for the Fintan Lalor Club'. We finally get a report on 16 October in the minutes written by Daniel O'Brien, which was a cutting from the 10 October issue of the *Workers' Republic*. It is recorded that Stewart had nothing else to add. With regards to the issue of delegates' credentials, the report states:

> Each nationality verified the credentials of its own delegates. Owing to an oversight of some sort on the part of the Secretary to the Congress, the Irish delegates were not forwarded their admission cards before setting out for Paris, and as a result there was some difficulty in obtaining recognition as representing a distinct nationality. This error was however happily rectified, and so obviated the necessity of withdrawing from the Congress, as the only other course left open to us was to attend as a portion of the British Delegation, a course of action which could not have been entertained.[378]

It seems from this account that it was an administrative error rather than any malevolence from Hyndman that created the confusion over the ISRP's delegate status. Indeed, on 15 July, Louis Debreuilh, the secretary of the Socialist Party of France, which was hosting the Congress, wrote to Murtagh Lyng, as Secretary of the ISRP, enclosing particulars for the Congress.[379] This was followed up with admittance cards for ISRP delegates on 14 September.[380] Daniel O'Brien's delegate card survives, and can be found in the O'Brien papers, with the name of the organisation he is representing stated clearly as the ISRP.[381] The problem, it appears, is that the cards did not arrive in time.

Nor was the issue of the delegates' status raised before the Congress itself. The first contact between the SDF and the ISRP regarding the conference appears to be a letter sent by the SDF Secretary H.W. Lee to Connolly on 4 July. The tone is cordial. 'Dear Comrade,' writes Lee, 'Official invitations for the [Paris International Workers Congress, 1900] are now being sent out. As we are arranging for a party to go to Paris for the International Congress at special cheap terms, we venture to enclose particulars, in case your society is sending delegates who might care to accompany our party.'[382] It goes on to explain the terms of the deal, including transport fares, accommodation and meals, and the date of departure from London to Paris on Friday 21 September.

The SDF makes no mention of the ISRP's delegate status, separate or otherwise, but wishes to extend logistical support, as both organisations will likely travel via similar routes to Paris. If the issue of delegates' rights was to be contentious, we might expect it to have been raised beforehand, and not left to a wrangle at the Congress itself.

Even if the SDF did not challenge the ISRP's status as delegates representing Ireland as an independent nation, such recognition by the Congress was, positively, a proud achievement for the ISRP. It set a precedent for the international socialist movement to recognise Ireland's right to independence, which was confirmed again in 1918 at the Berne Congress, to which to the ISRP's successor party the Socialist Party of Ireland (SPI) sent a delegation.

Moreover, aside from the national question, the Congress was of wider political importance to the ISRP's development, Connolly included. The main issue of contention at the Congress was whether it was permissible for socialists to enter non-socialist capitalist governments. As Raymond Challinor, in his history of the British SLP writes

> British revolutionary socialism was born in Paris on 27 September 1900. There, at the congress of the Second International, delegates fiercely debated the propriety of Alexandre Millerand and two other French socialists joining the government of Waldeck-Rousseau. It was not merely that the government was pledged to administer capitalism, and would therefore inevitably carry out anti-working-class measures, but the cabinet contained General Gallifet, the butcher of the Paris Commune. Twenty thousand communards had been murdered at his command. This made left-wing delegates even more incensed. They heckled Jean Jaurès, the veteran French socialist, when he put the case for participation in the government.[383]

The context for the debate on 'Ministerialism' was, of course, the Dreyfus Affair. In 1894, Captain Alfred Dreyfus, a French artillery officer of Alsatian and Jewish background, was sentenced to life imprisonment for allegedly passing military secrets to the German Embassy in Paris. Evidence soon came to light that Dreyfus had been framed, and that a terrible miscarriage of justice had been covered up. The affair came to a head when writer Emile Zola penned the famous open letter, *J'Accuse*, to the French President in August 1898, accusing the government of antisemitism and the unlawful imprisonment of Dreyfus. The following year, Dreyfus was re-tried in an atmosphere of intense ideological polarisation in French society between largely Catholic pro-military 'anti-Dreyfusards' and their republican and anticlerical opponents.

It was against this background that Millerand accepted a post in government, bowing to the pressure to 'defend' the Republic from the reactionary opposition. In doing so, however, he took a seat around the table alongside General de Gallifet, the Minister of War, who had been the butcher of the Paris Commune in 1871. This latter issue in particular exerted a strong emotional pull in the socialist movement and the general controversy over participation in bourgeois governments became an international dividing line. The left at the Congress 'taunted the supporters of Millerand with shouts of "Vive la Commune" and "Go to Chalons" – a reference to the place where French soldiers had recently killer strikers'.[384] In attempt to heal the burgeoning division, Kautsky, the outstanding theorist of German Social Democracy, put forward a compromise motion which condemned class collaboration but added: 'If in some special instance the political situation necessitates this dangerous experiment [of entering capitalist governments], that is a question of tactics and not of principle.'[385] The compromise motion was greeted with derision on the left. The Russian Social-Democrat Vladimir Lenin sarcastically dismissed it as being made from 'Kaoutcouch' ('caoutchouc' being India rubber, known for its elasticity), and when it passed, by 29 votes to 9, the left exploded in anger.[386]

One of the British delegates, George S. Yates of the SDF, sided with the left wing of the Congress in opposing the compromise resolution. Yates, who represented the Leith branch of the SDF, was described by one contemporary as an 'exceptionally clever worker'. An engineer by trade who had studied at the University of Edinburgh, Yates was 'a fluent speaker, he was well informed on Marxism, economics, history, philosophy, logic and literature. He read and spoke French and German fluently.'[387] Yates was also a dedicated internationalist, and brought the words and music of the socialist anthem *The Internationale* back with him to Britain. It proved to be immediately popular. The SDF General Secretary H.W. Lee reported that,

All the British comrades who were at the International Congress were much taken with the Socialist song 'L'Internationale'. It has, indeed, a thoroughly good swinging air, which is also a capital marching tune. The job [he continued] will be to translate the verses in to English. Whoever sets the tune going here, whether it be choir or band, had better start it at a good pace and, having once heard it taken at a spirited time, perhaps we shall avoid with the 'Internationale' the droning, methodistical, dirge-like funereal rendering which is the curse of most Socialist singing in this country.[388]

The ISRP delegates, too, sided with the left, joining forces with Jules Guesde's POF and De Leon's SLP. Soon after the congress, Connolly wrote in the pages of *Justice* that, by the letter of the new policy, in entering a capitalist government, 'Millerand could still logically claim to be considered a good socialist, differing only in tactics from the socialists of the world, who agreed with him in principle'. Instead, Connolly urged acceptance of the principle 'that the revolutionary proletariat should, through its delegates, accept no governmental position which it cannot conquer by its own strength at the ballot box'.[389]

Yet, there was no getting away from the fact that the Second International was having to face some serious ideological and political questions. In theory, the International was based on the revolutionary philosophy of Marx and Engels, according to which the conquest of political power by the Social-Democrats would start the process of abolishing class society itself. Yet, this revolutionary aim often seemed remote from the perspective of its national parties' day-to-day activity, especially as socialist parties found increased success within the framework of capitalist parliamentary systems.

These tensions crystallised with the 'Revisionist Controversy' in 1898. With the lifting of Otto von Bismarck's anti-Socialist laws in 1890, the German SPD was soon polling millions of votes, and was fast on the way to becoming Germany's largest political party. One of its key theorists, Eduard Bernstein, a protégé of Engels himself, had been based in London due to the repressive conditions in Germany. While in Britain, he was influenced by the reformist Fabians and sought a revision in the SPD's political theory to bring it into line with what he saw the party doing in practice. Bernstein developed his views in a series of articles between 1896 and 1898. Bernstein was perceptive about some of the changes in the Germany of the 1890s. Rising real wages, technological development, the centralisation of capital into larger and larger firms, and the growing integration of industrial and financial capital, all pointed in his view towards the optimistic prognosis that progress could be made without recourse to revolutionary break with the existing state and economic system. The movement for reforms, for Bernstein, 'was everything; the end goal, nothing'.

However, as his main theoretical interlocutor, Kautsky, pointed out, Bernstein's mistake was to generalise from these short-term tendencies to throw out aspects of Marxism's overall critique of capitalist society. The centralisation of capital into trusts and monopolies, far from mitigating the potential of crisis, made possible crisis on a deeper and more extended scale and the possibility of war through intense imperialist competition. On the more radical wing of the International, Rosa Luxemburg replied in her

Reform and Revolution that 'people who pronounce themselves in favour of the method of legislative reform in place and in contradistinction to the conquest of political power and social revolution, do not really choose a more tranquil, calmer and slower road to the same goal, but a different goal'.[390]

With Millerand's entry into government, and the theoretical controversy ranging in German Social-Democracy, Yates argued that a 'big wave of opportunism is passing through the ranks of the international socialist party'. In *What is to be Done?* written in the autumn of 1901, the Russian Marxist V.I. Lenin concurred that two trends were taking form in international Social-Democracy, one reformist and the other revolutionary, and wrote that:

> the strife of the various trends within the socialist movement has from national become international. Formerly, the dispute … remained confined within purely national frameworks, reflecting purely national features, and proceeding, as it were, on different planes. At the present time (as is now evident), the English Fabians, the French Ministerialists, the German Bernsteinians and the Russian Critics – all belong to the same family, all extol each other, learn from each other, and together taken up arms against 'dogmatic' Marxism.

This framing of the problem as a question of tendencies *within* national parties, cutting *across* national affiliations, rather than a battle *between* parties as a whole, is a useful one. The rebels – De Leon, Yates, Lenin, Rosa Luxemburg – all represented tendencies of thought within the larger Social-Democrat movements of their respective countries. In voting with Yates at the Paris Congress, and in the arguments that followed, the ISRP put itself on the radical left of the Second International.

The impossibilist revolt in the SDF

In the UK, the international bust-up at the Paris Congress was the spark for a quite profound re-alignment in the matrix of British socialism. Fresh from Paris, Yates returned to Britain convinced of the need to found 'a new party, as we have no ambition to swim with the tide'.[391] Yates took aim at the leadership of the SDF, who had backed the Kautsky resolution in Paris, and his views found echo in branches across Scotland and in London. They would lead eventually, as we shall see, to no fewer than two splits from the SDF itself.

A decisive influence, and a source of ideological ballast, for those gathered around Yates was the radical left wing of the American socialist movement, Daniel De Leon's SLP, which we mentioned earlier.[392] It is worth detailing De Leon's views in some depth, given the importance of his thinking on Connolly's subsequent political development.

Born in the Dutch colony of Curacao, off the coast of Venezuela, in December 1852, De Leon was educated in law in Germany and the Netherlands. He moved to the United States in 1874, finding work as a lecturer until his support in the 1886 New York mayoral election for populist land reformer Henry George cost him his part-time teaching job at Columbia University.

In 1890, De Leon joined the SLP, becoming the editor of its newspaper *The People* and the SLP candidate for governor of New York the following year. He soon established himself as a prominent figure in the party, advocating a form of revolutionary Marxism. This was too much for some on the right of his party, led by trade unionist Morris Hillquit, who split in 1899. Soon afterwards, they merged with the SDP of Victor Berger and Eugene V. Debs, founding the SPA in 1901, which soon became the USA's largest and most successful socialist organisation.

Under De Leon's influence, the SLP refined its revolutionary programme, but with decreasing influence amongst the wider working class. Rather than its members involving themselves in the American Federation of Labor (AFL), the De Leonites advocated a policy of 'dual unionism', setting up their own revolutionary socialist union, known as the Socialist Trades and Labor Alliance (STLA). Non-socialist trade unionism, or what AFL leader Samuel Gompers called 'pure and simple' unionism, was bitterly derided by the SLP, its leaders denounced as 'labor fakirs', and union officials as the 'labor lieutenants of the capitalist class'. In politics, the De Leon's SLP held no brief for palliative reforms, believing them to be a distraction from the battle for socialism. Reformist socialists in the rival SPA were known as the 'kangaroos' for their predilection to jump from one reform to another.

Even before the 1900 Paris Congress, the ISRP too was growing increasingly close to the American SLP. William O'Brien recalls that when he 'joined the ISRP in June 1899' he 'found the members very interested in the affairs of the SLP of the USA'.[393] Indeed, connections between the two parties went back to as early as 1896, when the ISRP was formed. The attraction was obvious. Not only did the SLP stand for the same uncompromising revolutionary socialism that Connolly advocated in these years but, given the large Irish-American population in the United States, it was clear that the ISRP could gain much from the relationship. As the SLP's national secretary Henry Kuhn explained to the ISRP at the time of its formation, there was no better way of promoting Connolly's new organisation 'than by promoting it here in America'.[394] Connolly would go on to contribute a number of articles for the SLP's *Weekly People*. In return, De Leon's newspaper would promote the ISRP's manifesto in the US and contribute financially to support the *Worker's Republic* newspaper. Thus was forged between the parties of Connolly and De Leon's an 'important link ... between like-thinking English-speaking militants on both sides of the Atlantic'.[395]

These connections between the ISRP and the SLP 'set the stage for [their joint] support of those militants in the S.D.F. who ultimately wished to break with the policies of the S.D.F.'s entrenched old guard'.[396] De Leon's writings were exhilarating stuff for the mostly young, left-wing critics of the ageing and complacent SDF leaders, and De Leonism spread quickly. According to one historian of the SDF: 'Links between Scottish SDFers and the American Socialists had been established in 1898 when J.P. Douall of the Edinburgh branch had visited the United States and returned with some SLP literature.'[397] By the end of 1900, 'the American SLP with its weekly and daily *People* and De Leon's pamphlets had exercised considerable influence on the SDF branches in Scotland'.[398]

Not surprisingly, given his criticism of the SDF delegates at the 1900 Paris Congress and his own links with De Leon, Connolly identified strongly with Yates's side of the argument. From the summer of 1901 onwards, until he left Britain and Ireland for the United States, Connolly would play a leading role as an *éminence grise* in the battle of ideas in the SDF, advising the left-wing critics of the SDF leadership, touring Britain to propagate their doctrines, and printing their newspaper, *The Socialist*, from the ISRP presses in Dublin.

Observing the language used in the SDF in this period, it is absolutely clear that this was not simply a parochial fight, limited to British issues. Though, with the exception of the Millerand issue, the focus would naturally be on those within the British labour movement, the activists on the radical left saw themselves as part of a wider transnational opposition to growing reformist tendencies within the Second International, which manifested itself in the various national parties. Indeed, their opposition was, in turn, seen as such by their more moderate opponents.

Tom Bell, a young follower of Yates, who later went on to become a founder of the Communist Party of Great Britain (CPGB) remembered that in the battle in the SDF, the two sides soon adopted the factional terminology of the French socialist movement. 'In France the fight against Millerand had been led by Jules Guesde,' he explained, 'who was then a thorough-going

Marxist. The Guesdists had been named the "Impossibilists" in contrast to the pure and simple reformists, dubbed "Possibilists".' Veteran SDF leader Harry Quelch would denounce his young critics as 'impossibilists' for their uncompromising revolutionary politics, a label they would adopt as a badge of honour. 'In retaliation for being called "Impossibilists",' Tom Bell remembered, 'we styled the reformists "Kangaroos" because they kept jumping from one reform to the other, and would never be definite on anything.'[399] Thus, in the struggle against the alleged reformism of the SDF leadership, the Scottish 'impossibilists' would develop and apply De Leon's ideas and, somewhat incongruously, his eccentric vocabulary of 'fakirs' and 'kangaroos', to the British situation. The appropriation of factional epithets was not limited to France and the US. The German party, too, was invoked. In 1902, when the future Labour Party leader George Lansbury, then a member of the SDF, expressed doubt about continuing to stand independent SDF candidates in general elections, he was denounced by the left for having advocated 'an alliance with radicals entirely in the Bernsteinian spirit'.[400]

Besides the vote at the 1900 Paris Congress, a number of specific national issues made the SDF a ripe target for left-wing criticism from within its ranks. Though a pioneer of socialist organisation and propaganda in Great Britain, by the turn of the twentieth century the SDF was stuck in a rut. It had missed the opportunities provided by New Unionism in the late 1880s to root its Marxism deeply in the working-class movement. Instead, the main beneficiary of the upsurge in workers' organisation had been the non-Marxist ILP. It had received little return from its various electoral efforts and the outbreak of the Boer War in 1898 saw the party membership start to decline. Shaken by the wave of jingoism, the party's energy was directed into defensive struggles against the breaking up of socialist meetings, as it attempted to swim against the stream.

These factors served to increase SDF's isolation and the demoralisation of its activists. Yet, ironically, it was the steps taken by the leadership to redress the problem which made it a further target for Yates and his comrades. The dissidents were younger, more working class, and impatient with the ageing, middle-class SDF Executive. They 'objected to what they saw as attempts at illusory short cuts to Socialism, the discarding of principles in the hope of immediate gain'.[401]

One issue of contention, therefore, was the attitude of the SDF towards the Labour Representation Committee (LRC). In February 1900, the Executive of the SDF decided to participate in the conference to launch the LRC, a body which aspired to bring together trades unions and socialist organisations such as the ILP to win increased labour representation in parliament. Initially, the SDF took an open-minded view and affiliated.

Immediately, the decision led to divisions within the SDF, and Scotland soon established itself as the restless hotbed of opposition. In 1898, a Scottish District Council of the SDF had been formed in Edinburgh to arrange local and national speakers for socialist propaganda meetings. Yates was an influential figure in the Scottish SDF and was horrified that the national party would involve itself in a body such as the LRC with the non-socialist trades unions. On 10 March 1901, he successfully carried a resolution at the Scottish District Council meeting in Falkirk, withdrawing the Scottish SDF from the Scottish Workers' Parliamentary Committee, a parallel organisation to the LRC. The latter body, argues Yates, had already 'obliterated the few shreds of class consciousness with which it began'. This was a marked turnaround from the Scottish District Council's position adopted the previous year, which was to send SDF delegates and 'work steadily along with the other bodies in this movement'.[402]

As well as facing opposition from within its own ranks, the SDF soon found itself in conflict with the ILP over what policy the LRC should adopt. The SDF moved a resolution calling for the LRC to recognise the existence of the class war and adopt an explicitly socialist objective. It was, however, defeated by 59 votes to 35, with the ILP delegation arguing such a declaration at an early stage would alienate the trades unions. The SDF was furious, 'that the delegates of an avowed Socialist organisation ... should deliberately and boastfully repudiate the principles they were presumably sent there to support [is] as incomprehensible as it is deplorable.'

In August 1901, delegates assembled in the Birmingham Town Hall for the 21st Annual Conference of the SDF, which would be the opening battle in a war which would ultimately split the organisation. Unsurprisingly, the SDF's support for the Kautsky compromise resolution at the Paris Congress was an issue of major contention. The leadership first sought to deal with the issue bureaucratically: a motion from Yates's Leith branch was ruled out of order by the executive. However, another 'impossibilist', L. Cotton from the Oxford branch, moved an amendment to another motion, repudiating the actions of the SDF delegates at the Paris Congress on the grounds that Millerand's entry into the French government was an issue of principle, not merely a question of tactics. The amendment was seconded by Yates, who noted that Millerand's Ministry 'had many times sent troops against the working classes, whose leader Millerand posed as being'. In this, he was supported by John Carstairs Matheson, a Falkirk schoolteacher, and good friend of Connolly's, who 'protested against the wave of moderatism which had swept over the Socialist Parties of the whole world and of which the Kautsky resolution was the highest expression'.[403]

Quelch, clearly irritated by the criticism, responded with a demagogic defence. The record of the conference states that:

> He [Quelch] maintained strenuously that we were not impossibilists, and circumstances must determine our policy. We must adopt any and every means to realise Social-Democracy. He himself was in favour of any means, from the ballot-box to the bomb, from political action to assassination. (Cheers) Oh, yes, the movers of the resolution cheered assassination, but they would not allow a Socialist to enter a Ministry.

Cotton's amendment fell by 37 votes to 8 after Quelch's forceful intervention. Yates then immediately switched to another line of attack. *Justice,* the SDF newspaper, was in fact owned by Twentieth Century Press, a company in which Hyndman and his allies had a controlling stake. In an effort to deprive the leadership of its monopoly over the party press, Yates moved a resolution that the party should take control of *Justice* directly. It was a repeat of a similar move by the Leith branch at the previous year's conference.[404] Quelch replied that 'the motion was an attack on the conduct of the paper and on the policy of the S.D.F.' and 'challenged Yates, instead of writing letters full of gibes and sneers, to write something educational for the paper. Yates replied and the motion was lost by 41 votes to 17.'[405]

Perhaps surprisingly, given its subsequent importance for historians, the LRC issue caused relatively little dissension. Following the earlier failure of the LRC to adopt a socialist objective, the conference voted 54-14 to secede from the body. Most historians, and many participants, now agree that this was a fatal error. H.W. Lee, who wrote the official history of the SDF, reflected that abandoning the LRC was a mistake:

> All the propaganda that we did afterwards, all the influence we were able to bring to bear in a Socialist direction, would have been very much greater indeed had we carried it on and exercised it as an integral part of the LRC, and not as an outside body at which many supporters of Independent Labour Representation looked a trifle askance because of our withdrawal from the LRC.[406]

For all their merits, of which there were many, the comrades who later formed the SLP in fact contributed to a hardening of the SDF's already sectarian position on an issue of cardinal importance to the working-class movement. It is, in part, their responsibility that the Labour Party would develop without the vigorous intervention of a coherent Marxist current shaping its course.

On the LRC issue, then, the 'impossibilists' were not alone, and made a united front with the leadership against the Lancashire branches. The leadership, represented by Harry Quelch, had moved the motion to pull the SDF out of the LRC, and it was easily carried. Yet, this could not disguise the widening gulf between the leadership and its 'impossibilist' critics. The official report in *Justice* described the conference as:

> in many respects one of the most critical in the history of our body, as we here had developed and brought in to the light of day an attack on the whole policy of the S.D.F and JUSTICE, which has long been in preparation by a few who wish to sidetrack the Socialist movement in this country into the impossibilism which seventeen years ago led to the formation and, later, to the collapse of the Socialist League.[407]

Though largely routed on the votes, the 'impossibilists' had reason to be cheerful. The Birmingham conference had extended their reach outside of Scotland to SDF branches in London and Reading. Both branches readily invited Connolly to lecture for them in October 1901. Bell recalled Connolly from this period with admiration, writing that

> [his] quiet, reticent disposition concealed the store of knowledge he had acquired from extensive reading and wide travel. But, provoked into discussion or debate, he would route opponents with incisive and merciless logic ... A proletarian of proletarians, he had none of that snobbery and pretentiousness that mar so many of our leaders. He was ... devoted and self-sacrificing for the cause of the workers' emancipation from capitalist slavery.[408]

Connolly encouraged his enthusiastic young followers to deepen and develop their knowledge of socialist theory. According to Challinor, 'he always encouraged his listeners to read the *Weekly People,* buy the Marxist classics being published by the New York Labor News Company, and start economics classes to get down to serious study'. By these means, 'Connolly hoped not merely to make converts, but also to have workers who, being more knowledgeable and trained, were likely to be of greater effectiveness in the struggle'.[409]

Encouraged by their growing support, the 'impossibilists' dug in, developed their organisational infrastructure, and prepared for further skirmishes with the SDF leadership. By now, Yates and his allies had taken over the Scottish District Council, and they took advantage of their position to promote Marxist economics classes throughout the Scottish branches. They put much of the emphasis on Marxist education. Matheson, reporting on the progress of the Falkirk branch in *Justice*, wrote that 'the principle aim of our members ought to be to gain a complete grip of scientific Socialism and to thoroughly assimilate the truth according to Marx before seeking to indoctrinate others'.[410] In order to further this work, Yates established the International Labour Literature Depot in Glasgow as an agency of the New York Labor News Co., and used it to import quantities of De Leon's *Weekly People* for sale in Scotland and London. It had the desired effect: 'Through the economics classes and the *Weekly People* as well as Connolly's lecture tours the impossibilist movement grew up both in Scotland and London and became a serious menace to the official S.D.F.'[411]

The growth of De Leonite influence in the SDF did not go unnoticed. In April 1901, *Justice's* column 'Topical Tattle' was prompted to complain that ever since 1896, 'the chiefs of the S.L.P. in New York have, in their paper, persistently engaged in attacks on the movement in this country … in which all the men who were known for their work in the movement were described as "freaks", "fakirs", "skates," and other quaint but not particularly edifying names'. In the aftermath of the 1900 Paris Congress, it noted, 'these attacks have increased in vehemence and frequency'. However, the paper attempted to make light of them: 'Generally they have been too outrageous and absurd to awaken anything but a feeling of amused imagination.'[412]

The SDF's reserves of good humour would soon run out. Round two of the fight between the leadership and the 'impossibilists' took place at the 22nd SDF Conference in the Blackburn Town Hall at the end of March 1902. The SDF leadership took some pre-emptive action to damage their critics, by re-publishing correspondence from an 'impossibilist' SDF member to De Leon's *Daily* and *Weekly People* written in the wake of 1901's SDF conference. Designed to stir up delegates' distrust of the 'impossibilists', *Justice* wrote that 'it is useful as showing the unscrupulous malignity of what our friend [Theodore] Rothstein called the "unholy Scotch current", and members of the S.D.F. will be able to understand the true inwardness of certain proposals which are being put forward in favour of drastic changes in the policy and programme of the S.D.F. Their real object,' concluded the article, 'conscious or otherwise, is disruption.'[413]

Matheson responded weeks later, suggesting that there was no proof the letter (signed by 'X.X.X') was not a fake. He complained that the comments made:

> upon an anonymous letter which appeared in the weekly *People* over three months ago and held over for publication by yourself until almost of the eve of the annual conference, point to the existence of a spirit of rancour and party hatred which augurs very badly against the prospect of a calm and dispassionate ...[414]

In the last issue before the Blackburn conference, the SDF leadership went further, publishing comments from a member of Matheson's Falkirk branch opposed to the 'impossibilist' policy, accusing them of preparing a split. Referring to an unnamed 'leader' of the 'unholy Scotch current', presumably Yates, the Falkirk member wrote that the '"leader" referred to had the audacity to admit that when the time was ripe, which was not yet, they would form a branch of the S.L.P.; indeed, they are at the present time raising funds to start a paper on lines analogous to the *Weekly People*, and, of course, in direct opposition to JUSTICE, which is being boycotted'.[415]

Another important context for the Blackburn conference was the Dewsbury by-election which had taken place two months earlier in January 1902. Quelch was put forward by the SDF as the 'Social Democratic and Trade Union Candidate' and the ILP felt obliged to withdraw their own candidate. Quelch, though defeated, garnered 1,597 votes, and regarded this as a positive sign that the SDF could unite the British socialists under its own leadership. The by-election also proved to be the occasion for the total breakdown in relations between Connolly and the SDF leadership. Connolly's role in stirring up discontent within the organisation had clearly strained things, but the issue came to a head during the election campaign.[416] The ISRP had recently published its own election manifesto for the Dublin municipal elections. It was sent to *Justice* to be printed for the benefit of British socialists but it did not appear. Connolly immediately suspected that Quelch feared the ISRP document would cost him voters in the election. Though he was assured this was not the case, Connolly replied guardedly in a letter to *Justice* that: 'I, of course, accept your statement that you never saw it. But, seeing that a marked copy of it was posted to you in a regularly sealed and addressed envelope, you will admit that our assumption that you had received it was by no means a rash one.' Pointing out that the manifesto 'was noticed favourably in the Socialist press of Germany, France, and America', he noted 'that it should be ignored by the English Socialists to whom it was addressed was not calculated to the promotion of fraternal feelings between us'.[417]

Fresh from the respectable by-election result, a mood of Socialist Unity was in the air as the delegates arrived in Blackburn for the SDF conference. At the opening of the meeting, the SDF leadership proposed to send fraternal greetings to the ILP conference, which was being held at the same time in Liverpool. The resolution was carried by 52 votes to 22 but the notion of unity with the non-Marxist ILP was rejected out of hand by the 'impossibilists'. At the Blackburn conference, the Scottish and London 'impossibilists' supported each other, and three were elected to the SDF executive. Again, aligning with the SDF leadership to reject a motion supportive of the LRC, the Scottish 'impossibilists' then went further, and unsuccessfully demanded that the SDF adopted the De Leonite position of 'dual unionism', in other words, the formation of separate socialist trade unions.[418]

After the Blackburn conference, the Scottish and London 'impossibilists' moved to formalise their friendly relations. Percy Friedberg of the Finsbury Park branch became the liaison agent for London to work in conjunction with the Scottish members. Quickly, however, the tensions with the SDF leadership came to a head. The impossibilists felt that the official report of the Blackburn conference, which was both hostile and dismissive towards the 'impossibilists' contained inaccuracies.[419] Friedberg wrote to *Justice* to have them corrected. When Quelch refused to publish his letter, it was sent to New York, and the *Weekly People* published it as part of its report on the SDF conference. Incensed, the SDF Executive passed a resolution on 20 May expelling Friedberg. The Finsbury Park branch stood by him, and it too was threatened with expulsion. At this point, Con Lehane, the former secretary of the Cork branch of Connolly's ISRP, preached caution and advised the Finsbury Park branch to avoid any danger of being expelled. The branch spurned his advice, continued to stand behind Friedberg, and soon found itself expelled from the SDF.

Though undoubtedly a setback for the 'impossibilists', and one which led to the London and Scottish-based comrades going their separate ways, the expulsion of the Finsbury Park branch did have one benefit. As early as March 1901, the Scottish District Council of the SDF had resolved to establish a new socialist paper supported by the Scottish branches. The idea was parked for want of sufficient funds but, in the summer of 1902, the newly-independent Finsbury Park branch agreed to set aside part of its membership subscriptions to fund the new paper. James Connolly agreed to print it in Dublin on the presses of the ISRP and, after some logistical frustrations, the first issue appeared in August 1902, printed by the Workers'

Publishing Co., Dublin, and published by the Scottish District Council of the SDF in Edinburgh.

The Socialist was a four-page broadsheet and owed much to both Connolly and De Leon. Moreover, it was an equal opportunities newspaper: 'The impossibilists were impartial in their attacks on all union and socialist leaders as "fakirs" – whether they belonged to the official S.D.F., the I.L.P., the L.R.C., or the trade unions, all provided abundant material for their bitter criticism.'[420] Connolly's influence is shown clearly by the strident republican tone of the first issue. On the occasion of King Edward's coronation in 1902, the SDF had published in *Justice* a remarkable 'Open Letter to the King', which stated: 'by using your position to improve the well-being of Englishmen at home and to save from utter ruin their greatest dependency abroad ... you can secure for yourself in history which mankind will look back to with admiration and respect.' A blistering reply came from the pen of Matheson in *The Socialist,* to the effect that: 'Monarchy or any other non-elective office or position is an insult to the sovereignty of the people. It is the very citadel of capital in times of revolutionary energy, as at present.' Meanwhile, De Leon's articles were borrowed constantly from the *Weekly People,* his longer works serialised, and the September 1902 issue advertised 'American Pamphlets for Sale' from the SLP.

Connolly had moved a long way since his socialist apprenticeship back in Edinburgh a decade previously. It is a measure of the distance that his old mentor, John Leslie, was among the most forthright critics of the 'impossibilist' tendency in Scotland. In a letter to *Justice* in the wake of the Blackburn conference, Leslie wrote that:

> The S.D.F. is to be congratulated on its emphatic condemnation of the insolent and ruffianly Yankee interference. But there is another outside interference nearer home, which while neither ruffianly or insolent, is none the less to be deprecated.[421]

Leslie was purposefully vague but it is a reasonable inference that the outside interference is Connolly, and the professedly friendly organisation was the ISRP.

The London 'impossibilists' had initially agreed to part-fund the new paper on the basis that it would have a say over the articles printed. It soon became clear that the Scottish comrades were moving faster towards a reckoning with the SDF leadership than was first imagined by their allies in England. The March 1903 issue of *The Socialist* contained an article from Yates entitled 'The Official SDF' which laid down the gauntlet to the SDF leadership on a number of questions. The following months, the London 'impossibilists' met at the Hope Coffee Tavern in Finsbury Park, and 9 out of the 16 present resolved that 'the Scottish section were forcing matters without having properly consulted the London men', and decided to hold a joint meeting on Easter Sunday when all would be present in London to attend the 23rd SDF Annual conference.

At the 23rd annual conference, held across three days in April at the Shoreditch Town Hall in east London, the SDF leadership were in no mood to indulge the 'impossibilists'. The eve of conference edition of *Justice* contained a letter with the ominous headline 'The Impossibilists: what will we do with them?' which complained of Yates and his comrades:

> Their language is free and choice, they have a jargon of slang peculiar to themselves and bespatter with their verbal mud all whom they differ with. They possess a monthly paper – a gutter-sheet – whose columns recently, among other literary garbage had a scurrilous article on 'The Official S.D.F'. Now, sir, is it not time to put an end to this sort of thing?[422]

The letter was prophetic. In advance of the conference, Yates was told that he was to be expelled. Such was the mood, 'some of the Impossibilists, believing it might be forcibly done, brought along a contingent of Scottish workers, who sat at the back of the hall, silent and watchful, lest the gathering turn violent'.[423] In the event, Yates was accused of obstructing steps towards Socialist Unity with the ILP, of refusing to sell *Justice,* and for writing the editorial in *The Socialist* attacking the SDF; he was, however, otherwise unharmed. On 11 April, the motion to expel him from the SDF was carried by 56 votes to 6, and the impossibilist presence on the party executive was wiped out. In the official conference report in *Justice,* the victorious SDF leadership did not hold back:

> What has recently occurred in the S.D.F. once more recalls the really serious 'split' of 1884. The Federation to-day has to put out from its midst a knot of ignorant and unseemly vilifiers of whom nobody ever heard until they set to work to calumniate and lie about those who were doing the work of the party, of whom very few have heard even now, and who will very soon be forgotten ... They were rather a nuisance in our body; they are a joke outside. How different, we say again, from losing such people as Morris and Bax and Scheu and Eleanor Marx ... most of whom afterwards came back to us.[424]

Back in Scotland, when party members in Glasgow got the telegram to say that Yates and his allies had been routed, they painted out the letters 'SDF' from the local headquarters, renaming themselves temporarily as the Glasgow Socialist Society. Meanwhile, that evening, the joint meeting between the Scottish and London 'impossibilists' was held at the Cock Hoop Tavern in Mile End. Yates, unsurprisingly, urged the formation of a new party, and a liaison committee was formed to explore this possibility. One London member, Fitzgerald, was not happy. Though he was elected to the liaison committee, he wrote that the meeting had revealed that:

> during the whole time they (the Scottish members) were supposed to be working with the London section for the re-organisation of the S.D.F., they were playing a double game by forming a new organisation in secret ... The London section were no more ready to blindly follow would-be geniuses from Scotland than 'highly educated' leaders from Queen Anne's Gate [Hyndman's residence].[425]

Unity between the London and Scottish comrades soon broke down, and the May 1903 issue of *The Socialist* announced that a conference would be held the following month in Edinburgh to found a new party. The majority of the London 'impossibilists' stayed with the SDF. However, at the subsequent SDF Annual Conference, held in Burnley in April 1904, the SDF leadership expelled them too. Soon afterwards, at a meeting at the Printers' Hall in Fetter Lane, the London 'impossibilists' formally announced the creation of the SPGB.[426]

At first, the Scottish 'impossibilists' did not have a name for their new organisation and were worried that they would simply be denounced as tools of De Leon if they called it the Socialist Labour Party. The American SLP was, indeed, the dominant influence on the new organisation, and in its founding 'Manifesto to the Working Class', Matheson defined the new party's idea of socialism, differentiating it from the SDF, the ILP and the Fabians:

> By this we do not mean what is variously called 'State Socialism', 'Public Ownership' or 'Municipalism' – that is, the ownership of certain public utilities by a community in which capitalism is still dominant. A worker is as much exploited by a capitalist state or corporation as by a private employer – as Post Office or municipal employees can testify. We insist upon the political overthrow of capitalism as an absolutely necessary preliminary to the emancipation of the working class.[427]

As for the name of the new organisation, 'It was Connolly', wrote Bell, 'who with characteristic directness, proposed the Socialist Labour Party. It doesn't matter what you call yourself ... You'll be dubbed the S.L.P. anyway.'[428] De Leon welcomed the new party to the family of satellite parties which orbited his own American SLP, proclaiming that the 'new Movement took the name that designates the revolutionary Socialist organization of Australia, American and Canada – "Socialist Labor Party" – thus completing, with a link in Great Britain, the chain of S.L.P. organizations in the English speaking world'. He praised his new comrades, writing: 'Its membership is active, well posted, serious and determined. Theirs is the S.L.P. attitude everywhere – the sword drawn, the scabbard thrown away.'[429]

However, the charge that the Scottish 'impossibilists' were slavish clones of De Leon was unfair. Raymond Challinor rightly argues that 'right from the outset Connolly and his comrades thought for themselves and asserted their political independence'.[430] At the founding conference on 6 and 7 June 1903, a major debate broke out over whether the party programme would include immediate demands for reforms. This issue also divided the Scottish party from the London-based SPGB who rejected all so-called 'palliatives', another reason why both groups of impossibilists went their separate ways. Theirs was a view shared by the Edinburgh comrades 'but most delegates realised the importance of the new party relating itself to the needs of the working class. Immediate demands had to be included if progress was to be made.' Accordingly, several immediate measures were included in the programme of the new party: 'the legal eight-hour day, abolition of child labour, gradated income-tax, nationalisation and democratic control of all industries, abolition of all hereditary authorities, national referendum on foreign affairs, full enfranchisement of the people.' While the American SLP strongly proclaimed its opposition to their inclusion in the programme, 'this had no effect on the inaugural conference. Deviations from the American line often happened subsequently.'[431] Also at the June conference, Connolly was elected chairperson and Neil Maclean the National Secretary. Initially, the party had four branches – Edinburgh, Falkirk, Glasgow and Leith – and soon afterwards, they were joined by Kirkcaldy, Southampton and East London, formerly the Bethnal Green branch of the SDF.[432]

The 'impossibilists' were prescient in anticipating criticism for adopting the name of De Leon's American organisation. In the wake of the split, *Justice* gloated that the 'prompt action of the SDF in dealing effectually with those malcontents who are bent upon following the lead of the German-Venezuelan Jew Loeb, or "de Leon", to the pit of infamy and disgrace, is regarded with much satisfaction on this side'.[433] In June 1903, Connolly himself hit back in *The Socialist* that the SDF was 'directly appealing to racial antipathies and religious prejudices' and that the attack on De Leon accurately reflected 'the mental conditions and methods of the men in charge of [*Justice*]'. If De Leon was 'a German-Venezuelan-Jew, or a Cockney-Irish-Scotsman, or even, horror of horrors, an Anglo-Saxon, what is it to us or to Socialists generally?' Of the SDF, he broadened his attack, adding that:

> this is no new trick of its policy. We all remember how, when the late Boer war was being launched upon this country, *Justice,* instead of grasping at the opportunity to demonstrate the unscrupulous and bloodthirsty methods of the capitalist class, strove to divert the wrath of the advanced workers from the capitalists to the Jews; how its readers were nauseated by denunciations of 'Jewish millionaires', 'Jewish plots', 'Jew-controlled newspapers', 'German Jews', 'Israelitish schemes', and all the stock phrases of the lowest anti-Semitic papers, until the paper became positively unreadable to any fair-minded man who recognised the truth, viz, that the war was the child of capitalist greed, and inspired by men with whom race or religion were matters of no moment.[434]

As this episode shows, Connolly was years ahead of many of his socialist contemporaries in understanding the pernicious evils of antisemitism.[435] His defence of De Leon personally shows an understanding of antisemitism as a racialised antipathy to individual Jews. More than this, however, Connolly's insistence that the Boer War was 'the child of capitalist greed' and nothing to do with 'Jewish millionaires' shows a nuanced understanding of how antisemitism also functioned, in the phrase often attributed to German SPD leader August Bebel, as a sort of 'socialism of fools' which displaced a true understanding of capitalism. Antisemitism is, thus, an enemy of socialism on several levels: as a particular threat to Jews, as a form of racist division in the working class and, on account of its 'pseudo-emancipatory dimension', a source of mystification which precludes a true scientific understanding and critique of capitalism.[436]

Connolly had demonstrated his opposition to antisemitism in practice the previous year. In the 1902 municipal elections to the Dublin Corporation, Connolly stood in the Wood Quay ward as a representative of the United Labourers' Union, though reserving the right to make his own socialist propaganda. Wood Quay ward, as Manus O'Riordan has written, was home to many of the small Dublin Jewish population, which was increasingly rapidly in these years as refugees fled Tsarist antisemitic pogroms in eastern Europe. Numbering only 352 in 1881, within a decade it reached 1057 and by 1901 was at 2169.[437] For the election, the ISRP wrote to Boris Kahan, secretary of the East London Jewish Branch of the Social Democratic Federation, who produced for them a Yiddish-language leaflet calling on Jewish workers to vote for Connolly because

> the Socialists are the only ones who stand always and everywhere against every national oppression. It is the socialists who went out onto the streets of Paris against the wild band of anti-Semites at the time of the Dreyfus case. In Austria and Germany they conduct a steady struggle against anti-Semitism. And in England, too, the Socialists fight against the reactionary elements who want to shut the doors of England against the poorer Jews who were driven to seek a refuge in strange land by the Russian government's brutality and despotism … Jewish workers! No matter how small your numbers you can achieve much. Do your duty and work earnestly hand in hand with your Irish brothers. Canvass for votes, vote yourself and persuade others to vote on the 15th of January for the Socialist candidate, James Connolly.[438]

Connolly won a respectable 431 votes against his United Irish League opponent P.J. McCall, who won 1434 votes after a dirty and divisive campaign. The party was subjected to vilification from the Church who, said the ISRP, invoked 'all the terrors of religious against all those who voted for Mr. Connolly'. The following year Connolly reminded the electors:

> how the paid canvassers of the capitalist candidate – hired slanderers – gave a different account of Mr. Connolly to every section of the electors. How they said to the Catholics that he was an Orangeman, to the Protestants that he was a Fenian, to the Jews that he was an anti-Semite, to others that he was a Jew, to the labourers that he was a journalist on the make, and to the tradesmen and professional classes that he was an ignorant labourer; that he was born in Belfast, Derry, England, Scotland and Italy, according to the person the canvasser was talking to.[439]

To America

In 1902, the SLP's National Secretary in the US, Henry Kuhn, wrote to the ISRP asking if they would send a speaker for a national tour. Connolly was already known in socialist circles in the US; as previously noted, the SLP had printed the ISRP *Manifesto* and Connolly's *Erin's Hope*. The appendix to the first American edition of the latter indicates the growing political affinity between the ISRP and De Leon's organisation. After calling for

Irish-American voters to support the SLP, Connolly wrote the party 'carries its banner in America as the Irish Socialist Republican Party does in Ireland. Given the triumph of one and the other is within sight of its goal.'[440]

Explaining why, despite its small size, he was drawn to the SLP, Connolly wrote:

> To me it was sufficient that the S.L.P. was following in America the same line of action which we in Ireland had mapped out for ourselves before we came in touch with S.L.P. literature, that although Ireland and Bulgaria were the only countries which at the International Congress had voted solid against the Kautsky resolution, yet the S.L.P. had followed the lead of France, Poland and Italy, and had backed us up by one vote, and that as long as their cause was just it did not matter whether the S.L.P. vote was 34,000 or the million which the S.D.P. did not poll in 1900. I believe firmly that the revolutionary Socialist movement will always be numerically weak until the hour of revolution arrives, and then it will be as easy to get adherents by the thousands as it is now to get single individuals.[441]

Connolly agreed to go, hoping to raise funds and increase subscriptions to the *Workers' Republic.* The tour lasted three and a half months, and took in New Jersey, Connecticut, Rhode Island, Massachusetts and New York on the east coast, before moving through the Mid-West to California, Arizona and Colorado, and Canada.

The first date was on 15 September, when Connolly was officially greeted at the Cooper Union in New York. Asked by one reporter – used to well-worn tales from Ireland – where his ancestors were from and whether they had any castles, Connolly replied: 'I have no "ancestors". My people were poor and obscure like the workers I am speaking to now.' Visibly affected by the enthusiastic cheers welcoming him to America, Connolly made clear to his audience: 'I represent only the class to which I belong … I could not represent the entire Irish people on account of the antagonistic interests of these classes, no more than the wolf could represent the lambs or the fisherman the fish.'

The tour was a success, and the offices of the ISRP back in Dublin were flooded with letters from appreciative audience members, complementing Connolly for his eloquent orations. From Duluth, Minnesota, Salt Lake City, Chicago, Delta Colorado and more, American comrades wrote to the ISRP to praise the tour dates and take out subscriptions to the *Workers' Republic.* 'I have heard Comrade Connolly at Union Hill, N.J.', wrote Ernest Aviyone of West Hoboken, New Jersey. 'I can say that he is an excellent speaker,' he continued, enclosing a subscription card for the paper.[442] Timothy McMahon, of Bridgeport, Connecticut concurred, congratulating the ISRP 'for having the good fortune of having such a man as Mr Conley [sic] to represent them in America. He is making it a success.'[443] In Detroit, an SLP comrade by the name of Sullivan reported that Connolly 'was applauded all through his address and in answering questions he is really witty and lucid.'[444]

It is clear that having Connolly speak boosted the confidence of the local branches of the SLP. Jeremiah Devine of North Abington, Massachusetts wrote to the ISRP on 2 October, that he 'went to Boston (19 miles from here) to see, and hear Comrade James Connolly, and as a member of the Socialist Labor Party I would freely say that I fully endorse him. He is a very convincing speaker.'[445]

The De Leonite character of Connolly's speeches can be gleaned from one letter, from an unidentified sender postmarked Chicago, who wrote to Dublin that 'the way our Comrade Connolly handled the freaks, frauds, fakers and Kangs was a treat, and a pleasure indeed.' He continued that:

Our comrades had a long talk over question of the movements in the British Isles, and it was hoped that the time is not far off when there will be a strong national movement all over Great Briton, and put an end to the fake socialist parties in Old England, such as the S.D.F., and I.L.P. and have a Socialist Labor Party in fact as well as in name. Let the Irish socialist cry be, Down with the fakers wherever you meet them ...[446]

After the high of his American tour, Connolly returned to Ireland to find the ISRP in a perilous state. Much of the money he raised from the tour had been spent plugging the deficit in a licensed bar – anathema to the strictly tee-total Connolly – that party members had opened on the premises. The paper, meanwhile, was appearing irregularly, and inadequate financial accounts had been kept in Connolly's absence. Having sold subscriptions to American comrades for the *Workers' Republic*, Connolly was affronted that the paper may cease to appear.[447] To make matters worse, the ISRP finances suffered yet another blow when the Scottish 'impossibilists' decided to print the *Socialist* in Edinburgh, rather than on the ISRP's press in Dublin – a decision which Connolly complained bitterly about to Matheson.[448]

Against this backdrop, Connolly's vote in the Wood Quay Ward in the January 1903 municipal elections was down from 431 in the previous election to 243, and this despite backing from the United Labourers Union and Griffith's *United Irishmen*. For a party which placed so much emphasis on advancing socialism through the ballot box, the poor results could do little but drain morale, with explanations centred on the calumny of opponents increasingly failing to convince the party rank-and-file: 'The constant failure at the polls and the party's inability to come up with any other strategy to forward the cause of socialism in Ireland were among the central reasons for the ISRP's eventual failure.'[449] It appears, too, that the internal regime in the ISRP had hardened to more closely resemble that of De Leon's SLP. The party expelled Joseph Treacy on 27 January 1903 for 'assisting the capitalist candidate in the North City Ward election' and expelled John Leon on 3 February for 'neglecting to vote for the nominee of the ISRP in the North City Ward'.[450]

In February 1903, Connolly took steps to remedy the dire financial situation. He proposed payment of the rent arrears on the party's offices so that they would avoid the loss of its Wharfdale printing machine, the latter a necessity if the party wished to continue printing the *Workers' Republic*. Connolly insisted 'that while I am ready as anyone to laugh at dodging creditors when we have no money, I yet think that the policy of refusing payment when we have money should not be tolerated.' Connolly lost the argument. In frustration and anger, he resigned from the party that he had founded. If his threat to resign was a gamble designed to shake up the rest of the leading members then it failed, as the resignation was accepted. Lillie Connolly refused to believe that the rest of the party would accept the resignation of its founding member. 'They did;' said Connolly, 'it hurts, Lillie.' Connolly later recalled that it felt like the loss of a child.[451]

Connolly then made an application to join the SDF, keen to continue his activism as part of a socialist organisation. However, before long, signs of a reconciliation appeared, and it looked as if Connolly would be accepted back into the fold. This was too much for E. W. Stewart, who had emerged as a staunch opponent of Connolly in the fight just gone. Stewart tendered his own resignation, and William O'Brien, Tom Lyng and others dropped out of the party.

The ISRP had, for all intents and purposes, come to an end. The *Workers' Republic* ceased to appear in May 1903 and in September 1903 the remaining members of the ISRP voted to affiliate the party to the British SLP and rename the party the Irish Section of the International Socialist Movement. As with all such splits, it is difficult to disentangle the political issues from organisational questions and personal animosities. While one recent historian of the ISRP, David Lynch, largely justifies Connolly's conduct, he does admit that 'Connolly did seem to show a lack of empathy with the everyday problems faced by volunteer members of the organisation'.

Having 'sacrificed so much of his own existence to help the ISRP to carry out its political work', Connolly 'could not countenance any perceived lack of commitment on the part of other party members'.[452]

However, at the time Connolly did see some underlying political issues. In a letter to Matheson, he saw Stewart representing a growing 'Kangaroo', or reformist, tendency. Stewart's later political development does seem to bear Connolly out. After leaving the ISRP in April 1903, Stewart threw himself into activity with the Dublin Trades Council, eventually becoming Treasurer in 1908. However, he would afterwards emerge as a bitter critic of Jim Larkin and syndicalism, defending conservative craft unionism and reformist politics.[453]

In April 1903, Connolly arrived in Edinburgh. He spent his time studying linotype operation to develop his skills as a printer, and became the first chairperson of the SLP following the split in the SDF. Connolly worked as the national organiser for the new party, for which he was paid 30 shillings a week, though the money was not always forthcoming. His schedule was punishing, and Tom Bell recalled that in addition to his literary work, 'Connolly never demurred to speaking anywhere, or at any time.' Bell admitted that 'he was shamelessly exploited by us' as the young SLP 'had not yet trained many speakers' and availed of Connolly's skills as a lecturer to build the organisation.[454]

Struggling to find the means to support his family, and doing up to a dozen meetings a week for the new Scottish SLP, Connolly decided to move to the US. Bell recalled that: 'We were all filled with emotion when he sailed from the Broomielaw one September night, in the Irish boat, to go to Dublin, in preparation for emigration to New York.'[455] Connolly's cousin, Margaret Hume, forwarded him the money for his passage, and on 18 September, Connolly embarked for the United States.

In his absence, the remainder of the ISRP decided that the 'best appreciation of Connolly's work for Socialism in this country we can offer him is to carry on the work of socialist propaganda by the party which he founded and for which he sacrificed so much' and tried to re-start its propaganda routines.[456] In early 1904, the two sides of the ISRP split tried to re-unify, but could not agree a name. Stewart, however, soon abandoned his followers to pursue his trade union career, and thus removed a major obstacle to re-unification. On 15 March 1904, the Socialist Party of Ireland was formed, under William O'Brien's leadership, and ensured that Irish revolutionary socialism did not wither completely with the emigration of Connolly.

Chapter 4

Connolly in America

Connolly stepped on to a steamboat in Dublin on 18 September 1903 and departed for the United States of America. As Connolly sailed across the Atlantic to New York, he joined a huge wave of transatlantic migration, pushed by Old World poverty and pulled by the promise of work, opportunity and a better life. Ireland represented an outsize proportion of this European migration wave and Connolly joined more than three million Irish immigrants who had entered the United States in the half century following the Irish Famine. By 1900, an estimated five million first- and second-generation Irish were settled in the United States, more than on the island of Ireland itself. By this time, at the turn of the twentieth century, more Irish people lived in Brooklyn and Manhattan than in Dublin.[457]

Despite huge personal hardship – tragically, Connolly's eldest daughter suffered fatal burns just before her departure for America – Connolly's time in the United States between 1903 and 1910 was to be decisive in his development as a socialist and a trade union organiser.[458]

In the summer of 1903, immediately before he set sail for the United States, Connolly was clearly impressed and enamoured by the American SLP. Tired and disillusioned by the faction-fighting in the British labour movement, he wrote an article in the British SLP's newspaper *The Socialist*.[459] It nailed his political colours to the mast, drawing out what Connolly thought were the key differences between De Leon's organisation and the SDF of Hyndman, from which he had acrimoniously split earlier that year.

Firstly, the SDF was slammed by Connolly for its lack of democratic party control over the privately-owned *Justice*. By contrast, Connolly was impressed by the SLP, which 'conducts a daily paper in the English language, a weekly paper, and a monthly paper in the same language', as well as German, Swedish and Yiddish publications, all 'owned and controlled entirely by the party membership'. Further, the SDF was criticised for its lack of strict working-class political independence. Hyndman's party, Connolly charged, 'professes to be a political party independent of all others' yet 'has never had the courage to engage in a parliamentary candidature without soliciting the help of the ILP and playing for the votes of the Radicals'. The SLP, on the other hand, 'declares itself to be the only genuine Socialist Party in the United States, and acting on that belief, it opposes every other part, and fights them at every election'. At the same time, while the SDF leadership recoils from criticism of the trade union leaders, the SLP 'declares pure and simple trade-unionism to be played out, and acting on that belief, it attacks and exposes the treacheries and sophistries of the trade-union leaders'. It attempts to organise trade unions 'on Socialist lines' and refuses membership 'to anyone who identifies himself with its antagonists by accepting office in pure and simple trade-union'. Finally, wading into arguments in the American socialist movement, Connolly identifies himself with the SLP over its rival, the newly-unified SPA. Comparing the latter to Hyndman's SDF, Connolly writes: 'Inconsistency and sacrifice of principle for the sake of votes mark both organisations, and "Be all things to all men" might be the watchword of either.'[460]

When Connolly arrived in the United States, then, he could rightly have expected a warm reception in the United States, having played a key role in the formation of the new SLP in Scotland. He was to be disappointed. The SLP did little to help in settle and find work, and De Leon greeted him coolly. Carl Reeve, in his study of Connolly's period in the United States, argues plausibly that the reason for De Leon's coldness was that Connolly had previously disagreed publicly with a minor point in the SLP leader's pamphlet Socialism vs. Anarchism. Later, in December 1908, by which time Connolly had definitively broken with the SLP, Connolly recalled the incident in a letter to Matheson. 'You will remember,' he wrote, 'that it was a criticism of his work that first set De Leon up in arms against me.'[461]

Relations only turned from bad to worse. On 23 March 1904, Connolly wrote a letter to the SLP's paper entitled 'Wages, Marriages and the Church'. Stating that while he was proud to be a member of the SLP, he had nevertheless encountered positions put forward by party comrades that he disagreed with. Having heard the view expounded by an SLP agitator in a debate with a 'Kangaroo' (reformist Socialist) that trade union wage struggles were pointless as higher wages would always be cancelled out by an increase in prices, Connolly wrote:

When the Kangaroo quoted from Marx's Value, Price and Profit to prove the contrary, our S.L.P. man airily disposed of Marx by saying that Marx wrote in advance of, and without anticipation of the present day combinations of capital. I am afraid that the S.L.P. speaker knew little of Marx except his name, or he could not have made such a remark. The theory that a rise in prices always destroys the value of a rise in wages might sound very revolutionary, of course, but it is not true. And, furthermore, it is no part of our doctrine. If it were, it knocks the feet from under the S.T. & L.A. and renders that body little else than a mere ward-heeling club for the S.L.P ... Until the party is a unit upon such points our propaganda in one place will nullify our propaganda in another.[462]

Undoubtedly Connolly had Marx's *Value, Price and Profit* on his side in this dispute. This short work, a collected series of speeches to the First International on the subject of wages, was published in 1865, just two years before *Capital,* and can therefore be taken as Marx's relatively mature view on the question.[463] It held that 'the value of labour itself is not a fixed but variable magnitude ... the fixation of its actual degree is only settled by the continuous struggle between capital and labour'.[464]

De Leon was only able to 'prove' otherwise by tendentious misreading and misleading edits. In fact, De Leon's view here (he had expressed different views in the recent past) was closer to the 'iron law of wages' propounded by the nineteenth century German socialist Ferdinand Lassalle. Lassalle saw trade union action on the economic front as a distraction from the ultimate goal of socialist revolution, rejecting it in favour of a wholly political battle to win state power. Lassalle's views had been hugely influential in the German socialist movement, which is reflected in the inclusion of the 'iron law of wages' in the 1875 Gotha Programme of the newly-founded SPD. Lassalle's influence on the SPD was heavily criticised by Marx and Engels, who complained that:

> There is not a word about the unions. And that is a very essential point, for this is the real class organisation of the proletariat in which it carries on its daily struggles with capital, in which it trains itself.[465]

De Leon did not go so far as to reject trade unions out of hand and, indeed the SLP had its own union federation, the STLA, organised along socialist lines. However, his position downgraded completely the importance of the day-to-day struggle for wages and conditions, the means by which many workers often first become conscious of their status as an exploited class.

For Connolly, this dispute had a real practical importance; a theoretical error in this area could lead to sectarian isolation from the working class and its everyday class battles. In his original letter to the *Weekly People* he said as much, arguing that his disagreement 'was an attempt to free [the

STLA] from the incubus of a false doctrine, and enable it to take a real live part in the struggles of the workers'.[466] Connolly at this time did not yet demur from De Leon's insistence on the need for explicitly socialist trade unions, as opposed to 'pure and simple' (non-political unions). However, he also recognised that short of this, the working class

> perpetually rises in protest ... organises to reduce the stealings of the Masters, and ever and anon throws down its tools, and enters on a bloodless insurrection against the conditions of its servitude ... that the Class War is the one, great fact in the modern world.[467]

When, for example, the 1904 SLP National Convention passed a resolution recognising all other trade union organisations, with the exception of the STLA, as 'pure and simple trade unions' and condemned 'the International Socialist Congresses of Brussels, Zurich and London for calling on "the duty of all wage earners to join the unions of their trade"', Connolly apparently told his ISRP comrade John Lyng that, in Lyng's words, he 'disagreed with the sectarian spirit of this resolution'. Lyng recalled that Connolly 'was always ready and willing to lend a hand to any section of the working class. No matter what the intellectual level of the man – as long as he was *striking a blow against* capitalism. Connolly stood with him. He was out to organise the working class, not a sect.'[468]

Connolly was on less sure ground when on the other two issues of contention in his dispute with De Leon, the questions of marriage and of religion. These questions will be treated separately and in greater depth in relation to Connolly's wider politics on religion and women's liberation.

The consequence of the dispute with De Leon was to sour Connolly's view of the SLP and its leadership. As important, if not more so, in angering Connolly than the theoretical controversy was the way in which De Leon dealt with the issues. De Leon denied Connolly access to the party's newspaper, effectively denying him the right to respond to criticism of his initial letter. This was too much even for some SLP members who took De Leon's side on the substance of dispute. One SLPer, Frank P. Janke, wrote that it was unfair to 'ask a man questions which demand an answer and then deny him the means to answer them'.[469]

Disciplinary proceedings were opened against Connolly in his local Troy section of the SLP, but Connolly's defence statement convinced the Troy comrades of his position. Instead, the local section demanded that the party's National Executive Committee publish Connolly's defence statement. De Leon refused, and the 1904 party convention upheld De Leon's position, though no action was taken against Connolly.

De Leon's victory, however, owed not a little to bureaucratic manipulation and Connolly's non-attendance at the convention. 'Of course I could not be present, was not a delegate, and had my nose too close to the grindstone of exploitation to attend anyway,' he wrote Matheson on 22 July 1904:

> Dan played a very smart trick ... He read my correspondence, paragraph by paragraph, *adding his own criticism in between* so that the delegates could not discern where I ended and *my quotations* began ... As a result, he had no difficulty in tearing me to pieces – and thus succeeded by this trick.[470]

Connolly expressed his bitterness in class terms, writing that 'neither in Great Britain nor America can a working-class Socialist expect common fairness from his comrades if he enters into a controversy with a trusted leader from a class above them'. The scale of his disaffection with the SLP is that he saw fit to compare the leadership styles of Hyndman and De Leon, whereas only a year previously he had drawn an absolute distinction between the two men. Connolly complained that the 'howl that greets every such attempt' to criticise these party leaders is vocalised in 'the accents of any army, not of revolutionary fighters but of half-emancipated slaves'.[471]

Nevertheless, for Connolly, politics trumped his personal sense of wounded pride. He still shared a political philosophy with De Leon and believed that the SLP still remained the best vehicle through which it could be realised. The formation of the IWW in June 1905, of which more below, offered an opportunity for these politics to reach a wider working-class audience. As Connolly explained to Matheson: 'I am convinced that the position taken up by Dan towards the I.W.W. is correct ... but I utterly disagree with his attitude towards the membership of the S.L.P.'[472]

In the same letter, Connolly lays out his own philosophy for building a revolutionary socialist party and movement. It is markedly more democratic in spirit, concerned with developing and *expanding* the size and capacity of the working-class vanguard:

> I believe that the duty of a true Socialist, editor or trusted leader, is to train as many comrades as possible to fill his position, to train and make editors, and writers and propagandists, and to encourage every member to develop the cool-headedness and readiness needed in a revolutionary moment; in short that it is the duty of a man in Dan's place to train comrades and equip the movement that there should be scores ready to fill his place in the case of death or removal in any form.[473]

Already here we see some of the underlying tensions which would lead to Connolly's ultimate break with De Leon in 1907. Not least was a yearning on Connolly's part to transcend the sectarianism of the SLP and reach a wider working-class audience. The experience of the Industrial Workers of the World (IWW) was cause for a temporary and uneasy truce between the two men, as De Leon initially played a constructive educative role in shaping the new revolutionary union organisation. At the same time, the IWW would give Connolly direct experience of the class struggle as a union organiser and introduce him to a much wider spectrum of the American labour movement. This in turn created the conditions for his eventual exit from the orbit of the SLP.

The Foundation of the IWW

The IWW, a revolutionary new trade union organisation, was formed in June 1905 at a convention at Chicago. The convention brought together some of the most militant sections of the American working class. Two hundred delegates, representing 43 organisations, were present to listen to William 'Big Bill' Haywood of the Western Federation of Miners (WFM) call the convention to order:

> This is the Continental Congress of the working class. We are here to confederate the workers of this country into a working class movement that shall have of its purpose the emancipation of the working class from the slave bondage of capitalism.[474]

The emergence of the IWW, writes Verity Burgmann, was 'an intelligent response from within the labour movement to the increasing centralisation of American capital and industry, a concentration of labour power to meet a concentration of ownership'.[475] Those who laid the basis for the new union, such as Haywood, Eugene V. Debs (formerly of the American Railway Union), and William E. Trautmann (from the United Brewery Workers), were convinced that a brand new organisation was required because the existing AFL could not be transformed in the necessary direction. 'The old form of pure and simple unionism,' declared Debs at the IWW's founding convention,

> has long since outgrown its usefulness; that it is now not only in the way of progress but that it has become positively reactionary a thing that is but an auxiliary of the capitalist class ... We are here for the purpose of uniting the working class, for the purpose of eliminating that form of unionism which is responsible for the conditions as they exist today.[476]

The AFL's high dues and initiation fees put membership out of reach for many workers. Dubbed the 'American Separation of Labour' by IWW militants, it was a federation mainly of craft unions, and prided itself more on its benefit funds than its capacity to fight the bosses. Its president Samuel Gompers and its officials co-operated with the National Civic Federation, bringing trade unions and industrialists such as J.P. Morgan together 'to settle disputes between capital and labour'.[477]

The IWW struck a very different tone. Its founding convention adopted the famous Preamble to the IWW constitution, which declared:

> The working class and the employing class have nothing in common. There can be no peace so long as hunger and want are found among millions of the working people and the few, who make up the employing class, have all the good things of life.[478]

Unlike the exclusive AFL, which organised on a narrow craft basis, the IWW set about creating 'an organization formed in such a way that all its members in any one industry, or in all industries if necessary, cease work whenever a strike or lockout is on in any department thereof, thus making an injury to one an injury to all'.[479] This inclusiveness extended to organising amongst immigrant workers, placing class unity above the divisions of race. The AFL, by contrast, took a reactionary approach to immigration, scaremongering about the 'yellow peril' and calling for immigration controls. In doing so, it put the interests of settled white workers ahead of the unity of the working class as a whole. This approach, of course, excluded huge swathes of the multi-ethnic American working class.

Though groundbreaking, the IWW did not drop from the sky. Its development, writes one historian of the movement, 'was rooted in American experience and shaped by American events,' notably the experience of the WFM and the American Labor Union.[480] The WFM, for instance, led a number of strikes in the mining camps of Colorado in 1903 and 1904, which went down to defeat though a lack of solidarity from other unions. Chastened by the experience of divisions, the 1904 Convention of the union instructed its Executive 'to take action necessary to bring organised labor together in one general organization'.[481] Added to this was the particular 'dispossessed labour force of young, semi-skilled or unskilled migratory workers' which had emerged with the development of capitalism in the American created a 'roaming army of several million not attached to any particular locality'. Rootless, voteless, and beyond the reach of the AFL, these 'lumberjacks, construction workers, miners and agricultural labourers moved from job to job', hitching a ride in freight trains, carrying with them all their worldly possessions. To such workers, militant direct action through industrial organisation appeared to be 'their only weapon against the system that oppressed them'.[482]

On this basis, however, it has been argued by some that the IWW was a purely American phenomenon, not influenced by wider syndicalist or revolutionary ideas from Europe and elsewhere. In one early study of the IWW, Brissenden, for example, writes that the 'main ideas of I.W.W.-ism – certainly of the I.W.W.-ism of the first few years after 1905 – were of American origin, not French, as is commonly supposed'.[483]

A strictly national focus, however, does not fully grasp the character of the IWW. As the delegates met in Chicago at the founding convention of the IWW, a revolutionary strike wave in Russia was growing and reverberated in the hall. The revolutionary labour organiser Lucy Parsons, who had also been married to one of the Chicago anarchists executed following the Haymarket affair in 1887, told the delegates: 'You men and women should be imbued with the spirit that is now displayed in far-off Russia and far-off Siberia where we thought the spark of manhood and womanhood had been crushed ... Let us take example from them.'[484] As Parsons understood, the IWW was the particular local expression of more general trends. The IWW was inspired by the use of the general strike by Russian workers, and saw it as a vindication of industrial unionism and the capacities of workers' economic power.[485]

In particular, the first two decades of the twentieth century saw the rise of a new form of explicitly *revolutionary* trade unionism. This was in response to international changes in the structure of industry and the labour process, the growing and often violent intervention of the state in labour disputes, and the perceived failure of political action to check the decline in workers' standard of living. As historian of syndicalism Bob Holton has written:

Between the 1890s and the 1920s there grew up in many parts of Europe, the USA, Latin America and Australia a distinctive group of social movements called "revolutionary syndicalist", anarcho-syndicalist and "industrial unionist". It was their common aim to overthrow capitalism through revolutionary industrial class struggle and to build a new social order free from economic or political oppression. Unlike many contemporary radicals who looked to parliament and the state to institute socialism, they concentrated instead on the revolutionary potential of working-class economic organisation, notably the trade union or industrial union. Such bodies would serve a two-fold function, acting both as organisers of class warfare and as the nuclei of the post-revolutionary society. The emancipation of the working class was to be achieved not by parliamentary pressure or political insurrection leading to state socialism, but by direct action and the general strike leading to workers' control over the economy and society.[486]

The IWW, then, fits into a wider chronology. The French *Confédération Générale du Travail* (General Confederation of Labor; CGT), formed in 1895, was the pioneer organisation. By the turn of the twentieth century, it was led by revolutionaries, such as Victor Griffhuelhes and the anarchist Émile Pouget, and became an inspiration for similar movements following in its wake, such as the IWW. The Wobblies, in turn, inspired Jim Larkin when the ITGWU was established in 1908. Revolutionary syndicalists were instrumental, too, in founding the *Confederación Nacional del Trabajo* (CNT) in Spain in 1910, and the *Unione Sindacale Italiana* (Italian Syndicalist Union; USI) followed in 1912.

As the above description suggests, 'for all its regional and national variations, syndicalism was an international movement' both in its near-simultaneous growth across four continents and in the profound overlap in its basic aims and philosophy.[487] Despite important differences, all promoted a vision of revolutionary class-struggle based on working-class self-activity and self-reliance, with faith in the creativity of workers themselves, organised at the point of production, to control and administer their own affairs. Crucially, however, for syndicalists or revolutionary industrial unionists, trade unionism was not simply a matter of fighting for better wages and conditions within the framework of capitalism: it was the means by which workers could overthrow the capitalist state and build a post-capitalist, socialist, society in its place.

The spread of revolutionary unionism was facilitated by a new phase of capitalist globalisation in the late nineteenth and early twentieth century, spurred on by revolutionary new developments in technology and communication. Workers, including radicals such as Connolly, increasingly searched the globe for work, or to escape from poverty and persecution. Often following the trail of expanding global labour processes, workers such as dockers and sailors, encountered and spread new ideas, including the gospel of revolutionary unionism.[488] It is no surprise, therefore, that many of the IWW's rank-and-file militants were migrants, who carried with them, for example, anarchist or syndicalist ideas from Italy and Spain.[489]

Contrary to Brissenden's assertion that the IWW was a particularly American phenomenon, it is clear that many of its leaders 'drew sustenance and inspiration from, networked within and significantly contributed to a wider transnational world'.[490] William Trautman, who wrote the initial document which became the basis of the IWW's first manifesto, and did much to shape the organisation in its formative years, was the key figure in translating French syndicalist ideas in to a specifically American register and organisational form. Trautman, writing a 1903 Labor Day address in the Brewery Workers' journal, *Brauer-Zeitugn*, advocated an 'industrial government', an idea held by the 'Socialists abroad' who 'build the labor organizations' in order to create 'the instruments for the management of the Socialist republic'. Trautman insisted that members of 'the continental Industrial Unions of Europe' be invited to the first I.W.W. Convention. He corresponded with Emile Pouget, the secretary of the CGT, and received syndicalist literature directly from the source. In founding the IWW, Trautman was open that he wished 'to establish among ... workers ... a unity of action ... similar to that now existing in France'.[491]

Trautman's advocacy of revolutionary syndicalist ideas saw him removed from the Executive of the Brewery Workers' Union. At this point, De Leon defended Trautman publicly, and published his writings in the columns of the *People*. De Leon, too, had more direct contact with French and Italian syndicalist ideas, as evidenced by the articles he republished in the SLP press. He spoke directly, too, about the French syndicalist journal, *Le Mouvement Socialiste*, at the SLP's tenth annual congress in 1900. The journal, edited by Hubert Lagardelle, carried articles by the big names of French syndicalism, such as Pouget, Griffuelhes and the theorist Georges Sorel, and De Leon republished articles from it in the *People* as early as July 1899. It is fair to conclude, as one historian has, that 'both before and during the period that De Leon was revising his political theory, he clearly had knowledge of the syndicalist principles which in the summer of 1905 he chose to amalgamate with his earlier Marxism'.[492]

It is worth spelling out what this revision of De Leon's political theory was because many of De Leon's post-1905 ideas were reflected in Connolly's own blend of revolutionary industrial unionism. Any understanding of Connolly's politics from this point on relies on a grasp of De Leon's innovations.

De Leon, as we have seen, stood on the uncompromising revolutionary socialist wing of the Second International. The SLP was distinguished primarily by its sharp hostility to reformism, to the class collaboration of socialist ministers in capitalist governments and its vanguardist conception of the party as the guardian of strict revolutionary principle. The SLP nevertheless shared with the Second International mainstream a stress on the primacy of political methods, such as contesting elections at the ballot box, and the view that the socialist revolution meant the conquest by the working class of the political state. 'The proletariat will use its political supremacy,' as Marx and Engels wrote in the *Communist Manifesto*, 'to wrest, by degree, all capital from the bourgeoisie, to centralise all instruments of production in the hands of the State, i.e., of the proletariat organised as the ruling class.'[493] Up until 1905, De Leon would not have disagreed. For De Leon, the consciousness of the American proletariat would mature, aided by to the socialist propaganda of the party. From there, it would be a relatively straightforward step towards achieving a majority in elections, socialising property and moving towards a socialist system of administrating society.

The process of founding the IWW in 1905 marked a step-change in De Leon's thinking in a number of respects, despite his attempts to square it with previous Marxist orthodoxy. On 10 July 1905, in an address to the Union Temple in Minneapolis, later published by the SLP under the title 'The Socialist Reconstruction of Society', De Leon laid out some of his new thinking about how the revolution in the United States would be made. Most important was the primacy De Leon gave to the economic organisation, the trade union. This was a reversal of his previous position, in which the unions, including his own STLA, were strictly subordinate to the political party. The political party would still carry out propaganda to raise the 'political temperature', and the level of socialist support would then be tested at the ballot box, with a view to capturing political office. However, now in De Leon's vision, 'the final, the consummating act of working-class emancipation must be achieved by the toilers "taking and holding" the product of their labor through an economic organization of the working class, without affiliation with any political party'.[494] If the capitalists sought to override the democratic process, and block the socialist movement from taking power, using 'the might conferred and implied by the industrial organization of their class, the working class would forthwith lock out the capitalist class'.[495] Political power, in this scheme, however, 'is to be taken for the purpose of abolishing it', along with 'the capitalist governmental system of territorial demarcation'. In its place, will be the 'central administrative organ of the Socialist Republic … not being political, but exclusively administrative of the producing forces of the land …'[496] Thus: 'The mining, the railroad, the textile, the building industries, down or up the line, each of these,' wrote De Leon, 'regardless of former political boundaries, will be the constituencies of that new central authority the rough scaffolding of which was raised last week in Chicago. Where the General Executive Board of the Industrial Workers of the World will sit there will be the nation's capital.'[497]

In other words, the combination of workers' political strength, as measured at the ballot box, combined with their economic strength in the workplace, would allow an immediate leap from the capitalist political state to a purely administrative socialist society. Dispensed with would be what Marx described as 'the period of the revolutionary transformation' between 'capitalist and communist society', the 'political transition period in which the state can be nothing but the revolutionary dictatorship of the proletariat'.

As we shall see below, De Leon's fusion of Marxism and syndicalism would have a profound influence on Connolly. First, however, let us look at Connolly's own involvement in the IWW.

Connolly and the IWW

Following the foundation of the IWW, Connolly chaired a number of SLP meetings with De Leon, to spread the gospel of the new organisation in New York and Newark, New Jersey.[498] Connolly followed this up with a series of open-air propaganda meetings, assisted by Patrick Quinlan, an Irish SLP member whose Longshoreman's Protective Association, an STLA local, would join the IWW. Quinlan, born in Limerick in 1883, but whose family moved to the US when he was four, had worked as a coal miner, steel worker, longshoreman, machinist and in a number of other jobs, before becoming involved in the labour movement.[499] He would soon become a close political collaborator of Connolly's, and the two men set up IWW locals in the Newark area.

The growth of the IWW's activities in New Jersey was a cause for optimism in the local labour movement. Soon, a growing feeling emerged promoting the unity of the two socialist parties, the SLP and the SPA, as joint activity began to mitigate the mutual distrust and suspicion between members of the rival organisations. Both Connolly and Quinlan were enthusiastic supports of the idea, and Quinlan was elected as a delegate to a Unity Conference to discuss the political basis on which the New Jersey SLP and SPA organisations could merge.

The New Jersey Socialist conference took place over six sessions between 17 December 1905 and 4 March 1906.[500] A New Jersey SLP state convention was called to authorise the talks and elect delegates to the unity conference. Connolly attended the SLP convention as a delegate from Paterson, and supported the idea of closer socialist unity. His close comrade Quinlan was elected at this convention to represent Essex County at the forthcoming unity conference.

The Unity Conference ultimately came to nought, due to opposition from the SPA's national leadership. However, its shows that even as early as 1905 and 1906, Connolly was trying to find a route to mass working-class politics on the basis of industrial unionism.

Events, however, soon provided another cause around which socialists could rally. On 30 December 1905, the former governor of Idaho, Frank Steunenberg, was assassinated by a bomb attached to the front gate of his home in the city of Caldwell. Steunenberg, a former Populist who had subsequently aligned with corporate interests, was a notorious enemy of organised labour. In 1899, he had used the federal government to break the miners' strikes in the state of Idaho. Following his assassination, suspicion immediately fell on the WFM. Soon afterwards, an itinerant miner by the name of Harry Orchard was arrested in his hotel room in the city, and detectives found bomb-making equipment, consistent with that used to make the bomb that killed the former governor.[501]

What happened next set the stage for one of the worst attempted frame-ups in American labour history. In January 1906, the current governor hired James McParland, of the Pinkerton Detective Agency, as the chief investigator for the state. McParland was a longstanding enemy of the labour movement and had for many years worked for the Mine Owners' Association of Colorado. Indeed, he had been a key figure in the trial of the Molly Maguires in 1877, which saw ten Pennsylvanian miners hanged. McParland immediately sensed a chance to frame the WFM. He went about doing so by obtaining a 'confession' from Orchard, to the effect that the miner had been put up to it by the leaders of the Federation. Orchard was promised that if he specifically named 'those cut-throats known as the Inner Circle of the Western Federation of Miners [then] the State would gladly accept your assistance as a State witness and see that you are properly taken care of afterwards.'[502] On the basis of this 'confession', Charles H. Moyer was arrested boarding a sleeper train to South Dakota, where he was travelling for union business, on 17 February. Haywood and George A. Pettibone were picked up shortly afterwards. All three men had been arrested without warrants, amounting effectively to kidnap, and put on a special train straight to Idaho penitentiary, where they were held in solitary confinement on death row.

The labour movement immediately sprang into action. The IWW distributed a leaflet on 20 February entitled 'Shall Our Brothers Be Murdered?', which charged that the arrest was 'the result of a conspiracy pre-meditated by the capitalist pirates of the West, led by the mine owners and backed by the Standard Oil Co'. It urged 'mass indignation meetings' and called for a defence fund to be established immediately. Debs' paper

The Appeal to Reason, also joined the campaign, warning in March that 'If they attempt to murder Moyer, Haywood and their brothers, a million revolutionists will meet them with their guns'. A month later, the American newspapers published a telegram from the Russian author and revolutionary Maxim Gorky, who was in the United States to raise funds for his comrades in Russia: 'Greetings to you, my brother Socialists. Courage! The day of justice and delivery for the oppressed of all the world is at hand. Ever fraternally Yours.'[503]

While Gompers and the AFL leadership resisted calls for action from the rank-and-file, much of the rest of the socialist and labour movement established Moyer-Haywood defence committees in many large cities across the country. The committees brought together the IWW, the SPA and the SLP, with many unions and labour bodies associated with the AFL. A defence fund of $87,000 was soon raised by subscription. One contemporary observer described the effect the Haywood-Moyer-Pettibone case had on the labour movement, as follows:

> During the past few years ... the radical class spirit of the western labor unionists has been spreading to other parts of the country. This has been due chiefly to agitation occasioned by prosecution of the officers of the Western Federation of Miners for murder of the late Governor Steunenberg of Idaho, and to the activity of employers' associations in fighting certain phases of trade-unionism. During the past year the attention of all organized labor has been turned to the trial of the officers. Meetings have been held in all large cities and industrial centres to raise funds and to arouse sympathy for the prisoners. These meetings, which have been generally promoted by socialists, have reached thousands of trade-unionists who had hitherto looked upon the labor problem as a craft, rather than a class, problem.[504]

In New Jersey, the SLP organised a conference to protest the 'impending legal murder' of the WFM leaders. Connolly attended as a delegate and joined the press and literature committee of the Newark Haywood-Moyer Defence Committee. Quinlan became its secretary. On 1 April, Connolly took the chair as De Leon addressed a packed meeting at Kurz's Coliseum in the city. As the date of the trial approached, rallies were held in every major city, including 50,000 people in Boston, and 20,000 in New York. Despite an eve of trial intervention from President Theodore Roosevelt, branding Haywood and Moyer 'undesirable citizens' the jury in July 1907, stirred by the soaring oratory of defence lawyer Clarence Darrow, returned a verdict of 'Not Guilty' for Haywood. In January 1908 Pettibone, too was acquitted.

In the end, Moyer was never tried. With the forces of the capitalist class and its state lined up against it, the labour movement had won what Debs hailed 'one of the greatest legal battles in American history'.[505]

From these activities in New Jersey sprang the Newark Workingmen's Defence Committee, which held a number of meetings addressed by Connolly. It was through his work that Connolly would become acquainted with the *Federazione Socialista Italiana del Nord America* (Italian Socialist Federation; FSI), which published the journal *Il Proletario* from its headquarters in Philadelphia. The FSI was largely concerned with Italian affairs, both in the sense of attacking bourgeois institutions of Italian-American life and in reporting on political developments back in Europe. It was marked by an insularity common to the emigre politics of recently settled migrants, compounded by language difficulties and exacerbated by the exclusionary and often racist practices of much of the mainstream labour movement. Its secretary, Carlo Tresca, became an enthusiastic supporter of FSI members joining the IWW. Tresca himself recalled, though, that 'though living in America, my thoughts, my talks, my habits of life, my friends and my enemies were all Italian'.[506]

In Newark, Connolly drew the FSI into joint activity, which served to break down some of the barriers between migrant communities in the city. On May Day 1906, the police seized a red flag from a demonstration organised by the Italian comrades, arresting two of their members. Later that month, the FSI had its premises raided and property unlawfully seized. In the name of Quinlan, as Secretary, and Connolly, as President, the Newark Workingmen's Defence Committee, 'representing the progressive trade unions and labor bodies of Newark and vicinity issued a letter of protest to the Mayor to unqualifiedly condemn the high-handed actions of the police on the occasions named'. It went on to brand them as 'direct attacks upon the Constitutional rights of our Italian fellow-citizens', the consequence of 'ignorant race prejudice', and resolved to offer

> the Italian workingmen our moral and material support in any effort they make to obtain redress, and to maintain the equal rights guaranteed by the Constitution of the United States, to every citizen regardless of race, language or country of origin ...[507]

On 23 June, an open-air protest meeting was held. Elizabeth Gurley Flynn, the teenage Irish-American socialist and labour organiser, whom Connolly first met through the Haywood-Moyer Defence Committee, recalled that the Italian comrades, strongly anti-clerical, held Sunday morning meetings as 'a substitute for church'. Local socialists were invited to address the largely Italian-speaking audience. Turning to Connolly, Flynn asked: '"Who will speak in Italian?" He smiled his rare smile and replied, "We'll see. Someone, surely".' After a short break, she recalled, 'we returned to the platform and Connolly arose. He spoke beautifully in Italian to my amazement and the delight of the audience who "viva'd" loudly.'[508]

After its second convention, the IWW stepped up its efforts to recruit foreign-born workers. Material was issued in a number of languages, foreign-language branches were established, and organisers hired from among various immigrant communities, including the Italians. It was in part because of the activity of IWW members such as Connolly that the FSI endorsed industrial unionism and instructed its members to join the IWW. A few years later, when Chicago's FSI-aligned journal La Propaganda published an article inspired by the discussion at the FSI's executive committee about whether to affiliate to the SLP, SPA or IWW, Connolly was the author of the reply in the IWW's Industrial Union Bulletin of 16 May 1908. While remaining neutral on the question of political party affiliation, Connolly reminded the Italian comrades that the IWW 'offers to the Italian immigrant on the first day he lands an opportunity to become fully possessed of all the rights and powers to act of a member of the economic revolutionary organisation, and therefore of an active fighter on the field of the class struggle' whilst, at the same time, 'he has no political rights for five years after landing and his field and period of activity hampered and circumscribed'. Connolly urged 'every section of the Italian Socialist Federation should at once form itself into a language local of the I.W.W. and set itself to organise the Italian workers into their respective Industrial Unions, according to their daily occupations'.[509]

In November 1906, Connolly found himself victimised for socialist and trade union activities. When he first arrived in New Jersey, he worked at the Metropolitan Life Insurance Co. Soon, however, Connolly found a job at the Singer typewriter factory and attempted to organise the plant. In early November, an SLP organiser visited the city and was invited to address a meeting at the gates of the factory. By the second day, according to Greaves, 'the word has spread. Workers bolted their lunch and came out to listen. A literature stall was set up and an appeal was mode for fifty men to picket the gate for trade unionism and the SLP.' One consequence, however, was that Connolly became 'a marked man in the factory. In the following month his foreman was under continuous pressure to dismiss him, and finally Connolly resigned rather than jeopardise his colleague's appointment.'[510]

One silver lining of his dismissal was that Connolly was now free to spend more time on labour movement activity. He was appointed as an organiser in the Building Section of the New York IWW and commuted daily from Newark. Soon afterwards he moved with his family to a tenement in the Bronx, near where Flynn and her family were resident. Connolly launched into his work for the IWW with gusto, 'revealing aptitudes which surprised even his friends'.[511] The IWW's industrial sections were not strict when it came to demarcation, and Connolly, working out of 60 Cooper Square in Manhattan, soon found himself organising 'tramwaymen, moulders, garment workers, milkmen and dockers'.[512]

A flavour of Connolly's activities and approach to trade union organising is found in his 'Notes from New York', a series of contributions to the *Industrial Union Bulletin*, the Chicago-based publications of the IWW. Seeking to build IWW membership amongst the unorganised, Connolly often found himself in conflict with the craft unions in the building trades, who were part of the AFL, and whose members often refused to work with 'Wobblies'. 'Scarcely a week passes,' reported Connolly, 'without seeing [IWW] members fired off jobs as a result of the section of the walking delegates of the pure and simple building trades.' On one occasion, the secretary and delegates of the AFL's Architectural Iron Workers, Housesmiths and Bronze Erectors, Local 52, prevailed upon the proprietor of a venue used by the IWW's bronze workers to refuse hire of the hall. Connolly reported in the bulletin how:

The two first worthies got the floor and emitted a series of growls, like the utterances of a bear with a toothache, in which the only intelligible words seemed to be 'dual organization', 'organized by the bosses', 'scabs', 'join our organization', 'we should stick together.' In fact, at once time they seemed to urge that we should join them, at another that we were organized by the bosses to harm them and would ourselves be thrown down when we had served the turn of the capitalist enemy.[513]

The IWW was, indeed, a 'dual organisation', establishing itself as a rival union centre to the AFL. In its very first year, the bulk of IWW recruits came, not from among the ranks of the unorganised, but from existing AFL-affiliated unions, largely from workers dissatisfied with the conservatism of their union leaderships. As Connolly's experience shows, this created scope for tension between workers in rival trade union organisations. However, though the national AFL leadership attempted to drive IWW members out of labour movement bodies, many rank-and-file AFL members were inspired by the industrial unionists' message, even if they did not formally join the IWW. Despite some undoubted instances of sectarianism on the part of IWW organisers, some AFL members will have been impressed, too, by the acts of solidarity they received from their 'Wobbly' counterparts. In Newark, for example, IWW shoemakers refused to work alongside strike-breakers who had been recruited to defeat the strike of AFL members. As historian Philip Foner comments, 'Such examples of working-class solidarity stood in sharp contrast to the policy of several A.F. of L. Unions whose officials engaged strikebreakers to take the places of I.W.W. Strikers and placed boycotts against goods made in factories where I.W.W. members worked.'[514]

As Connolly understood, the manner in which the AFL organised its own members was also a major source of division. Take, for example, the strike of the trolley-men on the Yonkers tramway, in which Connolly attempted to intervene. On their own initiative, Connolly reported in the *Industrial Union Bulletin* in December 1907, 'when the discontent which had been fermenting so long at last came to a head,' the workers formed a strike committee and presented their demands to the manager, 'intimating that if these were not acceded to not a man would go to work and not a car would leave the yards.' The manager, accustomed to the methods of arbitration characteristic of the AFL unions, asked the men to go back to work and appoint a committee to negotiate with him. '"Yes," said one of the deputation, "and while we are working you will be securing scabs."' Connolly reported:

So they struck. It was a complete tie-up. Not a wheel turned that day, and for the time the capitalist was at his wit's end. The spontaneous instinct of the workers had achieved a completer stoppage of industry than is usually achieved by 'organized' pure and simple leadership.

However, the 'organised' workers, the electricians and engineers, were in the employ of another company contracted to supply power to the tram system. 'Of course,' wrote Connolly bitterly,

they remained at work. You see, they had a contract with their employers, and their employers had a contract with another company, and so, and therefore, and for that reason, d'ye see? They took a tight grip on their union cards and – scabbed it on the men on strike.

With the strike undermined, the AFL leadership entered an agreement for the tramway men to return to work pending arbitration. The union leadership cried victory, and Connolly commented acidly, 'not for the strikers, but for the employers and the pure and simple union'. The AFL now had 'a few hundred more dues-paying dupes', while the employer could 'rest content knowing that their men were now organized in a union that could be trusted to prevent their taking their bosses by surprise by striking at a moment's notice'. It was, he wrote, 'only a few hundred more of our class delivered over, bound hand and foot, to be preyed upon and their veins sucked dry by the foul parasites that fatten upon labor'.[515]

The experience of the AFL's Brotherhood of Carpenters only reinforced Connolly's conviction in favour of industrial unionism. With their contract due to expire at the end of 1907, the employers were attempting to enforce a fifty cent per day reduction in the rate of pay. By waiting on the contract to expire before taking action, Connolly warned that the carpenters were 'being called upon to strike in the worst period of the year, when thousands of men will be idle necessarily as a result of climatic conditions'. The workers' 'unfortunate tactical mistake,' he wrote, 'has been forced upon the workers as a result of the trade union contract with the bosses'. Connolly at this time took an absolutist approach to never signing employment contracts with the bosses, an approach which was consistent with IWW policy. While it is common sense only to strike, if possible, at a time most advantageous to the workers, the 'principle' of never signing contracts undoubtedly led to the IWW's failure, in the long run, to consolidate its membership anywhere, nor to build on a routine of 'day to day' union work as well as in the situations where workers require immediate redress through direct action. However, Connolly's conclusion is a just one:

> Surely it does not need the wisdom of a Solomon to see that if all the workers in that industry were united in one union, and that union refused to sign a contract, but instead bided its time and at the opening of the busy season, or at its height, presented to the bosses the collective demands of all the workers, with the intimation that refusal to agree to any one of these demands would mean a strike of the entire body, then the chances of victory would be a million times greater than they are under the present criminally stupid division of forces.[516]

That same month, December 1907, Connolly wrote to the IWW secretary, Trautmann, with a proposal to set up a meeting to consider organising the New York harbour workers in to the IWW. Trautmann wrote to the IWW's General Executive Board that he and the union's national organiser, Vincent St. John, believed 'the suggestion involved in the affairs of transportation workers and shoe workers, with the culmination brought about by this year's propaganda among these workers, is the most important matter that ever confronted the IWW since its inception'.[517]

Unfortunately, Connolly's potential breakthrough with these workers would be a casualty of a renewed round of sectarian bloodletting in the IWW, which resulted in Connolly's final departure from the SLP.

Leaving the SLP

Connolly, it will be remembered, last crossed swords with De Leon in 1904 over the question of 'wages, marriage and the church'. It would be the first of these issues, the question of whether trade union action could successfully fight for higher wages, which led a bitter dispute within the IWW, beginning in the summer of 1907 and spilling well into the following year.

It began with an SLPer Frank Reed arguing the De Leonite case that the high wages would merely lead to higher prices. A New Jersey IWW organiser, James Thompson, replied to the effect that either Marx was correct, or Reed was correct – it could not be both. In October, Connolly finally entered the fray on Thompson's side with 'a contribution so conclusive that not one correspondent replied'.[518] Connolly recalled the previous dispute within the SLP and STLA, when the party's mistaken attitude towards trade union struggles was 'fast reducing their organization to a negligible quantity as an economic force'. With this in mind, Connolly hoped that the IWW 'might not make the mistake of confounding revolutionary phraseology with true revolutionary teaching', and warned of the danger that 'a wrong stand upon this point might easily eliminate from us large numbers of our fellow-workers whose sympathetic adhesion had been gained by our agitation'. Once again, Connolly cited the authority of Marx.

Capitalists may recover profits lost through higher wages, Connolly conceded, 'by speeding up, by new machinery, by improved methods, by the levelling process of economic crises, reducing wages again before the former level, and by many other means'. This is not done typically, however, through a general rise in prices, as most workers are not employed producing only 'the barest necessities of life of which they are the retail purchasers'. Rather, Connolly argued, 'the market price of labour (wages) is determined by the value (price) of the necessities of life,' not the other way around: in other words, 'prices invariably go up first, and wages slowly climb after them'. Connolly concluded strongly:

> Thus economic science, based upon and in alliance with the facts of life emphatically refutes the contentions of the writers of Marx's day as well as

those of the charlatans of our day who revamp the same arguments to prove the same point.[519]

Connolly's article appeared in October. By the time it came for the General Executive Board of the IWW to hear Connolly's plan to welcome the harbour workers into the union on 22 December, De Leon was spoiling for a fight. Connolly reported that around a quarter of the harbour workers in New York and Hoboken – some 12,000 men – had been influenced by the IWW through the work of 'vigilant organisers and committees and by the distribution of pamphlets'.[520] The Board agreed to take them into the IWW, and Connolly was excused to go and present the decision to the harbour workers' committee. On the second day of the Board's session, Connolly reported that the workers could not consider the matter until their next meeting in January. Ill, Connolly then left the meeting and went home. In his absence, De Leon took the floor and launched a tirade against the absent Connolly, stating his opposition to Connolly's work among the harbour workers, viewing it as a plot to flood the union with Irish and Italian Catholics, as part of a Jesuit plot to demoralise the IWW. Connolly, De Leon intimated, was a 'police spy', provoking Trautmann to protest against the 'continuation of star chambers proceedings, at which the most serious and grave charges are presented against another member of the IWW, without the accused having a chance to hear the charges or defend himself'.[521]

The session was adjourned until the following day when, with Connolly in attendance, De Leon presented his case. Connolly was 'a man with one foot in the SLP and with the other in the IWW', guilty of attacks on the SLP in the *Industrial Union Bulletin,* and of dragging party affairs into the union. Moreover, he had been 'a destroyer and wrecker of any movement had had been connected with', and had 'ruined the Socialist Labor Party in Ireland'.[522] At this point, the chair ruled that all matters relating to the SLP and the movement in Ireland were 'political' and accepted a proposal that the Board could not act constitutionally until De Leon had gone through the full administrative process of complaining first to Connolly's local branch, and appealing their decision if necessary.

In a way, Connolly was vindicated. De Leon's charges did not stick, and the SLP leader had discredited himself with a vicious personal attack on Connolly. On the other hand, the affair meant that tensions between the IWW and the SLP came to a head everywhere, and it was considered wise for Connolly to discontinue his 'Notes from New York' column in the *Industrial Union Bulletin.* According to Nevin, during the first eight months of 1908, 'the IWW locals in New York district were in turmoil occasioned by the charges and counter-charges arising from the Connolly affair'.[523]

Even without all this rancour, the IWW was not in a healthy position. A financial crash in October 1907 led in turn to a depression, hitting wages hard and throwing hundreds of thousands out of work. As unemployment spiralled, Connolly commented that the 'great American institution today is the bread line'.[524] This had a severe impact on the ability of unions to fight back. 'The crisis,' according to one historian of the union, 'almost wiped the I.W.W. out of existence.'[525]

The economic downturn, however, was not the only factor contributing to the weakness of the IWW. Prior to the crash, the IWW had gone through another period of internal conflict, which had changed the balance of political forces inside the union. At the 1906 convention, a struggle had been waged by De Leon and those of a more syndicalist inclination to oust the moderate and ineffectual president of the union, Charles Sherman. Sherman, however, was from the WFM, one of the founder organisations of the IWW. His removal had the negative effect of provoking the departure of many industrial unionists from the mining federation and the SPA. One of the most high-profile departures was Eugene V. Debs, stalwart of the SPA's left wing and the party's presidential candidate. In what was left of the IWW, the direct-actionist and anarcho-syndicalist elements were strengthened. Their ideological hostility to political parties increasingly found common cause with rank-and-file members frustrated by the political disputes that were increasingly consuming the energy of IWW organisers. 'Why does the I.W.W. not grow faster?' asked one member, rhetorically: 'Too many political squabbles fill the Bulletin, taking away valuable space from organisational activity.'[526] The anarcho-syndicalist current ranged against De Leon could only agree.

The new balance of forces within the union, combined with growing irritation towards the SLP, set the scene for a bitter split with De Leon and the proponents of 'political action' at the Fourth Convention in September 1908. In Portland, Oregon, IWW organiser John H. Walsh 'started a movement which ensured De Leon's defeat'. On 1 September 1908, a team of 19 men and one woman gathered in the Portland railway yards, 'all dressed in black overalls and jumpers, black shirts and red ties, with an I.W.W. book in his [sic] pocket and an I.W.W. button on his [sic] coat'.[527] Traveling east, hopping between a cattle car and freight trains, this self-proclaimed 'Overalls Brigade' arrived in Chicago in time for the opening of the convention. Joining forces with St. John and Trautmann, the anti-political workers from the West denied De Leon a seat at the convention by means of a spurious technicality. De Leon, the opponents of political action argued, was 'not a member of the local of the industry in which he is working', on the grounds that, as an editor, he should have been a member of the Printing Workers' Local Union, not the Office Workers' Local Union. The convention accepted the recommendation from the Credentials Committee to refuse De Leon a seat as a delegate by 40 votes to 21. Forthwith, the SLP withdrew from the IWW once and for all, setting up a rival organisation with its headquarters in Detroit.

Not all of those opposed to De Leon were opponents of political action. Nevertheless, by a narrow vote, 32 to 25, all mention of political action was removed from the IWW's Preamble, and announced that:

The I.W.W. refuses all alliances, direct or indirect, with existing political parties or anti-political sects, and disclaims all responsibility for any individual opinion or act which may be at variance with the purposes herein expressed.[528]

Connolly's trusted friend John Carstairs Matheson, editor of *The Socialist*, the newspaper of the British SLP was worried about the fight in the IWW and wrote to Connolly with his concerns. 'I do hope your side has not been led, through their natural irritation at the tactics of your opponents,' warned Matheson, 'into adopting the impossible position of antipolitics.'[529] Matheson was alarmed not only at the growth of anti-political syndicalism and anarchism in the United States but had more local concerns. Demonstrating the transatlantic character of radical networks at this time, the British SLP was inspired by the formation of the IWW in 1905 to set up a body promoting revolutionary industrial unionism in Britain. In August 1907, the Advocates for Industrial Unionism (AIU) was established in Birmingham, as a propaganda body independent from but supported by the party. A decision was made to establish a journal, the *Industrial Unionist*, which first appeared in March 1908.[530]

Many of those drawn to the AIU had more of an anti-political bent than members of the SLP were comfortable with. To many of the AIU's new members, 'politics was synonymous with parliamentary politics, the cavortings of Ramsay MacDonald & Co, who supported the Liberal government when it attacked the workers'.[531] This position was encouraged by E.J.B. Allen, a charismatic SLP member increasingly influenced by French syndicalism. The anti-political faction soon had the upper hand and dominated the line of the *Industrial Unionist*. Matheson complained to Connolly on 2 April 1908 that the AIU had fallen into the hands of 'a coterie of London antipolitical theorisers, glib-tongued cockneys who are "smart" talkers, who have the "patter" at their finger-ends and who are also about as shallow as the cockney often is'.[532] He worried that Connolly's fight against De Leon in the American SLP was being used by the anti-political faction of the AIU in Britain, who were in touch with Trautman and other anti-political IWW members, against the SLP there. The following month, the AIU would split, with Allen and others forming the more explicitly syndicalist Industrial League.

Although Connolly's relationship with De Leon had reached an end, Connolly assured his old friend Matheson that he is 'not an anti-political, nor in any danger of becoming so'. Connolly remained an advocate of political action even after his break with the SLP, and confirmed to Matheson that he 'would have been as well-pleased had the old preamble stood', though he admitted its wording had caused confusion.[533] The following year, addressing the issue in the *International Socialist Review,* Connolly would argue that 'if at any time the conditions of a struggle in shop, factory, railroad or mine necessitates the employment of political action those workers so organised will use it, all theories and theorists to the contrary notwithstanding'.[534]

In this letter to Matheson, however, Connolly did provide the key to his subsequent political development. 'Our loathing for De Leon did not turn us into anti-ballotism,' Connolly wrote, 'but did set our mind to work to discover the method by which the working class could control its own political party, and put the non-working class elements where they belong.'[535] Before we consider this, let us look at the final factor in the break and mutual 'loathing' between Connolly and De Leon.

The Irish Socialist Federation

Precipitating Connolly's final departure from the SLP was a row over his role in founding the Irish Socialist Federation (ISF), and its organ, *The Harp.* The ISF, its name clearly inspired by Tresca's Italian federation, was a group designed to reach Irish-American workers and attract them to socialism. The ISF held its inaugural meeting in the house of Elizabeth Gurley Flynn's father at 795 East 139th Street in New York in March 1907, and a committee was elected comprising Connolly, former ISRP member Jack Mulray, Elizabeth Gurley Flynn and Patrick Quinlan. That summer, a series of indoor and outdoor meetings were held in New York, and in January 1908 the first issue of *The Harp* appeared. Six months later, Connolly took to the road in yet another lecture tour, covering 3,000 miles, speaking to audiences about socialism and urging support for the SPA Presidential candidate, Eugene V. Debs.[536]

Though Connolly was still an SLP member when the new organisation was founded, the ISF refused to affiliate itself initially to either of the two major socialist parties in existence, the SLP or the SPA. The ISF was 'not founded for political action', Connolly explained, but 'for propaganda; it is not in existence to fashion a political machine, it is in existence to present Socialism as a historical development from capitalism and as the only remedy for the wage slavery of the workers'. It called for the unity of socialists, a course of action 'for which a strong sentiment already exists in the rank and file of both existing parties'. For Connolly, this would not 'be realized by an amalgamation of the existing parties'. With a dig aimed squarely at De Leon, he wrote:

> There are too many leaders, save the mark! Too many 'saviors of the working class' whose reputations have been built upon disunion; too many petty personal ambitions which might be endangered did the rank and file have an opportunity to know and understand one another ....

Nevertheless, for the ISF, 'neutrality on the political field [was] not extended to the economic'. The Federation fully endorsed the idea of industrial unionism, and more particularly, voiced its support for the IWW. The IWW, in fact, was seen as providing the basis on which socialist were ultimately to unite. 'On the day that the IWW launches its own political party,' explained the first issue of *The Harp*, 'it will put an end to all excuse for two Socialist parties and open the way for a real and effective unification of the revolutionary forces.'[537]

The Harp did cover American topics, containing some of Connolly's most developed thoughts in this period on industrial unionism and its relationship to political action. However, its focus was on Irish history and issues, constituting 'almost a mental return to the old country, before the physical return that was soon to follow'.[538] It was in America, however, not in Ireland, that 'Connolly encountered the first significant urban Irish working class'.[539] By 1900, there were more people of Irish descent in New York City than in Dublin, and more in the United States than in the whole of Ireland.[540] The purpose of the ISF was to reach these Irish-American workers and inculcate in them, as the ISF's statement of purpose put it, with 'a knowledge of Socialist principles, and to prepare them to co-operate with the workers of all other races, colours and nationalities in the emancipation of Labour'.[541]

This was easier said than done. Driven from rural Irish life by famine, and hurled across the Atlantic to what Connolly described as 'the cruel unfeeling environment of a new world, mad for hold, of a world basing all its activities and relations upon a "cash nexus" upon a calculation centring around the dollar,' the Irish coped with the experience of emigration by clustering in distinct urban enclaves.[542] In cities such as New York, Boston and Chicago, they constructed a highly developed communal support network. This stability gave the Irish the advantage of 'the networking and social organisation required to exert social, political, and economic influence', through Tammany Hall (the New York Democratic Party political machine), the AFL, Church groups and other civil society institutions. In 1910, the social reformer Emily Balch observed that, 'newcomers, encountering Irish policemen, Irish politicians, Irish bureaucrats, Irish saloon keepers, Irish contractors, and Irish teachers could be excused for thinking that "Irish" equaled "American"'.[543]

Moreover, nativist hostility to the Irish, was a powerful factor in breaking down local and regional distinctions in favour of self-consciously 'Irish' identity. This hostility came from Protestant gangs in the east coast in the 1830s and 1840s, the anti-immigrant 'Know-Nothing' movement of the 1850s and, later, from the Ku Klux Klan.[544] In an article about the 'Know-Nothing' movement, Connolly attempted to tap into this emigrant experience to engender an open and internationalist outlook amongst Irish-American workers. He pointed out that the Irish had 'in their day of weakness in this country, to suffer all the insults, abuse and ignominy now poured so freely upon the Italian, the Pole, the Hungarian, the Slav and the Jew'.[545]

Yet, as 'America's first ethnic group' the position of the Irish was privileged in comparison to more recent arrivals. The Irish, for example, dominated the leadership and officialdom of the AFL far in excess of their numerical weight. Though confined to stable but relatively low-paid manual positions, Irish influence in craft unions assured them control of apprenticeships and employment. Irish foremen, on building sites or in factories, could provide jobs for relatives and friends, and parish organisations provided a fertile ground for newcomers to make contacts who could 'put in a good word'. Such communal networks were, by definition, exclusionary towards outsiders. This could, on occasion, spill over to violence, as Irish workers sought to drive other ethnic groups – first, African-American workers and, later, Italians and eastern Europeans – off building sites and other workplaces.[546]

Politically, the Irish community followed the Democratic Party in US politics. In 1907, Mayor of New York City George B. McClellan Jr boasted, with some exaggeration, that '[t]here are Russian Socialists and Jewish Socialists and German Socialists! But thank God! There are Irish

Socialists!'[547] Connolly, for his part, hoped that the ISF would encourage Irish workers to rely on organisations of their own class. We must, he wrote, 'let the capitalist parties know that the Irish workers are not married to the Democratic Party [and] secure a divorce on the grounds of "incompatibility of interests"'.[548]

This assertion of independent working-class politics also applied back home in Ireland. For Connolly, the ISF had an important role to play, 'to assist the revolutionary working-class movement in Ireland by a dissemination of its literature'.[549] This meant, in particular, challenging the influence of the Home Rulers. Those Irish immigrants, concerned about Britain's oppression of Ireland, and with one eye fixed back to the home country, more often than not came under the influence of the United Irish League of America (UILA), linked to the nationalist UIL back in Ireland. Connolly complained that '[t]he Irish are the only race in America among whom are organised associations for the express purpose of assisting capitalist parties in the old country'.[550]

Though Connolly highlighted the discrimination against 'the Italian, the Pole, the Hungarian, the Slav and the Jew', there was one relative blind spot in his coverage of race and racism in *The Harp* – the position of African-American workers and the legacy of slavery in the United States. Connolly was largely based in the American North, where a relatively small number of black workers in this period co-existed with a much wider multi-ethnic working class, concentrated in the lowest-paid jobs and excluded from AFL unions by widespread racism. In the South, black workers were forced into cotton fields and lumber camps and terrorised by beatings and lynchings.[551]

Connolly's paper was not completely silent on the question. In July 1908, Connolly cited a report in the SPA journal the *Appeal to Reason*, which stated that the 'Socialist movement has repeatedly declared against discrimination with reference to color and sex' and stands for 'equality of economic opportunity for all'.[552] This was, however, a citation of another journal and was in the general context of an argument about the need for economic democracy. Delving any further, it is, in fact, rather difficult to trace references to the struggles of black workers in *The Harp*. This is because, as Carl Reeve has commented, 'consistently, no distinction is made between black and white Americans'.[553] Thus, in June 1908, Connolly cited an article from the *Chicago Socialist* about peonage in the cotton fields in the American South, protesting that 'Little children five years old have to go out and hoe cotton in May, June and July' with only a short break for schooling, after which 'the cotton picking begins' again in September. 'Connolly passionately protested against these conditions,' wrote Reeve, denouncing their 'awful conditions.' Nevertheless, there was no emphasis on 'the super exploitation and social discrimination' imposed on black workers, or any comments about the racial division of labour in the United States. Nor did Connolly discuss the situation in the North of country where, in cities such as Chicago, Philadelphia and New York, there were often severe tensions between Irish-American and African-American communities.[554]

As Reeve argues, *The Harp*'s approach to this question 'is typical of the Socialist movement, even the left wing, in the years in which Connolly was in the United States'.[555] The underdeveloped nature of Connolly's views, therefore, was part of a wider issue within American socialism in the era of Debs. The movement at this time has faced subsequent criticism – some of it fair, some of it less so – for its lack of attention to the issue of racism.[556] Debs, to be clear, was an unyielding opponent of racism. In 1903, he wrote that 'the history of the Negro in the United States is a history of crime without a parallel' and that the fact the 'white heel is still upon the black neck is simply proof that the world is not yet civilized'. [557] He refused to address segregated labour movement events and was a forceful advocate for open borders against immigration controls.[558] This was to his huge credit in a party which contained segregated local branches in some Southern states and included figures such as Milwaukee Congressman Victor Berger, who defended segregation generally on the grounds that 'Negroes and mulattoes constitute a lower race …'.[559]

At the same time, Debs famously argued that the Socialist Party has 'nothing special to offer the Negro, and we cannot make separate appeals to all the races'.[560] In other words, Debs refused to see the issues of black oppression as a particular question requiring specific answers from socialists, beyond the general struggle for socialism: 'there is no Negro question outside of the labor question – the working class struggle,' he argued. 'Our position as Socialists and as a party is perfectly plain … "The class struggle is colorless". The capitalists, white, black and other shades, are on one side and the workers, white, black and all other colors, on the other side.'[561]

This was, as Paul Heidemann has written, 'an unsatisfactory account of the relationship between Black liberation and class struggle', even if Debs's theoretical underdevelopment in this area did not imply an indifference to racism.[562] Nevertheless, according to Ira Kipnis's classic account of the American socialist movement, taken as a whole, 'despite their theoretical stand for Negro equality, the Left [in the SPA] made virtually no effort to use the party in a struggle for Negro rights'. Those 'Socialists who felt the urgency of work among minorities', he noted, 'turned more and more to the Industrial Workers of the World as the organization that was not afraid to fight'.[563]

It is clear that the contradictory, inconsistent and – sometimes – downright racist approach of the American socialist movement failed to attract black workers in significant numbers. Reeve is surely correct that 'the lack of energetic campaigns against lynching, disenfranchisement, union and job discrimination, southern peonage, etc., was a basic reason for the small number of Blacks in the socialist organizations of the day'. A report in *The Harp* provides some evidence of this. On 1 June 1908, ISF member Bernard McMahon reported back from the SPA's National Convention. Tellingly, he noted that California 'was positively unique in sending the only negro delegate, Woodbury from San Diego, on the Mexican border.'[564]

The ISF immediately became the subject of sharp political disagreement in the SLP, and not just because of its studied neutrality between the party and its main rival. Writing in the *People*, a De Leon supporter J.A. Stromquist stated his opposition to 'Race Federations', condemning the ISF as 'not only absurd, but disruptive and harmful'.[565] Connolly replied to Stromquist that he was 'as much opposed to Race and Language branches within the S.L.P. as any one can be; I would vote to abolish them all'. However, outside the SLP, he wrote, 'as strongly as I am opposed to Language Branches in the party I am in favor of Race and or Language Federations to organize all the sections of our heterogenous population'. Highlighting the political grip which capitalist organisations such as the UILA had over the Irish-American community, Connolly added: 'We propose to fight these tricksters with weapons somewhat like their own; to the capitalist organizations of Irish-America we will oppose a Socialist organization of Irish-America.' He concluded noting the 'enthusiastic outpourings of the Irish to hear a speaker from Ireland, and their readiness to buy literature from Ireland'. Connolly added:

> it will be part of our duty to take advantage of this tendency to push such Socialistic literature from Ireland as will broaden and develop the mental horizon of our countrymen and prepare them to take their place in the revolutionary army of the American proletariat.[566]

From Connolly's defence of the ISF in the pages of the *People*, it is clear that he did not envisage a separate Irish section of the SLP, comparable to the aspirations of the General Jewish Labour Bund in the *Rossiyskaya sotsial-demokraticheskaya rabochaya partiya* (Russian Social Democratic and Labour Party, RSDLP) before 1903 or the position of the semi-autonomous 'Language Federations' which would be established inside the SPA in 1911. Far less did he intend an independent political party for Irish-American workers. Rather, Connolly's vision was more integrationist. The ISF was seen as a bridge from the 'heterogenous population' to the organised socialist movement, and a means of challenging the influence of capitalist Irish-America in the community. The justification for this came from the failure of the socialist movement to make inroads into Irish-America, especially on the east coast. Those Irish workers who did become socialists, Connolly charged, then isolated themselves from the wider Irish community.[567]

Finally, it must be noted that the ISF, as a loose political centre grouped around *The Harp*, rather than a political organisation with a more defined revolutionary programme, lacked some of the political sharpness and clarity of Connolly's earlier endeavours. Partly this was down to the Connolly's awkward position as a member yet critic of the SLP. As he wrote to Matheson, 'when endeavouring to understand *The Harp*, remember that an SLP man cannot edit a *political* paper. So I have to be *very* impartial.' [568] Yet, as we shall see, it did reflect real and more fundamental changes in Connolly's politics which cannot be fully explained with reference to SLP party discipline alone.

Political re-thinking

In April 1908, amidst the faction-fighting with De Leon in the IWW, and tired of the SLP's attacks on *The Harp*, Connolly finally left the SLP and joined the SPA. The seemingly disparate issues involved in the final break with the SLP – the role of everyday trade union struggles over wages, and the creation of a loose propaganda body aimed at Irish-American workers – in fact flowed from the same underlying shift in Connolly's politics. Implicit in the debate with De Leon over wages was, as Owen Dudley Edwards noted perceptively, 'the distaste of the evangelist for dogmatist'.[569] Throughout his final years in America, Connolly sought to break out of the debilitating sectarianism of the SLP and reach the mass of workers with socialist ideas. We have seen above how Connolly aspired to greater socialist unity and saw the industrial unionism of the IWW as a means to reach this. Moreover, Connolly undoubtedly got a taste for mass work through his experience as an IWW organiser in New York, gaining in stature in the movement as a result. This notion of reaching wider layers of the working class was paralleled nicely in Connolly's attitude to the socialism's cultural output. 'Until the movement,' he wrote in an introduction to a pamphlet of revolutionary songs published in 1907, 'is marked by the joyous, defiant, singing of revolutionary songs, it lacks one of the most distinctive marks of a popular revolutionary movement, it is the dogma of a few, and not the faith of the multitude.'[570] It was to this goal, establishing socialism as a mass force, that Connolly increasingly aspired.

From the middle of 1908, then, Connolly began to work out a new approach, navigating the waters between the Scylla of sectarianism and the Charybdis of opportunism. Connolly elaborated his thinking in a series of articles published in *The Harp* between April 1908 and December 1908, and these were collected into a pamphlet, *Socialism Made Easy,* in 1909.

In 'Industrial and Political Unity', published in December 1908 (though it appears first in part two of *Socialism Made Easy*), Connolly advances that argument that 'the division of the workers on the political field is but the reflex of the confused ideas derived from the practice of the workers in strikes and lock-outs'.[571] In other words, the division of workers into craft unions, each pursuing their own sectional interests, makes it impossible for workers to 'realize the oneness of the interests of the working class as a whole against the capitalist class as a whole, and vote and act accordingly'.[572] Connolly compared the solidity of the Swedish labour movement with what he saw in America, citing the recent strike of the Longshoremen of the Port of New York which was undermined when scabs were imported by the Shipping Trust to undermine the dispute. 'A scab longshoremen unloaded the ship,' Connolly wrote, and 'union teamsters with union buttons in their hats received the goods from their hands, loaded them into their wagons, and drove them merrily away.'[573] The lesson, Connolly concludes, is that '[p]olitical division is born of industrial division; political scabbery is born of industrial craft scabbery; political weakness keeps even step with industrial weakness'. Therefore, as 'political parties are the reflex of economic conditions, it follows that industrial union once established will create the political unity of the working class'.[574]

This is a bold claim to make of any form of trade union organisation. Connolly, however, goes even further in his case for industrial unionism. Industrial unionism will create the material preconditions for greater working-class consciousness, argues Connolly in 'Industrial Unionism and Constructive Socialism' in June 1908. But not only this: those who 'are engaged in building up industrial organizations for the practical purposes of to-day', in his view, 'are at the same time preparing the framework of the society of the future'.[575]

Connolly, therefore, attempts to tackle a key question for workers attracted to socialist ideas: what would socialism actually *look like*? 'Time was', Connolly wrote, 'when Socialists, if asked how society would be organized under Socialism, replied invariably, and airily, that such things would be left to the future to decide. The fact was that they had not considered the matter.'[576] This was true, but only partly so. In the *Communist Manifesto,* Marx had written 'that the first step in the revolution by the working class is to raise the proletariat to the position of ruling class to win the battle of democracy' and that the 'proletariat will use its political supremacy to wrest, by degree, all capital from the bourgeoisie, to centralise all instruments of production in the hands of the State, i.e., of the proletariat organised as the ruling class …'.[577] How this might work in practice was demonstrated by the Paris Commune of 1871. The Commune-state was 'formed of the municipal councillors, chosen by universal suffrage in the various wards of the town, responsible and revocable at any time,' drawn largely from 'working men, or acknowledged representatives of the working class.' Police and 'officials of all other branches of the administration' were 'turned into the responsible, and at all times revocable, agent of the Commune' and 'public service had to be done at workmen's wages' while the 'privileges and the representation allowances of the high dignitaries of state disappeared along with the high dignitaries themselves'.[578] Following the experience of the Commune, Marx clarified his earlier statements in the *Manifesto,* writing that 'the working class cannot simply lay hold on the ready made State machinery and wield it for their own purpose. The political instrument of their enslavement cannot serve as the political instrument of their emancipation.'[579]

More commonly in the Second International, however, it was assumed that the representative structures of the bourgeois state would largely be preserved in the transition to the Socialist Republic. Kautsky, in *The Class Struggle,* his authoritative commentary on the German SPD's Erfurt Program, summed up the aim of the Social-Democrat parties: 'to call the working-class to conquer the political power to the end that, with its aid, they may change the state into a self-sufficing co-operative commonwealth.'[580] How the state would be 'changed' was not exactly clear. Kautsky did, however, argue strongly against proponents of 'direct legislation' and asserted whenever 'the proletariat engages in parliamentary activity as a self-conscious class, parliamentarism begins to change its character' and 'ceases to be a mere tool in the hands of the bourgeoisie'.[581] Elsewhere, he goes so far as to argue that 'it is beginning to become clear that a genuine parliamentary regime can be as much an instrument of the dictatorship of the proletariat as an instrument of the dictatorship of the bourgeoisie'.[582] As for the 'state apparatus and the technical-administrative apparatus constructed by the modern bourgeoisie,' writes his biographer Massimo Salvadori, these 'could be used for different socio-political purposes, they could not be "shattered" and replaced by an "anti-bureaucratic" state and form of social organization'.[583]

Connolly would have none of this. De Leon's ideas had offered Connolly 'both a concrete structure and an ideology which provided a logical extension of his own, much more tentative thoughts on organised labour and revolution'. Now, in his industrial unionist phase, Connolly was able to 'focus his own radical but somewhat unconnected ideas on craft unionism, workers' control of industry and the shape of socialist society'.[584] For him, the 'political institutions of today are simply the coercive forces of capitalist society they have grown up out of …'. They represent 'no real natural division suited to the requirements of modern society' and are, therefore, 'totally unsuited to the needs of the new social order, which must be based upon industry'.[585] By contrast, argues Connolly,

> under a Social Democratic form of society the administration of affairs will be in the hands of representatives of the various industries of the nation; that the workers in the shops and factories will organize themselves into unions, each union comprising all the workers at a given industry; that said union will democratically control the workshop life of its own industry, electing all foremen etc … that representatives elected from these various departments of industry will meet and form the industrial administration or national government of the country.[586]

This system represents 'the application to industry, or to the social life of the nation, of the fundamental principles of democracy', which will 'begin in the workshop, and proceed logically and consecutively upward through all the grades of industrial organization until it reaches the culminating point of national executive power and direction'. This, Connolly argues, is a thoroughly democratic system: 'social democracy must proceed from the bottom upward, whereas capitalist political society is organized from above downward.' Moreover,

> It will be seen that this conception of Socialism destroys at one blow all the fears of a bureaucratic State, ruling and ordering the lives of every individual from above, and thus gives assurance that the social order of the future will be an extension of the freedom of the individual, and not the suppression of it. In short, it blends the fullest democratic control with the most absolute expert supervision, something unthinkable of any society built upon the political state.[587]

The final article collected in *Socialism Made Easy* was 'The Future of Labour', which originated as a lecture for the IWW Propaganda Leagues and was published in the *Harp* in June 1908. In this article, Connolly laid out his understanding of how the bourgeoisie came to power in the period of the classic bourgeois revolutions. He drew an analogy between this period of the past and the future socialist revolution. 'In Cromwellian England, in Colonial America, in Revolutionary France,' Connolly argues, 'the real political battle did not begin until after the bourgeoisie, the capitalist class, had become the dominant class in the nation. Then they sought to conquer political power in order to allow their economic power to function freely.'[588] In 1903, Connolly had argued that it was necessary to 'remember that the French Revolution was an uprising of the capitalist class, that their tactics may not be our tactics, and that their victory added another to the list of our enemies in power'.[589] Now, however, Connolly argued that the working-class, like the bourgeoise before it, would consolidate its economic power within capitalist society prior to capturing political power. The industrial union, Connolly argued, would 'build up an industrial republic inside the shell of the political State, in order that when the industrial republic is fully organized it may crack the shell of the political State and step into its place in the scheme of the universe'.[590]

One of the most radical implications of Connolly's new industrial unionist theory was that he downgraded the primary role of the political party. Previously, in the ISRP and the SLP, Connolly demonstrated a conception of the socialist party as a 'clear cut' ideological vanguard of the working-class movement. In April 1903, for example, he argued that any party which did not 'cherish as its dearest belief the doctrine that it and it alone ... was destined to carry the banner of Socialism to a triumphant issue' was bound eventually to 'die of dry-rot or become prey to the machinations of intriguers or the doubts of weaklings'. Indeed, Connolly even wrote admiringly of 'the bigot, the man of no compromise, the good hater, the relentless fighter whoever or whatever he may be the man who wars to the knife and the knife to the hilt'.[591]

This conception of the political party did not survive his experience in De Leon's SLP. While the ideological rigidity of the SLP may be 'absolutely sound in theory, and might be sound in practice if adopted by men of large outlook,' in practice, Connolly argued, its 'immediate effects have been the generation of a number of sectarians, narrow-minded doctrinaires, who have erected Socialism into a cult with rigid formulas which one must observe or be damned'. From this, Connolly drew the conclusion that the 'proper position' for revolutionary socialists is 'in the general Socialist, or rather Labour movement, as friendly critics and *helpers*, rather than in a separate organisation, as hostile critics and enemies'.[592]

This was the political basis on which Connolly joined the SPA. In his private correspondence with Matheson, he had elaborated his reasoning for joining:

> I believe in the necessity of an uncompromising political party of Socialists and I do not believe that the Socialist Party, of which I am a member, is *yet* such a body. But I believe that the conduct of De Leon has rendered impossible for any clear cut movement *in America* except as an evolution out of the SP for agitation, and for the final revolutionary act out of the IWW.[593]

Though this is a major shift in thinking, it should not be understood to mean that Connolly ceased to be a revolutionary, or 'clear cut', in his own politics. He insisted to Matheson that

> if before joining the S.P. I had to accept the compromising elements and their political faith, I could never have joined it. But it is not necessary to do so. In the S.P. there are revolutionary, clear cut elements (43 votes in the last Convention) and there are also compromising elements. Neither can claim the right to be the Socialist Party ... Neither attempt to expel the other.

Overall, however, Connolly 'felt that it was better to be one of the revolutionary minority inside the party than a mere discontented grumbler out of political life entirely'.[594]

Connolly's new approach, however, went further than merely insisting that revolutionaries should work within the wider labour movement. After 1908, Connolly would put primary emphasis on the industrial union and explicitly downgrade the importance of the socialist political party. There was 'no function performed by a separate political party', argued Connolly in The Future of Labour, 'that the economic organization cannot help it perform much better and with greater safety to working-class interests'. The industrial union would organise the workers 'in unions patterned closely after the structure of modern industries, and following the organic lines of industrial development ...'. Not only is this a more effective means of fighting the class struggle, but it 'prepares within the framework of capitalist society the working forms of the Socialist republic' and 'familiarizes [the worker] with the idea that the union he is helping to build up is destined to supplant that class in the control of the industry in which he is employed'.[595]

However, as Connolly repeatedly stressed in his correspondence with

Matheson, he was by no means 'anti-political'. Indeed, as Ralph Darlington writes,

> one of Connolly's distinguishing marks within the syndicalist tradition was his defence of the role of the political party. He believed that the party had two functions. It had the task of producing general propaganda to educate the working class in the period when industrial unity, and therefore full political consciousness, had not been fully formed. It should also stand for elections and try to win seats in parliament to support, albeit in an auxiliary fashion, the industrial struggle.[596]

Yet, until the industrial union had been perfected, the political party would be a mere propagandist and electoral auxiliary to the economic organisation. A 'Socialist Political Party not emanating from the ranks of Labour,' Connolly wrote is 'simply a Socialist sect, ineffective for the final revolutionary act …'. In a striking phrase, Connolly argued that 'until that day dawns' when workers are organised industrially, 'our political parties of the working class are but propagandist agencies, John the Baptists of the New Redemption …'.

Connolly makes his change of policy explicit in an article on 'Political Action' in the *Harp* in July 1908. 'Among many of the adherents of the clear cut policy,' Connolly explained, 'the conviction has gained ground that the political party which exists for the fight at the ballot box is primarily and essentially an agitational and destructive force, and that the real constructive work of the Social Revolution must come from an economic industrial organization.' This conviction leads to two further considerations:

> One, that since the economic organization was the constructive one, political action was unnecessary; another, that since the political party was not to accomplish the revolution but only to lead the attack upon the political citadel of capitalism, there no longer existed the same danger in the unclearness of its membership, nor compelling necessity for insisting upon its purification. In other words that Socialism at the ballot box is the dress parade of the army of Labor, Industrial Unionism is the same army with its service clothes on, ready for work.

Therefore, this implies: 'One Socialist party embracing all shades and conceptions of Socialist political thought. One Socialist Industrial organization drilling the working class for the supreme mission of their class – the establishment of the Worker's Republic.'[597]

The argument that a 'clear cut' party is not necessary because the economic organisation is the main 'constructive' force for socialists clearly provides the justification for Connolly's shift from the SLP to the SPA. He explicitly points to the model of the European parties of the Second International:

> In Europe the solution of this problem of uniting the political parties of Socialism has been sought in a unity which embraces both schools of thought and while not concealing their utter divergence provides in press and platform a means for discussion, as members, of the things that divide them, and insists that all must recognize the voice of the majority of the party as supreme.[598]

In another letter to Matheson, Connolly goes even further in his revision of previous political positions. 'I have come to the belief,' Connolly wrote in a definitive break with his SLP past, 'that Keir Hardie was wise in his generation when he worked to form the Labour Representation Committee.'[599] Matheson is clearly surprised, and not to say a bit shocked, at Connolly's abandonment of the political positions which the two men had long shared. Matheson replied that

> it is of deep interest to me as an S.L.P.'er to know the reasons which influenced a man who has fought for the S.L.P. position both in Britain and America, to depart from that position. Is it due to the internal administration of the S.L.P. of America, or to a change of view as to Socialist tactics? Do you think Hyndman and Hardie right and we wrong?[600]

On Hardie and the LRC, Connolly criticised the former's 'readiness to compromise, his truckling to certain prejudices, [and] his watering down of the revolutionary programme'. However, Hardie, Connolly argues, 'has demonstrated to us the real method of upholding a Socialist Labour Party,' that is to say, he understood that the party must be based on the wider labour movement. 'What we want to do is to show that the same method can be utilised in building up a revolutionary party, free of the faults and shunning compromises of the LRC.' Connolly explained the crux of his new position, which fused socialist political representation with the revolutionary industrial unionism of the IWW:

> If that body was dominated by Industrial Unionists instead of by pure and simplers; if it was elected by the Industrial Unions and controlled entirely

by them, and capable *at any moment* of having its delegates recalled by the union, and had also its mandate directly from the rank and file organised in the workshops, it would be just the party we want.[601]

As Darlington has argued, Connolly's new conceptions contain a measure of 'crude deterministic materialism'.[602] Industrial organisation is a determinate of political consciousness, and 'the fight for the conquest of the political state is not the battle, it is only the echo of the battle', the real fight taking place in the workplace. This determinism is revealed in Connolly's uncritical analogy between the bourgeois and socialist revolutions, and his view of the union's role in the latter. Just as the bourgeoisie built up its economic power within the womb of feudal society, Connolly argues, the working class will in a similar manner built up its industrial organisation so that 'every fresh shop or factory organized under its banner is a fort wrenched from the control of the capitalist class and manned with the soldiers of the revolution to be held by them for the workers'. Thus would industrial unionism 'transform the dry detail work of trade union organization into the constructive work of revolutionary Socialism, and thus make of the unimaginative trade unionist a potent factor in the launching of a new system of society'.[603]

However, one key difference between the bourgeois and socialist revolutions is that the transition from a society based on feudal private properly to bourgeois private properly did not require the conscious political agency of capitalists themselves. Once capitalist social relations began to take grip in a society, all that was required was the destruction or transformation of the old absolutist feudal states for capitalism to flourish. This was achieved in different societies at various points in the historical sequence of capitalist development by a whole manner of different social classes: from the artisans and small traders of Paris smashing the monarchy during the French Revolution to Bismarck carrying through a 'revolution from above' during the process of Germany unification 1866-71.[604]

The transition from capitalism to socialism is qualitatively different in that it requires a socialist-led working-class movement, *conscious* of its aim to purposefully and wilfully replace capitalist private property with socially owned and democratically administered collective properly. De Leon himself addressed this very point in his earlier pre-industrial unionist period, in the lecture *Two Pages from Roman History*. 'The Working Class, the subject class upon whom depends the overthrow of Capitalism and the raising of Socialism,' he wrote, 'differs from all previous subject classes called upon by History to throw down an old and set up a new Social System.' Under feudalism, he explained,

> the distinctive mark of the bourgeoisie, or the then revolutionary class, was
> the possession of the material means essential to its own economic system;
> on the contrary, the distinctive mark of the proletariat to-day is the being
> wholly stripped of all such material possession.[605]

The problem with Connolly's conception is that trade union organisation
within capitalism is not equivalent to the bourgeoisie's 'possession of
the means essential to its own Economic System', its literal ownership of
the means of production. An organised workplace does not pass into the
'ownership' of the workers, and nor do most workers join trade unions
because they wish to 'own' their workplaces. Under normal conditions,
workers join trade unions to fight for higher wages, within the framework
of wage-labour and of capitalism. To do this effectively, trades unions need,
in ordinary times, to organise as widely as possible from within the working
class – not just the radical workers who might be attracted by revolutionary
syndicalism. As Connolly himself recognises, union organisation 'must
be perfected until it embraces everyone who toils in the service of your
employer or as a unit in your industry'. The entrance requirements for a
union are, therefore, less than those of a political party. As Connolly writes,
'The fact that your employers find it necessary to secure the services of any
individual or worker is or ought to be that individual's highest and best title
to be a member of your union,' and what is required is both an 'open union
and the closed shop'.[606]

Yet, in Connolly's conception, the industrial union is not simply a trade
union; it aspires to the eventually economic management of society as a
whole. There is a tension here, between short-term and long-term aims.
Unless in a pre-revolutionary situation, it is unlikely that most workers
will be convinced of the need to take over society themselves. Therefore,
either the industrial union has a wide membership, so as to be effective
as a trade union, or it selects its members by a strict political criterion,
necessarily restricting itself to a 'militant minority' of the workforce. As one
IWW organiser, and later a founder of the US Communist and Trotskyist
movements, James P. Cannon, later reflected: 'One of the most important
contradictions of the IWW, implanted at its first convention and never
resolved, was the dual role it assigned to itself.' By this, he meant the IWW's
'attempt to be both a union of all workers and a propaganda society of
selected revolutionists – in essence a revolutionary party. Two different
tasks and functions, which, at a certain stage of development, require

separate and distinct organizations,' Cannon wrote, 'were assumed by the IWW alone; and this duality hampered its effectiveness in both fields.'[607]

Another problem with Connolly's optimism about the industrial union is the very nature of trade unionism under capitalism. Trade unionism has a bargaining function, to achieve for workers the best price for their labour-power *within* the framework of wage-labour itself. In the absence of widespread socialist convictions among union members, trade unionism alone keeps the working class within certain limits. This bargaining tendency is often reinforced by the full-time union bureaucracy which sees its role as an intermediary between workers and capitalists. De Leon perceptively called these officials 'labor lieutenants of the capitalist class'. In *Two Pages from Roman History*:

> He draws an analogy between antiquity and contemporary capitalism: the tribunes, while articulating some of the grievances of the Plebian masses, continued to accept the basic principles on which Roman society was founded and saw to it that any protests were kept within limits that did not endanger the system. In the same way, argued De Leon, Labour politicians and union leaders today serve merely as a safety-valve, permitting workers' grievances against capitalism to gain expression in a manner not threatening the existence of capitalism.[608]

Up until the point that the mass of workers is convinced politically of the need for socialism, it remains necessary for socialists to organise into a party for this very purpose. That is why the earlier De Leon put the emphasis on the subjective element, the political party, and the irreplaceable role of ideological struggle: 'Other revolutions could succeed with loose organization and imperfect information … Otherwise with the proletariat. It needs information for ballast as for sails, and its organization must be marked with intelligent co-operation ….'[609] For De Leon, the 'socialist republic is no predestined, inevitable development'. It depends upon 'material conditions', yes, but also on 'clearness of vision to assist the evolutionary process'.[610]

Connolly recoiled, understandably, from the intolerance and sectarianism of De Leon's organisation. There is much to be gained from his more open approach, and a refusal to view comrades with different ideas as necessarily 'wreckers' or 'spies' or somehow alien to the labour movement itself. Moreover, unlike most political socialists in the era of the Second International, Connolly reckoned seriously with the need to connect workers' day-to-day class struggles in the workplace with the ultimate aim of establishing a socialist state. Nevertheless, Connolly's uncritical belief that if workers choose 'aright or wrongly' the correct form of trade union organisation 'so will the development of class consciousness in their minds be hastened or retarded by their everyday experience in class struggles' puts too much store on the automatic generation of socialist class consciousness by trade union struggle alone. His conception of the party as a mere propagandist or electoral adjunct to industrial unionism contains a deterministic view of the development of working-class consciousness. For Marx, the 'ideas of the ruling class are in every epoch the ruling ideas'.[611] Challenging the dominant bourgeois ideas in society requires not only the correct form of trade union organisation but a determined struggle on the ideological front also. Although Connolly is correct 'that it is not the theorists who make history; it is history in its evolution that makes the theorists', there is nevertheless a key role for working-class socialist theorists and activists in interpreting this historical movement and consciously shaping the forms of struggle it produces.[612]

Socialism Made Easy and transnational syndicalism

For all the above criticisms of its component articles, Socialism Made Easy was a vivid and readable work. It was 'the textbook in which Connolly reconciled the new syndicalist influence of his thought with his older views', and it drew on the Harp discussed above, together with a collection of 'Workshop Talks' taken from the Workers' Republic between 1899 to 1901.[613] Connolly was rightly proud of it. He wrote to Matheson that he prided himself on that achievement. 'It is the first pamphlet advocating industrial unionism issued by a Socialist Party publishing house' and was 'on sale now all over America, in the meetings of the Socialist Party.'[614]

For J.T Murphy of the British shop stewards' network during the First World War, and future CPGB leader, Connolly's views were 'clearer and more precise than anything I had read or heard from other socialists'.[615] For this reason, it was Connolly's first widely read work, with editions appearing in the USA, Canada, Australia, Britain and Ireland. It inspired and influenced a transnational network of working-class activists, and shaped debates on the relationship between trade union struggle and the shape of the socialist future.

Tom Mann, the great British syndicalist leader, himself cited Socialism Made Easy as an influence. Mann had been in Australia since 1901, and had established himself as a high-profile socialist agitator and revolutionary trade unionist. In 1908-1909, Mann led the Broken Hill (New South Wales) Combined Unions Committee in a bitterly fought dispute between mine workers and the Broken Hill Proprietary Co. Ltd. The state sent armed police from Sydney to break the strike, and Mann was arrested on charges of sedition and unlawful assembly. The police had been transported by the organised railwaymen of New South Wales. Pained by the lack of solidarity between workers of different trades which was the cause of the strike's defeat, Mann began to reflect: 'During the latter part of 1909', he recalled:

I devoted special attention to industrial unionism. As a result of the Broken Hill experiences, I realised more clearly the need for perfecting industrial organisation. It was plain to me that economic organisation was indispensable for the achievement of economic freedom. The policy of the various Labour Parties gave no promise in this direction, nor did the spending of political activities to the extent type of trade-union organisation seem any more hopeful.[616]

The result was Mann's own industrial unionist pamphlet, *The Way to Win*. Then, Mann recalled in his memoirs 'barely two months since the pamphlet was published, and, a week later, a larger and better pamphlet on the same subject arrived from America.' He continued:

I received from James Connolly (later shot by the British Government for his activities in founding the Irish Republic), who was then in the United States, some copies of his pamphlets Socialism Made Easy and The Axe to the Root. His views were identical with those I had expressed in my own pamphlet. I had met Connolly in Edinburgh and in Dublin, and was greatly interested to find that he presented the industrial side of the position in the unmistakable and clear fashion he did.[617]

Both Mann and Connolly were intervening into what was becoming an international debate. Industrial unionism was emerging simultaneously in several countries, as radicals began to draw conclusions about working-class struggle based on their experiences. Their views were elaborated further and systematised within transnational networks of militants and ideas, often spreading through personal ties or the circulation of pamphlets and newspapers. As Mann recalled:

As showing how general this subject is, still another pamphlet came to hand the following week, this time from England. It is called Revolutionary Socialism, by E.J.B. Allen, The Industrial League, 25, Queensdale Road, Notting Hill, London W. Price 1d. Notwithstanding the title, the subject of the pamphlet is Industrial Unionism, on the lines sketched in The Way to Win. It is known to all who watch European developments that the French and Italian unionists are strong advocates of direct action, and this is spreading rapidly through the various countries.[618]

Connolly's choice of publisher of *Socialism Made Easy*, the Charles H. Kerr company, was not an accident either. The Kerr company has rightly been described as 'the most significant U.S. publishing venture of the socialist movement during the first two decades of the twentieth century'.[619] Initially, the company translated and published classic works such as Engel's *Socialism, Utopian and Scientific*, and was a crucial medium through which European socialist classics such as Kautsky's *The Social Revolution*, and important but lesser-known books such as Italian philosopher Antonio Labriola's *Essays on the Materialist Conception of History* became available in the English-speaking world.[620] It was not just in America that the Kerr company's influence was felt. Its cheaply priced and accessible publications 'reached everywhere an English-language publication could, not only in the U.S. but Canada, the UK, New Zealand, and Australia, not to mention territorial Alaska, Hawaii, and Puerto Rico'.[621] Back in England, showing the reciprocal influence of the company back in Europe, the young SDF member and future CPGB founder T.A. Jackson recalled that when the company was established,

> [a] group of us put our shillings together, bought a share, and ordered a batch of books. We were eager to get and study Morgan's *Ancient Society*, Marx's *Critique of Political Economy*, Engels' *Feuerbach*, and particularly his *Origin of the Family etc.* These and other things were obtainable nowhere else in English, and we were avid for them.[622]

The foundation of the IWW had radicalised Charles Kerr, who lent his support to the left-wing industrial unionist wing of the SPA, grouped around Debs and Haywood. Kerr's journal the *International Socialist Review* (ISR) provided crucial political coherence to the SPA's left wing. What had been a rather scholarly and detached publication increasingly featured shorter articles and more reports from rank-and-file readers in the form of a letters column, 'News and Views'. Ralph Chaplin, a young agitator and author of the Wobbly anthem 'Solidarity Forever' recalled how the 'growing tempo of class war as registered in the Review reports and articles gave me a burning desire to participate'.[623] The tone and content, punchier and more agitational, ensured that circulation increased 300 percent in the first year; it reached 40,000 in June 1911 and continued to grow.[624] Chaplin, who illustrated Connolly's *Socialism Made Easy,* would recall his first meeting with Connolly:

> At the Review office one day I was introduced to a 'fighting' Irish comrade, James Connolly by name. Connolly was big all right and could probably fight, but what impressed me most was his spicy humour and fine friendly manner. He had written a pamphlet, Socialism Made Easy, which the Kerr Company was about to publish. I was drawing the cover design. 'Any suggestions?' I asked him. 'None at all, my boy,' he chuckled, 'just so it's plenty Irish.' The cover I drew was full of runic decorations, shamrocks, and an Irish harp. Connolly was so delighted that he whisked me to be chairman at one of his open-air propaganda meetings.

Though for Chaplin, Connolly 'spoke too much like an Irish nationalist' for his own tastes at one open-air propaganda meeting, he recalled that Connolly was 'abundantly endowed with personality'. Despite the fact that Connolly 'didn't remain in Chicago long', Chaplin remembered that he 'left a lasting impression on me and everyone else with whom he had associated'.[625]

A political ally of Kerr's, Connolly endorsed the ISR's shift to take more account of the struggles of the working-class movement. 'Our Socialist writers,' he complained, 'seem in some strange and, to me, incomprehensible manner to have detached themselves from the everyday struggle of the toilers …' While there was a limitless supplies of 'Studies of Marx and popularizing (sic) of Marx, studies of science and popularizing of science, studies of religion and applicational of same with Socialist interpretations', the movement, Connolly argued, lacked any real 'attempts to apply the methods of Marx and of science to an analysis of the laws of growth and incidents of development of the organizations of labour upon the economic field'.[626] Connolly would contribute articles on labour movement organization and strategy himself to the ISR in 1909, 1910 and 1915.[627]

Connolly also lined up with Kerr and the revolutionary left in the SPA when it came to resisting calls to water down the party's socialist programme. Connolly, it is true, hoped that the finished form of the socialist party would be 'the union of the economic and political forces of Labour' on the 'foundation of the industrial union'.[628] This would be something closer to the European Second International parties, broad multi-tendency organisations, agreeing on common programme of socialism but differing in emphasis on tactical and strategic questions. Connolly was, however, strongly opposed to attempts by the SPA right wing to set up an American equivalent of the British Labour Party, a party based on the trade unions but without an explicit commitment to socialism.

The creation of a trade union-based 'Labor Party' was becoming a subject of debate towards the end of Connolly's years in America. AFL leader Samuel Gompers had traditionally been against political action, arguing that 'the trade unions pure and simple are the natural organizations of the wage workers to secure their present and practical improvement and to achieve their final emancipation'.[629] Yet, by 1906, even Gompers was beginning to consider the necessity of some form of political action. The AFL leadership, 'harassed by injunctions, menaced by anti-union employers, scorned by Congress, and inspired by British unionists' created a Labor Representation Committee to 'reward our friends and punish our enemies' at election time. Though they denied their Committee was a proto-Labor Party, it developed a Bill of Grievances, calling for the eight-hour day and other measures. It also, however, contained reactionary demands, calling for immigration controls, and specifically for the exclusion of Chinese labour.[630]

Many socialists, including Connolly, were hostile to Gompers' initiative, and suspicious of his motives. Though they held out the prospect of independent labor candidates as a threat against Republicans and Democrats, in practice the AFL merely bargained with bourgeois candidates. For instance, in 1908 it backed William Jennings Bryan's presidential bid on the Democratic Party ticket, and refused to support Debs.

After Debs' defeat in the 1908 presidential election, the right wing of the SPA began to consider the prospect of an AFL-backed 'Labor Party' as a way of achieving electoral success. This would be at the expense, however, of the SPA's explicit commitment to socialism. Algie Simons, previously the editor of Kerr's *ISR* journal but by now firmly in the right wing of the party, attended the November 1909 AFL convention. He reported back to William English Walling that he found there 'an intense hatred of the Socialist Party combined with a perfect willingness to accept the philosophy of Socialism'. Simons thought, however, that the delegates would accept the creation of a Labor Party but would never join the SPA, and that the 'demagogical politicians' of the left must be driven out of the latter. Simons misjudged. Walling was angry and sent the letter to Charles Kerr who published it in the *International Socialist Review* in January 1910. Right-wing leaders drew back, and the controversy essentially squashed any move towards a 'Labor Party' based on the AFL.[631]

In February 1910, Connolly addressed the controversy in the *ISR*. Underscoring his distance from the De Leonite manner of settling political disagreements, Connolly struck a tolerant note. He asked comrades 'to decry and dissociate themselves from, the somewhat acrid and intolerant manner in which this discussion is often carried on'. This sort of ideological tolerance reflected Connolly's growing conviction that political questions would be settled, in the long run, by the correct form of industrial organisation. On the 'Labor Party' question in particular, Connolly noted that there was, essentially, a degree of overlap between his position, the 'standpoint of an industrialist', and 'those estimable comrades [in the SPA] who pander to the old style trade unions to such a marked degree as to leave themselves open to the suspicion of coquetting with the idea of a "labour" party …'.[632] The similarity was this:

> Both realize that the Socialist Party must rest upon the economic struggle and the forces of labour engaged therein, and that the Socialism which is not an outgrowth and expression of that economic struggle is not worth a moment's serious consideration.[633]

The point of difference, however, was this: 'Can the present form of American trade unions provide the Socialist movement with the economic force upon which to rest, or can the American Federation of Labor develop towards industrialism sufficiently for our needs?' Connolly argued in no uncertain terms that it could not. Again, his emphasis was primarily on the form of economic organisation – industrial unions versus craft unions, rather than the specifics of the party's programme. 'The industrial union and the craft union are mutually exclusive terms,' Connolly argued because 'a craft union cannot recognize the right of another association to call its members out on strike.'[634]

In this, Connolly was at one with figures such as Debs and Haywood. Debs viewed efforts to win the AFL over 'as wasteful of time as to spray a cesspool with arran of roses'.[635] The rationale core of this case is that for many unskilled workers, it was virtually impossible to join the AFL, as Haywood argued, because of 'a vicious system of apprenticeship [and] exorbitant fees'.[636] While 'immigration and the gradual entrance of women, children and African Americans into the work force reshaped the gender and racial characteristics of the class', writes one historian of the AFL, at the turn of the twentieth century:

> one could see in the United States a bifurcated working class, dominated by a minority of skilled workers, predominantly white native-born men, who made higher wages and exercised more power on the shop floor than did other workers. These skilled craftsmen were also far more likely to enjoy full

political rights, exercising the franchise and participating enthusiastically in the era's partisan political culture. The labor organization they created, the AFL, not only stood at the centre of the labor movement by the end of the nineteenth century, it also excluded the vast majority of workers. Semiskilled and unskilled workers, those most likely to be female, new immigrants, or workers of color, seldom found the AFL a welcoming place.[637]

Nevertheless, as David Howell has written: 'It may have been racist, sectionalist and unavailable, but contrary to Connolly's dismissal of it as a "usurper on the throne of labour", it had established a reasonable firm presence amongst some of the most secure sections of the American working class.'[638] For socialists, then, the AFL could not simply be bypassed or ignored.

Some syndicalists, increasingly, drew this conclusion. One erstwhile IWWer who did was William Z. Foster, founder of the Syndicalist League of North America (SLNA) in 1911. Foster had travelled to Europe and witnessed the success of the French syndicalists in the CGT. He was also aware of the situation in Britain. The AIU transformed itself into the grandiosely titled Industrial Workers of Great Britain (IWGB), and had some minor success in organising in the Singer typewriter factory in Glasgow. On the whole, however, its 'dual unionist' approach was viewed as sectarian to the existing and deeply-rooted labour movement, leading to the isolation of militants from fellow trade union members. This lesson was learned by EJB Allen's Industrialist League and, in 1910, the Industrial Syndicalist Education League (ISEL) founded by Tom Mann following his return to Britain from New Zealand. The ISEL's focus on making propaganda for amalgamating existing TUC unions into industrial unions much impressed Foster, who made a sharp case for the 'boring from within' strategy back in the United States. In his 1912 pamphlet *Syndicalism*, Foster charged that the IWW has 'become obsessed with the notion that nothing can be accomplished in the old unions, and that the sooner they go out of existence the better it will be for the labour movement' and have largely abandoned them. 'The result', argued Foster,

is a calamity to the labour movement. It has been literally stripped of its soul. The militants who could inspire it with revolutionary vigour have been taken from it by this ridiculous theory. They have left the old unions, where they could have wielded tremendous influence, and gone into sterile isolation. They have left the labour movement in the undisputed control of conservatives and fakers of all kinds to exploit as they see fit ....[639]

By this point, however, Connolly had returned to Ireland. He did not need to face the same problems as the American syndicalists in transforming the existing trade union movement, as the ITGWU was built along more industrial class-struggle lines from the start.

Back to Ireland

In 1909 Connolly, on the strength of his journalism for the *Harp,* was offered a speaking tour for the SPA. He became one of six national organisers for the party, and the eleven-month tour brought him across the length and breadth of the United States. Though the tour was, by any measure, a success, Connolly's attentions were increasingly turned to Ireland. Correspondence with William O'Brien and other comrades fanned the flames of Connolly's desire to return home. He admitted to O'Brien in May 1909 that moving to America was 'the greatest mistake of my life' and that he 'been studying very attentively the situation in Ireland [and was] very much impressed with the believe that all the conditions are favourable for a forward move in our direction'. This thought, Connolly wrote to his old comrade 'has filled me with a burning desire to get back'.[640]

Connolly was worried, however, that he could not provide for his family without a stable income. Eventually, a plan was hatched to bring him back to Ireland. As Connolly reported in September 1909 in the *Harp,* the Socialist Party of Ireland had been formed at a large meeting in the Trades Hall in Dublin. O'Brien wrote to Connolly that he intended 'to do all I can to enable you to come back here' so that Connolly could organise and lead the new SPI.[641] The initial plans fell through, when the SPI membership, only a handful of whom knew Connolly personally, baulked at taking responsibility for moving him across the Atlantic before they were sure they could pay him. With some reluctance, in May 1910 Connolly eventually accepted a proposal from O'Brien to move to Ireland for a tour of Ireland, Scotland and England on behalf of the SPI.

Connolly had another reason to be excited. At the beginning of 1909, the Irish Transport and General Workers' Union had been formed by the Liverpool-born socialist Jim Larkin. The ITGWU combined the same militant spirit and industrial strategy favoured by Connolly, emphasising short, sharp and offensive strikes backed up by solidarity action. Connolly wrote to O'Brien in May 1910: 'Tell comrade Larkin that I believe his union to be the most promising sign in Ireland that if things were properly handed on those lines, the whole situation ... might be revolutionised.'[642]

Connolly saw in the ITGWU the potential of combining the existing unions into an all-Ireland workers' union. Paradoxically, the weakness and relative backwardness of the Irish labour movement, was an advantage for socialists of Connolly's stripe. Unlike in Britain, with a long-established and relatively conservative labour movement, the ITGWU could potentially take the field and transform the situation. Connolly could therefore put into practice the strategy and tactics he learned in the IWW, with less risk of the sectarian isolation which accompanied the latter's 'dual unionist' strategy.

The ISF held a leaving banquet for Connolly in New York. On 16 July he set sail for Ireland, arriving a week and a half later. He left Ireland in 1904 as the erstwhile leader of a marginal socialist organisation, embittered against his former comrades. He returned in 1910 a more rounded, more mature, labour movement leader, with a high profile as a socialist organiser and real experience of mass working-class struggle to his name.

Chapter 5

Connolly returns to Ireland

In his classic 1935 work on Edwardian Britain, *The Strange Death of Liberal England*, American journalist George Dangerfield wrote of a rally in the Albert Hall on 1 November 1913. The meeting took place at the height of the Dublin Lock-Out, and was organised by the syndicalist *Daily Herald* to demand the release of Jim Larkin, who had been imprisoned for his role in this most dramatic labour dispute. Speaking that night were James Connolly, the playwright George Bernard Shaw, the socialist feminist Dora Montefiore, *Herald* editor and future Labour Party leader George Lansbury, the poet and co-operative activist George Russell (Æ), trade union organiser Delia Larkin, militant suffragist and socialist Sylvia Pankhurst, and the socialist and suffrage campaigners Charlotte Despard and Frederick Pethick-Lawrence. Dangerfield was not wrong in noting that the rally 'presents us with a very convenient phenomenon, for on the speakers' platform sat, in serried ranks, the united grievances of England [sic]. For the first and the last time,' he wrote, 'Irish Nationalism, Militant Suffrage, and the Labour Unrest were met together.' The platform at the Albert Hall meeting was strikingly emblematic of the varied and swirling currents of unrest coursing through Great Britain and Ireland at this time. For Dangerfield, 'the vigorous and passionate oratory, rising in increasing volume and a variety of accents beneath the roof of the Albert Hall' represented 'the gathering of a heavy cloud, caught up out of some teeming sea,' and a concentrated expression of the forces arraigned against the Liberal establishment.[643]

Yet it was not merely a piece of convenient symbolism. This diversity of political forces united to demand the release of Larkin speaks to the web of personal and political connections between the most advanced layers of the labour and suffrage movements of the time. Occupying a central point in this network of connections was none other than Connolly himself, as a socialist at the head of the Dublin labour movement, an enthusiastic supporter of women's suffrage and, of course, a militant advocate of Irish independence. The later part of this book charts Connolly's return to Ireland, gripped by the developing Home Rule crisis, his support of the campaign for women's suffrage, his leadership – alongside Larkin – of the Dublin Lockout of 1913-14 and, finally, his anti-war activities which culminated in the Easter Rising of April 1916.

Socialist Party of Ireland and the Home Rule crisis

In April 1909, the Liberal Chancellor of the Exchequer, David Lloyd George, proposed his so-called 'People's Budget', inadvertently sparking a constitutional crisis which would bring Ireland to the brink of civil war. The budget was needed to pay for the introduction of old age pensions and other welfare measures and bolster the position of the Liberals against Tariff Reformers and the incipient Labour Party. It aimed to raise additional revenue by introducing progressive taxes on income, higher death duties on the estates of the rich, and heavy taxes on profits gained from the ownership and sale of landed property.[644]

The measures provoked the ire of Britain's landed aristocracy, with its power base in the House of Lords. The upper house looked set to defy constitutional precedent and block the budget. This prospect led to Lloyd George's remarkable attack on the upper chamber in October 1909. 'It will be asked why 500 ordinary men,' proclaimed the Chancellor, 'chosen accidentally from among the unemployed, should override the judgment – the deliberate judgment – of millions of people who are engaged in the industry which makes the wealth of the country.'[645]

When the Lords rejected the Budget by 300 votes to 75, the Prime Minister Herbert Asquith, had no choice but to call a General Election in January 1910. To the surprise of everyone, the Liberals lost seats and were forced to govern with the support of Labour and John Redmond's Irish Parliamentary Party (IPP). The price of Redmond's support was the removal of the House of Lord's permanent veto over legislation, which had spelled the doom of the first two attempts to introduce Home Rule in 1886 and 1893. A second general election, in December 1910, paved the way for the introduction of the 1911 Parliament Act, removing the Lords' power to veto money bills and replacing its right to block bills with the ability to delay them for up to two years. When Connolly landed in Derry on 25 July 1910, after sailing from New York, the full implications of the brewing constitutional crisis were as yet unclear. It would soon be clear that they would come to define his activity up until the outbreak of the First World War in August 1914.

Connolly, initially, had more immediate concerns. He had arrived in Ireland at the urging of his old comrade William O'Brien to undertake a speaking tour, addressing meetings on behalf of the recently re-formed SPI, a successor to the ISRP. The SPI was a rather loose propaganda organisation, described by the radical Irish journalist W.P. Ryan as 'a complex body – containing thoughtful, combative, doctrinaire, and racy elements – in which Peadar Ó Maicín, Francis Sheehy-Skeffington, Fred Ryan, Walter Carpenter, R.J.P. Mortished, and Seamus Ua Pice, were amongst the active spirits'.[646] As well as this, old ISRP stalwarts such as O'Brien and Tom Lyng were involved, having kept the flame alight in Connolly's absence. Desmond Ryan remembers visiting the SPI headquarters at 35 Parliament Street, prior to Connolly's return, recalling that

> One name and one presence pervades the little room: Connolly away in the States. He is the master spirit who has called and held these men together, but somehow they lack his reality and fire. There is something sterile about the group with their long phrases culled from their God over the mantel ... Only Lyng and William O'Brien seem conscious that they live in Dublin; the rest are a sect conning pamphlets and that long row of Marxist works in the bookcase yonder.[647]

It was hoped that Connolly's return would inject some increased vigour into the party. He achieved quick success in his tour, setting up a branch of the party in Belfast on 7 August, with recruits including William McMullen, a young shipyard apprentice, David Campbell, the president of Belfast Trades Council, and Tom Johnson, future president of the ITUC. From there, Connolly addressed meetings in Dublin under the auspices of the ITGWU, before speaking in Cork for the first time in nine years, attracting a crowd of over 2,000 at a public meeting during which 200 copies of his latest pamphlet, *Labour, Nationality and Religion,* were sold. Off the back of this activity, a branch of the SPI was established with 24 members, and by September 1910 talks were underway to establish a national delegate conference of the SPI.[648]

That same month the party released a manifesto drafted by Connolly and Sheehy Skeffington, reflecting some of Connolly's new political thinking. Since early 1910, while still in the United States, Connolly had developed a new set of political perspectives for the development of the Irish workers' movement. This involved a three-fold call for, firstly, a unified propaganda body for the dissemination of socialist ideas (the SPI); the establishment of an Irish Labour Party to represent Irish workers in any future Home Rule parliament; and, finally, the organisation of all who work for wages into one body of national dimensions and scope, under one executive head, elected by the vote of all the unions, and directing the power of such unions in united efforts in any needed direction.

On this first point, socialist propaganda, prior to his departure from America Connolly marked a departure from the highly principled positions, and perhaps sometimes sectarian practices, he had held in the ISRP and the SLP. Writing in *The Harp* in January 1910, Connolly argued that he continued to uphold 'our belief in the correctness of the principles for which we stood in Ireland from 1896 onward', namely 'that the only hope for Ireland, as for the rest of the world, lies in a revolutionary reconstruction of society'. Nevertheless, Connolly wrote, 'we have come to the opinion that in the struggle for freedom the theoretical clearness of a few socialists is not as important as the aroused class instincts and consciousness of the mass of the workers'. The task was to find a way of combining theoretical clarity with the growing working-class movement, indicating he was

willing to work and cooperate heartily with anyone who will aid us in arousing the slumbering giant of labour to a knowledge of its rights and duties ... even should the aim they set for such organisation be far less ambitious than our own.[649]

Connolly contrasted the situation in Ireland then, in 1910, with that at the turn of the century when the ISRP was formed. Though 'militant, enthusiastic and with a thorough knowledge of the causes of social and national slavery', the party was at the time too weak to influence the course of the developing political labour movement. Now, however, there was a 'strong socialist movement, representing some of the best intellects in Ireland, an independent socialist feeling and education on socialist thought in every city of industrial activity in Ireland, and a general feeling of comradeship and sympathy between the trade unions and the socialists'. In this context, he argued:

The times are ripe for a forward move! We suggest, then, the formation of a political party in Ireland which shall be composed of all bodies organised upon the basis of the principle of labour ... a party which shall act and be distinct from all others, and entirely guided by the interests of labour.[650]

SPI manifesto of September 1910 closely reflected this approach. It announced that it wished to 'organise the workers of this country, irrespective of creed or race, into one great PARTY OF LABOUR' and called on the Irish working class 'to follow the example of the workers in every civilised country in the world ... and organise itself industrially and politically [to gain] control and mastery of the entire resources of the country'.

Such was the aim. With regard to methods, the SPI espoused an essentially reformist political strategy of 'Political organisation at the Ballot Box to secure the election of representatives of Socialist principles to all the elective governing Public Bodies of this country ...'. As well as potentially standing candidates of its own, the SPI would 'assist in furthering every honest attempt on the part of Organised Labour to obtain representation through independent working-class candidates pledged to a progressive policy of social reform'.[651]

As Nevin has commented, notable in its absence 'was any reference to industrial unionism, Home Rule, of the future government of Ireland. In ideological terms the aims and methods were social democratic,' a substantial political concession on Connolly's part.[652] Though Home Rule is not addressed directly, a rather passive mention is made of the fact that 'More and more civic and national responsibility is destined to be thrust upon, or won by, the people of Ireland'. In this new situation, the Manifesto strikes an optimistic note, anticipating that:

> Old political organisations will die out and new ones must arise to take their place; old party rallying cries and watchwords are destined to become obsolete and meaningless, and the fires of old feuds and hatreds will pale and expire before the newer conceptions born of a consciousness of our common destiny.[653]

As we shall see, this scenario was not borne out by events. First, though, let us look more closely at Connolly's more developed position on Home Rule from 1911 onwards.

Connolly's position on Home Rule

Though in September 1910 it might have just about been possible to largely ignore the Home Rule issue, as 1911 continued it became clear that it would become politically central. William McMullen, whom Connolly had recruited to the SPI from the ILP, recalled later about this period that 'Home Rule for Ireland was being hotly debated, not alone in the British Parliament but from every political platform in the country as wide apart as from Portrush to Cork'.[654] It could no longer be ignored by socialists.

Connolly's position saw Home Rule as 'almost a certainty of the future', and he urged the working class to prepare to seize the opportunities of any Home Rule Parliament. Writing in a series of articles between March and May 1911 in the Glasgow ILP newspaper *Forward*, Connolly was optimistic that the settlement of the Home Rule issue would, finally, remove a major source of working-class division. paving the way for the development of class politics. For, he wrote, the 'question of Home Government, the professional advocacy of it, and the professional opposition to it is the greatest asset in the hands of reaction in Ireland, the never-failing decoy to lure the workers into the bogs of religious hatreds and social stagnation'. With Home Rule granted, and the barrier of the Union removed, it would 'throw the Irish people back upon their own resources, make them realise that the causes of poverty, of lack of progress, of arrested civic and national development, are then to be sought for within and not without ...'. It was the task of the SPI 'to prepare for it by laying now the foundations of that socialist movement, whose duty it will be to guide and direct the efforts of labour in Ireland, to find and fashion a proper channel of expression and instrument of emancipation'.[655]

Connolly was keen to stress, however, that this meant no political endorsement of the Irish Parliamentary Party, which was 'bossed locally by small sweating employers, slum landlords and publicans ...'. Indeed, ever since his early years in the movement, this had been a point of contention between Connolly and many British socialist supporters of Home Rule.[656] 'The fact that national political freedom is both desirable and necessary, Connolly argued,

blinds many people to the truth that the advocates of such freedom on the political field may be most intensely conservative on the social or economic field and, indeed, may be purblind bigots in their opposition to all other movements making for human progress or enlightenment.

The SPI, on the other hand,

recognises that national political freedom is an inevitable step towards the attainment of universal economic freedom, but it insists that the non-Socialist leaders of merely national movements should be regarded in their true light as champions of the old social order and not exalted into the position of popular heroes by any aid of Socialist praise or glorification.

While supporting the principle of Home Rule against the Unionists, socialists 'need not beslaver the United Irish League because we detest the Tories. We can detest them both', Connolly insisted:

In fact they represent the same principle in different stages of social development. The Tories are the conservatives of Irish feudalism, the United Irish Leaguers are the conservatives of a belated Irish capitalism. It is our business to help the latter against the former only when we can do so without prejudice to our own integrity as a movement.[657]

While the IPP was willing to vote with Labour and the Liberals for social spending commitments in the British House of Commons, the party was less keen when it became clear than Irish treasury would have to cover the cost of its own welfare measures in a Home Rule Ireland. Though voting for the 1911 National Insurance Act, as part of its pact with the Liberals, the IPP opposed the extension of the bill's medical provisions to Ireland. At the IPP's behest, Ireland was also excluded from the Sweated Industries bill and the Feeding of Necessitous School Children bill. Belfast trades council worried that this was 'a foretaste of what they were going to get in the future under Home Rule'.[658]

Connolly launched a bitter attack on Redmond over the IPP's record on social legislation. His heart, Connolly sneered, 'bleeds for the poor of Ireland, but he would not vote for the Feeding of School Children's Act to be applied to Ireland ...'. This issue was the subject of a campaign by the SPI in late 1911, as the extension of school meals bill to Ireland was opposed by both the IPP and the Catholic Church, who felt it was the family's job to keep children fed. At Connolly's suggestion, the Irish Women's Franchise League and *Inginidhe na h-Eireann* jointly approached the Dublin Trades Council with the SPI, and a conference was held at the Mansion House on 12 December calling for school meals for Irish children.[659] Connolly also attacked the Belfast West MP, Joseph Devlin, and had strong words to say about his organisation:

the A.O.H., supposed to be the Ancient Order of Hibernians, but by some believed to be the Ancient Order of Hooligans, [which] has spread like an ulcer throughout Ireland, carrying social and religious terrorism with it into quarters hitherto noted for their broad-mindedness and discernment.[660]

Connolly may have supported Home Rule, therefore, but it was from a distinct and independent working-class position, which necessitated no let-up in criticism of the bourgeois Irish nationalists, nor any cessation of the fight to assert working-class interests. As 'Socialists we are Home Rulers,' he wrote, 'but that on the day the Home Rule Government goes into power, the Socialist movement in Ireland will go into Opposition.'[661]

To make this opposition a reality, however, workers required their own political party. Connolly saw it as the duty of the SPI, therefore, 'to assist and foster every tendency of organised Labour in Ireland to found a Labour Party capable of fighting the capitalist parties of Ireland upon their own soil'. To this end, Connolly, along with Larkin, was part of efforts to have the ITUC establish the Irish Labour Party. In June 1911, a motion on independent political representation from the Dublin Trades Council was narrowly defeated, with delegates, at the urging of the Belfast ILP, persuaded instead to look towards the British Labour Party.[662] At the time, Connolly wrote that the 'unborn Labour Party of Ireland was strangled in the womb by the hands of I.L.P.ers.' and that 'the 32 votes for Walker's amendment represented the forces of reaction anxious at all costs to save the present political parties from the danger inherent in a proposal to give the political forces of Labour an Irish home and Irish basis of operations'.[663] This, amongst other issues, would be the subject of a public spat between Connolly and William Walker in the pages of Forward, which will be considered in more detail below.[664]

By the 1912 conference, the mood had shifted: a reflection of the growing strength of the 'Larkinites' and the importance of the ITGWU. Prior to this, the ITUC had been dominated by skilled workers and craftsmen – 'the constellation of butchers, bakers and candlestick-makers', in the words of labour historian Emmet O'Connor.[665] In May 1912, Connolly addressed the delegates at the nineteenth Irish Trade Union Congress at the Town Hall in Clonmel. Moving the important motion on political action, Connolly told the delegates that they 'all felt the disadvantage, and he might say the humiliation, involved in the fact that the working classes of Ireland were practically the only workers in any country in Europe to-day that had not a definite organised method of expressing its view upon the political field'. For this reason, they had missed out on the medical benefits of the new National Insurance Act. 'When the representatives of Ireland came to meet in the old historic building in Dublin, which they had heard so much about,' Connolly asked the hall, 'were the workers to be the only class that was not to be represented?' No; they should 'be ready to enter the new body to represent a definite organised labour opinion' and ensure that the 'years in which they would be waiting for Home Rule should synchronise with the preparation of labour for Home Rule'.[666]

The motion was opposed, Connolly reported later, 'from most strangely assorted forces. The Hibernians opposed it, the Orangemen opposed it, the All-for-Irelanders ... opposed, and the members of the Belfast Branch of the British I.L.P. opposed it in the name (wonder of wonders!) of international solidarity.'[667] Following Connolly's speech, however, delegates voted 49 votes to 18 to include 'the independent representation of Labour upon all public boards amongst its objects', and put in place the practical steps 'to give effect politically to this resolution'. The Irish Labour Party had, in effect, been formed; the ITUC would rename itself the Irish Trades Union Congress and Labour Party.[668]

Connolly and William Walker

From mid-1911 until the outbreak of the Dublin Lock-Out at the end of August 1913, Connolly's main area of activity was his political and trade union work in Belfast. It was here that Connolly would be confronted with the reality of a divided working class, and widespread working-class Protestant opposition to Home Rule. This situation would confound some of his optimistic predictions for the smooth development of class politics in a Home Rule parliament.

On 27 May 1911, the Connolly family, now re-united in Ireland, moved to the Falls Road area of west Belfast. Connolly had been appointed district organiser of the ITGWU by Larkin and set up an office on 112 Corporation Street. Connolly had some success, consolidating the union among the deep-sea dockers with a strike in July, and took 600 dock workers out on strike in solidarity with their colleagues in Liverpool in August, winning for themselves, Connolly boasted, an 'increase in wages all round, abolition of slave-driving, [and] full and complete unionising of all labour on foreign-going vessels. We have,' he continued proudly in an article in the *Irish Worker*, 'enforced union conditions for the Seamen and Firemen on all ships coming into the Low Dock.'[669]

In October, Connolly clashed with some of the more established craft unions in the city. He was approached by women involved in a wildcat strike in the linen mills, who were protesting part-time working. As the strike spread, the unskilled spinners were locked out and Connolly encouraged them to set up a strike committee. However, Mary Galway, the secretary of the craft union, the Textiles Operatives Society of Ireland (TOSI), urged them to return to work. Connolly then clashed with Galway when he organised the women into a new industrial union, the Irish Textile Workers' Union (ITWU), closely associated with the ITGWU.

On the political front, Connolly was making some inroads. The socialist movement in Belfast was dominated by the British-based ILP, whose moving spirit in the city had long been William Walker. Walker was the son of a boilermaker and had served as an apprentice joiner in Harland and Wolff. A regular outdoor speaker since the 1890s, Walker had helped build the socialist movement in the city from its initial propagandist beginnings on the steps of Custom House Square to achieve some success on a municipal level on the Belfast Corporation. Walker himself won election to the Belfast Corporation in 1904, and narrowly missed out on a parliamentary seat in Belfast North in the general elections of 1905 and 1906. William McMullen, a political opponent, described him as a 'highly intelligent man [and] a brilliant and gifted speaker, [who] was universally popular with the citizens as well as the workers, and was generally held in very high esteem'.[670]

Walker's positive contribution has been somewhat overshadowed, however, by his succumbing to Protestant sectarianism during the 1905 general election campaign. He was approached by Richard Brathwaite, secretary of the Belfast Protestant Association (BPA) with a questionnaire devised by the Imperial Protestant Federation in London.[671] 'The fourteen questions were of a nature, if answered in the affirmative, to antagonise catholic voters.' Walker, however, fearful of losing votes from supporters of the populist Independent Orange Order (IOO), 'answered the questions to the satisfaction of the BPA', committing himself, amongst other things

> against transubstantiation, to the inspection of convents and monasteries, to the exclusion of catholics from the office of lord lieutenant of Ireland, and to the statement that 'Protestantism means protesting against superstition, hence true Protestantism is synonymous with labour'.[672]

Walker's election agent, Ramsay McDonald, was so disgusted he threatened to withdraw his services from the contest and predicted that Walker would alienate Catholic voters and lose the contest. He was right. Walker lost 3,966 votes to the 4,440 votes of his opponent, Lord Mayor Sir Daniel Dixon. Over 1,000 Catholic voters lived in the constituency, and the consequent silence of Catholic political leaders on the contest 'probably lost Catholic votes that might have gained him the seat'.[673]

In May 1911, Connolly entered into what has been described as 'an ill-tempered and discursive polemic' with Walker in the pages of *Forward*, which lasted until the editor brought it to an end due to the increasingly personalised nature of the correspondence.[674] Ill-tempered it was but the political issues at stake were of crucial importance to the development of working-class and socialist politics in Ireland.

Connolly's initial article called for 'socialist unity in Ireland', calling for unity between the SPI and the ILP ahead of the introduction of Home Rule, and proposing a convention 'to debate and agree upon all questions of tactics, policy, and name for a new organisation to embrace all sections of the movement in Ireland'. The central issue dividing the parties, as Connolly understood it, was 'that the I.L.P. in Belfast believes that the Socialist movement in Ireland must per force remain a dues-paying, organic part of the British Socialist movement, or else forfeit its title to be considered a part of International Socialism …'. The SPI, on the other hand, 'maintains that the relations between Socialism in Ireland and in Great Britain should be based upon comradeship and mutual assistance, and not upon dues paying, should be fraternal and not organic, and should operate by exchange of literature and speakers' rather than in perpetuating Ireland's subject colonial relationship with Britain. At the core, argued Connolly, were competing conceptions of internationalism: the SPI's position for 'a free federation of free peoples', and 'that of the Belfast branches of the I.L.P. [which] seems scarcely distinguishable from Imperialism, the merging of subjugated peoples in the political system of their conquerors'. The latter was a conception propagated not by 'the spread of reason and enlightenment amongst the peoples of the earth' but spread through 'the flash of the sword of militarism, and the roar of a British 80-ton gun'.

In the course of his first article, Connolly, though expressing 'great admiration for Comrade Walker', nevertheless was 'glad that he was defeated in North Belfast', for the spectacle of an Irish Socialist MP voting against Home Rule in the House of Commons 'would have killed the hopes of Socialism among Irish Nationalists the world over'. He also attacked the Belfast delegates for planning, at the upcoming ITUC congress in June 1911, to once again vote against the establishment of an Irish Labour Party. A 'crime against the rise of a native Labour movement,' Connolly commented, which 'is committed in the name of Internationalism!!!'[675]

Not unsurprisingly, Walker responded. He defended Belfast municipal achievements and accused Connolly of holding 'an antipathy to Belfast and the black North', which led him to 'advocate reactionary doctrines alien to any brand of Socialism I have ever heard of'. Connolly, Walker charged, would disrupt relations between the Irish and British Labour movements. Studiously ignoring the relationship of domination between Britain and Ireland, he further argued that

[if] because of national characteristics, Ireland has a right to an Irish Socialist Party, by the same parity of reasoning Scotland also should have its Scottish

Socialist Party; and, to pursue the matter, a Highland and a Lowland Party, a Welsh Party, a Berwick-on-Tweed Party; and as York was once the seat of power, a Northern English Party and a Southern English Party?[676]

The exchange is notable for how Connolly situates his analysis of Irish Labour within the context of debates about the national question within the Second International. As David Howell has argued, Walker's contention that the Irish labour movement would thrive as part of the larger and more industrially developed United Kingdom 'reflected the incentive and crude Progressivism of much Second International thinking' and reproduced classical Unionist tropes about religiously-determined 'Northern growth and Southern backwardness'. This social-imperialist thinking was not unique to Walker, or even to Belfast Labour, however; even those in the British Labour movement, such as Arthur Henderson, who supported Home Rule, attached a positive value to the British Empire. The particular issue of Labour Unionism highlighted a wider problem, which was to gain a heightened significance after the outbreak of war in August 1914, namely the issue of 'a working-class movement tied materially and ideologically to an imperialist state'. This was a problem with labour movements in advanced capitalist states in general, which had very particular consequences for the division of the working class in the north of Ireland.[677]

There was another side to Second International thinking, however, which understood that economic development would not automatically eradicate national difference or solve questions of national oppression. Though there were important differences between leading theorists of the international, formally, at least, the 1896 London Congress of the Second International declared 'in favor of the full autonomy of all nationalities …'.[678] Though Connolly was not immune to charges of economic reduction at times, he nevertheless did put the emphasis in this case on more *subjective* considerations, such as the impact of national oppression on working-class consciousness in both oppressed and oppressor nations. Regarding Ireland in particular, Connolly appealed to the authority of Karl Marx, no less, citing a letter to Marx's friend and comrade Louis Kugelmann from November 1869, which Connolly had become aware of after it was reprinted in the German SPD's theoretical journal *Die Neue Zeit* in 1902. In the letter, Marx addressed the problem of how England's dominant position over Ireland binds its workers 'to the leading-strings of the ruling classes'. Marx was convinced that 'we shall never be able to do in England anything decisive' if English workers do not 'take the initiative in dissolving the Union founded in 1801, and replacing it by an independent Federative bond …'. Such an 'aim should be followed not as a matter of sympathy with Ireland,' Marx continued, 'but as a necessity based on the interest of the English proletariat' because, otherwise, '[e]very movement of the working class in England itself is crippled by the dissension with the Irish, who form a very important section of the working class in England itself'. In other words, putting an end to national oppression has important subjective significance, not just for the workers of the oppressed nation, but for those of the oppressor too.

Connolly continued, placing his demands for an independent Irish Labour movement in the context of the precedent set by the fact that at 'every International Socialist Congress a separate vote and recognition is given to such subject nations as Finland, Poland, and the various nationalities within the Russian Empire ...'. He pointed to the message of solidarity given at the 1907 Stuttgart Congress to the Indian independence activist Bhikaiji Cama. Connolly also pointed to how 'at the Paris Congress of 1900, the delegates from the Irish Socialist Party were seated, and given the same votes as the delegates of independent nationalities, such as Germany or England', before concluding:

> Such, in brief, is the real position of International Socialism towards subject nations. It is a concept based upon the belief that civilisation needs free nations just as the nations need free individual citizens, that the internationalism of the future will be based upon the free federation of free peoples, and cannot be realised through the subjugation of the smaller by the larger political unit.[679]

In his final article in the debate, Connolly also turned to an 1893 lecture, 'Socialism, Revolution and Internationalism' by the veteran French socialist Gabriel Deville. It had been published in translation by the Charles H. Kerr & Company in 1907. Deville, who did much to promote Marx's writings in France, started political life as a supporter of the revolutionary Jules Guesde, before affiliating himself in the late 1890s with the more moderate French socialist leader Jean Jaurès.[680] The lecture aimed to show that internationalism is not in conflict with 'patriotism' and that, 'so long as countries and classes exist it will be necessary for us, not to deny their existence in declarations, but to adapt our tactics to the facts which are the consequences of their existence'. Connolly also quoted Jaurès himself on the subject of the separation of Norway from Sweden, to show 'that the Socialists of a subject nation [Norway] were and are not only in the right in voting for the national independence of their country, but in defending it with their lives if need be'.[681]

Unionist opposition to Home Rule

'The strident tone which characterised the debate between Connolly and Walker,' argued Henry Patterson, 'was a reflection of the labour movement's increasingly embattled position as the Unionists mobilised against third Home Rule Bill.'[682] This pressure was felt, in the first instance, most keenly by Labourites of Walker's stripe, who found themselves in competition not only with the Unionists on one side but, on the other, when even 'within Belfast a current emerged which for the first time argued that the ILP should identify itself openly with Home Rule'. [683] The emergence of pro-Home Rule socialist voices was closely connected with the formation of the ITGWU and the growing weight of the southern trade union movement. The rupture between NUDL and what became the ITGWU in 1907 made itself felt in Belfast Trades Council, when David Campbell from the Belfast Socialist Society in 1909 backed Larkin's struggle for affiliation to the ITUC.[684] By 1911, Connolly too was a delegate to Belfast Trades Council, increasingly dominated by Campbell and his supporters, following a walkout by the Conservatives delegates to the Council. In this period, too, remembered William McMullen, though the ILP was 'the more popular organisation', Connolly, 'being on the spot and engaging in active propaganda, was attracting a number of the more thoughtful elements of the Socialist movement of the City to his standard'.[685]

On Easter Monday in 1912, Connolly finally got his wish for a conference on socialist unity, which was held in the Antient Concert Rooms in Dublin and chaired by Francis Sheehy Skeffington. In attendance, as well as the SPI were four out of the five branches of the ILP (excluding Walker's North Belfast branch, the biggest of the five) and the recently established Belfast branch of the British Socialist Party (BSP, the successor body to Hyndman's SDF). With Connolly from Belfast were Campbell, McMullen, Thomas Johnson, Danny McDevitt and James Mitchell, and the conference voted to set up a new socialist propaganda organisation, called the Independent Labour Party (Ireland), which had a similar programme to that of the SPI's, with the addition of syndicalist themes missing from the latter, advocating 'unity of action in the industrial field as a means to the conquest of industrial power, the necessary preliminary to industrial freedom'.[686]

These apparent successes, however, disguised the weakening of labour in general in the face of Unionist opposition to Home Rule, the decline of Belfast Trades Council which 'like its counterparts in the rest of the UK, was suffering from a decline in significance as the development of national collective bargaining structures undermined its industrial functions', and the widening gap 'between the politics and ideology of the Council and that of the majority of Protestant trade unionists'. As socialists such as Campbell and Connolly became the dominant influence, affiliations to the Council declined to the extent that by 1913 'Campbell and his supporters ruled an organisation which had ceased to reflect, even tangentially, the position of any substantial section of the Protestant working class'.[687]

The third Home Rule Bill was introduced by Asquith in the House of Commons on 11 April 1912, around the same time that Connolly was fighting to unify Irish socialists under the banner of the ILP(I) and establish a broad-based Irish Labour Party to prepare for a Home Rule Parliament. As Greaves has written, however, the 'conditions envisaged in the two Labour programmes never came into existence'.[688] With constitutional means of blocking Home Rule neutered with the passage of the Parliament Act the previous year, opposition to Home Rule now took the form of a naked show of force by the Tory establishment and the Ulster Unionists. The resistance of Ulster Unionists to their incorporation into an all-Ireland parliament was more powerful than the nationalists, Connolly or the Liberals had imagined, and utterly transformed the political situation in Britain and Ireland.

Ever since the foundation of the Ulster Unionist Council (UUC) in 1905, bringing together local Ulster Clubs, MPs, Orange lodges and skilled shipyard workers, the Unionists had been quietly consolidating a powerful cross-class movement against Irish self-government. The Unionist leader was Edward Carson, a Dublin barrister from a wealthy professional Anglican background. Though a southern Unionist, representing one of the two Dublin University seats in the House of Commons, Carson recognised the power of Ulster resistance to Home Rule. This brought him into a close alliance with the pugnacious Boer War veteran James Craig, son of a Presbyterian whiskey millionaire from County Down.

Craig had set the tone in September 1911, organising a demonstration of 50,000, at which Carson declared: 'We must be prepared … the morning Home Rule passes, ourselves to become responsible for the government of the Protestant Province of Ulster.'[689] Plans were made for a Provisional Government with the support and funding of Ulster's Protestant bourgeoisie. This rebellious talk was matched from the very citadel of the Tory establishment, when Andrew Bonar Law, with strong family links to Ulster, became the Conservative Party leader in November 1911. At the Duke of Marlborough's residence at Blenheim, Bonar Law denounced the British government as a 'revolutionary committee' and announced that his party 'shall use any means to deprive them of the power they have usurped … I can imagine no length of resistance to which Ulster will go in which I will not be ready to support them'.[690]

The Protestant working class was central to the Unionists' plans to resist Home Rule. Of special strategic significance were the predominantly Protestant Belfast shipyard workers who, at around 20,000, were 'the single largest group of male industrial workers', and their 'crucial role in the Belfast working class meant that their effective mobilisation would be a major factor in ensuring Unionist hegemony over the Protestant proletariat'.[691] Unionist Clubs to resist Home Rule were set up in the yards in early 1911, and by April 1912 police estimated that around 6,000 workers were actively involved in workplace-based Orange lodges and Unionist Clubs.[692]

By July 1912, as the marching season approached, and Unionist mobilisation against the Home Rule Bill increased, sectarian tensions were heightened in the mills and factories across the city. An attack by members of the sectarian nationalist AOH on Protestant schoolchildren on a day out in Castledawson provided a trigger for widespread violence, when it was widely publicised in the Unionist press. In response, loyalists began to expel around 2,000 workers from the shipyards, Catholics ('Fenians'), as well as a minority of Protestant socialists and supporters of Home Rule.[693] The climax of Unionist resistance was reached when on 28 September 1912, Carson led the signing of a Solemn League and Covenant pledging defiance of Home Rule. 237,368 men signed up, with a similar number of women signing a separate declaration.

'This is the background,' recalled William McMullen, 'against which Connolly and a few of us kept alive and engaged in active propaganda work, an Irish based political organisation, having as our dual purpose the spread of Socialist ideals and the securing of Home Rule for the country.'[694] Connolly himself recognised the difficulties, writing to William O'Brien that:

> Our fight is a fight not only against the bosses but against the political and religious bigotry which destroys all feeling of loyalty to a trade union … the feeling of the city is so violently Orange and anti-Home Rule at present that our task has been a hard one all along.[695]

The phenomenon of working-class Protestant resistance to Home Rule posed a difficult problem for Connolly's Second International Marxism, which linked economic and industrial development with the growth of workers' organisation and the forward march of socialism. Connolly himself recognised this, writing that:

According to all Socialist theories North East Ulster being the most developed industrially, ought to be the quarter in which class lines of cleavage, politically and industrially should be the most pronounced and class rebellion the most common. As a cold matter of fact it is the happy hunting ground of the slave driver and the home of the least rebellious slaves in the industrial world.[696]

In explaining this problem, Connolly viewed working-class Unionism as a sort of 'false consciousness', and the product of ruling-class manipulation. It may have had historical roots in the Protestant's position as 'strangers holding a conquered land in fee for rulers alien to its people' but its presence in the twentieth century was as an 'atavistic survival of a dark and ignorant past', owing to the 'perfectly devilish ingenuity of the master class ...' and the legacy of 'those pastors and masters who deceived [and] enslaved' the Protestant workers 'in the past'. [697]

It is clear that Connolly's understanding of the nature of Unionism significantly underestimated its strength and power. Connolly saw Unionism as the doomed ideology of the declining landowning class. 'A real Socialist movement cannot be built by temporising in front of a dying cause as that of the Orange ascendancy,' he wrote as late as August 1913, 'even though in the paroxysms of its death struggle it assumes the appearance of health.'[698] Underpinning this view was Connolly's extraordinary claim that 'there is no economic class in Ireland today whose interests as a class are bound up with the Union', implying that Unionist resistance to Home Rule was simply an anachronism. Its roots, he implied, were therefore shallow: 'Only the force of religious bigotry,' Connolly argued, 'remains as an asset to Unionism.'[699]

What this ignored, of course, were the material underpinnings of industrialised Belfast's opposition to Home Rule. Northern capitalists, it has been argued, perceived their interests 'as dependent on the continuing integrity of the British Empire', and were concerned about any weakening of ties between Ireland and the rest of the United Kingdom. Belfast, though an Irish city, was economically integrated in the more industrialised British economy, 'part of a developed industrial capitalism, one apex in a "golden triangle" completed by Liverpool and Glasgow'.[700] The Irish Home Rule movement, on the other hand, 'represented a coalition of agrarian, commercial, and petty capitalist interests', advocating a more protectionist economic policy.[701]

Connolly's view of Protestant resistance to Home Rule as essentially shallow licensed him to dismiss its seriousness, predicting, for example, that the 12 July parade in 1911 would 'be as the last flicker of the dying fire which blazes up before totally expiring'.[702] As Unionist resistance heated up, after the formation of the Ulster Volunteer Force (UVF) in January 1913, Connolly still took the view in July that 'the gun today is the wooden gun and the threats today can only terrify those who see things with the eyes of children ...'.[703] Moreover, he remained optimistic, even in May 1913 that 'with the advent of Home Rule ... the old relation of Protestant and Catholic begins to melt and dissolve, and with their dissolution will come a new change in the relation of either faith to politics'.[704]As late as April 1914, Connolly wrote that although it was necessary to 'be frank with ourselves and confess that the wooden guns of Ulster have, at least, succeeded in frightening the Liberals', he could nevertheless see fit to write that 'the Unionist Party is only a negligible quantity except in a small corner of Ireland, and in that corner it is not destined to be permanent'.[705]

McMullen admitted that Connolly 'no doubt, found the Northern environment trying and uncongenial and it was only with difficulty he could be patient with the odd stolid Orangeman whom he encountered in his propaganda work up to this'. He recalled Connolly's rather complacent reply to an Orange heckler at an open-air propaganda meeting:

> One such occasion was when he was speaking at Library Street on a Sunday evening and was expatiating on Irish history when one of this type interrupted him, and drawing a copy of the Solemn League and Covenant from his pocket brandished it in the air and remarked there would be no Home Rule for Ireland and that he and his thousands of co-signatories would see to it. Connolly, with a sardonic smile, advised him to take the document home and frame it, adding 'your children will laugh at it'.[706]

Connolly did, however, attempted to tackle the influence of Orange ideology within the Protestant working class, using two main methods. Firstly, he attempted to produce special 'literature that would be suitable for the conversion to Socialism of Orangemen', exploding what he saw as some of the myths of the Orange Order's claims to defend civil and religious liberty.[707] Secondly, Connolly attempted to use his limited foothold in the Belfast labour movement to mobilise workers against sectarianism through a combination of demonstrations, rallies and trade union struggles.

As an example of the first approach, in an article entitled 'A Forgotten Chapter of Irish History', Connolly aimed to show that in the 1770s the Protestant aristocracy defrauded their co-religionists, the tenantry of Antrim, through huge rent rises when their initial leases had expired. It was a story, wrote Connolly, which demonstrated 'the treatment of Protestant workers by Protestant exploiters in Ulster …'.[708] In another, 'July the 12th', Connolly outlined the religious persecution of Ulster's Presbyterians by the Anglicans, writing about how the 'planters were continually harassed to make them adjure their religion, fines were multiplied upon fines, and imprisonment upon imprisonment'. Connolly argued that 'the landlord and capitalist class now seek an alliance with these Protestants they persecuted for so long in order to prevent a union of the democracy of all religious faiths against their lords and masters'. In service of this aim, 'they seek insidiously to pervert history, and to inflame the spirit of religious fanaticism'. The answer was to remember that: 'The Irish Catholic was despoiled by force,' while the 'Irish Protestant toiler was despoiled by fraud' and that 'the only hope lies in the latter combining with the former in overthrowing their common spoilers, and consenting to live in amity together in the common ownership of their common ….'[709]

The appeal of this propaganda, however, could only have been limited. For one, it was published in *Forward,* a newspaper read almost exclusively by those who already considered themselves socialists. The ILP(I) was weak and in decline, with very little implantation in the wider Belfast labour movement, and Connolly's only other outlet in this period was the ITGWU's *Irish Worker,* which was largely a trade union paper with little focus on events in the North and was circulated predominantly in Dublin.[710]

Connolly did, however, within the limits of the forces available to him, make an active effort to tackle Orange bigotry through united working-class action. In response to the sectarian unrest and expulsions in the shipyards in July 1912, the ITGWU organised a march, led by its Non-Sectarian Labour Band, which had emerged during the 1911 dock strike, and Connolly addressed the rally at the end.[711] The *Irish News* reported speeches at the Custom House steps, noting that 'strong appeals were made … that all workers should put sectarianism aside and work in amity and harmony for the betterment of their conditions'.[712] Then, on 2 August, the ILP(I) held a meeting on 'The Present Situation at the Shipyards' in its office in Donegall Street, which called for united opposition of 'all progressive bodies, Liberals, Nationalists and all the freedom-loving organisations' against the expulsions.[713]

At times, Connolly does grasp towards a more materialist explanation of the phenomenon of working-class Unionism. He argued in August 1913 that when 'the skilled worker looked down with contempt upon the unskilled', the attitude of Orangemen to Catholics is, Connolly wrote, 'but a glorified representation on a big stage of the same passions inspired by the same unworthy motives'.[714]

Overall, however, Connolly's view of working-class Unionism as the product of ideological manipulation, while true, was one-sided. It underestimated its deep roots in Belfast's particular pattern of development. Henry Patterson has qualified the view of Orange ideology simply as 'an ideology which emphasises the common interest of employers and workers as Protestants threatened by Catholic power.' Patterson argues that Orange ideology 'was not simply productive of class peace. It also provided the main categories by which certain limited forms of class conflict could be expressed'. It functioned, therefore, 'both as an integrative mechanism and as a source of conflict'. This accounts for the prevalence of Orangeism in certain Belfast trade unions, as well as the phenomenon of the Independent Orange Order aligned to sections of the Belfast labour movement in the first decade of the twentieth century. As class conflict, however, it was severely limited, in that it was highly exclusionary and discriminated against Catholic workers, thus dividing the working class. Moreover, it rarely recognised the class struggle between workers and capital. Instead, it was a 'militant populism which expressed class conflict in terms of upper-class "betrayal" of the Protestant cause'.[715] Nevertheless, in the absence of a strong socialist movement in Ireland, Orange ideology had played an important role in shaping the culture and outlook of the Ulster labour movement.

Another problem for Connolly in understanding Unionism, however, as David Howell has argued, is that he 'became committed to a Gaelic interpretation of Irish identity' in which the north-east was a stubbornly awkward fit; Ulster, tellingly, is nowhere mentioned in Connolly's *Labour In Irish History*, published in 1910. Whereas in his earliest writings Connolly asserted that 'Ireland, distinct from her people, means nothing to me', by the period in question he was willing to embrace, in the context of the threat of partition, a geophysical concept of Ireland wherein the 'frontiers of Ireland, the ineffaceable marks of the separate existence of Ireland, are as old was Europe itself, the handiwork of the Almighty, not of politicians'.[716]

Missing from this is any conception the Protestants in the north-east were in any way distinct on national grounds. Indeed, in an article bemoaning that the socialists in the North take their cue in politics from the British labour movement, Connolly attempts to collapse the different national outlooks into a shared 'racial' background. He wrote, thus, that the 'problem does not arise out of any distinction of race; indeed, despite the prevalent opinion to the contrary, the Irish Protestants of the North are as purely Celtic as the Catholics of any part of Ireland'.[717]

Connolly was, of course, justified in supporting Home Rule on democratic grounds. Indeed, the Unionist campaign against Home Rule at this stage was motivated not by any democratic self-determination principles but to stop *all* of Ireland from gaining Home Rule from Britain. The Ulster exceptionalism came later on, when it was clear that a partition settlement was the most that Unionists could hope for. Nevertheless, Connolly's understanding of Unionism *simply* as an atavistic survival and a product of ruling-class manipulation was disarming and underestimated the force of Unionist opposition to Home Rule.

Moreover, though he placed his advocacy of Irish self-determination within the framework of Second International thinking on oppressed nations, Connolly did not seem aware of the innovations of socialists in this tradition, for example in the nations of the Russian Empire. There, Marxists faced with complex national questions and several nations inhabiting one state were developing more sophisticated slogans to break down the barriers between workers of different nations, within the framework of preserving maximum economic development which was seen as a prerequisite for socialism. Lenin, for instance, wrote that the 'great centralised state is a tremendous historical step forward from medieval disunity to the future socialist unity of the whole world'. Nevertheless, 'insofar as, different nations constitute a single state,' it was vital that this be a *democratic* form of centralism, with 'local self-government, with autonomy for regions having special economic and social conditions, a distinct national composition of the population, and so forth …'.[718] While Protestants arguably do not represent a separate 'nation', it is clear that the grip of Ulster Unionism on the Protestant population of the north-east complicated any attempt to assimilate them straightforwardly into an increasingly Catholic and Gaelicised Irishness.

What Connolly lacked, then, was a more thorough democratic programme beyond Irish self-determination. This could have granted some recognition to Protestants' distinctive position within the island of Ireland – perhaps reflected in autonomy for Protestant majority areas within the overall framework of Irish unity – to blunt the edge of Unionists' opposition to Home Rule. Admittedly, however, this would at most have been a propaganda exercise. The Unionist backlash was too strong, and the socialist movement too weak, to arrest the torrent of sectarianism which erupted in Ulster in the years before the First World War.

Connolly and women's liberation

As if Connolly did not have enough of a challenge on his hands, his first years back in Ireland also saw him develop another strand of his politics: a concern with women's liberation.

Connolly's involvement in the socialist movement coincided with the mass entry of women into the workplace, the development of working-class women's organisation, and its attendant theoretical expression within the socialist movement in Europe. Marxist understandings of women's oppression were developed in works such as Bebel's *Women Under Socialism* in 1879 and T*he Origin of the Family, Private Property and the State* by Engels in 1884, which traced the origins of women's oppression in the emergence of private property, inheritance traditions and the division of labour. Amongst the parties of the Second International, the German SPD led the way in building a working-class socialist women's movement. As early as 1891 the SPD advocated 'Universal equal and direct suffrage, with secret ballot, for all citizens of the Reich over 20 years of age without distinction of sex'. In 1894, it launched a programme of agitation, including demonstrations by socialist women, and unsuccessfully moved a bill in the Reichstag for women's suffrage.

At the same time, there were intense debates over the extent to which socialists should co-operate with 'bourgeois feminists'. Some socialists, such as Clara Zetkin and Eleanor Marx, argued against cross-class collaboration. Alongside this were struggles to convince socialist men to take the cause of women's liberation seriously. What hindered the Second International's efforts to come to terms with the issue, despite the best efforts of these comrades, was a rather economistic theoretical tendency, which reduced society to a simplistic class binary, meaning that 'a wide variety of other debates, such as those over religion, teetotalism and feminism, were defined as peripheral'.[719]

Britain's leading Marxist organisation at the time, the SDF, was heavily influenced by Second International traditions but on this issue, as in many other respects, it fell short of its European counterparts. An analysis of the SDF's position on women's liberation is necessary because it was within the bounds of this political tradition that Connolly first developed his Marxism. At the worst end of the scale, some of the SDF leaders, such as Belfort Bax, were outwardly misogynist. Ever since the 1880s Belfort Bax had been writing articles attacking feminism and the women's movement and advocating men's rights, which he saw as under attack. Typical is his 1913 screed entitled *The Fraud of Feminism*, in which he argued that demands for women's rights 'as formulated by suffragists as a reason why the vote is essential to the interests of women, amount to little if anything else than proposals for laws to enslave and browbeat men ...'.[720] Hyndman, who was not much better, saw leading socialist feminist Dora Montefiore as being worse than the 'impossibilists' who had split to form the SLP in 1903. He was of the view that women who demanded emancipation as a '"sex-question" ought to be sent to an island by themselves'.[721]

Hyndman and Bax may have been misogynists but a closer view of the SDF 'challenge[s] the assumption that the party as a whole can be characterised by the views of its male leadership'.[722] Its local branches were granted a considerable degree of autonomy, and the organisation contained within its ranks many comrades, such as Montefiore, Eleanor Marx and Charlotte Despard, who made a serious contribution to the development of Marxist feminism. Montefiore in particular had direct contact with the International Socialist Women's Bureau, established by Zetkin and others at the first International Conference of Socialist Women held in Stuttgart in August 1907, and was personal friends with another leading figure in the movement, Alexandra Kollontai. Nevertheless, that Bax was not subject to party discipline (indeed, his views were freely published in the party press) was symptomatic of a tendency to treat 'the woman question', as it was known to contemporaries, as one of secondary concern.

Historian Karen Hunt has argued that the 'dividing line between the "public" and "private" was of crucial importance for the SDF's analysis of the woman question'. This division, though both historically and culturally specific, nevertheless 'marked the limit of political activity ... The private sphere of the family, personal relationships and individual conscience provided an inner sanctum which was supposedly free from political dispute.'[723] This is indicated by the case of Edith Lanchester which forced the SDF to discuss a 'private' issue that had become 'public'. The affair also allowed for the expression of some of Connolly's earliest opinions on women's liberation.[724]

Edith Lanchester came from a prosperous family in Battersea, in south London, but committed herself to the socialist movement. She joined the SDF in 1892, rising to a position on its executive in 1895. Her socialist feminist convictions had led her to conclude that the wife's vow to obey her husband was oppressive and she was politically opposed to the institution of marriage. Acting on her convictions, Lanchester caused a storm when she announced that, in protest against Britain's patriarchal marriage laws, she was going to cohabit in a 'free union' with her lover, an Irish factory worker and fellow socialist, James Sullivan.

The union was to begin on 26 October 1895. Incensed, Lanchester's father and brothers barged into her house the night before, and forcibly subjected their daughter to an examination by Dr George Fielding-Blandford, a leading psychiatrist and author of *Insanity and Its Treatment*. After signing emergency commitment papers under the 1890 Lunacy Act, Fielding-Blandford had Lanchester imprisoned; her own father and brothers bound her wrists and dragged her to a carriage destined for the Priory Hospital in Roehampton. The psychiatrist explained his reasoning in a contemporary news report. Lanchester 'had always been eccentric, and had lately taken up with Socialists of the most advanced order. She seemed quite unable to see that the step she was about to take meant utter ruin', was in his opinion 'a monomaniac on the subject of marriage' and the psychiatrist believed that 'her brain had been turned by Socialist meetings and writings, and that she was quite unfit to take care of herself'.

Almost immediately a meeting was called by Lanchester's comrades under the auspices of the Legitimation League, a body set up to campaign to secure equal rights for children born outside of marriage. At the meeting, a resolution was passed against Fielding-Blandford, and Lanchester's landlady, the SDF activist Mary Gray, was urged to take legal action against her tenant's brother for assaulting her during the raid on her home. After four days of lobbying by the SDF, with the help of Lanchester's local MP, the former SDF member John Burns, the Commissioners of Lunacy proclaimed her sane though 'foolish' and released her.

Though the SDF did defend Lanchester, it felt the need to distance itself from the idea that 'free love' was an issue that the socialists would necessarily promote. The party moreover saw itself as vulnerable to misrepresentation by its opponents on this and related issues of marriage. The common recourse to an ostensibly neat division between 'private' issues, which were a matter of opinion, and 'public' issues on which more of a stricter party line should be enforced, is demonstrated by Connolly when Lanchester came to speak to the SDF's Edinburgh affiliate in February 1896.

In January of that year, a meeting had been held on the issue of 'Marriage Under Socialism' by a hostile opponent, the Rev. Jackson of Leith. Jackson 'gave what the Edinburgh Socialists regarded as "undue place" to the views of certain advanced socialist writers of the "free love" persuasion', sparking anger, including from Connolly. 'At the close, Comrade Connolly, amid loud applause,' reported the *Labour Leader*, 'took exception to the lecturer's method of treating Socialism, and pointed out that it could only apply if he was prepared to saddle christianity with the opinions and conduct of professing christians.'[725] Then, when Lanchester herself spoke at a meeting in the Operetta House on 2 February, Connolly from the chair complained that speaker 'assumed the representative character and used the phrase "We Socialists" far too much.' He assured the audience of the packed meeting that 'socialism had no connection with speculations on family life and was nowise responsible for the opinions of individual socialists on that subject.'[726]

In his earliest days, then, Connolly demonstrated views which were not far outside the SDF mainstream when it came to determining the issues which were of fundamental importance to socialists or not. It is likely, too, that his stance was culturally conditioned by his Catholic background, and a concern that socialists did not present themselves as unnecessarily *outré* to 'conventional' working-class morality. As a member of the Socialist League, he will have encountered the views of Edward Carpenter on homosexuality and, in the United States, the issue of birth control advocated by Margaret Sanger. He did not, as far as we know, leave a written record of his own position on these topics.

The 'public/private' dichotomy endured in Connolly's thinking around questions of women's liberation, at least up until the first decade of the new century. As expressed in his 1904 dispute with De Leon, Connolly's view on the question of the material basis of women's oppression was that:

> The abolition of the capitalist system will, undoubtedly, solve the economic side of the Woman Question, but it will solve that alone. The question of marriage, of divorce, of paternity, of the equality of woman with man are physical and sexual questions, or questions of temperamental affiliation as in marriage, and were we living in a Socialist Republic would still be hotly contested as they are to-day.[727]

Here, Connolly abstracts 'the economic side', in other words, the economic relations of production between humans in a given mode of production, from the supposedly 'private' sphere of the family and sexuality, as if one does not condition the other in multiple and complex ways. In doing so, despite his sensitivity to democratic questions such as national oppression, Connolly demonstrates a tendency on occasion to reduce Marxism to a theory concerned only with the strictly 'economic' sphere, rather than a materialist analysis of society as a whole. This leads directly to downplaying the importance of issues such as the right to divorce (which Connolly did not support), and workers' 'private' religious views, seeing them as questions that were not for socialists to address.

Conveniently, too, this position licensed an approach to Irish Catholic workers which avoided raising certain difficult issues in propaganda, for fear of alienating them from the socialist cause. In 1910, for example, Connolly polemicised against an attack on the socialist movement by a Jesuit, Father Kane, responding in his pamphlet *Labour, Nationality and Religion*. Connolly was vigorous in his attempt to steer the clergy away from issues – such as the economics of socialism – which they had no business meddling in, while conceding their right to pronounce on 'moral' issues such as marriage and the family. He agrees with Kane that:

> Socialists are bound as Socialists only to the acceptance of one great principle – the ownership and control of the wealth-producing power by the State, and that, therefore, totally antagonistic interpretations of the Bible or of prophecy and revelation, theories of marriage, and of history, may be held by Socialists without in the slightest degree interfering with their activities as such, or with their proper classification as supporters of Socialist doctrine.[728]

Responding to the allegation that there exists a 'socialist doctrine of divorce', Connolly, rather than upholding the *right* to divorce, concedes major ground. He argued that 'divorce is one of those non-essential, non-fundamental points upon which Socialists may and do disagree'. Moreover, conceding that divorce is an essentially negative phenomenon, he turns the question around and seeks to blame the capitalists for its rise. 'The divorce evil of to-day arises not out of Socialist teaching,' argued Connolly, 'but out of that capitalist system, whose morals and philosophy are based upon the idea of individualism, and the cash nexus as the sole bond in society.'[729]

Even given the standards of the contemporary socialist movement, Connolly's views here to do not age well. Nevertheless, despite his own personal morality, and his emergence within the context of the relatively theoretically backward British movement, Connolly was able to rise above many of his peers to become a staunch supporter of women's suffrage. The rise of the suffrage movement in Britain and Ireland was to set a test for the labour movement's capacity for solidarity; it was a test that Connolly met.

With the limited expansion of male suffrage by the 1867 Representation of the People Act, demands multiplied for the vote for women who owned property, encouraged by the granting of the municipal franchise to English women in 1869 and the first married women's property act in 1870.[730] Ireland was not immune from the effects of this agitation. The movement was, at first, mainly middle class and Protestant, with an emphasis on self-improvement through education and a strict adherence to constitutional methods. The widening of educational opportunities in the 1870s eventually 'resulted in a body of educated articulate women impatient for reform. Many of these women were found to the fore of the various political and cultural organisations that evolved in the first two decades of the new century'.[731] Though prominent women such as Maud Gonne and Constance Markowitz succeeded, after some difficulty, in establishing a place for themselves in the organisations of the Cultural Revival, opportunities for most women were narrow. The law, the civil service, and most other professions, were closed off; the predominant job for women in early twentieth-century Ireland was teaching, but supply far outstripped demand. Many worked as shop assistants, clerks or in domestic service.[732]

Up until 1908, the Irish suffrage movement largely followed the pattern laid down by its English counterpart, with the Irish Women's Suffrage and Local Government Association adopting militant tactics after the Pankhursts' Women's Social and Political Union (WPSU) did the same in 1903.[733] In 1908, however, Margaret Cousins and Hanna Sheehy-Skeffington established the Irish Women's Franchise League (IWFL) owing, Cousins recalled, to 'the different political situation of Ireland, as between a subject country seeking freedom from England, and England, as a free country'.[734] As the political situation in Ireland heated up, with the growing expectation of Home Rule in the second decade of the century, Cousins recalled that:

> We were as keen as men on the freedom of Ireland, but we saw the men clamouring for amendments which suited their own interests, and made no recognition of the existence of women as fellow citizens. We women were convinced that anything which improved the status of women would improve, not hinder, the coming of real national self-government.[735]

In other words, the IWFL set as its aim the attainment of women's suffrage for the election to any future Home Rule Parliament, which, to all at the time, seemed imminent. They had a fight on their hands, for the IPP was resistant to any attempts to raise the issue of women's suffrage. For some Home Rulers, it was thought that any confusion of the issues of women's suffrage and the creation of an Irish Home Rule parliament would be to the detriment to the prospects of the latter. Others were straightforwardly reactionary on the issue. Redmond's deputy John Dillon, for instance, told a deputation of Irish suffragettes that women's suffrage 'will, I believe, be the ruin of our western civilisation. It will destroy the home, challenging the headship of man, laid down by God. It may come in your time,' he intoned: 'I hope not in mine.'[736]

In May 1912, the IWFL set up a newspaper, the *Irish Citizen*, with Hanna Sheehy-Skeffington's partner, Francis, as one of the co-editors. Sylvia Pankhurst, who first met Francis in the offices of the paper, later described him as a 'small man in knee-breeches, jumping about as though on springs, with a red beard covering the greater part of his face'. This enthusiastic man, she wrote, was 'a citizen of the world, a comradely man with broad views and a quick intelligence', and was well respected for his commitment to the suffrage movement.[737] The motto of the *Irish Citizen* was 'For Men and Women Equally, The Right of Citizenship; From Men and Women Equally the Duties of Citizenship!' and it provided the movement 'with an essential means of communication, education and propaganda', opening its columns to a wide range of suffrage organisations, and publishing articles 'designed to educate Irish public opinion in the various aspects of feminism and the struggle for women's rights, detailing the victimisation of women workers, and highlighting and the legal and social obstacles to advancing women's status'.[738]

As well as organisations devoted explicitly to the cause of women's suffrage, there also emerged in Ireland in the early twentieth century a number of bodies devoted to asserting women's claim as co-equals in the national movement. The most important of these was *Inghinidhe na hEireann*, founded by Connolly's friend Maud Gonne in 1900. *Inghinidhe* had its roots in Gonne's committee to organise the Patriotic Children's Treat for the children in Ireland. The Treat was conceived to provide a nationalist alternative and opposition to the visit of Queen Victoria in April 1900 (which was designed to promote recruitment to the British Army, then currently engaged in the Boer War). *Inghinidhe* continued its agitation on republican and Irish cultural issues, establishing 'the first women's paper ever to be produced in Ireland', *Bean na hEireann* (Women of Ireland), edited by Helena Molony. It first appeared in November 1908, with Molony explaining the need for the new paper:

> The United Irishman, starting as a physical force separatist journal, had gradually changed its policy to one of reactionary social and dual-kingdom ideas ... We wanted a paper to counter-act this. We wanted it to be a women's paper, advocating militancy, separatism and feminism.[739]

Though committed to 'Freedom for Our Nation and the complete removal of all disabilities to our sex', not surprisingly, as a separatist republican organisation, *Inghinidhe* did not support, even critically, the attempts to win women's suffrage in Ireland through the Parliament in Westminster. The difference was stated in the following terms, with an *Irish Citizen* editorial arguing that 'there can be no free nation without free women', and the counter-argument being made that 'neither can here be free women in an enslaved nation'.

A third hybrid stream existed, which was socialist feminist in character. It was created by the growing identification between sections of the radical republican women's movement and the suffragists with the socialist and labour movements. The SPI proved an important sphere of overlap for all three groups. Francis Sheehy-Skeffington combined membership of the SPI with his role as editor of the *Irish Citizen*. Moreover, the IWFL rented rooms from the SPI, and one IWFL activist recounted how the party was 'very useful to the I.W.F.L. in a number of small things', noting that they were 'more friendly to the Suffrage agitation since Connolly took up the reins'.[740] Helena Moloney, editor of *Bean na hÉireann*, became acquainted with Connolly in 1908. She recalled that,

> I saw Connolly's *Harp*, which he edited in America, and wrote him enthusiastically about it, saying that I wished he were back in Dublin. I asked him for articles, too. Later I was shown letters from Connolly asking about our journal and my activities. No doubt this led to our coming together.[741]

Among the activist layers of these organisations, there was much overlap in this period, as Senia Pašeta makes clear. 'Molony was one of several Inghinidhe members who were by this time also becoming more likely to involve themselves in socialist politics.' Through Molony, Connolly was introduced to a number of other women who would soon come to prominence in labour movement politics:

> His close female confidantes came to include Molony, Markievicz, Perolz and Kathleen Lynn, all like him socialists, republicans and feminists ... They were all among the most radical and prominent participants in the opposition to the visit in 1911 of King George V and Queen Mary, often in co-operation with the Socialist Party of Ireland ...[742]

Molony, Lynn and Markievicz, too, would take up prominent positions in the Irish Citizen Army (ICA), the trade union defence force established during the 1913 Lockout, open to both men and women, which marched together with the Volunteers on Easter Monday 1916. Writing in 1927, Markievicz recalled Connolly's attitude towards women at this time:

> When he began to organise the Irish Citizen Army, he brought me along, treating me, as he got to know me, as a comrade, giving me any work that I could do, and quite ignoring the conventional attitude towards the work of women. This was his attitude towards women in general; we were never, in his mind, classed for work as a sex, but taken individually and considered, just as every man considers men, and then allotted any work we could do.[743]

But that is to get ahead of ourselves. Let us look closer at Connolly's evolving position on women's rights in this period, and his activity in support of the cause of women's suffrage.

'The soundest and most thorough-going feminist among all the Irish labour men'

The activity of the IWFL and *Inghinidhe* had a profound impact on Connolly, and he emerged as an unequivocal supporter of the cause of women's suffrage, treating the issue as a yardstick with which to judge others in the movement. 'I am unequivocally glad to hear that you are on the right side in this women's business,' he wrote to his old friend Matheson in June 1913. 'The attitude of most socialists, including the chief socialist press, in that matter is just beneath contempt. All glory to the women, say I! Their hearty rebellion is worth more than a thousand speeches of the doctrinaires ...,' he wrote, adding characteristically that 'I am with the militants, heart and soul.'[744]

On 1 June 1912, a mass meeting took place in the Antient Concern Rooms in Dublin to demand the including of women's suffrage in the Home Rule Bill. Among the organisations represented were the IWFL, the Women's Workers' Trade Union and the Irish Drapers' Assistants' Association. Speakers were drawn from all over Ireland, and messages of support were received from a range of organisations and individuals, including Maud Gonne, Helena Molony, and Connolly, on behalf of the ILP(I). 'Need I say,' went Connolly's message, 'that I heartily sympathise with the object of the meeting?' He continued:

A Home Rule Bill that excluded half of the people of Ireland from the franchise would be an anomaly in this age of progress, and would be a poor recompense to the women of Ireland for all they have done and suffered in the past for the freedom of Ireland.[745]

Connolly's support was not purely literary or verbal; it was also practical in character. In the July 1912, the Prime Minister, Herbert Asquith, was due to visit Dublin in connection with the Home Rule Bill. In the run-up to the visit, anonymous letters appeared in the nationalist press warning suffragettes not to protest his visit. One letter, signed 'Home-Ruler', warned Francis Sheehy Skeffington that 'should he and his suffragist friends begin their dirty tricks and surprises, they may expect to receive at the hands of Nationalists more than they bargained for'. In the event, the IWFL did stage a number of peaceful protests during the visit. What escalated the situation, however, was the actions of three English WSPU members, who travelled to Dublin without the knowledge of the Irish suffragettes. During the Asquith visit, the WSPU members threw a hatchet at the Prime Minister's carriage, in which Redmond was also travelling. It narrowly missed Asquith, with Redmond suffering slight grazes to his ear. Next, there was an arson attempt on the Theatre Royal, where Asquith was due to speak, followed by an explosion in the building.

Though the Irish suffrage societies distanced themselves, in varying degrees, from these actions, they nevertheless served as the signal for an indiscriminate wave of nationalist hooliganism. The effect was that 'all suffragists in Dublin, irrespective of method or nationality, were suspect and for a time become the objects of mob-violence'. In Dublin, an IWFL meeting held in the Antient Concert Buildings drew a large crowd which 'included a considerable element of organised hostility. A stone was thrown at Mrs. Cousins,' reported the Irish Citizen, and even when the culprit was arrested, a 'great deal of noise, however, was kept up throughout the meeting, and speakers had great difficulty in obtaining a hearing.'[746] The following day, at a meeting in Phoenix Park, Connolly spoke alongside Miss Laird, and the disruption was 'even noisier, and only those in the immediate vicinity of the speakers could hear anything'.[747]

During the wave of Home Ruler mob violence, the backbone of which was provided by the sectarian AOH, the labour movement, most notably in the form of the ITWGU, stepped forward as an ally to the suffrage movement, providing venues and protection for meetings. As one historian wrote of the transport union's efforts, 'the burly figures of the dockers deterred many a heckler'.[748] Connolly's support for the suffragists was not forgotten. In January 1913, when Connolly stood in the Belfast municipal election, he received a ringing endorsement from the IWFL. 'In Belfast, the candidate of most interest to women is that of Mr. James Connolly for Dock Ward,' wrote the Irish Citizen:

Mr Connolly is undoubtedly the ablest Labour Leader in Ireland; he is also the strongest supporter of woman suffrage to be found in the ranks of Irish Labour. Both in Dublin and Belfast he has done much to educate his party on the vital importance of the women's fight for freedom. Last summer, while the organised opposition to suffragist meetings was at its height in Dublin, Mr. Connolly travelled specially to Dublin to speak at one of the Phoenix Park meetings of the I.W.F.L. at considerable risk and inconvenience, to testify to his support of the fight for free speech and political emancipation.[749]

In his election address, Connolly stood for independent working-class representation, and made his position as a socialist clear, stating that he wished 'to see capitalism abolished, and a democratic system of common or public ownership erected in its stead'. As well standing 'in favour of Home Rule' and the belief that 'Ireland should be ruled, governed, and owned by the people of Ireland', he also made clear his support for equal suffrage, stating 'that men and women having to face the battle of life together, could face it better were all enjoying the same political rights'.

Tying together the themes of class, national and gender oppression, he concluded:

> If you are content to be represented by men belonging to some section of the master class, then do not vote for me, but if you want your cause represented from Dock Ward by one of your own class, who will battle for your rights, who is the determined enemy of the domination of class over class, of nation over nation, of sex over sex, who will at all times stand for the cause of the lowly-paid and oppressed, then vote for [James Connolly].[750]

Connolly was supported in his fight against his opponent Jones, a butcher, by the dockers and millworkers in the ward. According to Ellen 'Nellie' Gordon, an organiser with the Irish Textile Workers' Union, which Connolly founded in 1911 for the women workers in the linen mills, one of the millworkers wrote a ballad for Connolly's election campaign:

> We'll send Jones home tonight
> To take the wrinkles out of his tripe
> And we'll all vote for Connolly in
> the morning ...'

'There was about six verses,' she recalled, 'and Connolly liked it so much that he got copies printed.'[751]

Of course, this is not to say that the socialist and labour movement as a whole were in step with Connolly's views on women's suffrage and the cause of women workers generally. Craft unions were particularly opposed to admitting women, for fear that it would drive down the wages of men. This explains, in part, why organisations such as the IWFL and the *Inghinidhe* insisted on the necessity of maintaining an independent profile, despite providing extensive coverage in its press about labour movement issues, especially those concerning working-class women.

Unbelievably, too, the ITGWU did not at this stage admit women workers. To attempt to solve the problem of organising women workers, the Irish Women Workers' Union (IWWU) was established on 5 September 1911, and Delia Larkin became its secretary. The move caused some dissension, however. Louie Bennett, a key figure linking the worlds of suffrage and labour, defended the existence of a separate union on the basis that it was 'futile to deny a latent antagonism between the sexes in the world of industry' and a 'disposition amongst men workers not only to keep women in inferior and subordinate positions, but even to drive them out of industry altogether.' The opposite view was expressed by Cissie Calahan, an activist in the Linen Drapers' Assistants Association, who wrote to

> remind Miss Bennett that the pioneers of the suffrage movement did not seek to establish a separate parliament for women, but demanded a place in the nation's parliament. If women in the industrial world [she argued] want a place in the labour movement, they must seek it in the Labour Parliament, shoulder to shoulder with the men, and not in any separate organisation apart and isolated.[752]

But the question was how the labour movement could be transformed so that women could take their place as equals to men, and have their concerns recognised and taken up by the movement has a whole.

The IWFL, despite many of its members such as the Sheehy-Skeffingtons aligning themselves as individuals with the labour movement, was not a predominantly working-class organisation. Sympathetic to the cause of labour, it was nevertheless drawn from the ranks of educated middle-class women. There was nothing in Ireland at this time exactly paralleling the work of Sylvia Pankhurst in east London, whose East London Federation of Suffragettes (ELFS) rooted itself deeply inside the working class, raising the demand for universal suffrage, and connected the struggle for the vote to wider social conditions. As Pankhurst herself wrote, the ELFS fought

> not merely for votes but towards an egalitarian society – an effort to awaken the women submerged in poverty to struggle for better social conditions and bring them into line with the most advanced sections of the movement of the awakened proletariat.[753]

Connolly, while strongly supporting the efforts IWWU was clear that the ideal situation would be men and women organised together. In 1915, he sketched out the need for an industrial union in Ireland, 'embracing all workers in each industry must replace the multiplicity of unions which now hamper and restrict our operations, multiply our expenses and divide our forces in face of the mutual enemy'. On the basis of this principle, 'branches can be formed to give expression to the need for effective supervision of the affairs of the workshop, shipyard or railway; each branch to consist of the men and women now associated in Labour upon the same technical basis as our craft unions of today'.[754]

Connolly's 1915 pamphlet *The Re-Conquest of Ireland*, which contains an analysis of the women's movement, including a spirited defence of women's self-organisation: 'None so fitted to break the chains as they who wear them, none so well equipped to decide what is a fetter.' Connolly argued that

> in its march towards freedom, the working class of Ireland must cheer on the efforts of those women who, feeling on their souls and bodies the fetters of the ages, have arisen to strike them off, and cheer all the louder if in its hatred of thraldom and passion for freedom the women's army forges ahead of the militant army of Labour.

Nevertheless, Connolly was clear that 'whosoever carries the outworks of the citadel of oppression, the working class alone can raze it to the ground'.[755]

Though the women's and labour movements in Ireland did work closely together, Connolly is surely exaggerating the identity of the two when he asserted that 'the women's cause is felt by all Labour men and women as their cause; the Labour cause has no more earnest and whole-hearted supporters than the militant women'.[756] The Irish women's movement was not rooted in the labour movement; at the same time, the labour movement itself was not unanimous in its backing for women's demands.

On the class character of suffragism more generally, both the Second International's Stuttgart Congress in 1907 and the first Socialist Women's International meeting that year supported agitation for adult suffrage and came out strongly against limited women's suffrage. This influenced socialist feminists in the SDF such as Dora Montefiore, who left the WSPU after growing concerns with the authoritarian leadership of the Pankhursts.[757] While Montefiore threw herself into activity as a tireless speaker on behalf of the Adult Suffrage Society (ASS), the tendency in *Justice* was to counterpose adult suffrage with women's suffrage, decried as 'fine-lady suffrage', with very little positive activity on either front.[758] For the likes of Montefiore, adult suffrage was intended as a *socialist* demand and not an anti-woman demand. However, the SDF's lack of activity in agitating for even this measure, as well as its continued refusal to enforce party discipline against misogynist opponents of women's suffrage within its ranks, did little to salvage its reputation amongst contemporary suffrage activists and historians alike.[759]

Connolly was distinct from either position – adult suffrage or a sectarian or misogynist rejection of questions around women's suffrage in general. He was clearly influenced by Montefiore. His famous comment in the *Re-Conquest of Ireland* that while 'the worker is the slave of capitalist society, the female worker is the slave of that slave' very closely echoes Montefiore's own in 1909 that 'though under capitalism the working man is the wage-slave, yet his wife is the slave of the slave …'.[760] Nevertheless, unlike Montefiore, Connolly backed the militant suffrage movement's demands for limited women's suffrage more uncritically and on their own terms. He did this primarily because the movement represented a general spirit of militancy and rebellion. Even though the Irish TUC & Labour Party position was for universal adult suffrage, Connolly stated at the 1914 ITUC Congress 'that he was in favour of giving women the vote even if they used it against him as a human right'.[761]

However, despite his position on limited women's suffrage, it goes much too far to say that Connolly's 'perspectives did not include a central role for working class women at the point of production'.[762] If we look beyond his published works to his activities and speeches, it is clear that Connolly did approach a perspective of building a specifically working-class women's movement. In March 1914, Connolly addressed an Irish Women's Suffrage Society meeting on the theme of 'A Labourer's Advice to Suffragettes'. Connolly 'insisted at the outset', ran a report, 'that all who were in servitude must work out their own salvation,' and he put forward his own suggestions for consideration. Laying out a strategy to win suffrage reform through the use of 'economic force', Connolly

> pointed out that the prosperity of the North of Ireland rested chiefly on the linen industry, that industry in turn being largely dependent on the labour of women. He suggested that suffragists should make it their business to organise the women factory workers industrially and at the same time to emphasise their inferior economic position as unenfranchised women. [It was necessary] that propaganda for the vote must be accompanied by the more immediate prospect of better conditions of labour and better pay. Then, when the organisation of the women on these lines was sufficiently advanced … it would be possible by holding up the linen industry, owing to a general strike of the workers, to demand the vote as the price of a return to work.

It was a characteristic blend of industrial unionism, political action and support for women's rights; a combination which marks out Connolly, in many ways, as an embodiment of the radical movements of the time. But we get a sense from the report that the audience considered Connolly's suggestions novel, and perhaps a bit extreme. 'The discussion which followed was most animated,' we are told, 'and will be taken up again at a subsequent meeting when members will have had time to suggest Mr. Connolly's suggestions.'[763]

Labour, Nationality and Religion and Labour in Irish History

Finally, Connolly's return to Ireland in 1910 coincided with the publication of two of his most considered works of historical and political analysis, *Labour, Nationality and Religion,* and *Labour in Irish History.* Both have a clear bearing on his political activity in Ireland, relating as they do to two of the key issues of the day: the influence of the Catholic Church and the dominance of the national question in politics.

Labour, Nationality and Religion, published in July 1910, was one of Connolly's most substantial pamphlets. Written in response to the Lenten Discourses against socialism delivered by the Jesuit priest Father Robert Kane in Dublin that year, it is primarily of interest in laying out Connolly's views on the relationship between socialism and religion.[764] Connolly's own private views on religion are contained in a letter to his friend John Matheson at the beginning of 1908:

> though I have usually posed as a Catholic, I have not gone to my duty for 15 years, and I have not the slightest tincture of faith left. I only assumed the Catholic pose in order to quiz the raw freethinkers whose ridiculous dogmatism did and does annoy me as much as the dogmatism of the Orthodox. In fact, I respect the good Catholic more than the average free thinker.[765]

It is difficult to know how straightforward Connolly is being here, even in this private correspondence. Even if he did not have faith in God, Connolly's overall outlook, from his conception of Irish nationality to his own personal morality, is suffused with the Catholicism of his upbringing in the Irish community of Edinburgh. There are grounds to believe, then, that it may in part be his atheism here that is the 'pose' to his strict Marxist friend and comrade Matheson. Nevertheless, if privately Connolly *was* an atheist, he makes clear in his letter that he rather opportunistically let it be assumed he was a Catholic so as not to erect an additional barrier between the socialist movement and the mass of Irish Catholic workers. Thus, for example, when Connolly engaged in a polemic with a Jesuit priest, Father MacErlean S.J., in the pages of the *Catholic Times* of London in 1912 he did so in terms which suggested he was, himself, a Catholic, speaking at one point of '*our* Catholicity'.[766]

As one historian has commented, 'his pose is itself a remarkable testimony to the powerful hold that Catholicism had over the loyalties of Irish working men and women, both at home and in America'.[767] In several European countries, such as France, Italy and Spain, socialism was generally associated with anti-clericalism. This was because the Catholic Church was straightforwardly a pillar of a reactionary establishment. The Irish Catholic Church, while no less reactionary on social or political matters, developed differently. The Church, and the majority of the Catholic Irish, were oppressed by British colonialism and the Protestant Ascendancy. The development of Irish nationality, in opposition to that oppression, was intertwined with Catholicism, reinforcing the hold of the Church over the Irish people.

Nevertheless, in adopting this pose, Connolly was already on the defensive. He had to argue that socialism was not a complete system of thought, rival to that of Catholicism, thus narrowing down the scope of socialism's materialist critique of society. Indeed, in his polemics with Kane, he quotes with approval the priest's contention that 'we must understand a Socialist to be that man, and only that man, who holds the essential principle of Socialism, i.e. that all wealth-producing power, and all that pertains to it, belongs to the ownership and control of the State'. As we have seen above in the discussion of women's liberation, Connolly agrees with Kane that 'Socialists are bound as Socialists only to the acceptance of [this] one great principle' of state ownership and matters such as antagonistic interpretations of the Bible or of prophecy and revelation' are excluded as defining criteria.[768] On this basis of erecting a rigid separation between public and private, Connolly argued that priests would be best off 'abandoning their attempt to dominate the public, as they have long dominated the private life of their fellow-Catholics'.[769] This is an old argument, put forward by both the Fenians in the 1860s and the Parnellites of the 1890s. However, the public/private distinction is never absolute. On the one hand, socialists cede too much ground to the clergy in giving up the field of 'private' morality; on the other, the clergy may obviously protest that 'public' matters have a clear 'private' moral significance.[770]

Even here, Connolly couches his argument explicitly in terms which suggest his approach is *mutually* beneficial, both to society as a whole and the Church itself. Thus, Connolly writes, 'Whenever the clergy succeeded in conquering political power in any country the result has been disastrous to the interests of religion and inimical to the progress of humanity'. As Bernard Ransom has commented, 'at certain points it is clear that he argued primarily from a Catholic standpoint, and only secondarily as a Marxist'.[771] This line of argument, however, did not go down well with some Scottish comrades of a Catholic background, such as Harry McShane or John Wheatley, whose experiences produced a more explicitly anti-clerical bent in their politics. McShane remembered that Connolly was 'well known in Glasgow ... for his fight with the Irish bishops and his argument that catholics could be socialists'. However, while *Labour, Nationality and Religion* 'was widely read', McShane 'thought that Wheatley's attitude on this was more uncompromising'.[772]

Nevertheless, Connolly did try and reconcile his position with his own particular understanding of the Second International's approach to religion. In 1901, for example, Connolly wrote that the ISRP

> prohibits the discussion of theological or anti-theological questions at its meetings, public or private. This is in conformity with the practice of the chief Socialist parties of the World, which have frequently, in Germany for example, declared Religion to be a private matter, and outside the scope of Socialist action.[773]

This was a comment on the 1891 'Erfurt Programme' of the German SPD that declared religion a private matter. The presentation is, however, a misleading one. As Lenin commented in 1909, while some ultra-leftists in Russia wished to proclaim a one-sided 'war on religion', some socialists

> managed to give rise to a new distortion of Marxism in the opposite direction, in the direction of opportunism. This point in the Erfurt Programme has come to be interpreted as meaning that we Social-Democrats, our Party, consider religion to be a private matter, that religion is a private matter for us as Social-Democrats, for us as a party.' Yet, Friedrich Engels had 'deliberately underlined that Social-Democrats regard religion as a private matter in relation to the state, but not in relation to themselves, not in relation to Marxism, and not in relation to the workers' party.'[774]

Shortly after this, Connolly published his must substantial work, *Labour in Irish History*, a polemical though scholarly account of Irish history. Upon publication, *Labour in Irish History* was hailed as a classic of Irish socialist historiography. In a contemporary review in the SDF newspaper *Justice*, Jim Connell, author of the *Red Flag*, wrote that *Labour in Irish History* 'is a book which in the near future will be regarded as the beginning of a new departure in Irish politics and sociology'.[775] The liberal *Manchester Guardian* was similarly impressed, noting that Connolly 'has given us a study of Irish history from a fresh and, so far as we know, absolutely original point of view'.[776] The Unionist *Belfast News-Letter,* however, was less keen, writing that it 'did not know what class in Ireland will welcome this book, for it is more Socialist than Nationalist, and it is not intended for Unionists'.[777]

Labour in Irish History is a bracing, polemical work. Far from offering a synthesis of Irish nationalism and socialism, it set out to destroy the myths of the former, leading one contemporary socialist reviewer to fret that Connolly 'runs the risk of repelling Irish Nationalists' by his trenchant analysis of figures such as Henry Grattan and Daniel O'Connell.[778] This is due, largely, to the book's explicitly working-class perspective. 'Irish history has ever been written by the master class – in the interests of the master class,' argued Connolly in the opening chapter, and

> whenever the question of labour and its wrongs figured in the writings or speeches of our modern Irish politicians, it was simply that they might be used as weapons in the warfare against a political adversary, and not at all because the person so using them was personally convinced that the subjection of labour was in itself a wrong.

The book's sixteen chapters pay particular attention to before the Act of Union of 1801 – the period of Grattan's Parliament, the United Irishmen rebellion and its aftermath – with material on O'Connell, Irish utopian socialism and the Young Ireland movement.

The book was long in development, with chapters appearing sporadically between 1898 and 1903 in the *Workers' Republic,* and later in the *Harp* in 1909 and 1910.[779] Fundamentally, *Labour in Irish History* recapitulates on a broader historical canvass the thesis on Irish history that Connolly had developed in *Erin's Hope: the ends and means* in 1897. That is, according to Connolly, that the Irish question is no mere quarrel for political independence but 'is a social question, the whole age-long fight of the Irish people against their oppressors resolves itself, in the last analysis into a fight for the mastery of the means of life, the sources of production, in Ireland'. He continued:

Without this key to the meaning of events, this clue to unravel the actions of 'great men', Irish history is but a welter of unrelated facts, a hopeless chaos of sporadic outbreaks, treacheries, intrigues, massacres, murders, and purposeless warfare. With this key all things become understandable and traceable to their primary origin; without this key the lost opportunities of Ireland seem such as to bring a blush to the cheek of the Irish worker; with this key Irish history is a lamp to his feet in the stormy paths of to-day.[780]

In contrast to contemporaries, such as the Scottish ILP's Tom Johnston, whose historical writing was a 'scholarly, rather antiquarian treatment of the conditions of working people in Scotland in the medieval and early modern periods', Connolly's work was in Ransom's words 'undeniably teleological in tone – one might almost say, eschatological'. Above all, it attempted, as another review in *Justice* put it, to '[apply] the materialist conception of history to Ireland'.[781] Indeed, Connolly wrote that the book would be guided by the 'key to history, as set forth by Karl Marx, the greatest of modern thinkers and first of scientific Socialists'. For Connolly, this 'key' was:

That in every historical epoch the prevailing method of economic production and exchange, and the social organisation necessarily following from it, forms the basis upon which alone can be explained the political and intellectual history of that epoch.[782]

Connolly here was closely paraphrasing Engels' 1888 preface to the English edition of the *Communist Manifesto*. This approach, developed by Marx and Engels, is often described as the 'materialist conception of history'. It focuses, as Connolly rightly says, on how social relations of production – how humans produce and distribute the means of material life – condition the development of society as a whole, including its political and ideological superstructures. Thus, as well as Connolly's own contention that the work could be considered part of the Gaelic Revival, *Labour in Irish History* also sits in the context of Second International Marxist historiography. Basing themselves, for instance, on Marx's approach in the historical sections of *Capital* and Engels's analysis of the German Peasant War of the 1850s, some Second International theorists produced works of considerable merit. Kautsky wrote on the *Foundations of Christianity* and on Renaissance 'communism', while Eduard Bernstein wrote a history of the English Revolution. Though open to charges of a crude economic reductionism, the 'vulgar Marxism' of many of the Second International writers broke new historical ground, opening up huge vistas which would only be fully explored by generations of historians following in their wake. The 'materialist conception of history', highlighting as it did the struggle between classes, the ultimate determination of politics and culture by society's economic underpinning, and a concern with the long-term shape of historical development represented, in Eric Hobsbawm's words,

> concentrated charges of intellectual explosive, designed to blow up crucial parts of the fortifications of traditional history, and as such they were immensely powerful – perhaps more powerful than less simplified versions of historical materialism would have been ...[783]

Modern Irish historian Professor J.J. Lee has commented, 'Nobody has overcome so many material obstacles to write so illuminating about Irish history'.[784] It is in this context that any critical remarks on *Labour in Irish History* should be considered.

That being said, Connolly's approach to historical materialism is at times both extremely orthodox ('economic conditions have controlled and dominated our Irish history', Connolly writes at one point) and idiosyncratically heterodox.[785] One problem lies in Connolly's amalgamation together of two distinct modes of production, the 'feudal' and the 'capitalist' into the compound 'feudal-capitalist'. Marxism recognises the specificity of each mode of production, loosely distinguished by the means by which the 'unpaid surplus-labour is pumped out of the direct producers', a relationship of exploitation which 'determined the relationship of rulers and ruled, as it grows direct out of production itself and, in turn, reacts upon it as a determining element'.[786] Thus, in the *Communist Manifesto*, Marx and Engels write famously:

> The history of all hitherto existing society is the history of class struggles. Freeman and slave, patrician and plebeian, lord and serf, guild-master and journeyman, in a word, oppressor and oppressed, stood in constant opposition to one another ...[787]

Connolly's methodology is different. As in *Erin's Hope*, Connolly sets out the fundamental conflict as one between the English 'feudal-capitalist' system and a Gaelic communal social order, represented at various points in Irish history by the forces of 'labour'. Thus, Connolly writes, 'This book does not aspire to be a history of labour in Ireland; it is rather a record of labour in Irish History'.[788] For Connolly, however, 'labour' is not simply synonymous with the working class but with *all* forces which have fought for 'the mastery of the means of life, the sources of production, in Ireland'.[789] This includes, for instance, early modern peasant struggles and the Land League's nineteenth-century fight against landlordism. In a key passage, Connolly reads this eternal conflict between 'labour' and the 'feudal-capitalist' system into several centuries of Irish history:

> The fight made by the Irish septs against the English pale and all it stood for; the struggle of the peasants and labourers of the 18th and 19th centuries; the great social struggle of all the ages will again arise and re-shape itself to suit the new conditions. The war which the Land League fought, and then abandoned, before it was either lost or won, will be taken up by the Irish toilers on a broader field the sharper weapons, and a more comprehensive knowledge of all the essentials of permanent victory. As the Irish septs of the past were accounted Irish or English according as they rejected or accepted the native or foreign social order, as they measured their oppression or freedom by their loss or recovery of the collective ownership of their lands, so the Irish toilers henceforward will base their fight for freedom, not upon the winning or losing the right to talk in an Irish Parliament, but upon their progress towards the mastery of those factories, workshops and farms upon which a people's bread and liberties depend.[790]

This has startling implications for Connolly's understanding of the Irish bourgeoisie.[791] In effect, they are written out of the picture, due to the fact that the patriotism of the 'Irish capitalist class' is an 'apostate patriotism ... arising as it does upon the rupture with Gaelic tradition ...'.[792] When Connolly does consider bourgeois revolutionary figures such as Wolfe Tone, their social radicalism is exaggerated, and the physical-force republican tradition is scripted into the historical *telos* of the age-old struggle between rival property forms. Thus, Connolly constructs a tradition which encompasses the 12th century landlord, Laurence O'Toole, Abbot of Glendalough and Archbishop of Dublin, the 18th century bourgeois revolutionary Wolfe Tone, the Land League and the modern Irish labour movement.[793]

In his denial of an indigenous Irish capitalist interest, Connolly dangerously underestimates the capacity of the Irish bourgeoisie, both historically and at the time of his writing. If, as Connolly writes, the Irish capitalist class was formed from a rupture in the fundamental pattern of Irish development, and 'the capitalist system is the most foreign thing in Ireland', then the prospect of an independent capitalist Ireland is severely diminished. Though Connolly at one point admits that 'Communal ownership of land would undoubtedly have given way to the privately owned system of capitalist-landlordism, even if Ireland had remained an independent country,' nevertheless, he argues,

> coming as it did in obedience to the pressure of armed force from without, instead of by the operation of economic forces within, the change has been bitterly and justly resented by the vast mass of the Irish people, many of whom still mix with their dreams of liberty, longings for a return to the ancient system of land tenure – now organically impossible.[794]

Overall, in diminishing the possibility of a contemporary Irish capitalism, Connolly in turn exaggerates the inevitability of socialism as a return on a higher level to historic Irish communal forms of a property. Viewed in this lens, while constitutional reformers are consistently denigrated as bourgeois charlatans, while the social radicalism of separatist figures such as James Fintan Lalor and John Mitchel, and the Fenian movement, is overstated. Politically, this contains a disarming implication – though left largely unstated – that physical-force separatism contains an imminent tendency towards socialism.

Several commentators have compared Connolly's position in *Labour in Irish History* to Trotsky's theory of 'permanent revolution'.[795] The phrase originates from Marx's analysis of the 1848 revolution in Germany, during which they called on the working class to 'make the revolution permanent until all the more or less propertied classes have been driven from their ruling positions, until the proletariat has conquered state power ...'.[796]

This analysis would play a central part in debates over the 'class character and political alliances of the Russian revolution in 1903-7' within Russian and German Social-Democracy.[797] Though associated most closely with Trotsky, the concept of 'permanent revolution' was first introduced into Russian Social-Democracy by David Ryazanov in 1902 and developed by Alexander Parvus. A similar analysis of the motive forces of the Russian revolution of 1905 would come to be shared by influential figures such as Kautsky and Luxemburg in the German party.[798] Nevertheless, Trotsky would give the idea its most systematic treatment in a series of works in 1906, 1907 and 1930.[799]

Trotsky, in common with other Russian Marxists, whether Bolshevik or Menshevik, argued that the coming revolution in Russia against the Tsar would be a bourgeois revolution, 'that is, a revolution produced by the contradictions between the development of the productive forces of capitalist society and the outlived caste and state relationships of the period of serfdom and the Middle Ages'.[800] However, the 'bourgeois character of the revolution could not,' argued Trotsky, 'answer in advance the question of which classes would solve the tasks of the democratic revolution and what the mutual relationships of these classes would be.'[801]

Where Trotsky broke new ground was in arguing that the working class, once in power, would be compelled by the logic of the struggle to go beyond the limits of the bourgeois revolution; that the tasks of the democratic revolution could only be solved through 'the dictatorship of the proletariat as the leader of the subjugated nation, above all of its peasant masses'.[802] Thus the bourgeois revolution, with the workers at its head, would, through working-class activity, be converted 'uninterruptedly' into a socialist revolution: 'the democratic revolution grows over directly into the socialist revolution and thereby becomes a permanent revolution.'[803] Socialist construction was not possible, however, in a backward country such as Russia. The revolution could only be consolidated if it spreads beyond national borders. 'The way out for it lies only,' wrote Trotsky, 'in the victory of the proletariat of the advanced countries.'[804]

This strategic hypothesis was based on Trotsky's analysis of the Russian social formation. The 'combined and uneven development' of Russian society saw a reactionary Tsarist absolutism promote economic development under the military pressure of its capitalist rivals. Importing large quantities of largely foreign capital had created a social structure in which the native Russian bourgeoisie was numerically and socially weak and tied to the old regime. At the same time, by the beginning of the twentieth century the working class was increasingly strong. Whereas the Mensheviks saw the model for Russia as the French Revolution of 1789, when feudalism was smashed and a revolutionary bourgeoisie took power, Trotsky argued that the Russian bourgeoisie appeared too late on the scene and was unable and unwilling to put itself at the head of the workers and peasants in a revolution against the Tsarist system.

In *The Permanent Revolution*, a book-length polemic in 1930 against Karl Radek, a fellow member of the Left Opposition who was on his way to capitulating before Stalin and the new bureaucratic rulers of the Soviet Union, Trotsky generalised his theory from specifically Russia conditions to apply more widely to societies such as semi-colonial China. 'With regard to countries with a belated bourgeois development, especially the colonial and semi-colonial countries,' wrote Trotsky,

the theory of the permanent revolution signifies that the complete and genuine solution of their tasks of achieving democracy and national emancipation is conceivable only through the dictatorship of the proletariat as the leader of the subjugated nation, above all of its peasant masses.[805]

Thus, the permanent revolution was not just a nineteenth-century German phenomenon or theory of early twentieth-century Russia, but a potential strategy for revolution internationally.

What, then, of Connolly and Ireland? It is too much to say, as Austen Morgan does, that it is 'a travesty to try to tease out a theory of permanent revolution from his writings'.[806] Though there is no evidence Connolly was aware in any detail of the debates in Russian and German Social-Democracy over the character of the 1905 Russian Revolution, it is plausible that a certain 'elective affinity' exists.[807] That is to say, socialists facing situations with a certain structural similarity – weak or belated capitalist development, with a seemingly supine bourgeoisie, and a number of outstanding unresolved 'tasks' – drew more or less similar conclusions about the role of the working class. In this sense, Connolly's theory certainly bears a familial resemblance to the theory of permanent revolution. Crucially, it foregrounds working-class agency in the fight for national liberation, arguing that the bourgeoisie is unwilling or unable to solve this democratic task itself. In *Labour in Irish History*, Connolly put forward 'two propositions upon which this book is founded', firstly, that:

in the evolution of civilisation the progress of the fight for national liberty of any subject nation must, perforce, keep pace with the progress of the struggle for liberty of the most subject class in that nation, and that the shifting of economic and political forces which accompanies the development of the system of capitalist society leads inevitably to the increasing conservatism of the non-working-class element, and to the revolutionary vigour and power of the working class.

Secondly, that:

the middle class, growing up in the midst of the national struggle, and at one time, as in 1798, through the stress of the economic rivalry of England almost forced into the position of revolutionary leaders against the political despotism of their industrial competitors, have now also bowed the knee to Baal, and have a thousand economic strings in the shape of investments binding them to English capitalism as against every sentimental or historic attachment drawing them toward Irish patriotism.

Consequently, Connolly argued, 'only the Irish working class remain as the incorruptible inheritors of the fight for freedom in Ireland'.[808]

It must be stressed, however, that Connolly reached this conclusion through a completely different series set of steps than Trotsky. Trotsky based himself on the theory of combined and uneven development, which emphasised the historic belatedness and weakness of the Russian bourgeoisie and the strategic power of the working class. Connolly's 'two propositions', included in the Foreword written after the bulk of the book was completed, feel tacked on, rather than running like a thread through the work as a whole. Connolly lacks the sort of rigorous analysis of the social formation and its class dynamics that can be found with Trotsky. Connolly's overall argument is premised, rather, on a cluster of related claims: the oppression of Ireland is both political and social; the Irish bourgeoisie developed on the basis of a historic rupture with Gaelic civilisation and is therefore 'apostate'; Irish history is characterised fundamentally by a struggle between two competing forms of property; and that therefore the national revolution would also be a socialist revolution in effecting a return, on a higher historical plane, to forms of communal property.

Whether the theory of permanent revolution is applicable to Ireland depends, above all, on the specificity of the Irish social formation. Methodologically, Trotsky placed great importance on the need to 'deduce the character of [a revolution] not from *a priori* definitions and not from historical analogies, but from the living structure of [a given] society and from the dynamics of its inner forces'.[809] It follows, therefore, that permanent revolution is a schema applicable only in certain circumstances, namely 'countries with a belated bourgeois development, especially the colonial and semi-colonial countries …'. In particular, a key dynamic in Trotsky's theory was the failure of the bourgeoisie to solve the land question. Indeed, Trotsky wrote, 'in a backward country the numerically weak proletariat could not attain power if the tasks of the peasantry had been solved during the preceding stage'. Rather, 'the dictatorship of the proletariat appeared probable and even inevitable on the basis of the bourgeois revolution precisely because there was no other power and no other way to solve the tasks of the agrarian revolution'.[810] The Russian working class, then, was able to take power on the back of a peasant land war, promising to turn over the land to the peasants. This unsolved land issue provided a veritable powder keg, enabling the Russian working class, through a strategic alliance with the peasantry, to overthrow the Tsar and the bourgeois Provisional Government in March and November 1917.

Ireland, of course, historically *did* have a land issue. In 1905, Michael

Davitt, leader of the Land League, entitled his book about the struggle of the peasants against the landlords *The fall of feudalism in Ireland*. This was not much of an exaggeration, given that before the reforms introduced by successive British governments between 1870 and 1903, landlords could simply confiscate the fruits of any improvements by tenants through rack-renting and evictions. Without a lease or any protection from eviction, 'tenants were unwilling to finance improvements on the land because the landlord, as owner of the land, reaped all the benefits upon eviction'. Such a state of affairs 'thwarted the process of capital accumulation necessary for the development and modernization of Irish agriculture'.[811]

From the standpoint of permanent revolution, what makes the Irish case more complex, however, is the role of British imperialism in attempting to solve the land question itself. After 1870, the British government set out, in Gladstone's words, 'to pacify Ireland', under pressure from Fenian terrorism and the growth of Michael Davitt's radical movement for land reform. It saw through a form of 'bourgeois revolution from above', pushed forward by land reform, and inaugurated a system under which tenants could use loans to buy out their landlords, thus transferring land ownership from the landlords to a new class of Irish smallholders and capitalist farmers. Arguably, these reforms undercut a key dynamic of the agricultural revolution which would have made the strategy of permanent revolution operable in Ireland. As one historian has commented, the social and political aspects of the revolution were severed:

> Between 1879 and 1923, Ireland experienced two revolutions. The first – beginning with the Land War in 1879 and arguably not completely until 1984 when the Land Commission suspended its activities – constituted a social revolution. In effect, the ownership of the land was transferred from the landlord to the tenant, and the class structure was therefore transformed. The second – beginning in 1916 and ending in 1923 – was a political revolution, involving the transfer of state power from one elite to another.[812]

The British government, through its land reform, worked to soften and prevent the outbreak of radical revolution in rural Ireland. Thus, the schema of permanent revolution – understood as a harnessing of the power of the democratic revolution to drive forwards into the socialist one – became ever less telling in these years. If the permanent revolution is understood as this harnessing, the British government, through its land reform, had dampened the powder of the democratic revolution, removing a powerful source of revolutionary energy. As we saw in chapter 3, Connolly did try to theorise a link between the working class and the Irish peasantry. This proved difficult, however, given the attachment of the peasantry to peasant proprietorship. As Connolly had long recognised, this had negative implications for his formulation of socialism. 'Land for the people' in the form of peasant proprietorship meant that 'there are now 40,000 more individuals interested in maintaining private ownership of land than there were in 1885.'[813]

Indeed, as we have seen, in 1902 Davitt himself acknowledged and regretted that his own proposals for land nationalisation had failed because of the hunger for individual proprietorship amongst the peasantry. A 'plan of Land Nationalisation such as I hoped amidst the many pleasing dreams of Portland Prison might forever solve the Irish agrarian problem,' Davitt wrote, 'will not recommend itself to the people of Ireland. There are some faiths which cannot move Irish mountains,' he complained, 'and I have to confess that mine has proved to be one of them.'[814]

In less than a decade, however, a rather different faith was to move Irish mountains: working-class militancy in the form of 'Larkinism'.

Chapter 6

The Dublin Lockout

So far we have considered two of Dangerfield's 'grievances' against the British Liberal government: Irish nationalism and the campaign for women's suffrage. Now let us turn to the third, the tremendous wave of working-class struggles which erupted in Great Britain and Ireland in the years immediately preceding the First World War. As we shall see, the wave of strikes which spread across these isles reached their pinnacle in the Dublin Lockout of 1913-14.

This four-month struggle convulsed Ireland's capital and captured the imagination of radical workers in Great Britain and beyond. The Lockout posed the question of which class would rule a post-Home Rule Ireland: the working class, organised primarily through Larkin and the IGTWU, or the Irish Catholic bourgeoisie, headed by the predominant Dublin capitalist, William Martin Murphy. As Connolly said at the height of the Lockout: 'The Dublin fight is more than a trade union fight; it is a great class struggle, and recognised as such by all sides.'[815]

The struggle divided Ireland, forcing all political movements to pick a side. During the course of the dispute, Connolly reported, with some satisfaction, that 'all the intellect, the soul and the spirit of the nation ... had been drawn gradually as if by a magnet' to the side of the workers. He continued: 'Publicists of all kinds, philanthropists, literary men, lovers of their kind, poets, brilliant writers, artists, have all been conquered by the valiant heroism of the Dublin workers, have all been drawn within the ranks of the friends of the fighters of labour ...'[816] As well as this moral support, during the Lockout, the IWFL in particular gave practical help, running soup kitchens at Liberty Hall, the strike headquarters. 'That gesture,' writes the biographer of one leading IWFL activist, Hanna Sheehy-Skeffington,

> had nothing to do with charity and everything to do with the expression of solidarity in the class struggle ... The experience did much to cement ties

between militant feminists and others who would concentrate on forging links between nationalists and the labour movement.[817]

This chapter will examine how the solidarity movement for the Dublin Lockout drew on the connections between the most radical sections of the British and Irish labour and socialist movements, to create a movement which shook the Irish capitalist class, the British government, and the British trade union bureaucracy to its core. First though, let us consider the background to the Lockout, and how its outstanding leader, Jim Larkin, arrived in Ireland.

'Larkinism'

'A spectre is haunting all Europe!' declared the December 1913 issue of the Chicago-based *International Socialist Review*:

> Parliaments are debating on how to fight it. Kings and emperors are concerned with its menacing significance. The capitalist class is arming to protect itself against it. The spectre is what the daily newspapers call fearfully 'Larkinism'.[818]

Jim Larkin was the man most responsible for transformation of the Irish labour movement in this period. Born in Liverpool to poor Irish parents in 1876, Larkin left school at the age of eleven, and found work as a docker in the late 1890s. Already Larkin was a socialist, having joined the Independent Labour Party before he turned seventeen. 'For the next fifteen years,' wrote his biographer, 'he was always to be found in the front rank of militant British Socialists, preaching and prophesying the coming of the Social Revolution.'[819]

Thought it might seem strange in light of his later career, young Larkin had little time for strikes. He saw them largely as a distraction from the ultimate goal of socialism, which was to be achieved primarily through political action.[820] Such was the disconnect between the end goal and the trade union movement that Larkin worked as a foreman, with a reputation for driving the dockers hard. Larkin was far from alone in this; he was shaped by the character of the socialist movement of that time. As Connolly, who himself had seen strikes as a mere palliative in his earlier period as a socialist agitator, later recalled,

> [if] it were now possible to examine the socialist speeches of that period we would find that an inordinately large proportion of time was given up

in them to a belittling of industrial action and to what was practically an exaggeration of the ease and facility with which the working class could achieve its rights at the ballot-box.[821]

Though Larkin remained a political socialist, it was as a trade union leader that he would come to prominence and make his greatest impact. Larkin's active involvement in trade unionism came in 1905 as a result of hard experience. As a member of the NUDL, Larkin was sacked following a dispute in which his employer withdrew recognition from the union, and Larkin took a leading role on the strike committee. Blacklisted for his efforts, and without work, he was taken on by NUDL as an organiser for the ports of Scotland and Ireland.

In 1907, Larkin arrived in Belfast, where he was to have early success. Through the use of militant methods, such as the sympathetic strike, a practice whereby workers not directly involved in disputes refuse to handle 'tainted goods' from employers whose employees are on strike, Larkin had within months recruited 2,900 dockers and carters in Belfast and 1,000 in Derry.[822] In May 1907, dockers working for the Belfast Steamship Company walked off the job in pursuit of higher pay, shorter hours and union recognition. With the larger companies on the docks not prepared to negotiate, the strike spread. In response to attempts to break the strike by importing scab labour, Larkin extended the action to the carters in early July. The strike temporarily transcended the sectarian divide, with the mainly unskilled and Catholic dockers and carters being joined by skilled Protestant shipyard workers on the picket lines and in demonstrations in working-class areas of the city. As the struggle intensified, even the Royal Irish Constabulary (RIC) mutinied, prompting a flood of troops into the city that resulted in serious fighting leading to the death of two Catholic bystanders on 12 August.

Larkin's methods, though they won the support and loyalty of the workers, were anathema to the NUDL leadership, headed by James Sexton. Sexton was a one-time radical whose comfortable position as NUDL general secretary since 1893 led him eventually to a knighthood, a seat in Parliament and a place in the political establishment. Well down this road by 1907, seeing his role as managing class tensions rather than prosecuting workers' struggle, Sexton persuaded the carters to return to work with increased pay but no recognition, leaving the dockers to go down fighting alone. It was a betrayal, and one that Larkin would never forget.

Meanwhile, Larkin was also at work establishing the NUDL in Dublin, and was engaged in a dispute involving both dockers and carters in November and December 1908. Before long, 'Larkin and his supporters had established NUDL branches in every major port in Ireland'.[823] His militant methods, however, including the use of aggressive picketing, which led to clashes with both strike-breakers and the police, brought Larkin increasingly into conflict with Sexton and the union's executive. On 7 December, relations between the two men broke down completely, and Sexton suspended Larkin from his position in the union.

In response, Larkin moved quickly. On 28 December 1908, a meeting took place 'of delegates representing the carters, dockers, and other trades of Dublin, Dundalk, Cork, and Waterford for the purposes of forming a new Irish Trade Union for those engaged in the distributive trades'.[824] Up until this point, Larkin's conception of international solidarity meant, for him, remaining in British unions and he had opposed the formation of a separate Irish union when floated by some radical trade unionists, including William O'Brien, in early 1908. There were indications, however, that as 1908 went on, Larkin was starting to revise this position. According to O'Brien, Larkin had commented that 'it might be that the best way to bring Irish workers into line with the workers of the world was to organise them on Irish lines first. He couldn't say yet whether he would put his hand to the plough – but if he did he would not turn back.'[825]

Sexton's actions essentially made Larkin's mind up for him. There would be no turning back: Larkin broke with NUDL, formally establishing the ITGWU on 4 January 1909. The union soon won members from NUDL in most of the ports in Ireland. Sexton tried to crush the ITGWU at birth, including by colluding with employers in Cork to have Larkin imprisoned in a row over the use of funds during the Dublin carters' strike. These efforts backfired, however, and Larkin quickly emerged as a national focus for a growing wave of militancy.

Larkin's allies, too, were becoming an increasingly influential voice in the wider labour movement. In the years immediately before Larkin arrived in Ireland, a group of more progressive young trade unionist had emerged: 'the forward element', including O'Brien, P.T. Daly, Michael O'Lehane, William Murphy and William P. Partridge, and had established a base in the Dublin Trades Council (DTC). Along with his allies, Larkin now began to transform the wider Irish labour movement. By 1909, the tide was turning with Daly, O'Brien and Murphy on the executive of the ITUC. The following year the ITGWU finally won recognition at the ITUC Congress.[826] In 1911, the ITGWU established itself on a sure footing, growing from 5,000 to 18,000 members by the year end.[827]

As Emmet O'Connor has argued, the ITGWU made a virtue out of the necessity of breaking from NUDL, and set out 'explicitly to decolonise labour consciousness, arguing that Irish workers should rely on their own resources to build a movement geared to tackling native conditions'.[828] Forming the new union, asserts a more recent account, 'was a separatist act in itself and was the basis for the socialist republicanism that emerged in the following decades' as a specific labour movement ideology, as distinct from the turn towards left-wing populism within the Irish Republican Army (IRA) during the Irish Civil War 1922-3.[829] Larkin's view on nationalism and internationalism was expressed succinctly in the union's newspaper, the *Irish Worker,* in a debate about forming an Irish Labour Party, a proposal which Larkin and his allies strongly supported. It was an abuse, Larkin argued, of the word 'Internationalism' to claim

> that the Irish working class should sink their identity as a Nation, and join the English Labour Party. Whilst I agree that the formation of the English Labour Party was, and is, the best thing the English Workers have ever done, so too, the formation of the Irish Labour Party would be the best day's work ever attempted by the Irish Workers. The World cannot afford to allow the Irish Nation to be obliterated. Internationalism means *Internationalism* not *one* Nationalism.[830]

Yet, though its Irish roots are crucial, at the same time, 'Larkinism' as a phenomenon should rightly be regarded as part of the wider explosion of militancy internationally and within the British Isles. In one sense, 'Larkinism gave an Irish expression to an international acceleration of class conflict' associated with the rise of syndicalism in Europe and the United States.[831] Connolly himself recognised this wider dimension when describing the tactics employed by the ITGWU in the Belfast shipyards during a dispute over the responsibility for a workplace accident. 'We have just had, and taken, the opportunity in Belfast,' he reported in the *Irish Worker* on 16 September 1911,

> to put into practice a little of what is known on the Continent of Europe as 'Direct Action' … ignoring all the legal and parliamentary ways of obtaining redress for the grievances of Labour, and proceeding to rectify these grievances by direct action upon the employer's most susceptible part – his purse.[832]

More precisely still, 'Larkinism' has been described as representing what Bob Holton has termed 'proto-syndicalism', that is, 'something less than social revolutionary but more than trade union consciousness'. Newsinger has described it as a 'combination of very diverse elements: syndicalism, industrial unionism, labourism, socialism, republicanism and Catholicism', all held together by 'the principle of working-class solidarity ... the central ethnic of the ITWGU, the core around which everything else revolved'.[833] This principle of working-class solidarity was concretised, in the form of the tactics, by the practice of the sympathetic strike. As Connolly defined it, the sympathy strike was a recognition

> that the capitalist cannot be successfully fought upon the industrial field unless we recognise that all classes of workers should recognise their common interests, that such recognition implied that an employer engaged in a struggle with his workpeople should be made taboo or tainted, that no other workers should cooperate in helping to keep his business growing, that no goods coming from his works should be handled by organised workers, and no goods going to his works should be conveyed by organised workers. That he should, in effect, be put outside the pale of civilisation, and communication with him should be regarded as being as deadly a crime as correspondence with an enemy in war time.[834]

This sort of trade unionism came as a nasty shock to the Dublin bosses. W.P. Ryan, the socialist writer and early historian of the labour movement, wrote how the employers viewed Larkin's practices as

> not only revolutionary, but incomprehensible. They regarded the social and industrial system they knew as part of the order of nature ... they could understand working men (and to some extent even working women) desiring more wages, for from time to time they had come up against this hunger of the proletariat. But there was a regular way to present these demands ... The sudden 'sympathetic' strike, the impudent refusal to handle 'tainted goods', and all such methods of 'Larkinism' and Connollyism were on a par with conspiracy and assassination.[835]

The tactic, Connolly insisted, was not born of 'mere cool reasoning' but 'out of our desperate necessity'. That the labour movement in Dublin made pioneering use of the sympathetic strike 'is due to the fact that in this city what is known as general or unskilled labour bears a greater proportion to the whole body of workers than elsewhere'. Hence, the workers are a more moveable, fluctuating body, are more often as individuals engaged in totally dissimilar industries than in the English cities, where skilled trades absorb so great a proportion, and keep them so long in the one class of industry.[836]

A modern evaluation of the 1911 census bears this analysis out. Emmet O'Connor writes:

Of some 900,000 employees, 348,670 were classed as agricultural or general labourers, 170,749 were in domestic or related service, and 201,717 worked in textiles and dressmaking. Thus, over seven out of every nine employees were to be found in largely unorganised, subsistence-waged employment. Trade unions were located mainly in the shipbuilding and engineering trades (30,234 workers); construction (which included 49,445 craftsmen); the tiny skilled grades in textiles and clothing; and the constellation of butchers, bakers, and candlestick-makers who held such a high profile in the pre-Larkinite ITUC.[837]

What Larkin realised was that among the 'general workers, those employed in transport and essential services, who operated at the hinges of commercial infrastructure where strikes would have an immediate and widespread effect, were most favourably placed to take successful industrial action'. These workers would, in turn, act as a bridge to organising other workers, with the ultimate ambition of establishing One Big Union.

Within the British Isles, 'Larkinism' anticipated by a few years an unprecedented wave of militant industrial action, which soon swept Great Britain too. As Walter Kendall has described it:

The mass strike wave of 1910 to 1914 remains unique in British history. A wild, elemental, pent-up force seemed suddenly let loose, disregarding precedents and agreements, impatient of compromise, shaking the old complacent trade unionism by the ears, sometimes, as in the rail strike of 1911, forcing conservative leaders ahead of it like fallen leaves driven before an autumn wind. The trade union leaders, almost to a man, deplored it, the government viewed it with alarm ... yet disregarding everything, encouraged only by a small minority of syndicalist leaders, the great strike wave rolled on, threatening to sweep away everything before it.[838]

In this context, the Dublin Lockut should also be seen as part of a dynamic cross-channel interaction with events in the UK.[839] Indeed, the Lockout had huge potential to encourage widespread rank-and-file activity in the British labour movement, spurred on by the radical syndicalist current of the British labour movement represented by the *Daily Herald*. As we shall see, this potential source of strength also represented a challenge to the position of the British trade union leaders. Their role in misdirecting and demobilising the movement of solidarity for Dublin was one of the reasons for the Lockout's ultimate defeat in early 1914.

The strike begins

The Dublin Horse Show opened on Monday 25 August 1913. 'The social side,' wrote the nationalist *Freeman's Journal,* 'is always one of its great attractions, as this year, 'a more than usually large number of distinguished visitors' were expected. Hotels rooms were at a premium, as polite Anglo-Irish society looked forward to the week-long spectacle.[840] Yet, despite the display being prepared for the various dignitaries and visitors, beneath the surface all was not well in the British Empire's second city. The structure of Dublin's economy meant poverty and insecurity for the majority of its inhabitants. Employment in manufacturing in Dublin had declined in percentage terms throughout the course of the previous century and employed only 24 per cent of the city's working population in 1911. Dublin became, instead, a transport city, with many manual workers, in the words of one contemporary, making their living 'by carrying things from one spot to another', for low pay and in casual employment. While transport, general labouring and work at Dublin's port became increasingly important for its population, Dublin's position as a port city declined. 'In 1857 Dublin had been the largest port in Ireland and the fifth largest in Britain as a whole,' writes Newsinger, 'but by 1907 it had been overtaken by Belfast as Ireland's largest port and was twelfth in Britain.' The result was a city which could not provide sufficient employment opportunities for its own inhabitants, let alone for the surplus agricultural population.[841]

Much of Dublin's working-class population lived in overcrowded slum housing, with the 1911 census recording that 22.9 per cent of the city's population was living in one room. These statistics rank amongst the worst in Europe at the time, and tuberculosis was responsible for a death rate comparable, according to one study, 'with cities such as Cairo, Moscow or Madras'.[842] Of course, as Connolly himself was to comment,

> the high death-rate of Dublin is seen to be entirely due to economic causes, to rise and fall with economic classes. The rich of Dublin enjoy as long an immunity from death as do their kind elsewhere; it is the slaughter of

Dublin's poor that gives the Irish metropolis its unenviable and hateful notoriety amongst civilised nations.[843]

Amidst this bleak picture, Larkin and the ITGWU sought to restore a sense of dignity to Ireland's working population. As well as fighting for material improvements, the union aimed to raise the moral and cultural level of its members. Towards this end, it purchased Croydon Park, a house and three acres of land, to provide a recreational centre for its members. Along with a spirit of 'independence and self-reliance' in the workshop, commented the *Irish Worker,*

> also the workers are realising that they require a fuller and more enjoyable life. If employers and their families need lawns and gardens to sport in, then the workers and their families need them also … The idea may be revolutionary, but it is merely bare justice nevertheless.[844]

This had nothing to do with charity but had a direct bearing on working-class organisation and consciousness. By the eve of the Lockout, wrote Connolly:

> Out of this class of slaves the labourers of Dublin, the Irish Transport and General Workers' Union has created an army of intelligent self-reliant men, abhorring the old arts of the toady, the lickspittle, and the crawler and trusting alone to the disciplined use of their power to labour or to withdraw their labour to assert and maintain their right as men.[845]

The fantastic growth of the ITGWU saw it expand into new sectors, including agricultural labourers. By the summer of 1913, Larkin 'controlled almost all the unskilled labour in Dublin with the exception of the Corporation labourers and the builders' labourers, who were organised in their own unions'.[846] Not surprisingly, Larkin was boasting that Dublin was the best organised city in the world, with only Arthur Guinness's brewery and William Martin Murphy's Dublin United Tramway Company beyond the writ of the Transport Union. The British government's own report into what it termed the 'Dublin Disturbances' shows the rising level of the class struggle, and the increasing anger of the Dublin working class against the police:

> The year 1913 was a period of industrial unrest in Dublin. Between the end of January and the middle of August, 1913, no less than thirty strikes took

place in the City, many of which were accompanied by actual violence and intimation, resulting in prosecutions and convictions in some forty-five cases.[847]

The growing strength of the ITGWU did not go unnoticed by Dublin's employers. Murphy, a former Home Rule MP and 'the nearest thing Ireland had had to a multi-millionaire', was the owner of the *Irish Independent,* Ireland's largest department store, Dublin's most prominent hotel, and had railroad interests in Ireland, Africa and Argentina. Murphy also had interests in the municipal electric tramway systems in several British cities and was attacked variously by Larkin in the pages of the *Irish Worker* as the 'tramway tyrant', a 'capitalist sweater' and as a 'blood-sucking vampire'.[848] As should now be obvious, there was no love lost between the two men.

Conflict between Murphy and the Transport Union was inevitable, as the Dublin capitalist class sought to check the growth of 'Larkinism'. Murphy struck first. On 19 August, the magnate sacked 60 union members in the despatch department of the *Irish Independent* newspaper. When the ITGWU responded by 'blacking' the paper (instructing union members to refuse to handle it), Murphy sacked 200 union members working in the parcel department of the Dublin United Tramways. Murphy's intention was clear; he wanted to break the Transport Union, and this was only the beginning. The union quickly responded by formalising demands for higher pay, more time off and overtime for Sunday working but the company refused even to meet ITGWU union representatives.

On 23 August, the workers met at Liberty Hall and decided, by a large majority, to strike. Thus, on the second day of the Horse Show, at 9.40 in the morning, conductors and drivers in Dublin pinned the Red Hand badge of the ITGWU to their lapels and walked off the job, bringing the city's transport system to a grinding halt. The tracks connecting the city centre to its middle-class suburbs lay idle, and crowds looked on as fifteen empty trams blocked the tracks in Sackville Street under the shadow of Nelson's pillar.[849] Ireland's greatest labour conflict had begun.

Repression

On the day the strike began, Tuesday 26 August, Larkin announced in the press that the ITGWU would hold a huge meeting on O'Connell Street the following Sunday. It was promptly banned by the Dublin Metropolitan Police on the grounds that 'the object of such Meeting or Assemblage is seditious' and 'would cause terror and alarm to, and dissension between, his Majesty's subjects …'.[850] On Friday 29 August, Connolly arrived from

Belfast and, along with Larkin, addressed a crowd outside Liberty Hall, promising to defy the banning order. The following afternoon, the police arrested Connolly and charged him with incitement to cause a breach of the peace. 'Connolly refused to be bound over and informed the court that he did not recognise the English government in Ireland' and was subsequently given a sentence of three months.[851]

Connolly soon declared a hunger strike, taking inspiration from the struggle of the suffragettes in the WSPU. Contemporaries immediately drew the parallels between the two causes, with the *Irish Citizen* describing Connolly as the 'the first non-suffragette hunger-striker'.[852] As Hanna Sheehy-Skeffington recalled, Connolly 'did not hesitate to borrow the weapon used by the militant women, the hunger-strike, when occasion arose – at a time too when certain men leaders were condemning it scornfully as "womanish"'.[853]

At this time, the campaign for women's suffrage was reaching its height. In response to the widespread use of hunger strike tactics, the government resorted to force-feeding the imprisoned women. In the face of a widespread public outcry, it introduced the 1913 Prisoners (Temporary Discharge for Ill-Health) Act, commonly known as the Cat and Mouse Act, which allowed for the early release of prisoners at risk of death from hunger striking. Once recovered, they were to be recalled to prison, whereupon they commonly resumed their protest. When Connolly was released after seven days, the Irish suffragist movement reported that:

No attempt was made to feed him forcibly, or to apply the Cat and Mouse Act. Whereas in the case of Suffragist Hunger-Strikers, all 'privileges' … were withdrawn immediately on the commencement of the Hunger-Strike, Mr. Connolly was permitted to receive visitors for the first three days of his fast, until his weakness necessitated his removal to hospital; and his supply of newspapers and letters does not appear to have been interrupted.[854]

Suffragists pointed to Connolly's more lenient treatment, asserting that it was down to the potential electoral support wielded by the labour movement, as an argument for the necessity of struggling for the vote. A meeting was held in Belfast on 11 October outside the City Hall 'to protest against the Cat and Mouse torture being meted out to our women in Great Britain, the speeches being delivered from a waggonette decorated with the indomitable purple-green-and-white flags …'. According to a report in the *Irish Citizen,* one of the speakers contrasted the treatment of James Connolly, recently hunger-striking in Mounty, with that of the 'mice', and showed that the difference was due to the man carrying too many votes from his supporters to enable torture to be safe. She showed that the wicked Act has done away with forcible feeding, which has been condemned as physically disastrous and as an outrage on human dignity.[855]

As we saw with Connolly's imprisonment, from the very beginning the authorities were determined to respond to the strike using repression and force. On 28 August, Larkin and the rest of the ITGWU leadership were arrested and charged with seditious libel, seditious conspiracy and unlawful assembly. Released on bail, Larkin immediately went into hiding and announced his intention to defy the ban on the O'Connell Street meeting planned for Sunday 31 August. The night before, fighting broke out between striking workers and the police, and two union members, James Nolan and James Byrne, were clubbed to death. By the morning of the meeting itself, two men lay dead and 200 were injured. As the government commission reported: 'On the 30th and 31st August, and 1st and 21st September, 1913, fifteen separate and distinct riots took place in the City of Dublin.' As a result of these, 'two deaths are attributable to injuries received as a result of baton charges which took …The jury at the inquest found that death was caused by fracture of the skull, and compression of the brain.'[856]

Larkin, meanwhile, had been hiding out at the house of Count and Countess Markievicz in Rathmines, in Dublin's southside. Determined not to give in to the banning order, Larkin donned a disguise, dressing up as an elderly clergyman, complete with hair powder, a false beard and spectacles. Riding in a carriage, at 1.30 in the afternoon Larkin pulled up to the Imperial Hotel on O'Connell Street, owned by none other than William Martin Murphy. Accompanied by a young woman posing as his niece, Larkin 'made for the first floor, nonchalantly lighting a cigar as he went, sauntered into the dining room, walked to the French windows overlooking O'Connell Street, stepped out on to the balcony, and began to speak'.[857] Once the crowd recognised Larkin on the balcony, it surged forward excitedly. The police responded by violently clearing the streets, indiscriminately clubbing all in their wake. Within minutes, over 400 people were injured. When news of the police brutality spread throughout working-class Dublin, the police came under attack from angry crowds, sparking running battles which would last well into the next day.[858]

On 2 September, the situation escalated. What had started as a dispute between the ITGWU and Murphy's Dublin United Tramways company now became a general lockout, as the employers sought to press home their advantage in the wake of the police repression. Having agreed a lockout in principle on 29 August, the bosses put it into practice on 2 September when Dublin coal merchants locked out their workers. Other employers followed suit, ánd by the end of the month around 25,000 workers were locked out by other 400 employers.[859] Writing on the eve of the Lockout, as the press campaign was building in anticipation of the bosses' actions, Connolly was defiant: 'Let them declare their lock-out; it will only hasten the day when the working class will lock-out the capitalist class for good and all.' He added: 'if it is going to be a wedding, let it be a wedding; and if it is going to be a wake, let it be a wake: we are ready for either.'[860]

Solidarity efforts

One effect of the police's actions on 30-31 August was to thrust the events in Dublin into the consciousness of the international socialist movement. From exile, Lenin reported in early September in *Severnaya Pravda* that:

> The police have positively gone wild; drunken policemen assault peaceful workers, break into houses, torment the aged, women and children. Hundreds of workers (over 400) have been injured and two killed – such are the casualties of this war. All prominent workers' leaders have been arrested. People are thrown into prison for making the most peaceful speeches. The city is like an armed camp.[861]

The British TUC was meeting in Manchester from 1-6 September and, impressed by a deputation from DTC, resolved that a delegation 'be sent to Dublin to address meetings in favour of free speech, the right of organisation and free meetings, and to inquire into the allegations of police brutality'.[862] Keir Hardie, the British Labour leader, always instinctively sympathetic to the workers' side, arrived in Dublin on 2 September to visit Larkin in prison and attend the funeral of James Nolan. The situation in Dublin was, in his judgement, 'the most serious event the Trades Union Movement has had to face for at least a century'.[863] In response to its report to the TUC's Parliamentary Committee on 23 September, an appeal for funds was issued immediately, and donations flew in as a result of 'factory gate collections, shop stewards' speeches and explanations, band concerts, individual efforts at flower sales or a few pints taking a serious mood ...'.[864]

The TUC organised a relief effort, which saw a British food ship, the *Hare*, arrive in Dublin on 27 September. It brought a cargo of food worth £5,000 and considerable moral comfort and support to the Dublin workers, who realised that they did not fight alone. Between October 1913 and January 1914, food shipments worth £6,000 would travel to Dublin from the TUC-organised effort, accompanied by substantial financial assistance, and additional money was raised by individual trade unions and union branches, the Co-operative movement, trades councils and socialist organisations. One estimate puts the overall figure raised by the British labour movement for the Dublin workers at around £150,000, the equivalent of £10,000,000 in today's money.[865]

The *Daily Herald,* too, gave extensive coverage to the police events, written on the spot by its correspondent, Francis Sheehy-Skeffington. The newspaper was to become central to the campaign to build support for the Dublin workers in the British labour movement, with much of the activity driven by the Irish socialist W.P. Ryan, who was one of the paper's deputy editors. The *Herald* had begun as a strike paper during the January 1911 printers' dispute. It was relaunched on 15 April 1912, and soon reached a circulation of between 50,000 and 100,000 copies an issue, reaching 'a significant proportion of the most advanced sections of the British working class'.[866] The paper's 'outstanding characteristics', wrote one historian of the *Herald,* 'were established from its first issue. It was financially and organisationally anarchic and politically disinclined to take orders from anyone.'[867] Raymond Postgate, the socialist writer and historian, who worked as a journalist for the *Herald* after the First World War, remembered that 'to get into its columns a writer had only to be a rebel; he had to be an enemy of the existing capitalist system, and what he was in favour of mattered less'.[868] As such, argues Huw Richards:

> in a time of intellectual flux on the left, the *Herald* provided a forum for polemic among and between proponents of guild socialism, syndicalism, Christian socialism and even the distributivism of Hilaire Belloc and G.K. Chesterton. Women's suffrage and the independence movements of Ireland and India also found consistent support.[869]

Resolutely militant, the paper caught the mood of the times, with its one-time editor George Lansbury recalling that it 'could with truth be said of us that wherever a strike took place there we were in the midst'. In particular, the *Herald* promoted a policy of militant rank-and-file action and was not afraid to criticise moderate trade union or Labour leaders who stood in the way. In its syndicalist critique of the conservative role of the trade union bureaucracy, 'the policy of the paper was not merely unofficial,' said Lansbury, 'it was avowedly anti-official'.[870]

The paper urged a general strike in support of the Dublin workers and, all across the country, Herald Leagues, set up to support the paper financially, threw themselves into organising meetings and collecting funds in support of ITGWU. One of the most ambitious, and controversial, solidarity efforts undertaken by supporters of the *Herald* would be a scheme to re-house the children of locked-out workers with sympathetic families from the British labour movement. It is to this we now turn.

The Children's Exodus

The scheme for British labour movement families to look after the children of locked-out Dublin workers was the brainchild of Dora Montefiore. Dismissed outrageously in one account of the Lockout as 'a well-known social worker', Montefiore, as we have seen, was in fact an experienced labour movement activist, and a serious socialist feminist, acquainted with Clara Zetkin and other figures of international renown.[871] She would go on to become a founder of the CPGB, and serve as the only women on its first executive.[872]

The idea of the scheme was that supporters in labour movement and socialist organisations in Great Britain would make their homes available for the hungry children of Lockout Dublin workers, providing them with somewhere safe and warm to stay for the duration of the dispute. This was not a mere charitable effort but was based on labour movement tactics which had been employed to good effect in several European countries and very recently by the IWW in the Lawrence Textile Strike in January 1912.

In Lawrence, Massachusetts, 30,000 workers employed in wooden mills struck against attempts to drive down wages in response to state legislation restricting working hours for women and children. As the strike dragged on throughout the cold New England winter, 'a proposal was made by some of the strikers that we adopt a method used successfully in Europe – to send their children out of Lawrence to be cared for in other cities.'[873] According to the IWW newspaper *Solidarity*, the suggestion came from a Franco-Belgian striker, who told the strike committee of how the tactic had been used in labour disputes in Belgium.[874] It had been used to good effect, too, in the 1907-1908 agricultural workers' strike in Parma, during which the chamber of labour organised for strikers' children to board with sympathetic families throughout Northern Italy.[875]

The response was overwhelming. The children were accompanied by the chair of the SPA's Women's Committee, Margaret Sanger, a famous advocate of birth control, and were met by 5,000 people in New York's Grand Central Station. 'People wept when they saw the poor clothes and thin shoes of these wide-eyed little children,' and they were fed in the Labor Temple on East 84th before being introduced to their hosts.[876]

What transformed the situation in Lawrence, bringing much national public sympathy to the workers' cause, was the response of the authorities. On 24 February, the police intervened violently to stop a group of 40 children being accompanied from Lawrence to Philadelphia. Gurley-Flynn, again, recounts how police 'surrounded the station outside to keep others out. Children were pulled and torn away from their parent and a wild scene of brutal disorder took place.' 35 women and children were arrested, and the police station was besieged by strikers. 'It was a day without parallel in American labour history,' the IWW organiser later reflected. 'A reign of terror prevailed in Lawrence, which literally shook America.'[877] One recent history of the strike concurs, arguing that the authorities' response to the children's exodus 'proved to be the strike's turning point' in making 'the entire nation witness to the arrogance, stupidity and brutality of Lawrence's employers and public officials'.[878] Writers, political figures, and trade union leaders alike all denounced the police's actions. The events drew the attention of Congress, who investigated the workers' conditions, and the pressure was a factor in the calculation of the bosses to settle the strike in the workers' favour.

After its success in Lawrence, there was good reason to believe that the tactic could work in Dublin. In her autobiography, Montefiore recounts just how the 'children's exodus' idea came to play a role in the Lockout. On 10th October 1913 Montefiore shared a platform at the Memorial Hall in London with Larkin, who had come to appeal for solidarity for the locked-out workers from the British labour movement. 'As I listened to his appalling story,' she recalled, 'it flashed across my mind that here was a great opportunity for organised workers in England to prove their solidarity with the locked-out men in Dublin, by taking into their homes some of the children who were suffering so severely from the effects of industrial strife.' After Larkin's speech, Montefiore 'wrote out a slip of paper and passed it across to him, asking him if a plan like this which had already been successfully carried out by Belgian comrades, and in the Lawrence strike, in the United States, could be arranged through the *Herald* League, would it have his backing'.[879] Larkin agreed, and contemporaries immediately recognised the parallel with the IWW's tactics. 'Larkin took a lesson from the Lawrence strikers,' wrote IWW activist and birth control advocate Caroline Nelson in the *International Socialist Review*, 'and the strike committee planned to send the children of Dublin strikers to their comrades in England to be cared for till the battle was won.'[880]

Under the auspices of the *Daily Herald* and its supporting Leagues, a committee was established by Montefiore. It sent an appeal to a wide range of socialist publications, namely 'the *Clarion,* the *Labour Leader,* the *Citizen,* the *New Age,* the *Express, Justice,* and the Christian Commonwealth', and met a generous response. Montefiore recalls that 'among the letters offering homes many were from trades councils, branches of the Herald League, trade union branches, and other Labour organisations, stating that certain members of the organisation would provide the homes, and that the executive of the organisation would collect funds for fares, clothing, etc'.[881] Understandably wishing to set the record straight, in light of the scheme's eventual failure, Montefiore, 'in order to refute the accusation that our mission to Dublin was an irresponsible one,' stresses the support the scheme received from a range of organisations, and 'the quality of the homes also, and of the beautiful feeling of love for the children which inspired the offer of shelter to the hungry and the naked,' of which 'there can be no manner of doubt'.[882] Having made these arrangements, Montefiore travelled to Dublin to arrange for the transportation of the children. Working out of a room provided by Delia Larkin in Liberty Hall, Montefiore and union organiser Grace Neal began the work of registering children for the scheme. 'The passage leading to our room was blocked from morning till evening with women and children,' Montefiore recalled. 'We tried to let them in only one at a time, but each time the door opened the crush was so great that often two or three mothers forced their way in.'[883]

As Newsinger argues, there was 'every expectation of a great practical and propaganda success. No one expected the police to behave as the Lawrence police had.' But Dublin was not Lawrence: 'What they had miscalculated was the response of the Catholic Church.'[884] The Catholic Church whipped up a hysterical campaign against the proposal. Tapping into deep-rooted fears of 'soupers', Protestant evangelists during the Famine, priests denounced the plot to 'kidnap' good Catholic children and expose them to the malevolence of English Protestants.[885] On 21 October, the Archbishop of Dublin, William Walsh, published a letter in the *Irish Times,* condemning the scheme and warning any women considering taking up the scheme

> that they can be no longer held worthy of the name of Catholic mothers if they so far forget that duty as to send away their children to be cared for in a strange land, without security of any kind that those to whom the poor children are to be handed over are Catholics, or, indeed, are persons of any faith at all ...[886]

Walsh's intervention, one historian writes, was 'taken as a license for holy war by many Catholics'.[887] A wave of mob violence followed, organised by the reactionary AOH aided by priests, seizing their chance to 'get' Larkin and the ITGWU.

Put on the defensive by the Church, the ITGWU, in a major concession, decided instead to send some of the children to Catholic homes in Belfast. With any ostensibly 'religious' objection now satisfied, the anti-union bias of the Church was exposed when the agitation against Larkin continued. Montefiore recalled how, when she reached the train station with Larkin's sister and fellow union organiser Delia Larkin:

At one end of the platform, in front of the compartment into which the parents were attempting to get their children, there was a compact, shouting, gesticulating crowd of Hibs. In the centre of the crowd was the little party of children and parents, and among them were the priests, who were talking, uttering threats against the parents, and forbidding them to send their children to Protestant homes. Some of the women were upbraiding the priests for allowing the children to starve in Dublin; and according to an American paper, whose correspondent was on the platform, 'one woman slapped the face of a priest who was attempting to interfere'.[888]

Unlike the woman who delivered the slap to the face of the interfering priest, the ITGWU was ambivalent in its response to the Church. William Partridge, though complaining about 'the most undeserved and injudicious display of bigotry', nevertheless conceded the Church's right to interfere. The union, Partridge promised, 'would remove any child from a home in England not approved by the local priest there and undertake to place it in any home selected by him'.[889] In response to Walsh's letter, Connolly angrily denounced the Archbishop, writing that if he was 'as solicitous about the poor bodies of those children as we know you to be about their souls' then he would call on the bosses to negotiate an end to the strike.[890] Moreover, he defended Montefiore and Neal, writing that 'we must protest in the name of the whole labour movement of this country against the foul and libellous accusations brought against the noble-minded ladies who have been in charge of the scheme'.

At the same time, however, Connolly used the same article in the Glasgow ILP's *Forward* to not-so-subtly distance himself from the policy of Larkin and Montefiore. In the heat of the struggle, this was a questionable decision, bowing to clerical harassment and undermining Montefiore. Somewhat undercutting his solidarity with Montefiore, Connolly wrote that

[we] do not wonder at our British friends being surprised, nor at them being horrified, nor at them being scandalised and shocked at the treatment to which they have been subjected, and the vile aspersions cast upon their motives. For ourselves we anticipated it all, and have never been enthusiastic towards the scheme.[891]

What followed was an 'explanation' for the clerical intervention, which at times could be read as an apologia:

We realised that their children are about all the workers of Dublin have left to comfort them … and that to part with their dear ones would be like wrenching their hearts asunder. We realised, further … that Great Britain is still an alien country to Ireland, and that even the splendid comradeship and substantial aid of today can hardly expect to obliterate immediately the evil results upon our intercourse of long generations of oppression during the period when class rule stood in Ireland for Great Britain … And we also knew that some of the darkest memories of Ireland were associated with British attempts to stab the heart of Ireland through systematic abduction of the bodies and corruption of the minds of Irish children.[892]

Moreover, Connolly was careful to distinguish between individual Hibernians and priests and the Archbishop himself, who he flattered as a 'gentleman' with 'his own high sense of honour'.[893] It was the Archbishop's very intervention, however, which licensed the extreme reaction 'from below'. As one historian comments, to defeat the children's scheme, 'he allowed his priests to lie and slander, to whip up sectarian hatred and prejudice and to organise vigilante mobs. His responsibility for this cannot seriously be denied.'[894]

It was clear that Connolly was somewhat blinded to the essentially anti-socialist nature of the Church. Though the Archbishop was a nationalist and a supporter of the Land League, who had previously intervened positively in industrial disputes, he viewed the workers from the perspective of Christian charity – not as subjects of their own emancipation. Indeed, he told a meeting of the St. Vincent de Paul on 27 October that although 'the sight of poor ill-clad children makes a powerful appeal to the hearts of our charitable people', they must 'harden their hearts' and give only to respectable charities. Revealingly, the Archbishop complained that the scheme would make the children 'discontented with the poor homes to which they will sooner or later return …'.[895] George Russell, at the Albert Hall rally on 1 November, nailed the true motivations of the Catholic

Church in the whole affair:

> You see, if these children were, even for a little, out of the slums they would
> get discontented with their poor homes. Once getting full meals, they might
> be so inconsiderate to ask for them all their lives. They might destroy the
> interesting experiment carried on in Dublin for generations to find out how
> closely human beings can be packed together, on how little a human being
> can live, and what is the minimum wage an employer need pay him. James
> Larkin interrupted these interesting experiments towards the evolution of
> the underman, and he is in jail.[896]

Connolly's equivocation was indicative of his wider approach to
Catholicism, which attempted to draw a rigid firewall between the sphere
of individual faith – a domain which could be legitimately claimed by
the Church – and wider political questions, from which the Church
should refrain. However neat this division may be in theory, it drastically
underestimated the obstacles to socialism in the way in which religious
ideology – privately held or publicly proclaimed – bound Irish workers to
the Church as an institution, and by implication to the Catholic middle
class. Connolly believed that the Church was not intrinsically anti-socialist
and would ultimately come to the workers' side, just as it begrudgingly and
retrospectively made its peace with the rise of capitalism. 'In the future the
Church,' argued Connolly, 'when it realises that the cause of capitalism
is a lost cause it will find excuse enough to allow freedom of speech and
expression to those lowly priests whose socialist declarations it will then use
to cover and hide the absolute anti-socialism of the Roman Propaganda.'[897]

The subsequent experience of twentieth century Irish workers does
not bear this out. It is understandable that a small and embattled socialist
movement, under attack from the capitalist class, might want to avoid taking
on the Church in a such a deeply Catholic country as Ireland, where faith
and national consciousness were so closely bound together. This approach
was, however, ultimately self-defeating. The intense Catholicity of the Irish
Free State after 1922 would be mobilised against socialists and the labour
movement. In March 1933, one of the casualties would be Connolly House,
the headquarters in Dublin of the Irish Revolutionary Workers Group,
stormed and burned by a several hundred-strong Catholic anti-communist
mob.

Free Larkin

On 28 October, Larkin was imprisoned by the authorities for the charges made against him at the beginning of the dispute. Connolly took over the reigns as acting general secretary of the ITGWU. He quietly retired the 'children's exodus' scheme and immediately launched a campaign to 'Free Larkin', mobilising a tremendous movement of solidarity in Britain and abroad. In an interview with the *Herald* in the wake of Larkin's arrest, Connolly told the paper that

> [the] imprisonment of Larkin is having just the opposite effect to what the Murphy crowd expected. They thought and talked a great deal about the personal magnetism or the tyranny of Larkin as being responsible for the trouble, but they will now see that a strong Trade Union organisation has been quietly built up, and instead of its being weakened by Larkin's imprisonment, it has become more determined and enspirited.[898]

The centrepiece of the campaign was a huge solidarity rally organised in the Albert Hall on Sunday 1 November under the auspices of the *Daily Herald* and its supporters. The paper announced two days beforehand that 'James Connolly will make his first appearance before a great audience of London rebels and democrats, thousands of whom perhaps have but known him dimly so far. There will,' it added, 'be nothing dim in their picture of him henceforth.'[899] The ticket-only event attracted 12,000 people, with a further 20,000 reported to have been turned away, to hear Connolly himself, the playwright George Bernard Shaw, Dora Montefiore, George Lansbury, poet and co-operative activist George Russell (Æ), Delia Larkin, Sylvia Pankhurst, and the socialist and suffrage campaigners Charlotte Despard and Frederick Pethick-Lawrence. The *Irish Citizen* reported on the involvement of the suffragettes in the organising of the rally, commenting that:

> the labour movement which at the moment has its centre in Dublin has many points of interest for suffragists. It has been noted by all commentators, friendly or hostile, that the London demonstration in the Albert Hall, last Saturday, to aid the Dublin locked-out men and to demand the release of Mr. Larkin, was made a success largely through the work of the militant suffragists, both in organising, in stewarding, and among the audience.[900]

This was most strikingly demonstrated by the presence of Sylvia Pankhurst on the platform. Invited to speak by George Lansbury of the

Herald, Pankhurst recalled how she 'was glad to accept the invitation, as an opportunity to show solidarity with the Dublin workers, and to keep the women's side of the struggle to the front'. As well as a display of solidarity, Pankhurst had a further reason to appear, one which speaks to the interplay and mutual inspiration between the suffrage and labour movement struggles. There would be 'much piquancy, and I hoped some embarrassment, for the Government,' recalled Pankhurst, 'in my appearance side by side with two fellow hunger strikers, Connolly and Lansbury, both perfectly at liberty, whilst I was pursued under the "Cat and Mouse" Act.' Pankhurst was out on release under the terms of the Act, but her licence had expired. She was, then, liable to re-arrest and her appearance on the platform exposed her to risk. Her act of defiance electrified the crowd, and she 'for some time could not be heard, owing to the enthusiastic reception accorded her'. She later remembered that 'there was no great difficulty in escaping in a crowd of 10,000 people. I went out with Lansbury and the other speakers, and though the mounted police chased us about, I got away clear, and was at Hackney Baths next night, where the police were against overcome by the solidarity of our gallant crowd.'[901]

'Then', reported the *Herald,* 'came James Connolly. His speech was another masterpiece. Never a misplaced word, never a wasted adjective. Sheer massive argument, and brilliant summary of facts. Here,' its reporter enthused, 'was a man with more statesmanship in his little finger than the whole Cabinet heaped together.'[902] Pankhurst, too, was impressed. Describing Connolly as 'a thick-set, quiet-mannered, serious-looking man, who might have been taken for a comfortable farmer by his appearance,' she recalled that he 'gave a temperate, informative address, in striking contrast to the excitability of old Lansbury and the other speakers.' It was, she said, 'an evidence of the old adage that "still waters run deep"'.[903] As if to make George Dangerfield's point about how the rally drew together a diversity of struggles in a common cause, Connolly declared 'that he stood for opposition to the domination of nation over nation, of class over class, or of sex over sex'. In its coverage, the *Irish Citizen* commented that 'No sentiment of any speaker was so loudly cheered' as this.[904]

After the meeting, the *Herald* wrote excitedly that a 'great result of the militant Suffrage Movement has been to convince many people that the vote is not the best way of getting what one wants ... every day the industrial rebels and the suffrage rebels march nearer together'.[905] Not everyone in the suffrage movement agreed. According to one of Sylvia's biographers, 'Pankhurst's participation in the rally, her speech and the coverage by the *Daily Herald* were too much for the WSPU. These events precipitated the long-awaited split in the suffragette family that would lead to the expulsion of Pankhurst and the federation from the WSPU.'[906] In response to the *Herald*'s report, her sister Christabel angrily denied 'that the WSPU is marching nearer to any other movement or political party' especially the Herald League, 'a class organisation.'[907]

The row captured the essence of Sylvia's difference with her sister and mother in the WSPU leadership. As Sylvia herself argued in January 1914,

> we had more faith in what could be done by stirring up working women … while they had most faith in what could be done by people of mean and affluence … they said a deputation to the Labour Party was all very well for us, but one for the King was better for them.[908]

Another speaker who suffered consequences for his appearance on the platform was George Russell. Russell launched a blistering attack on the Dublin employers and the clergy and hailed the 'labour uprising in Ireland' as 'the despairing effort of humanity to raise itself out of a dismal swamp of disease and poverty'. Larkin, he said, 'may have been an indiscreet leader. He may have committed blunders, but', proclaimed Russell,

> I believe in the sight of heaven the crimes are on the other side. If our Courts of Justice were courts of humanity, the masters of Dublin would be in the dock charged with criminal conspiracy, their crime that they tried to starve out one-third of the people in Dublin, to break their hearts, and degrade their manhood, for the greatest crime against humanity is its own degradation.[909]

Russell's attacks on the priests with 'so little concern for the body at all, that they assert it is better for children to be starved than to be moved from the Christian atmosphere of the Dublin slums' provoked a storm, subjecting him to attacks in the press and an attempt by the Hibernians to close down his newspaper the *Irish Homestead*.[910] He responded with a letter on 11 November, which no Dublin newspaper would publish and was instead distributed as a leaflet. In it, Russell attacked the bias of the press and defended himself against the personal abuse heaped upon him for his stand in support of the workers. 'He withdrew nothing,' commented Newsinger, 'and rode out the controversy.'[911]

Meanwhile, Larkin was still in prison, and the campaign to free him continued. Another aspect of the strategy to win his release had been highlighted by Connolly in his Albert Hall speech. Against echoing the tactics of the suffragettes, Connolly called on working-class voters to punish the Liberal government by voting against them in a series of upcoming by-elections until Larkin was freed. 'We are at war,' Connolly expanded in an article published in the *Irish Worker* on 1 November:

Our enemy is the governing class; the political force of that enemy is the Liberal Government. Next year it may be the Conservative Government, and Sir Edward Carson may be again prosecuting Irish rebels as he did in the past; but this year and this moment it is the Liberal Government that fills the jury box with employers to try strike leaders; that sets policemen to ride roughshod over the law guaranteeing the right of peaceful picketing; who orders the bludgeoning of men and women in the streets of Dublin; that has turned Dublin into an armed camp, in which the citizens walk about in terror of their lives in the presence of uniformed bullies – in short, it is the Liberal Government that has lent itself to the employers to imprison, bludgeon, and murder the Dublin working class ... Therefore, the Liberal Government must go.

Connolly continued:

Larkin is in prison, jailed by this cowardly gang! We appeal to the workers everywhere in these islands to vote against the nominees of that government at every contested election until Larkin is released. To-day we are sending a telegram to the electors of Keighley, asking them, in the name of working class solidarity, to vote against the murderers of Nolan and Byrne, against the bludgeoners of the Dublin working class, against the jailers of Larkin.[912]

On 9 November, the Liberals lost the Reading by-election to a Conservative, while they clung on only narrowly in Linlithgowshire. As the results came in, fireworks went up from the roof of Liberty Hall, celebrating the government's defeat.[913] 'There are explanations,' rued Liberal Chancellor of the Exchequer David Lloyd George, 'the most prominent of which is, probably, Jim Larkin.'[914] Under pressure, the Cabinet gave in. Larkin was released, after serving only seventeen days of his seven-month sentence. He walked free at 7 a.m. on 13 November, less than 24 hours after the Cabinet decision.[915]

Later in the day, Larkin told a crowd of supporters gathered at Beresford Place that the government 'had made a mistake in sending me to prison and have made a greater mistake in letting me out'. That same night, with Larkin resting, Connolly was the main speaker at a huge rally to celebrate Larkin's release. It was, in Padraig Yeates's words, 'one of the largest demonstrations of working-class power ever seen in Dublin'.[916]

Connolly, emboldened, was in a particularly militant mood. 'I am going to talk sedition,' he told the crowd. 'The next time we are out for a march I want to be accompanied by four battalions of trained men with their corporals and sergeants.' Highlighting the discrepancy between the repression meted out to the Dublin workers with the Liberal government's tolerance towards Sir Edward Carson's open defiance of its Home Rule policy, he asked: 'Why should we not drill and train our men in Dublin as they are doing in Ulster?' Connolly's speech foreshadowed the formation of the ICA, the workers' militia which would go on to play an active role in the Easter Rising. '[Every] man who was willing to enlist as a solder in the Labour Army,' Connolly continued, 'should give his name when he drew his strike pay this week-end, and they would be told when and where to attend for drilling. They had got competent officers ready to instruct and lead them, and they could get arms any time they wanted.'[917]

The ICA arose first and foremost as a trade union self-defence force in the heat of the Lockout, 'for the purpose of protecting the working class and preserving its right of public meeting and free association,' as Connolly explained it.[918] The idea had been in circulation for some time, with Larkin floating the idea of a 'workers' army' to defend against the police during the 1908 Dublin carters' strike. In light of the violence of the DMP during the Lockout, the idea had ready appeal. The immediate spur for the formation of such a force in November 1913, however, had a rather unlikely source.

Captain James (Jack) Robert White, D.S.O., was a retired British Army Captain, and son of late Field-Marshal Sir George White, hero of the Siege of Ladysmith during the Second Boer War. A Home Ruler in politics at this point, White suggested to a meeting of the Civic League (a moderate middle-class body concerned to bring the strike to an end through conciliation) 'the formation of a citizen army, as a means by which to bring discipline into the distracted ranks of labour'. The 'title Army was not intended to suggest military action', recalled Rev. R.M. Gwynn of Trinity College who hosted the meeting, 'but merely drill on military lines to keep unemployed men fit and self-respecting'.[919]

White then approached Connolly, as acting general secretary of the ITGWU, and found ready acceptance for his idea. 'Only a figure as politically naive as White,' commented one historian of the Lockout, 'could have failed to realise the direction in which men such as Connolly would take his project.'[920] Even the name, Citizen Army, concealed a dual meaning. At once denoting a sense of civic responsibility, as befitting the worthy enthusiasts of the Civic League, it had at the same time an altogether more radical political resonance. As William O'Brien recollected, 'the name Citizen Army was first introduced in the early '80s in Great Britain. When the Social Democratic Federation was formed it was one of the items on their platform,' and 'their conception of the Citizen Army was an alternative to the standing army of the state.'[921] The SDF position was one common with the parties of the Second International; the German SPD, for example, called in its highly influential Erfurt Program of 1891 for the creation of a *Volkswehr*, a 'people's army in place of the standing armies' and the 1896 London Conference of the Second International endorsed a call for the 'simultaneous abolition of Standing Armies and the establishment of a National Citizen Force'.[922] This concept of the Citizen Army, O'Brien argued, 'is where the title came from'.[923]

Solidarity and bureaucracy

By now, mid-November 1913, the Lockout had been dragging on for well over two months, and conditions were only worsening for the workers and their families. The 'children's exodus' had been a setback, though not a fatal one, and the campaign to free Larkin was a much-needed boost from morale. While Larkin was in prison, however, a new development seriously threatened the prospects for victory: the employers began to import scabs from Britain to replace the locked out workers.

Rumours of such a plan were in the air in late September but did not materialise then. With Larkin in prison, however, the employers now seized the initiative, bringing 50 scabs from Manchester to work in the timber yards on 29 October, protected by the police and allowed to carry pistols with impunity. A week later, a further 160 scabs arrived from Liverpool aboard the Shipping Federation's ship *Ella*. Dublin, further, was flooded by police and troops to protect them, instituting something akin to martial law in the city.

In response, Connolly issued a manifesto, which was plastered across the city, condemning the plan 'to import English scabs to take the bread out of the mouths of Dublin men, women, and children, and to reduce them to slavery'. In it, he appealed to the workers to 'Rally and fight as you never fought before' and, beginning on 10 November, called them to begin mass pickets 'outside the doors or gates of their former employment at the usual hours of labour, commencing at the first hours of opening in the morning'. Connolly's appeal ended:

> Fellow-workers – the employers are determined to starve you into submission, and if you resist, to club you, jail you, and kill you. We defy

them! If they think they can carry on their industries without you, we will, in the words of the Ulster Orangeman, 'Take steps to prevent it'. It is your duty to find the ways and means. Be men now, or be for ever slaves.[924]

The appeal failed. The workers, beaten down, both by hunger and repression, did not respond to the union's call. The ICA, which was formed to protect the pickets from the armed scabs, fought bravely, but against the odds. The situation was critical. From the very moment the bosses generalised the tramway strike into an all-out war to break the Transport Union in early September, Larkin had 'quickly realised that the only way the union could escape being ground down in an unequal war of attrition was if the dispute could be spread to Britain'.[925] What was true in September was even more true in November, given the added urgency of the situation. If the union was not to go down to defeat, the strike had to spread – now.

To this end, Larkin crossed the Irish Sea and embarked upon what he called a 'Fiery Cross' crusade to convince British workers to take industrial action to prevent the bosses sending scabs to Dublin. The first stop on his tour was a rally in the Free Trade Hall in Manchester on 16 November. 'Manchester is ablaze!' reported the *Daily Herald* correspondent covering the meeting. 'Jim Larkin with his fiery cross has come,' and never had the reporter seen a meeting 'so moving, so thrilling, and so momentous as to-day's.' With 4,000 people inside the building and a further 20,000 waiting outside, a wit commented that it 'was easier to get Larkin out of gaol than to get into the meeting'.[926]

Also on the platform that night was an international visitor, Connolly's old comrade from the IWW, Big Bill Haywood. Haywood had been in Paris meeting with leaders of the French syndicalist union federation, the CGT, when he received a letter 'like a call to arms' from *Daily Herald* editor, Charles Lapworth. Lapworth was already known to Haywood from his time touring the United States on the 'Red Special', as Eugene V. Debs' 1908 presidential election campaign train was known. The IWW leader left for England bearing 1,000 francs and a stirring letter of solidarity from Leon Jouhaux on behalf of the CGT praising the Dublin workers' 'great fight [as] an example and encouragement', and sending 'fraternal and international greetings'. Jouhaux's letter concluded with a stirring rallying cry: 'Long live the Union of all proletarians, educated in one and the same hatred of exploitation and one and the same hope of the ultimate and complete victory of Labor.'[927]

Larkin and Haywood met in the Clarion Cafe in Manchester for the first time. A picture exists of the meeting, with Connolly and Ben Tillett also attendance. 'We were not strangers,' Haywood added, 'being acquainted with each other's work.' Haywood recalled the Free Trade Hall rally, in all its excitement:

> So great was the enthusiasm and desire to see and hear Larkin that an overflow crowd of 20,000 stood in the drizzling rain, ankle deep in mud, waiting for him to conclude his speech in the Hall. And what a speech! He described the condition to which capitalism had brought the workers in Dublin, Belfast, Sligo, in Cork and throughout the entire industrial region of the little Green Isle. It was a terrific indictment. The torture and indignities imposed upon the locked-out workers in Dublin by William Martin Murphy and the rest of the Citizens Alliance of Ireland's capital were equalled only by some of the labor struggles that we have known so well in this country.[928]

Key, however, was Larkin's call for workers to take action, speaking over the heads of the trade union leaders themselves: 'You have sent money and moral assistance,' Larkin said, referencing the food ships organised by the TUC and other labour movement bodies. 'You have got me out of jail,' he continued. 'You can get those out of jail who are still in, and get the scabs out of Dublin, and you can get us what we are fighting for – the right to combine. You can do it, and men and women like you ...' Coming to the crucial point now, Larkin told his audience:

> We want to carry out the fundamentals and ethics of Trade Unionism, so don't 'scab' us. Are you going to allow us in Dublin to be offered up as a sacrifice? If not send a message to your leaders and tell them that the employing class in Dublin will not get any help from this side of the water.[929]

From Manchester, Larkin embarked on a widespread tour of working-class Britain. He was intent, reported Haywood,

> [on] carrying his message throughout the length and breadth of Great Britain. The workers in all the great industrial centres such as Cardiff, Swansea, Bristol, Sheffield, Birmingham, Hull, Liverpool, Leicester, New-Castle-on-Tyne, Leeds, Wakefield, Preston, Glasgow, Edinburgh, heard his call for Solidarity, and his demand that British trade unionists should no longer scab on the Transport Workers of Ireland by loading or unloading ships for Dublin or other ports that would affect the strike.[930]

The speaking tour stirred up remarkable interest, with the liberal *Manchester Guardian* commenting

[when] a man's imprisonment raises such a storm of protest that Cabinet Ministers and Members of Parliament cannot speak in the remotest parts of the country without having his name shouted at them, when the chance of hearing him speak fills the Free Trade Hall, and leaves thousands blocking the street outside for a sight of him, even the most convinced and implacable opponent, if he is honest, must admit that he is a man to be reckoned with – must admit, too, that a personal influence so extraordinary must be backed by a cause or a principle that deeply moves his fellow-countrymen.[931]

At the Sheffield rally, Larkin made a lasting impression on one young engineer, Jack Murphy, who heard him speak alongside George Lansbury. 'Six-foot Jim Larkin with his powerful, torrentially passionate eloquence swept the audience off its feet,' recalled Murphy. 'He finished his speech with a rendering of William Morris's *The Day is Coming*.

I had never heard an orator of this calibre before, not seen an audience so roused to demonstrative enthusiasm. It was not the kind which greatly appealed to me at the time. I preferred the colder analytical speeches and was sceptical of emotionalism. But it was impossible to be unimpressed by this man. Here was the fighting leaders, bearing in his person all the marks of battle, who would storm hell himself.[932]

Murphy, later known as J.T. Murphy, was one of the most prominent leaders of the CPGB in the 1920s. Then a young militant in the Amalgamated Society of Engineers (ASE), Murphy travelled to Liberty Hall, where he met Connolly and came away 'wanting to know all that this man had ever said or written, for he spoke as one having the authority of experience; of having put his theories to the test of practice'.[933] Inspired to read Connolly's works, his blend of syndicalism and political socialism 'seemed to me clearer and more precise than anything I had read or heard from other Socialists', Murphy wrote in his autobiography.

It invested the daily work of the trade unions with a vision and a purpose that made it worthwhile. It appeared to me that here was the way to make democracy real and to ensure individuality in co-operation, the way in which men, individually and collectively, could really be masters of their own fate. I had now a faith and reasons for the faith that was in me.[934]

Murphy, influenced by Connolly's ideas, joined the SLP in 1916. He soon emerged as a leader of the Sheffield Workers' Committee, a rank-and-file shop stewards committee which mobilised thousands of workers to take strike action during the war in defence of their conditions, at a time when strikes were viewed by the government and conservative trade union leaders as a threat to national security.[935]

Less impressed by Larkin's 'fiery cross' crusade, however, were the leaders of the British trades unions. Larkin and Connolly's style of trade unionism, with its aggressive use of the sympathetic strike, combined with radical socialist politics, was anathema to moderate trade union leaders, such J.H. Thomas of the National Union of Railwaymen (NUR) and J. Havelock Wilson from the National Sailors' and Firemen's Union (NSFU). Throughout the 'Great Unrest', these leaders had been struggling to keep a lid on working-class discontent, which had bubbled up repeatedly, with strike action by miners, railway workers, dockers, seamen, and many others, including the hitherto non-unionised. Often in the face of opposition from full-time union officials, this wave of working-class assertion was motivated by a strong ethic of solidarity, and eschewed existing contracts, established channels and incumbent leaders. Each year between 1910 and 1913 saw around 10 million days lost to strikes, with the figure climbing to over four times that number in 1912, the year of the national miners' strike. According to Darlington, between 1910 and 1914 'somewhere between 25 and 30% of the British workforce went on strike', with a success rate of over 85%, a period which utterly transformed British trade unions, increasing membership 'from 2.4 million at the end of 1909 to 4.1 million by the end of 1913'.[936]

'It is against this backcloth of an assertive and growing trade union movement,' it has been argued, 'that the high level of solidarity for the Dublin dispute can be understood.'[937] Calls for solidarity action were promoted by a growing and active left wing in the trade union movement, which was both organisationally and politically heterogenous but shared a core belief in the efficacy of asserting working-class economic power, and in bypassing the conventional 'collaborative' arrangements between employers and union leaders to take on the bosses and the state directly.

While the number of members of explicitly syndicalist organisations, such as Tom Mann's ISEL, was never more than the low thousands, support for radical trade unionism could be found across a range of organisations, such as the left wing of the ILP, the Plebs' League and the Central Labour College – set up to promote radical independent working-class education. Added to this was the *Daily Herald,* with its network of around 300 local

Herald Leagues.[938] Noah Ablett, a Welsh miner from the Rhondda Valley, who played a leading role in establishing the Plebs' League while a student at Ruskin College in Oxford, was introduced to Marxist ideas through his exposure to SLP literature.[939] Ablett was the main author of *The Miners' Next Step,* a broadly syndicalist programme for transforming the South Wales Miners' Federation, published by the rank-and-file Unofficial Reform Committee, which was critical of the old-style leadership of William 'Mabon' Abraham.[940]

Larkin's call for the 'blacking' of goods bound for Dublin, aimed over the heads of the union leaders towards the rank-and-file, contributed directly to an ongoing battle for control *within* the British trade union movement between the radicals and the more conservative leadership and officials. Earlier in the dispute, an incident in Liverpool demonstrated the potential (or, from the union leaders' perspective, the danger) of the Dublin dispute to reshape the British trade union movement. On 16 September, railway workers in Liverpool began a general refusal to handle Dublin traffic. The *Herald*'s correspondent gleefully reported that 'despite the passionate plea of Mr. T. Loath to allow the strike negotiations to be settled by the executive committee and ratified by the men afterwards', the workers insisted on rank-and-file representation on the negotiating committee. They decided 'to appoint a negotiating committee consisting of representatives of the executive committee and three special representatives appointed by the men', a move described by the *Herald* as 'a big blow to the policy of Unity House [NUR headquarters], for it shows that the Liverpool strikers intend to make a settlement on their own account without too much deference to the officials'.[941]

Though the action started in Liverpool, 'within days it had spread to places as far away as Birmingham and Sheffield. By 19 September, 10,000 men were out in the Midlands and another 3,000 or 4,000 in the North-west'.[942] Even at this early stage, J.H. Thomas condemned the strikes and ordered the men back to work, condemning the action as 'sectional and local'. Leading figures in the Parliamentary Labour Party, too, such as Philip Snowden, condemned the strike in the right-wing newspaper the *Morning Post.* Snowden had, that year, devoted a pamphlet to condemning syndicalism as 'fantastic and impractical', and argued during the Lockout that the energy put into supporting Dublin could more usefully be expended by supporting the Labour Party.[943]

Ahead of Larkin's tour, the ITGWU published a manifesto in the *Daily Herald* on 14 November, signed by Larkin and Connolly. Though vaguely worded, the paper took the call for British workers to 'go ahead and strike while the iron of revolt is hot in our souls' as an endorsement of its call for a general strike in support of Dublin. The same issue of the paper reported that

> meetings of railwaymen to discuss the subject of Dublin 'tainted' goods will be held to-morrow at Liverpool, Birmingham, Holyhead, Swansea, Bristol, Heysham, Manchester, Kentish Town, Cricklewood, Clerkenwell, Bermondsey, Nottingham, King's Cross, Crewe, Derby, Sheffield, Leeds, Newcastle, and other places.

They were expected to discuss 'the appointment of vigilance committees' to monitor suspected goods and decide 'the nature and extent of any action that is to be taken by the railwaymen to deal with Dublin goods'.[944]

This tide of rank-and-file activity could not but make an impression on the official labour movement. The TUC Parliamentary Committee met four days later, on 18 November. 'That the rank and file were taking more than ordinary interest in the meeting … was shown by the large crowd which assembled … outside the offices in Aldwych,' reported the *Daily Herald*. 'The deputation from Dublin awaked considerable interest,' it added, 'and Larkin especially came in for the cheers of the crowd.'[945] Inside the meeting itself, the demands of rank-and-file activists were felt, with the secretary of the committee recording that 'he had received many letters asking the committee to call a conference for the purpose of considering the question of a general "down-tools' policy" in support of Dublin'.[946]

The TUC was hoping that it could persuade the ITGWU to meet the employers, but the Irish delegation was having none of it. William MacPartlin declared that they 'were in favour of a fight to the finish' and Larkin called for a conference to decide on action: 'We ask you in no uncertain way that the working class of England be called together, and be asked to give their opinion, and we will abide by whatever verdict they give.' Larkin added that: 'There was not a rank and file man of any value who was not prepared at this moment to aid them in their struggle.'[947]

The meeting ended acrimoniously on 19 November, with Larkin clashing with members of the British unions. In the end, it was decided to call a Special TUC Conference, but delay it three weeks until 9 December. The ostensible reason for the delay was to enable unions to meet to mandate their delegates, so that any decisions taken would be genuinely representative. In reality, the delay was so that the TUC could force a resolution to the dispute, and it had the effect of postponing much-needed solidarity action. The *Daily Herald*'s comment was scathing, declaring that the Parliamentary

Committee 'declared for Conference, but allows the enemies of the people period of twenty days which to play batons, blacklegs, class-law bitterness, and the other vicious factors for all they are worth'.[948]

The bluntness of the *Herald*'s message reflected its position as the mouthpiece for the radical rank-and-file movement urging solidarity with Dublin against the wishes of the TUC leadership. The same day as the Parliamentary Committee ended its session, the Heraldites held a show of strength in the Albert Hall, addressed by Larkin and Haywood. The mood of distrust with the TUC's motives is demonstrated by the following report of the rally:

> A striking scene ensued when Mr. Naylor said that the Parliamentary Committee of the Trades Union Congress had come a decision that afternoon – (derisive cries) – to call a special national conference of the Unions – (cheers) – to meet the challenge of the employers to Trade Unionism. That conference, however, was not to be held for three weeks – (fierce groans and hisses, which prevented the speaker proceeding for several minutes, during which the chairman appealed for order. His appeal was followed by shouts for a revolution.) When silence was restored Mr. Naylor said that the conference should have been called in three days – (cheers) – that if the Trade Union leaders were in earnest. At a time like the present no other alternative would have any effect on the present Government short of national stoppage labour. (Applause.)[949]

The paper, for its part, commented that the 'Parliamentary Committee started to rise to the occasion, and then fell pitifully'. It warned its readers that 'the rank and file must ever be alert and ardent and prepared to do their own leading when avowed leaders fail ...'.[950]

Larkin, frustrated by the continuing delay, issued a manifesto on 22 November which the *Herald* duly published. By this point, Larkin clearly expected nothing of the main union leaders, and directed his appeal squarely at the membership. He launched a remarkable attack on the union leaders, accusing them having forgotten

> that they worked at the bench, in or out of the factory, on the dock, or in the stokehole. They have forgotten the footplate and the engine. They have forgotten the laborious work of the goods yard. They seem to think that Round Table Conferences, nice language, beautiful phrases that fall trippingly from the tongue, Conciliation Boards and Agreements are the be-all and end-all of life.

He concluded his statement with a call to act: 'Send resolutions, send instructions, send demands to you leaders that they strike a true and honest note, that they shall lead from the front and not from the rear, that they will give voice to the beliefs of the rank and file.'[951]

Debate has raged subsequently about the tactical wisdom of attacking the trade union leaders, with some arguing that Larkin built a rod for his own back. Bill Moran comments, however, that while Larkin may not have helped himself in his intemperate attacks on the moderate trade union leaders, 'in reality his behaviour was used as a justification for rejecting policies which trade unionists like Thomas and Havelock Wilson, had set their minds against in any case'.[952] Personality clashes, of course, play a role but they simply exacerbated a real and existing tension between the left-wing direct-actionists amongst the rank-and-file and the trade union leadership and officialdom who were ever keen to put a damper on the struggle.

In the run-up to the TUC Special Conference, another incident demonstrated just what was at stake in the fight to commit the British labour movement to support for Dublin. In 1911, Llanelli, south Wales, was the site of one of the key confrontations in the national railway strike that year. Traffic was brought to a standstill, prompting the state to send in troops. Soldiers of the Worcester regiment opened fire on strikers who were attempting to prevent a train from passing through the station. Two men were killed, with others sustaining injuries, prompting an outburst of working-class anger that saw police, troops and targets associated with the Great Western Railway Company attacked.

In November 1913, a driver and member of the Associated Society of Locomotive Engineers and Firemen (ASLEF), George James, refused to handle coal which was destined for Dublin. He was suspended and then dismissed. Soon, another driver would receive the same treatment from the employers. The *Herald* captured the mood, reporting that when it

> first became known that these men were be dealt with in this way the feeling among their mates has been rising gradually, and at the present time the majority of the men in the South Wales and Monmouthshire district are ready to take any action necessary to secure the reinstatement of their mates.[953]

Before long, thirty thousand railwaymen struck in sympathy, paralysing railway traffic in south Wales. One Tory paper, the *Sheffield Daily Telegraph*, complained that 'Dublin, indeed, is responsible for this latest disturbance' and, decrying the increasingly tendency of workers to take unofficial action, noted that the National union Executive, 'of course, has not been consulted; it never is in these fervent days'.[954]

J.H. Thomas, true to form, had no intention of allowing unofficial action in support of Dublin. He argued that because the ancillary importance of the railways for the functioning of other industries, a policy of blacking 'tainted goods' would involve railway workers in virtually every dispute, regardless of which industry it took place.[955] On a more fundamental level, Thomas and the union bureaucracy saw their role as arbitrators between workers and employers and were therefore motivated by a desire for respectability in the eyes of the latter. As a contemporary newspaper observed, such 'spasmodic outbreaks' as the south Wales dispute 'have for some time been uncomfortably frequent' and warned that, 'if the National Union is unable to protect itself, and the public, against this sort of thing, [it] cannot expect to be regarded by employers or by anybody else, as an authentic representative of railway labour'.[956]

Thomas, in the words of the NUR's semi-official history, 'went down and turned the table on the malcontents'.[957] He branded the drivers 'a disgrace to the trade union movement' and even called for NUR members to take the ASLEF members' jobs. In the end, the NUR and ASLEF secured the reinstatement of all workers sacked as a result of the action, except the original two drivers. 'There was for some time afterwards,' wrote G.D.H. Cole and Robin Page Arnot in their history of the railway unions, 'considerable anger in South Wales against Mr. J. H. Thomas, who was mainly responsible for the settlement.'[958] Coming three days before the special TUC conference, the setback, in the judgement of one historian, 'considerably undermined the momentum for sympathetic action'.[959]

When the 600 delegates, representing 350 unions, assembled on 9 December, it became clear almost immediately that the TUC was not going to sanction industrial action in support of Dublin. R.M. Fox, in his memoirs of the period, expressed it best when he wrote that 'the Labour officials called a special conference to decide what was to be done about Dublin. In reality it was to decide what was to be done about Larkin.'[960] The conference, in effect, was rigged. Despite the given reason for the three-week delay in holding the conference being that unions needed time to consult their members, labour historian Bill Moran in researching the event was unable 'to trace a single one who had been formally elected or mandated'. Instead, the 'majority were selected from delegates at the previous annual conference or were appointed by the executives of their unions'.[961] For example, Robert Williams of the NTWF, and a supporter of Larkin, complained that he 'was refused admission, presumably because my opinions did not square with those of the official gang'.[962] Connolly knew the game was up in a lunchtime interview given to the *Daily Herald*. 'Ninety-nine per cent of the delegates,' he admitted, 'have come here to-day with the intention of settling – Larkin.'[963]

Such a gathering was never likely to mobilise sympathetic action, but what happened next was in many ways the most shocking turn of events. In the morning session, before any action in support of Dublin had been discussed, Ben Tillett took the stage. The left-wing dockers' leader had accompanied Larkin on platforms during his 'Fiery cross' crusade and had indulged in some of headiest rhetoric at the rallies in support of the Dublin workers. Nevertheless, he moved a motion condemning 'the unfair attacks made by men inside the Trade Union movement upon British Trade Union officials'. Regardless of Tillett's intention, the floodgates were now open for union leaders such as Thomas and Havelock Wilson to attack Larkin in the strongest possible terms. Shaking with anger, Larkin responded, addressing the conference as 'Mr. Chairman and human beings', and giving as good as he got. The motion, however, was carried overwhelmingly, with only six votes against. The morning's proceedings having set the tone, the afternoon session provided yet another blow to Larkin. While it was agreed that financial support should be maintained, 'a crucial amendment to secure a ban on the handing of goods bound to and from Dublin was crushed 2,280,000 votes to 203,000'.[964]

Defeat

The TUC conference, in effect, spelled the inevitable end of the Dublin Lockout. On 16 December, Connolly ordered ITGWU members to return to work whenever it was possible to do so without having to sign the document repudiating the union. With the exception of Murphy and Jacob's Biscuit Factory, most employers had by now dropped the demand that ITGWU sign the hated document. For the union, the resolution of the dispute, then, largely involved settling terms for reinstatement, and avoiding as far as possible the victimisation of striking workers.

The defeat of the Dublin Lockout, which left the ITGWU virtually bankrupt, and its members demoralised, had a profound effect on Connolly. In a series of articles, Connolly drew several conclusions from the experience about the nature of the trade union bureaucracy and the structure of the British trade union movement. Connolly recognised that the British trade union movement, and especially its rank and file, had provided invaluable assistance to the Dublin workers. 'Never was seen such enthusiasm in a labour fight,' Connolly reflected. 'Trade unionists, socialists of all kinds, anarchists, industrialists, syndicalists, all the varying and hitherto discordant elements of the labour movement found a common platform, were joined together in pursuit of a common object.' In its response to the call from Dublin for solidarity, 'the working class movement of Great Britain reached its highest point of moral grandeur ...'.[965]

However, Connolly reflected bitterly, this attitude was not mirrored by the trade union leaderships. 'We asked for the isolation of the capitalists of Dublin,' he wrote, 'and for answer the leaders of the British labour movement proceeded calmly to isolate the working class of Dublin.' Despite the splendid and heroic support of British workers, 'sectionalism, intrigues and old-time jealousies damned us in the hour of victory, and officialdom was the first to fall to the tempter'. He concluded dramatically:

> And so we Irish workers must go down into Hell, bow our backs to the lash of the slave driver, let our hearts be seared by the iron of his hatred, and instead of the sacramental wafer of brotherhood and common sacrifice, eat the dust of defeat and betrayal ... Dublin is isolated.[966]

What lessons did Connolly draw from this? Firstly, he further developed an industrial unionist critique of the way that the British union movement was structured. Connolly argued that 'the multiplicity of unions and executives' encouraged each set of union leaders and officials to follow 'the immediate material interests of their union, instead of the broader material and moral welfare of their class'. This attachment to institutional interest over the class struggle imperilled the tactic of the sympathy strike and made it difficult to mobilise class-wide solidarity because each 'union not immediately engaged in the conflict is a union whose material interests – looked at from a narrowly selfish point of view – are opposed to being drawn into the struggle'.[967] To remedy this state of affairs, Connolly called for 'the amalgamation of all forces of labour into one union, capable of concentrating all forces upon any one issue or in any one fight, [that] can alone fight industrially as the present development and organisation of capital requires that labour should fight'.[968]

In calling for amalgamation, Connolly lined up with radical currents in the British labour movement, such as Tom Mann's syndicalists, who wanted to reshape the unions into more effective vehicles for militant forms of struggle.[969] In 1910, the NTWF was established, linking up the various unions in the 'sea-going, waterside and road transport trades'.[970] Connolly commented that the NTWF was in part the fruit of industrial unionist activity, and prior to its establishment 'Great Britain was the scene of the propagandist activities of a great number of irregular and unorthodox bodies, which, taking their cue in the main from the Industrial Workers of the World, made great campaigns in favour of the new idea'.[971] This was only the beginning of what became a growing force. As G.D.H. Cole wrote, in addition to transport, 'powerful movements for promoting amalgamation on industrial lines were launched in the railway, building, printing, engineering and other industries'.[972]

However, there were limitations to this 'Amalgamation Movement' and to amalgamation as a solution to the problems Connolly posed. The example of the NUR, led by Larkin's nemesis J.H. Thomas, makes this clear. The NUR itself was an industrial union that was created in 1913 by the merger of the Amalgamated Society of Railway Servants, the United Pointsmen and Signalmen's Society and the General Railway Workers' Union. Despite this, executive power was concentrating in the hands of leaders such as Thomas, who were hostile to the sympathetic strike. Connolly himself understood this, noting that 'the amalgamations and federations are being carried out in the main by officials absolutely destitute of the revolutionary spirit, and that as a consequence the methods of what should be militant organisations having the broad working-class outlook are conceived and enforced in the temper and spirit of the sectionalism those organisations were meant to destroy. Into the new bottles of industrial organisation,' Connolly argued, 'is being poured the old, cold wine of Craft Unionism.'[973] Later he noted how the 'frequent rebellion against stupid and spiritless leadership and the call of the rank and file for true industrial unity seems to have spurred the leaders on, not to respond to new spirit but to evolve a method whereby under the forms of unity it could be trammelled and fettered … a scheme to prevent united action rather than facilitate it'.[974]

Yet, it was not simply a question of having the 'wrong' officials in charge. A problem which revolutionary advocates of industrial unionism had to face was that the centralisation of unions to better fight the class struggle risked creating cumbersome and bureaucratic structures, with their own interests and at an increased distance between the rank-and-file and the leadership. Sidney and Beatrice Webb, in their *History of Trade Unionism*, commented that the growth of trade union organisation during the 1910-1914 'Great Unrest' swelled the membership of trade unions from 1,436,000 in 1894 to 3,918,809. At the same time, between 1892 and 1920, the number of full-time officials ('a Civil Service of the Trade Union world') increased from some 600-700 to 3,000-4,000. The trade union official, they wrote, 'occupies a unique position' in belonging 'neither to the middle nor to the working class'.[975] As Darlington writes, the development of institutionalized collective-bargaining machinery effectively gave full-time officials a dual role, on the one hand of negotiating better terms for their members, and on the other of delivering the goods to management for the duration of the agreement in terms of orderly workplace relations.[976]

At least with the 'much-condemned small Unions of the past' Connolly conceded, 'they were susceptible to pressure from the sudden fraternal impulses of their small membership'. By contrast, in a larger, more bureaucratic union,

> As the General Executive cannot take action pending a meeting of delegates, and as the delegates at that meeting have to report back to their bodies, and these bodies again to meet, discuss, and then report back to the General Executive, which must meet, hear their reports, and then, perhaps, order a ballot vote of the entire membership, after which another meeting must be held to tabulate the result of the vote and transmit it to the local branches, which must meet again to receive it, the chances are, of course, a million to one that the body of workers in distress will be starved into subjection, bankrupted, or disrupted, before the leviathan organisation will allow their brothers on the spot to lift a finger or drop a tool in their aid.[977]

In place of 'the mere amalgamation of certain unions' and 'the creation of those much more clumsy federations and amalgamations now being formed', Connolly called for the 'organisation of all workers in any one industry into a union covering that entire industry, and the linking up of all such unions under one head'.[978] Drawing an analogy with the modern Cabinet, he called for a 'system of organisation … which will leave to the unions the full local administration, but invest in a Cabinet the power to call out the members of any union when such action is desirable, and explain their reasons for it afterwards …'.[979]

Even in this proposal, there is an implicit tension between the need for centralisation, necessary to effectively co-ordinate disputes, and the decentralising prerogatives of democratic accountability. 'The only solution of that problem,' Connolly argued,

> is the choice of officers, local or national, from the standpoint of their responsiveness to the call for solidarity, and, having got such officials, to retain them only as long as they can show results in the amelioration of

the condition of their members and the development of their Union as a weapon of class warfare.

What is arguably missing is a recognition that, as organisations established to negotiate wages within the system of wage-labour, many trade unions have an inherent tendency towards bargaining with the capitalist class. This sets limits on militancy and risks the absorption of trade union officials into arbitration structures which simply seek to manage relations within the framework of capitalism. Connolly understood that 'it is scarcely humanly possible that these executives should act otherwise if the consciousness of class solidarity has not entered into the minds and hearts of their membership', and 'whatever be our form of organization, the spirit of sectionalism still rules and curses our class'.[980] He nevertheless puts a lot of store in the structure of trade unions to guarantee a militant spirit. However, in order for workers to choose 'officers, local or national, from the standpoint of their responsiveness to the call for solidarity' and be replace them when they fail to maintain this standard, a permanent organisation of the rank and file, independent of the official structures, would be required. Though the Herald Leagues and individuals in the socialist parties did sterling work in support of the Lockout, the BSP was hamstrung by its propagandist approach and the SLP by its 'dual unionist' sectarianism to the wider labour movement. Socialists did not yet see their role as organising independent rank-and-file structures within established trade unions on any systematic basis.

Many of the same issues are considered, in great detail, in the remarkable pamphlet produced in 1912 by the Unofficial Reform Committee of the South Wales Miners' Federation, *The Miners' Next Step*. Like Connolly, this document, too, notes how 'the policy of conciliation gives the real power of the men into the hands of a few leaders', meaning that 'control of the organisation by the rank and file is far too indirect'.[981] While Connolly's remarks are of a more general character, *The Miners' Next Step* sets out a comprehensive set of reforms to its union structures, overcoming sectionalism by establishing a 'united industrial organisation' and a 'constitution giving free and rapid control by the rank and file acting in such a way that conditions will be unified throughout the coalfield'.[982]

Connolly was part of the same upsurge of working-class militancy which challenged the power of capital and, through pamphlets such as *The Miners' Next Step*, questioned the prerogatives and conciliating tendencies of the trade union bureaucracy. Connolly's own writings, especially *Socialism Made Easy*, had a shaping effect on leading militants such as Tom Mann and those, such as J. T. Murphy, who would go on to play leading roles in the wartime Shop Stewards' Movement. More practically, in taking charge of the ITGWU during the Lockout, Connolly contributed directly to a key event of the Great Unrest, one which provided significant impetus to rank-and-file militants across Great Britain in the movement of solidarity with the Dublin workers.

Chapter 7

War and the International

On the morning of Sunday 28 June, a bullet fired from the pistol of a young Serbian nationalist killed Archduke Franz Ferdinand, heir presumptive to the Austro-Hungarian throne. The assassination set off a chain reaction, provoking a general conflict between Europe's leading imperialist powers, who had for decades been locked in economic and political rivalry. The Austro-Hungarian Empire declared war on Serbia on 23 July, with the promise of German backing if Russia joined the war. Russia subsequently mobilised its troops on 31 July, prompting Germany to declare war on Russia and France. The German invasion of Belgium led directly to Britain declaring war on 4 August. The First World War had begun. It would last until 11 November 1918, by which point around 40 million people had been killed or injured in war.

As tensions mounted in the capitals of Europe many, Connolly included, had looked towards the socialist movement to prevent a drift towards war. 'In the confused and restless years preceding World War I,' wrote the French historian Georges Haupt,

> the Socialist International was considered the most important anti-militarist political force in the world: the International did not merely declare 'war on war', but believed itself capable of mobilizing an army of five million organised workers in the active struggle for peace.[983]

The International's own public pronouncements on war reflected this aspiration. In 1907, at its Stuttgart Congress, the International passed a resolution on war and militarism, first drafted by August Bebel. 'In case of war being imminent,' it read, 'the working class and its parliamentary representatives in the countries concerned shall be bound ... to do all they can to prevent the outbreak of war, using for this purpose the means that appear to them the most effective ....' In a final paragraph, sharpened by an amendment drafted by Rosa Luxemburg, Lenin and the Menshevik Julius

Martov, the resolution stated

> [if] war should break out notwithstanding, they shall be bound to intervene for its speedy termination, and to employ all their forces to utilize the economic and political crisis created by the war in order to rouse the masses of the people and thereby hasten the downfall of capitalist class rule.[984]

This view was reinforced in subsequent resolutions in 1910 and in 1912, but also through public demonstrations. In 1912 alone, 'there were labour movement protests against war in Bohemia, Hungary, Italy, England, Sweden, Denmark, Spain, Germany, France, and the Netherlands. About 100,000 marched in Paris, while meetings in forty-three German cities brought together 300,000.'[985]

Viewed from the vantage point of early August 1914, the International seemed at the height of its power. Connolly recorded that 'anti-militarist resolutions of socialist and international trade union conferences have become part of the order of the day and are no longer phenomena to be wondered at. The whole working class movement stands committed to war upon war – stands so committed at the very height of its strength and influence.'[986] Such resolutions and demonstrations, however, only served to make what happened all the more shocking to those on the revolutionary left of the International. When war actually broke out, the International failed to rise the occasion. 'The anti-militarist resolutions voted at previous International congresses,' wrote Haupt, 'remained a dead letter.' Worse, with some noble exceptions, the national parties of the Second International joined with their 'own' bourgeoisies to support their respective nation's war efforts. 'On 4 August 1914, the social democrats in the Reichstag voted for war credits; Emile Vandervelde, the president of the International, joined the Belgian government; and the Union sacrée triumphed in France.'[987]

Connolly, when the war broke out, was profoundly shocked at the rapid collapse of the Second International. It is difficult to overstate the importance of this event for his politics between 1914 and 1916. Connolly entered politics in 1889, the year of the International's founding. Even in his most syndicalist moments, the Second International, taken together as its parties, resolutions, networks and activities, formed a vital political reference point and framing for Connolly's politics.[988]

His first reaction to the war was a sense of shock about the International's failure to uphold the banner of revolutionary internationalism: 'And now, like the proverbial bolt from the blue,' he despaired, war is upon us, and war between the most important, because the most socialist, nations of the earth. And we are helpless!

Civilisation is being destroyed before our eyes; the results of generations of propaganda and patient heroic plodding and self-sacrifice are being blown into annihilation from a hundred cannon mouths; thousands of comrades with whose souls we have lived in fraternal communion are about to be done to death; they whose one hope it was to be spared to cooperate in building the perfect society of the future are being driven to fratricidal slaughter in shambles where that hope will be buried under a sea of blood.[989]

Connolly's shock soon turned to anger, and a grim determination to rouse the working class, in Ireland and more widely, against the conflict. His initial response was also impeccably internationalist. 'To me,' Connolly wrote,

the socialist of another country is a fellow-patriot, as the capitalist of my own country is a natural enemy. I regard each nation as the possessor of a definite contribution to the common stock of civilisation, and I regard the capitalist class of each nation as being the logical and natural enemy of the national culture which constitutes that definite contribution.

He treated, too, with sarcasm and contempt the argument that socialists 'did their whole duty when they protested against the war, but that now that war has been declared it is right that they also should arm in defence of their common country …'.[990] To this, Connolly protested:

When the German artilleryman, a socialist serving in the German army of invasion, sends a shell into the ranks of the French army, blowing off their heads; tearing out their bowels, and mangling the limbs of dozens of socialist comrades in that force, will the fact that he, before leaving for the front 'demonstrated' against the war be of any value to the widows and orphans made by the shell he sent upon its mission of murder? Or, when the French rifleman pours his murderous fire into the ranks of the German line of attack, will he be able to derive any comfort from the probability that his bullets are murdering or maiming comrades who last year joined in thundering 'hochs' and cheers of greeting to the eloquent Jaurès, when in Berlin he pleaded for international solidarity?[991]

Closer to home, the British labour movement, too, swung behind the government's war effort. On the eve of the war, Keir Hardie and Arthur

Henderson, leaders of the British Labour Party, had put their name to a document issued in the name of the British Section of the International Socialist Bureau (the permanent executive organisation of the Second International) calling on workers to hold 'vast demonstrations against war in every industrial centre' and to 'conquer the militarist enemy and the self-seeking Imperialists to-day, once and for all'.[992] Upon the outbreak of war, however, the TUC and Labour Party leadership declared an industrial and electoral truce. Henderson replaced James Ramsay MacDonald, who opposed the war, as leader of the Parliamentary Labour Party (PLP) and entered the wartime coalition government with the Conservatives and Liberals in May 1915. Even the left-wing BSP initially supported the war, though an anti-war faction gained the upper hand by 1916, leading to the departure of the pro-war supporters of Hyndman. Hardie, along with the ILP as a whole, maintained an anti-war stance, though largely from a pacifist (as opposed to a revolutionary) perspective.[993] As Connolly wrote, '[with] the honourable exception of the Independent Labour Party (ILP) and the Socialist Labour Party (SLP), the organised and unorganised Labour advocates of Peace in Britain swallowed the bait and are now beating the war drum'.

A similar story, he reported, was true on the European continent:

the French socialists protested against the war – and then went to the front, headed by Gustave Hervé, the great anti-militarist; the German socialists protested against the war – and then, in the Reichstag, unanimously voted 250 million to carry it on; the Austrians issued a manifesto against the war – and are now on the frontier doing great deeds of heroism against the foreign enemy; and the Russians erected barricades in the streets of St. Petersburg against the cossacks, but immediately war was declared went off to the front arm in arm with their cossack brothers.

Such a policy, argued Connolly,

means that the socialist parties of the various countries mutually cancel each other, and that as a consequence socialism ceases to exist as a world force, and drops out of history in the greatest crisis of the history of the world, in the very moment when courageous action will most influence history.[994]

Revolutionary opposition to war

In Ireland, however, the prominence of Connolly and his allies, as well as the country's colonial relationship with one of the major belligerents, ensured that the official Irish labour movement would adopt an internationalist response to the war. The Irish TUC and Labour Party released a statement opposing the conflict on 10 August 1914: 'A European war for the aggrandisement of the capitalist class has been declared. Great Britain is involved. The working-class will, as usual, supply the victims that the crowned heads may stalk in all their panoply of state ....'[995] In doing so, the Irish joined the Russian Bolsheviks, Mensheviks and Trudoviks, the Serbian Social-Democrats, the Bulgarian Tesnyaki, the Italian Socialist Party, the smaller of the two Dutch socialist parties, and a few others in opposing the war wholesale. In other countries, syndicalist organisations such as the Spanish CNT, and minority movements within established socialist parties such as the group around Rosa Luxemburg, Karl Liebknecht and Franz Mehring which later became a nucleus for the *Kommunistische Partei Deutschlands* (Communist Party of Germany, KPD) also flew the flag for revolutionary internationalism.

Connolly's earliest pronouncements on the war were addressed squarely at 'the working-class democracy of Ireland', a fact he wished to emphasise 'because I believe that it would be worse than foolish – it would be a crime against all our hopes and aspirations – to take counsel in this matter from any other source'. The Home Rule leader John Redmond had declared in the House of Commons that his movement would join the Unionists of Ulster in defending Ireland from Britain's enemies. For Connolly, this was tantamount to promising that 'the Irish slaves will guarantee to protect the Irish estate of England until their masters come back to take possession'. The 'advanced Nationalists' meanwhile, 'have neither a policy nor a leader,' and could not be looked towards to give a lead. It was up to the working class to act. 'Should the working class of Europe, rather than slaughter each other for the benefit of kings and financiers, proceed tomorrow to erect barricades all over Europe, to break up bridges and destroy the transport service that war might be abolished,' Connolly wrote, 'we should be perfectly justified in following such a glorious example and contributing our aid to the final dethronement of the vulture classes that rule and rob the world.'[996]

At a public meeting held on 30 August to commemorate the deaths of James Nolan, John Byrne and Alice Brady, who were killed during the Dublin Lockout, Connolly openly proclaimed the need for rebellion. 'You have been told you are not strong, that you have no rifles,' Connolly told the crowd. 'Revolutions do not start with rifles; start first and get your rifles after.'[997]

Short of this scenario, however, Connolly put forward a more limited programme to defend workers' interests. It was the duty of the labour movement, he insisted, 'to take all possible action to save the poor from the horrors this war has in store'. Connolly rightly predicted that the war would lead to increased food prices, and that though 'the Irish farmer like all other farmers will benefit by the high prices of the war ... these high prices will mean starvation to the labourers in the towns'.[998] Indeed, in Dublin, the price of sugar overnight rose from 2 1/2d a pound to 6d, with increases too for butter, flour and bacon, creating great hardship for the workers, while war profits increased.[999] To counter this attack on workers' standards of living, Connolly called on the labour movement 'to refuse to allow agricultural produce to leave Ireland until provision is made for the Irish working class'. He warned the readers of the *Irish Worker* that this 'may mean more than a transport strike, it may mean armed battling in the streets to keep in this country the food for our people. But whatever it may mean it must not be shrunk from.'

Working-class action of this sort in Ireland, Connolly hoped, would have European-wide significance, leading ultimately to socialist revolution: 'Starting thus, Ireland may yet set the torch to a European conflagration that will not burn out until the last throne and the last capitalist bond and debenture will be shrivelled on the funeral pyre of the last war lord.'[1000]

A week later, writing for a wider socialist audience in *Forward*, Connolly argued that 'no insurrection of the working class; no general strike; no general uprising of the forces of Labour in Europe, could possibly carry with it, or entail a greater slaughter of socialists, than will their participation as soldiers in the campaigns of the armies of their respective countries'. If workers must die, Connolly asked, 'would it not be better to die in their own country fighting for freedom for their class, and for the abolition of war, than to go forth to strange countries and die slaughtering and slaughtered by their brothers that tyrants and profiteers might live?'

Drawing on the 1905 revolution in Russia for inspiration, Connolly hoped that 'ere long we may read of the paralysing of the internal transport service on the continent, even should the act of paralysing necessitate the erection of socialist barricades and acts of rioting by socialist soldiers and sailors, as happened in Russia in 1905'. He continued that:

Even an unsuccessful attempt at social revolution by force of arms, following the paralysis of the economic life of militarism, would be less disastrous to the socialist cause than the act of socialists allowing themselves to be used in the slaughter of their brothers in the cause.

A great continental uprising of the working class would stop the war; a universal protest at public meetings will not save a single life from being wantonly slaughtered.[1001]

As one biographer has pointed out, however, there is a seeming paradox that 'calls for an immediate general strike once war was declared came from the more vacillating elements of the Second International' such as Hervé, who later became a French chauvinist, and Hardie, who saw in the call the potential for pacifist opposition to war. The danger with this approach, however, was that when 'an immediate stoppage failed to materialise there was no other socialist strategy available' and the 'most militant calls for strikes could easily turn into despair and demobilisation'.[1002] As we shall see, Connolly did despair of the Second International parties. Yet in part because of this, he was driven to insurrectionary conclusions.

The failure of the Second International

By March 1915, Connolly was forced to admit that 'the socialist forces in the various countries failed so signally to prevent or even delay the outbreak [of war]'. He penned an article, 'Revolutionary Unionism and War', for a North American audience in the *International Socialist Review*, which was the fullest statement of his views on the topic. In it, he reflected that 'the signal of war ought also to have been the signal for rebellion, that when the bugles sounded the first note for actual war, their notes should have been taken as the tocsin for social revolution'. However, admitted Connolly, 'that possibility has receded out of sight ...'. His primary explanation for 'the failure of European socialism to avert the war' was that there was a 'divorce between the industrial and political movements of labour ... The socialist voters having cast their ballots were helpless, as voters, until the next election.' Connolly wrote:

> as workers, they were indeed in control of the forces of production and distribution, and by exercising that control over the transport service could have made the war impossible. But the idea of thus co-ordinating their two spheres of activity had not gained sufficient lodgement to be effective in the emergency.
>
> No socialist party in Europe could say that rather than go to war it would call out the entire transport service of the country and thus prevent mobilisation. No socialist party could say so, because no socialist party could have the slightest reasonable prospect of having such a call obeyed.[1003]

Connolly's polemic, however, reads better as a piece of general propaganda for revolutionary industrial unionism than as an explanation of the failure of the Second International. His analysis of the importance of the industrial wing of labour does not explain why, for instance, the preeminent syndicalist union federation, the CGT, backed the war. Nor does it do justice to parties such as the German SPD, which was not simply a political party. As well as its 1,085,905 members in 1914, it received more than 4,250,000 votes and had over two million members enrolled in the trade unions associated with the party. As historian Pierre Broué has written,

> Around it, its activists knew how to build a broad network of parallel organisations; these organised at different levels nearly all wage-earners, and extended into every sphere of social life: associations of socialist women, the youth movement, people's universities, libraries and reading societies, leisure organisations and open-air movements, publishing houses, newspapers, journals and magazines.[1004]

The failure of the Second International was, in many senses, more profound and more political; it could not be reduced to mere forms of organisation. Firstly, despite its real and performative internationalism, the Second International was 'a loose association of autonomous working-class parties' for whom the 'arena of action was first and foremost the nation-state'. As Kevin Callaghan has persuasively argued, its internationalism was, in effect, a hyphenated 'inter-nationalism' which affirmed

> that the unit of the nation constitutes the rudimentary category of identification within the context of internationalism. A socialist movement is preoccupied with its national prerogatives and then understands the development of its own movement as a contribution to the larger international cause.[1005]

A focus on the nation state as the natural terrain of struggle, and an increasing emphasis on the electoral arena, built up a sizeable party bureaucracy whose interests lay in maintaining the organisation as an institution. In the case of the SPD, understandably proud of the party's journey from harassed underground movement under Bismarck to the largest party in Germany, the leaders wished to keep it that way, and saw a confrontation with the state as a risky proposition. Anticipating this somewhat, the SPD member and sociologist Robert Michels warned in 1911 that 'it is far from obvious that the interests of the masses which have combined to form the party will coincide with the interests of the bureaucracy in which the party becomes personified'.[1006] This was borne out in 1914, when out of a concern for the self-preservation of the SPD as an institution, the parliamentary group voted for war credits. Predicting a short war, Kautsky sought to justify an abstention on the grounds that 'the International cannot be an effective instrument in time of war: it is essentially a peace-time instrument', and it should keep its forces intact until after the conflict.[1007]

It was not only the professionalisation and bureaucratisation of the parties which provided a reformist drag on their revolutionary aspirations; a similar process operated within the trade unions, which Connolly had seen first-hand with the British unions during the Lockout. The reason why, if a call was made for a transport strike to paralyse military mobilisation, 'no socialist party could have the slightest reasonable prospect of having such a call obeyed' was not only down to the electoralist focus of the parties but also the moderating influence of the trade union bureaucracy.

Taking Germany, the Second International's most powerful labour movement, as an example, it was the unions which had long acted as a major reformist brake on a nominally Marxist political party, the SPD. During 1902 and 1913 the membership of the German free trade unions aligned with the SPD grew by 350 per cent but its bureaucracy by over 1,900 per cent. 'In any search for the increasing conservatism of the free trade unions,' wrote one historian of the SPD, 'these figures play an important part. For most of this bureaucracy the movement was everything, the end nothing.'[1008] At the SPD's Mannheim Congress in September 1906, Karl Kautsky, who was by and large still allied with the left, worried that if 'the trade unions want peace and quiet, what perspectives open up for us if they are fastened to the already cumbersome part body as brakes?' The Congress produced a compromise which gave the union leaders a de facto veto over the use of a mass political strike by German Social Democracy. One radical SPD journal, the *Leipziger Volkszeitung*, concluded glumly that after struggling against revisionism in the party for a decade, 'the revisionism we have killed in the party rises again with greater strength in the trade unions'.[1009]

The growth of the parties and unions as large self-interested bureaucracies, increasingly enmeshed in the parliamentary structures of their respective bourgeois nation states, had a deadening effect on the International's paper policies of revolutionary internationalism. These policies, too, had their ambiguities, and could be exploited in service of social chauvinist ends. Once the war actually broke out, many socialists drew on patriotic traditions to argue that 'their own' nation was fighting a war of national self-defence. As

Marc Mulholland has argued, the legitimacy of wars for self-defence, in the abstract, was never questioned by the International. Indeed, as late as the 1910 Copenhagen conference, for example, the International re-affirmed its recognition of the right to 'self-determination of all peoples and their defence against armed attacks and violent repression'.[1010] Added to this was a sense of nationalist cultural superiority among the pro-war socialists in the warring nations; the SPD leadership portraying the war as a struggle of progressive Germany against Tsarist despotism, while Hyndman warned that the 'Prussian Goth is at the gate'.[1011]

Connolly himself recognised, in the context of a world conflict, that if each national labour movement claimed self-defence, 'the socialist parties of the various countries mutually cancel each other'. Moreover, Connolly placed the war in a wider context, arguing that it was an imperialist war:

> The war of a subject nation for independence, for the right to live out its own life in its own way may and can be justified as holy and righteous; the war of a subject class to free itself from the debasing conditions of economic and political slavery should at all times choose its own weapons, and hold and esteem all as sacred instruments of righteousness. But the war of nation against nation in the interest of royal freebooters and cosmopolitan thieves is a thing accursed.[1012]

On similar grounds, revolutionary critics within the International, such as Lenin, argued that in 'a genuinely national war the words "defence of the fatherland" are not a deception and we are not opposed to it'. However, 'in this war "defence of the fatherland" is a deception, an attempt to justify the war'.[1013]

An Irish Lenin?

As Bill Anderson notes in his perceptive study, Connolly's position on the war has 'frequently been compared with Lenin's'. For Bernard Ransom, 'Connolly's internationalist stand on the war was substantially similar to that of Lenin', and Peter Beresford Ellis stated in his introduction to a collection of Connolly's writings that 'Like Lenin, Connolly completely denounced the imperialist holocaust'. This is especially true, however, for C. Desmond Greaves and others in the Irish Stalinist tradition, who have attempted to portray Connolly as an 'Irish Lenin', whose 'thought ran parallel with Lenin's ... almost phrase by phrase'.[1014]

This 'Irish Lenin' position, which has greatly shaped popular attitudes to Connolly, owes less to what Connolly actually wrote and more to the ideological requirements of the CPGB, of which Greaves was a long-time member. As a national hero, Connolly was a useful vessel for transmitting Marxist-Leninism into Ireland, especially through the CPGB's Connolly Association, which was set up in the 1940s to attract Irish workers in Britain to Stalinism by adapting to Irish nationalist sensibilities. This was not the only use for Connolly, however. The British Communists even went so far as to publish a selection of Connolly's writings on the war in early 1941, at a time when Stalinist Russia (and therefore the CPGB) was in an alliance with Nazi Germany.[1015] The collection did not, however, remain in print for very long. The Nazis invaded Russia on 22 June 1941 and soon afterwards the book was pulled by its publisher, Lawrence & Wishart, as the Stalinists rolled full square behind Winston Churchill's war effort. Though much more scholarly, and based on valuable primary research, Greaves's influential biography *The Life and Times of James Connolly* is nevertheless part and parcel of this ideological project.

Withholding judgement for the moment regarding the merits or otherwise of Connolly's position, an examination of the evidence – or merely an attentive look at Connolly's contemporary articles in the *Irish Worker* and the *Workers' Republic* – renders the 'Irish Lenin' argument unsustainable. Moreover, it displays an unfortunate tendency to downplay the complexity and richness of the revolutionary left in the Second International, by viewing it backwards and in a reductionist fashion through the prism of later developments.

The equivalence of Connolly and Lenin is flawed in at least three respects. Firstly, in terms of Connolly's overall characterisation of the First World War; secondly, with regard to his position on whether it was permissible for the socialist movement to take sides between the major two sets of belligerents in the war; and thirdly, in respect of the related question of Connolly's particular attitude towards Imperial Germany.

As we have seen, there was an important overlap between Connolly and other revolutionary critics of the war on its characterisation as an imperialist conflict. Flowing from this was the argument that slogans such as 'defence of the fatherland' were inapplicable to this war on the ground that they led to the socialist movement collapsing into support for their respective national governments. Moreover, Connolly rightly insisted on the hypocrisy of Britain and its allies' claim that the war was being fought in the name of the self-determination of small nations. He blasted the affected piety of the Allied powers' commitment to national freedom, writing in a leaflet published in Belfast in 1914 that

Britain guaranteed the independence of Belgium. Yes, as she guaranteed the independence of Egypt, and then swallowed it up and slaughtered and imprisoned its patriot sons and daughters. Britain guaranteed the independence of Belgium. Yes, as she guaranteed the independence of Persia, and then encouraged her Russian ally to invade it and drown its freedom in a sea of blood.[1016]

Connolly also cited a statement by the Russian Socialists in opposition to the war, which railed against the Tsar's 'suppression of the liberties of Finland, his continued martyrdom of Poland, his atrocious tortures and massacres in the Baltic provinces, and his withdrawal of the recently granted parliamentary liberties of Russia'. Cutting to the heart of the matter, Connolly commented that the 'Russian Government and the British Government stand solidly together in favour of small nationalities everywhere except in countries now under Russian and British rule'.[1017]

However, for Connolly, within the wider bracket of viewing the war as an inter-imperialist conflict, the First World War was also more narrowly 'the war of a pirate [Britain] upon the German nation'. It had its roots as much in the development of global imperial capitalism as in the fact that, in the earliest twentieth century, 'other nations began quietly to challenge the unquestioned supremacy of England in the markets'. This competition, he argued, led Britain to determine 'that since Germany could not be beaten in fair competition industrially, it must be beaten unfairly by organising a military and naval conspiracy against her'.[1018] Rather than viewing imperial rivalry in general as the issue, Connolly seems to imply that the major problem was Britain's unwillingness to play fairly, and lays particular blame at the feet of the British ruling class. Characterising the war thus, as an offensive war by Britain, Connolly proclaimed to cheers at a meeting of the Irish Neutrality League (INL) in October 1914 that 'Germany was fighting for the commerce of the seas and for the means of building up a sane civilisation in Europe …'.[1019] It is no surprise that Ireland's colonial relationship to Britain, and the crimes of the British ruling class, would loom largest in the minds of an Irish socialist, but the difference between Connolly and Lenin on this point is clear and should be noted in any discussion of their respective positions.

On the second aspect of the question, whether it was permissible for the working-class to take sides, Connolly's writings display two conceptions which sit in tension with one another. As we have seen, writing for a wider British socialist audience in *Forward*, Connolly wrote that the consequence of socialists backing their 'own' side in the war was 'that the socialist parties of the various countries mutually cancel each other, and that as a consequence socialism ceases to exist as a world force …'.[1020] Co-existing with this position was the view, expressed in his very earliest comments on the war in the *Irish Worker* on 8 August, that:

> Should a German army land in Ireland tomorrow we should be perfectly justified in joining it if by doing so we could rid this country once and for all from its connection with the Brigand Empire that drags us unwillingly into this war.[1021]

Connolly did raise the slogan 'We Serve Neither King Nor Kaiser' on the masthead of the *Irish Worker* and on a banner outside Liberty Hall, and later argued that 'we do not wish to be ruled by either empire'. Nevertheless, Connolly did pick a side in the war and he picked Germany.[1022] His lesser-evilism was explicit: 'the instinct of the slave to take sides with whoever is the enemy of his own particular slave-driver is a healthy instinct, and makes for freedom.'[1023]

This contrasts, again, with Lenin's position. With respect to Russia in particular, Lenin's view was that 'for us, Russian Social Democrats, there can be no doubt that, from the point of view of the working-classes and of the toiling masses of all the Russian peoples, the lesser evil would be a defeat of the Tsarist monarchy'. However, as a general position for the international socialist movement, it was, Lenin argued,

> impossible to determine, from the standpoint of the international proletariat, the defeat of which of the two groups of belligerent nations would be the lesser evil for socialism … The conversion of the present imperialist war into a civil war is the only correct proletarian slogan.[1024]

Connolly's position in favour of a German victory has come in for criticism. First of all, as Brian Hanley has argued, it could, and did for Connolly, lead to a position that 'eulogised Germany as a modern, progressive state and ignored or played down the reactionary nature of German imperialism'.[1025] We will discuss Connolly's view on the German state below but on German imperialism Connolly wrote that the German Empire, was 'a homogenous empire of self-governing peoples' which contained 'more of the possibilities of freedom and civilisation than' Britain's.[1026] This completely ignored Germany's colonial dependencies in Africa, and downplayed the brutality of German atrocities. In a remarkable passage, too, Connolly suggests that if Belgium had not resisted the German invasion and 'had contented herself with protesting at the passage of German troops through her territory',

> she would now have all her fortresses and cities in her own hands, her
> soldiers would all be alive and in a position to act with effect when the war
> had exhausted both sides, none of her civilian population would have lost
> their lives ... and her neutrality and independence would be effectually
> maintained.[1027]

From an internationalist perspective, another potential problem is
evident. If the victory of Germany is the lesser evil, or indeed represents a
positive development in itself, this logically justifies the position not of the
anti-war Marxist German left but the pro-war SPD right. Indeed, at times
Connolly followed this logic to its conclusion. In the *Workers' Republic*, he
published without comment a speech from the pro-war SPD deputy Edouard
David, one of the original revisionists, denying that Germany was waging a
war of conquest and placing the burden on Germany's opponents to make
peace.[1028] Connolly even went so far as to reprint a gushing interview with
the Kaiser by another pro-war German Social Democrat Anton Fendrich.
In it, the Kaiser described the socialists as 'splendid fellows' and Fendrich
asserted of the German ruler that 'there is no doubt that he understands the
aims of the Radical Left in parliament far better and has more sympathies
for them than the world knows'.[1029]

Brendan Clifford has gone so far as to argue that Connolly's embrace
of Germany led to a fundamental revision, in the final years of his life, to
his basic ideas of what a socialist society should look like. From his earliest
critiques of the Fabian equivalence of state ownership and control with
socialism, to his De Leonite-inspired industrial unionism, Connolly had
always insisted that socialism was the application of democratic and co-
operative principles to social life, to be fought for by workers themselves,
through their own political parties and trade unions. He was suspicious
of the notion of 'a bureaucratic State, ruling and ordering the lives of
every individual from above', arguing that industrial unionism, building
democracy from the workshop up to the national level 'gives assurance that
the social order of the future will be an extension of the freedom of the
individual, and not the suppression of it' and 'blends the fullest democratic
control with the most absolute expert supervision, something unthinkable
of any society built upon the political State'.[1030]

Clifford's argument is that in 1915 and 1916 Connolly's 'idea of socialism
was definitely concretised' and he 'began to see in Germany the essential
features of a socialist society'.[1031] It is true that Connolly published uncritical

articles in the *Workers' Republic,* such as a *New York Times Magazine* review of Frederic C. Howe's *Socialized Germany,* which argued that: 'The State socialism of Germany ... is the explanation of German's victories in Russia, France and Belgium', its 'victories in manufactures, trade and shipping'.[1032] Connolly later excerpted the concluding chapter of the book, which stated that an 'emphasis on human welfare is one of the remarkable things about the German idea of the state' and lauds 'the many social services which are supported by taxation' and the 'labour exchanges which eliminate much of the waste of unemployment'.[1033]

However, at the same time in 1915 Connolly published and promoted his last important book, *The Re-Conquest of Ireland,* in which he goes into his syndicalist-inspired vision for an Irish socialist state in some depth. Though the book was written before the outbreak of the war, Connolly still decided to publish it, and presumably stood by its contents. The concept of the one Big Union, 'embracing all workers in each industry' and federating these industrial unions nationally into one organisation was 'not only the outline of the most effective form of combination for industrial warfare to-day, but also for Social Administration of the Co-operative Commonwealth of the future'. Outlining a libertarian rather than an authoritarian statist conception of socialism, Connolly explained that:

> A system of society in which the workshops, factories, docks, railways, shipyards, &c., shall be owned by the nation, but administered by the Industrial Unions of the respective industries, organised as above, seems best calculated to secure the highest form of industrial efficiency, combined with the greatest amount of individual freedom from state despotism.[1034]

In addition to expanding industrial unionism, Connolly continued, 'Labour must necessarily attack the political and municipal citadels of power'. He envisages a scenario in which the labour movement expands its political control over the state, but the working class organised economically, at the point of production through industrial unions, acts as a guarantor of democracy and safeguards against bureaucratic state socialism:

> Every effort should be made to extend the scope of public ownership. As democracy invades and captures public powers public ownership will, of necessity, be transformed and infused with a new spirit. As Democracy enters, Bureaucracy will take flight. But without the power of the Industrial Union behind it, Democracy can only enter the State as the victim enters the gullet of the Serpent.[1035]

This democratic conception of socialism was consistent with the industrial unionism Connolly had espoused for the best part of a decade previously. Indeed, as Marc Mulholland has argued, the Irish conception of the 'Workers' Republic' and the 'Co-Operative Commonwealth' had a particularly democratic quality, in a country suspicious of state socialism.[1036] Moreover, it fits into a much wider contemporary critique of the 'servile state'. In 1912, the Catholic intellectual Hilaire Belloc published a book, *The Servile State,* which saw an authoritarian tendency inherent in the New Liberal social legislation. In particular, he saw the system of Labour Exchanges introduced by the Liberal government as a 'coming nearer to the establishment of compulsory labour among an unfree majority of non-owners for the benefit of a free minority of owners …'.[1037] Though Belloc was an anti-socialist reactionary, 'his acute identification of the servile tendencies of "welfare" legislation became the common property of the progressive opponents of state socialism: industrialist unionists, syndicalists, guild socialists' and, in particular, the SLP.[1038] While Belloc's pre-war writings bordered on the hysterical, they were given an added salience by the massive expansion of the state's wartime powers during the war. In particular, state power and private capital were increasingly interlocked within the Ministry of Munitions, as the government took over production of food, coal and most other raw materials, as well as shipping and rail transport, capital markets, wages and rents.[1039] The Defence of the Realm Act 1914, as Connolly wrote, 'gives the military authorities power to arrest civilians and try them by Courtsmartial, sets aside all the ordinary safeguards of civil liberty, and empowers these Courtsmartial to inflict the death penalty or any lesser sentence'.[1040] The Munitions Act 1915, moreover, banned strikes in war industries and made arbitration compulsory.

As we shall see in the next chapter, this wartime expansion of the state's powers was a major concern for Connolly, and it pushed him towards his view that a pre-emptive insurrection was necessary if the labour movement and a separate sense of Irish nationality were to be preserved. In this context, it seems unlikely that his conversion to 'German state socialism' was genuine, rather than a revision of his long-standing suspicion of bureaucratic state socialism, Connolly's publication of articles on the German economy was more 'pro-German' than 'pro-statism', in the context of his support of the German side in the war.

Some further comments are, however, necessary. Imperial Germany was not Nazi Germany, and 1914 was not 1939. If problematic from an international socialist perspective, Connolly's preference for a German victory was explicable from the perspective of one struggling for Irish self-determination. There is nothing wrong, in principle, with an oppressed nation exploiting the divisions between imperial powers in order to win self-determination. The issue came when this spilled over into positive political support for a German victory, and in Connolly's attempts to theoretically justify his backing for the Germans. This, at times, slipped into apologism for Germany's conduct of the war and special pleading regarding the nature of the German Empire. Connolly was not unique in this. His position fits into a wider context of widespread pro-German attitudes within the separatist movement, which was a milieu he was hoping to influence. The ICA sang 'The Germans Are Winning the War, Me Boys', a song written by 'Countess Markiewicz to the tune of "The Young May Moon"', which Scottish republican Margaret Skinnider recalled 'had a great effect in Dublin, before the rising, in preventing the British from getting Irish recruits'.[1041] Even the pacifist and socialist Francis Sheehy-Skeffington held, in a letter to William O'Brien, that 'This war means the end of the British Empire. If Germany wins, that is obvious. But if Russia wins, Russia will speedily turn on India, and end matters that way. I am hoping against hope for a German victory …'[1042]

Finally, there are some qualifications to the above discussion which can be made. Connolly had a tendency on a number of issues to exaggerate particular emphases or arguments in order to gain a better hearing for his position. The most famous example is his admission to Matheson that he 'posed' as a Catholic so as to not offend the religious sensibilities of Irish workers. Connolly was party to talks as early as September 1914 about conducting a rising with German backing, and German support was the most obvious form of military assistance for such an undertaking. Though he certainly was sympathetic to the German side, could Connolly's pro-German propaganda also in part be a similar 'pose' to soften up the target audience for his propaganda for the prospect of a German-backed insurrection? Patrick Pearse certainly expressed doubts as to the sincerity of Connolly's views on this matter. He complained at Christmas 1915 that 'Connolly is most dishonest in his methods. In public he says the war is a war forced on Germany by the Allies. In private he says that the Germans are as bad as the British.'[1043] This is reinforced by his repeated claim, even in public, that 'we do not wish to be ruled by either empire' and the expression of independence contained within the slogan 'We Serve Neither King nor Kaiser but Ireland'.

Connolly's clear internationalist instincts also come through in public statements, despite his occasional promotion of the pro-war Germany SPD. When erroneous reports surfaced early in the war that the revolutionary anti-war German SPD deputy Karl Liebknecht had 'been shot in Germany for refusing to accept military service in the war', Connolly hailed 'our continental comrade, who, in a world of imperial and financial brigands and cowardly trimmers and compromisers showed mankind that men still know how to die for the holiest of all causes – the sanctity of the human soul, the practical brotherhood of the human race!'[1044] Moreover, he later approvingly quoted Liebknecht's appeal in the anti-war British newspaper the *Labour Leader* which decried that 'many Socialists in the belligerent countries – for Germany is not an exception – have in this most rapacious of all wars of robbery willingly put on the yoke of the chariot of Imperialism just when the evils of capitalism were becoming more apparent than ever'.[1045]

There are clear suggestions too, that Connolly hoped for the overthrow of the German state by its own socialist movement. Though he warned his readership not to 'let anyone play upon your sympathies by denunciation of the German military bullies,' he added: 'German military bullies, like all tyrannies among civilised people, need fear nothing so much as native (German) democracy. Attacks from outside only strengthen tyrants within a nation.' He went on to speak of the German people 'rapidly forging weapons for their own emancipation from native tyranny', which can only mean the Kaiser. This article, entitled 'On German Militarism', is all the more important for having been published in the *Irish Worker*, i.e. for an Irish audience, rather than a British socialist audience, as with Connolly's articles in *Forward*.[1046]

There is a final piece of evidence, from shortly after the Easter Rising, that Connolly still approached the question of Germany as an international socialist. In May 1916 Sir Horace Plunkett, the pro-Home Rule MP and promoter of agricultural co-operation, arrived in London. On 11 May, he met Sir Basil Thomson, the deputy commissioner of the Metropolitan Police, who recorded the meeting in his diary. Plunkett had with him a report from a doctor in Dublin Castle who had seen Connolly prior to his execution. According to Thomson's diary entry:

[Connolly] told the doctor that the Germans were going to win the war; that he liked the Hohenzollerns no better than the doctor did, but when the war was over they would join the German socialists to turn the Hohenzollerns out. The doctor said that Ireland geographically could never be independent of England, to which Connolly replied: 'In a few weeks, there will be no British Empire'.[1047]

Though one of Connolly's biographers cites this as evidence that Connolly was, to the end, 'embroiled in nationalism', it is more straightforwardly evidence that Connolly held little truck for the Kaiser and looked forward to his overthrow by the German socialists after the war – even if this was lower in his order of priority than defeating his immediate enemy, the British Empire.[1048] Though Connolly did not live to see it, the Kaiser was in the end overthrown by a revolution in November 1918.

Anti-war activity

We have so far examined Connolly's response to the outbreak of war and the failure of the Second International to prevent it. In light of the comments of some of Connolly's biographers that upon the outbreak of war in August 1914 'Connolly became a revolutionary nationalist' and 'collapsed politically as a socialist', it is necessary to insist that, while his political world collapsed around him, Connolly's opposition to the war maintained an internationalist and working-class character, in a very difficult set of circumstances.[1049] In doing so, he made common cause with the anti-war socialist left in Britain, and was keen to highlight instances of socialist opposition to the war in the wider international movement.[1050]

The very early months of war also saw Connolly rise to positions of great power within the Irish labour movement, providing him with an unprecedented platform for his views. In October 1914, Larkin set sail for the United States, leaving Connolly as the acting general secretary of the ITGWU and the commander of the ICA. He rapidly promoted his close allies Michael Mallin and Helena Molony to influential positions in the ICA and the union, and took over the editorship of the *Irish Worker*.

The *Irish Worker* was part of a network of socialist newspapers that opposed the war, along with the SLP's *Socialist*, Keir Hardie's *Labour Leader* and *Merthyr Pioneer*, and the Glasgow ILP's newspaper *Forward*. Such anti-war activity was subject to state repression, much of it under the Defence of the Realm Act 1914 (DORA), which had been passed by the British Government at the start of the war. DORA gave the British Government sweeping powers, including the censorship of the press and communications, the requisitioning of property required for the war effort, the suspension of trial by jury, powers of search without warrant, and penalties of imprisonment or deportation 'for activities calculated to undermine the war effort in any way'. Such powers, it is argued, 'severely hampered left-wing activists and publicists throughout the United Kingdom'.[1051]

Upon the publication of its 5 December issue, the *Irish Worker* itself was suppressed under DORA, as part of a drive to clamp down on anti-war publications in Ireland. The Dublin Metropolitan Police (DMP) warned the printer, William Henry West, that under the Act he would be held personally responsible for printing material considered by the authorities as 'likely to cause disaffection, or to interfere with recruiting' to the British Army. The printers of the IRB's *Irish Freedom* and several other republican newspapers were similarly warned. When West had refused to print an editorial by Connolly attacking the DORA, Connolly printed a blank space where the column would have been, inserting a notice that 'Home Rule is now on the Statute book. Martial law is now in force, and free expression of opinion forbidden.'[1052] At this, the newspaper was banned. As a group of Huddersfield anti-war socialists put it, 'the military despots took a childish revenge on it [the *Irish Worker*], thus exposing the lie that this war is a war of liberty'.[1053] The suppression of the *Irish Worker* also meant that Connolly found it necessary to end his association with *Forward*, lest it meet the same fate. In a letter to the editor, Tom Johnston, Connolly expressed how 'proud [he] was to have been associated, ever so slightly with the little paper that held so close to the idea of Internationalism when so many who had given that principle lip service had so basely deserted it'.[1054]

Not willing to allow state repression to deprive him of a newspaper, Connolly turned to his old comrades in the Glasgow SLP. The *Irish Worker*'s short-lived replacement, *The Worker*, was printed on the SLP press in Renfrew Street. 'Each week, thousands of copies were taken over on the Irish boat by Arthur MacManus – disguised as glass shipments – for distribution in Dublin.'[1055] *The Worker* contained some of Connolly's most hard-hitting anti-war pieces. These included an important editorial in January 1915, 'In this Supreme Hour of Our National Danger', urging Dublin workers to remember their class position amidst the horrors of the war and vote for the Dublin Labour Party in the municipal elections. Reproducing a quote from the *Irish Times* on the horrific conditions in slum housing in the city, Connolly wrote that it is 'our duty to our own class, to our country, and to ourselves to see that the voters do not so forget' such horrors, which 'degrade and destroy many thousands of their lives'. On the contrary, workers must 'seize the opportunity given them by the elections to strike as hard a blow as they can at the system responsible for such atrocities, and at the political parties which uphold that system'.

What follows is a stirring example of Connolly's socialist anti-war journalism, in advocating the independent interests of the workers against both the Irish capitalist class and the war for the British Empire:

Of course, we will be told that 'now in this supreme hour of our national danger', etc, all ideas of war between classes should be laid aside and we all should co-operate harmoniously together. In answer we would ask – has any capitalist or landlord shown any forbearance towards the workers more than they have been compelled to by the force of law, or by the power of labour unions? Is it not the fact that 'in this supreme hour of our national danger' the employers are seizing eagerly upon every pretext to reduce wages and victimise the workers?

Connolly proclaimed:

War or no war those slums must be swept out of existence; war or no war those slum landlords are greater enemies than all the 'Huns' of Europe; war or no war our children must have decent homes to grow up in, decently equipped schools to attend, decent food whilst at school ... war or no war the most sacred duty of the working class of Ireland is to seize every available opportunity to free itself from the ravenous maw of the capitalist system and to lay the foundations for the Co-operative Commonwealth – the Working Class Republic.[1056]

By now, the police were monitoring the SLP's Renfrew Street premises and discovered the source of this seditious material. On 15 January, the Glasgow police intercepted three large parcels containing around 4,000 copies of The Worker at the Caledonian railway station and removed a copy before letting the parcels continue on their way to Dublin. They were given to paper boys for sale in the streets, and Dublin Castle's view was no action needed since it was 'more anti-capitalist than anti-British'. On 4 February, however, the RIC received a tip-off from Glasgow that the latest issue would arrive on board the SS Puma in a box and parcel marked 'Socialist Labour Party' and 'Fry's coca chocolate'. Sir Matthew Nathan the under-secretary for Ireland, believed it was directed against the army and wanted action to be taken. The Army issued a suppression order and the DMP seized the container on the morning of 6 February, destroying all but ten copies to be kept 'for official purposes'.[1057]

By May 1915, however, Connolly was in a position to launch yet another newspaper, printed on a printing press stored in the basement of Liberty Hall. Connolly chose for its title the Workers' Republic, picking up a thread of continuity which had been broken when his previous paper with this title closed twelve years before. Introducing the paper on 29 May, Connolly described its mission as follows: 'To increase the intelligence of the slave, to sow broadcast the seeds of that intelligence, that they may take root and ripen into revolt, to be the interpreter of that revolt, and finally to help in guiding it to victory ...'[1058] To do this, Connolly reported on the struggles of Irish workers, such as the railway strike in Dublin, the dockers' strike in Derry and, most notably, the long drawn-out battle between the ITGWU and the City of Dublin Steam Packet Company, which Connolly himself conducted as general secretary of the union.

Though Connolly resolved to 'devote most of our space to the Labour movement in this country', his reportage did not stop at national borders. As David Convery has argued, even 'in the midst of the First World War with national and parochial views at their height, the Workers' Republic was exposing audiences of working-class people in Ireland to ... an international viewpoint'.[1059] It did this by carrying reports from 'a remarkable range of the international press'. While the Second International had failed to prevent the war, 'Connolly remained attuned to events worldwide' and printed stories from Sylvia Pankhurst's Women's Dreadnought, the Labour Leader, Forward, and the SDF's Justice in Britain; US publications such as the Call and International Socialist Review; the German SPD's Neue Zeit, La Guerre Sociale in Paris, and a piece from Russkija Wedomosti in Moscow.

Connolly also highlighted working-class and socialist resistance to the war internationally. As we have already seen, he hailed the bravery of the anti-war SPD's Karl Liebknecht. In September 1915, he also reprinted a piece from the Cleveland Citizen celebrating the anti-war speech in the Russian Duma from the Georgian Menshevik leader Nikolay Chkheidze.[1060]

That same month, an unofficial conference of 42 delegates from Second International parties opposed to the war met at Zimmerwald in neutral Switzerland. The delegates were divided between the views of Lenin and the Bolsheviks that the war should be turned into a revolutionary international civil war and a much more cautious pacifist opposition to the war on the right, with a centre group comprising Trotsky and Angelica Balabanoff in between. Nevertheless, all agreed to issue a manifesto to the working class:

Since the outbreak of the war, you have placed your energy, your courage, your endurance at the service of the ruling classes. Now you must stand up for your own cause, for the sacred aims of Socialism, for the emancipation of the oppressed nations as well as of the enslaved classes, by means of the irreconcilable proletarian class struggle.[1061]

Connolly published an account of the Zimmerwald conference in the Workers' Republic on 25 December 1915 from two French delegates,

Bourderon of the French socialist party and Merrheim from the Union of Metalworkers. Both were on the moderate wing of the French labour movement. Their statement was a blistering attack on the '*Union Sacrée*', which saw the French labour movement call a truce with the government for the duration of the war. Rather than revolutionary action, however, the French statement called for 'international, common and simultaneous action of the working classes in all countries' to 'prevent the ruling classes from taking decisions as to the conditions of peace, which would be fatal to the interests of all workers'.[1062] But as Peter Petroff, an internationalist opponent of Hyndman in the BSP, commented at the time, the Zimmerwald Manifesto was 'one step in the right direction' but 'does not call for definite revolutionary action. It simply invites the Socialists of the various countries to carry on a campaign for peace.' Thus, 'in this respect,' Petroff noted, 'the manifesto bears a strong resemblance to the platitudes of which many of the leaders of the Old International were so enamoured'.[1063]

Though Trotsky would write in 1930 that 'the hitherto unknown name of Zimmerwald was echoed throughout the world', Connolly can perhaps be forgiven for not treating the anti-war conference more seriously.[1064] The means – simultaneous action – would have struck Connolly as unrealistic, given the collapse of the Second International; the ends – pressure on the ruling class for peace – too hopelessly moderate to meet the requirements of the situation. While Connolly may have seen the full text of the Manifesto in *Justice* or the *Labour Leader,* it took time for Zimmerwald's true significance in cohering the anti-war left of the International and preparing the ground for a new International to become clear. By this time, of course, Connolly had already set his sights on a rising.

Though increasingly despairing of the Second International parties, Connolly also remained in contact with British socialist opponents of the war, and the *Workers' Republic* circulated widely in Scotland, promoted by members of the ILP. Connolly was considered an important ally by the Glasgow socialists. In September 1915, the Glasgow-based socialist John Maclean was imprisoned under DORA. His comrade, Harry McShane, then went on the run and 'before he left the city he was given a letter of introduction, signed by both Maclean and James MacDougall, addressed to James Connolly'.[1065] It was hoped that Connolly would hide him, though McShane in the end did not reach Dublin. Then, in November, Glasgow ILP, SLP and BSP members were co-operating on anti-conscription activity in the city and hoped to involve Connolly in their campaign. McManus wrote to him and received a friendly reply assuring him that Connolly 'would gladly accept [his] offer and invitation to address an anti-conscription meeting in Glasgow were it at all possible. But,' wrote Connolly, 'every moment in Dublin just now is full of tragic possibilities, as our beneficent Government is becoming daily more high-handed in its methods, and my presence is required here in constant watchfulness.' Connolly felt moved to decline but sent instead a message to McManus and 'all the Comrades who refuse to be led astray to fight the battles of the ruling Capitalist class'. He wrote:

Tell them that we in Ireland will not have Conscription, let the Law say what it likes. We know our rulers; we know their power, and their ruthlessness we experience every day. We know they can force us to fight whether we wish to or not, but we know also that no force in their possession can decide for us where we will fight. That remains for us to decide; and we have no intention of shedding our blood abroad for our masters; rather will we elect to shed it if need be in a battle for the conquest of our freedom at home.[1066]

Connolly's sense of solidarity with the British anti-war movement was borne of his view, expressed in a letter to the editor of Forward, that the 'moral and physical courage required to take up and maintain such a position', in Britain, the heart of the British Empire, was 'a hundredfold grander than anything on exhibition in the trenches from end to end of the far flung battleline of the warring nations'.[1067] Keir Hardie's paper, the Labour Leader, Connolly wrote, 'has covered itself with imperishable glory owing to the stand it has taken against the war'. This attitude was also on display in his heartfelt tribute to Keir Hardie, by whose loss, Connolly wrote, 'labour has lost one of its most fearless and incorruptible champions, and the world one of its highest minded and purest souls'. Recalling Hardie's support for the workers of Dublin during the Lockout, and celebrating his steadfast opposition to the war, Connolly wrote of how, when

the contending hosts of Europe were being marshalled by their masters for the work of murder, James Keir Hardie stood resolutely for peace and brotherhood among the nations – refusing to sanction the claim of the capitalist class of any nation to be the voice of the best interests of that nation.[1068]

Connolly's appreciation extended, too, to the south Wales miners, whose strike for higher pay against the war-time Coalition Government, Connolly held as 'proof of the strengths and invincibility of Labour when united'.[1069]

Moreover, Connolly argued, the victory of the Welsh miners had a direct bearing on the situation in Ireland. Congratulating 'our Welsh Comrades upon the successful outcome of their resistance to the attempt of the Government to dragoon them into submission', Connolly wrote that

> we realise that had the Government succeeded in terrorising them we might all have bidden a long farewell to our industrial liberties. Successful in Wales, the capitalist class that runs these islands would have been ruthless in Ireland.[1070]

Though he was full of admiration for the anti-war minority in Britain, developments in the wider British labour movement gave Connolly cause for pessimism. In March 1915, the union leaders reached the so-called Treasury Agreement with the government. Under the terms of the agreement, trade unions 'formally relinquished the right to strike for the duration of the war'. Moreover, 'all disputes that could not be settled in the normal way' would be referred to arbitration.[1071] As Connolly wrote scathingly, 'the workers have surrendered the only weapon they possess of immediate effective value in compelling a hearing for their demands'. There was no sign 'of the capitalist class giving up any of the power they possess over the lives of their employees. It is only the workers who are asked to surrender civic rights – rights hard won by generations of fighters.'[1072] Labour's Arthur Henderson joined the wartime Cabinet in May 1915, along with two Labour junior ministers. This only served to provide cover for further repression. In July 1915, the British government went further with the introduction of the Munitions of War Act, which gave legal force to the concessions freely made by the union leaders.

In September 1915, the TUC Congress met in Bristol. 'Time was,' Connolly commented, 'when the most beloved spokesmen of that Congress were those who most passionately declared that it was the duty of the workers to overthrow all the social, political and military tyrannies rooted in the capitalist system of which the British Empire is the perfected fruit.' Not now. The Congress backed its leadership in repudiating strike action for the war's duration. Connolly drew a stark conclusion:

> We have ere now looked hopefully to the British Trade Union Congress, but our hopes are gone. The British Empire is ruled by the most astute ruling class in the world; the British working class is the most easily fooled working class in the world. God help the poor Irish as long as they remain yoked to such a combination.

It must have been particularly galling for Connolly that some of his one-time allies in the radical British syndicalist milieu had abandoned their internationalism in favour of a pro-war position. The TUC Congress was an occasion at which 'a leader like Ben Tillett foams at the mouth against those who desire peace as a few months ago he foamed at the mouth against those who desired war'. In April 1916, Connolly quoted Tom Mann as having said at a meeting in Sheffield that 'the termination of the war at this moment would result in serious disaster'. Both Tillett and Mann, said Connolly,

> were before the war the greatest of internationalists, and rather despised our Irish love for our own nationality, as being mere sentimental slop and entirely out of date. Now they are raving jingoes, howling for the blood of every rival of the British capitalist class.[1073]

By then, however, Connolly had more pressing concerns than the political degeneration of his erstwhile syndicalist allies. Just over a week after these words were published, he would march his Citizens' Army into battle as part of the Easter Rising of April 1916.

Chapter 8

The road to the Easter Rising

In a very real sense, some sort of insurrection in Ireland was inevitable as soon as the First World War began. The question would be, however, what sort of insurrection, carried out by whom and with what programme. We have seen in the previous chapter that Connolly hoped the labour movement would exploit the opportunity provided by the war to launch a socialist revolution. His initial reaction to the war called in the *Irish Worker* of 8 August 1914 for the working class 'to erect barricades all over Europe, to break up bridges and destroy the transport service that war might be abolished'.[1074] In the very same edition of Larkin's newspaper, however, Connolly also argued that if a German army landed in Ireland, it would be justified to join with it to rid Ireland of its connection to the British Empire. This pointed to a still radical, but more limited, aim of winning Irish self-determination

To understand this, it may be helpful to consider Connolly's attitude as a 'dual perspective'. Both socialist revolution and national self-determination were held out as potential prospects on the horizon. Both aims were contingent, however, on creating social and political forces which could realise them in reality. In Connolly's view, it soon became clear not only that the Second International had failed to stop the war, but that the labour movements in Europe, Britain or Ireland did not seem capable of sparking a worker-led socialist insurrection. As the war continued, 'notions of socialism and national liberation continued to co-exist' in Connolly's mind; however, 'his socialist pronouncements remained propagandist exercises'.[1075] Of increasing practical importance for Connolly was the necessity to forge a practical alliance with the separatist republicans, who were in the process of being transformed from a fringe on the edges of the nationalist movement to a decisive force in the situation.

It is clear that Connolly hoped for some working arrangement with the republican movement from the very outbreak of the war. According to Cathal O'Shannon, who worked closely with Connolly in Belfast, when the news of war broke, Connolly was in his Belfast ITGWU office, and declared: 'This means war.' He announced, after a dramatic silence, that a blow for Irish independence must be struck.[1076] Similarly, William O'Brien recalls that Connolly discussed with him 'the desirability of acting with all those who would favour organisation for an insurrection' and promised to his comrade: 'I will not miss this chance.'[1077] Both men record that Connolly asked them to put him in touch with the IRB.[1078]

In this sense, therefore, those biographers who stress the outbreak of the war as representing a rupture point in Connolly's political development have a point.[1079] Prior to the war, Connolly had followed a three-pronged strategy of building the ITGWU as an industrial union, the Irish Labour Party as the trade union movement's political wing, and the SPI and then ILP(I) as a socialist propaganda organisation. Following the outbreak of the war, when this schema no longer applied, Connolly sought a path through an unprecedented and potentially disorienting situation. He was forced to reckon with the failure of the International to prevent the war, and what this meant for the capacity of the international working class as an agent of revolutionary change. At the same time, however, Connolly tried to ascertain the revolutionary possibilities of the crisis for Ireland, which provoked difficult questions about the nature of any Irish uprising and the alliances that would be necessary to carry it out.

Next we shall examine Connolly's attitude towards the IRB, as well as the position of this secretive republican organisation on the war and its growth to a position of influence over a significant minority of the wider nationalist movement.

Connolly, the IRB and the Volunteers

Like Connolly, the IRB also sensed that the war provided an opportunity which could not be missed. Indeed, as historian Fearghal McGarry wrote, a 'wartime insurrection, even one likely to fail, was not only rational but a moral and historical imperative if Fenianism was to retain any credibility or future'.[1080] Pearse summed up the general mood in separatist circles, writing in August 1914 that the 'European war has brought about a crisis which may contain, as yet hidden within it, the moment for which the generations have been waiting'.[1081]

For an organisation which would play such a decisive role in Easter 1916, the IRB was not in a strong position in the years leading up to the insurrection. As late as April 1912, when the third Home Rule Bill was introduced, one historian of the organisation wrote that 'the IRB in Ireland was essentially nothing more than the *Irish Freedom* newspaper, three small circles led by Denis McCullough in Belfast' and a small following around the energetic young organiser Bulmer Hobson.[1082] McCullough and Hobson, however, were part of a new generation who played a crucial role in reversing the IRB's decline. Part of their efforts involved a cull of the dead wood in the organisation. As McCullough, the Belfast-based President of the IRB, bluntly recalled: 'I cleared out most of the older men (including my father), most of whom I considered of no further use to us.'[1083] They were aided in this effort by the veteran Fenian Tom Clarke, who returned from Ireland in 1907 after spending almost a decade in the United States. Before that, Clarke had served fifteen years in British prisons after he was sentenced to penal servitude for life in 1883 at the Old Bailey for involvement in an IRB dynamiting campaign. Clarke, a strong 'physical force' militarist, encouraged several talented young activists (including his protégé Sean MacDermott) to focus their attentions away from the increasingly moribund Sinn Féin movement and into building the IRB.

What seriously transformed the prospects of the IRB, propelling it to a position of major influence over the national movement, was the formation in November 1913 of the Irish Volunteers. The Volunteers were an Irish nationalist militia organisation, pledging to defend Home Rule from any attempts to frustrate it by the Unionists or the British Tory establishment. The organisation was a response, in part, to the formation of the UVF by Sir Edward Carson and James Craig in January 1913, who threatened to declare a provisional government in Ulster if Home Rule for Ireland was introduced. Fronted by the more moderate figure of Eoin MacNeill, Professor of Early and Medieval History at University College Dublin, the idea for the Volunteers had come from the IRB and was the result of months of back-room planning. Rightly, the IRB saw in the Volunteer movement the potential to transform Irish republican separatism from what Hobson admitted was 'a little secret movement meeting in back rooms', into something far more dangerous to British rule in Ireland.[1084]

The launch of the Volunteers took place at a rally on 25 November 1913 at the Rotunda Rink in Dublin, just as the Dublin Lockout was reaching a crescendo. It is important to note for our analysis of the relations between the labour movement and the nationalists in this chapter that a number of Home Rule organisations were invited to take part but the ITGWU was not. Future playwright Sean O'Casey was, at this stage, 'a staunch Irish-Irelander, an active member of the IRB and a member of the ITGWU' and the Citizen Army.[1085] Having failed to bring the IRB into the fight against the employers, O'Casey was incensed to hear of his organisation's moves to establish a Volunteer organisation with men who 'had locked out their employees because they had ventured to assert the first principles of Trade Unionism'. Why, he asked, 'while every national body society and club,' such as the UIL and Sinn Féin, 'received invitation to attend the initial meeting ... the Transport Union, the largest union of unskilled workers in Ireland was ignored?'[1086] The answer was, of course, that the IRB hoped to keep the Volunteers as broad as possible, and that the inclusion of the ITGWU would alienate the bourgeois Home Rule nationalists who they hoped to attract to the new organisation. As Newsinger put it, 'with the conditions of class war prevailing in Dublin in November 1913, the IRB had to choose between the ITWGU and the home rulers of the United Irish League, and they choose the latter'.[1087]

Relations between the Volunteers and the ITGWU deteriorated further when the joint secretary of the Volunteers' provisional committee rose to speak on the night of the launch. Kettle had well-known anti-trade union views and, as part of the Lockout, his father Andrew, a prominent UIL politician, had even locked out union members in his own farm, replacing them with scab labour. When Kettle started speaking,

> A large contingent of ITGWU men had infiltrated the hall and drowned out his voice with heckling and cat-calls. Scuffles broke out between the hecklers and stewards. At the same time, another body of union men tried to invade the hall but were kept out by stewards armed with hurley bats.[1088]

This episode, which was covered prominently in the *Irish Worker,* left a residue of bitterness between the Larkinites and the Volunteers. There was admittedly a spectrum of views towards the Volunteers within the Citizen Army, with O'Casey undoubtedly representing the most hostile. Nevertheless, the period of early 1914 in general was characterised by mutual mistrust between the Transport Union's militia and the Volunteers. Moreover, this reflected the class divisions in Irish society as a whole, and the jostling between the labour movement and the nationalist bourgeoisie for primacy in an expected Home Rule Ireland. On the one hand, the Volunteers did not want to be associated with the ITGWU's radical syndicalism while, in the context of the murderous conduct of the DMP during the Lockout, O'Casey wondered out loud if Home Rule meant merely a transference of 'the stick which beats the worker' from British imperialism to the Irish Volunteers.

In addition to the ever-present class dimension, the spring of 1914 was characterised by growing uncertainty surrounding the Third Home Rule Bill. On 9 March, the British Prime Minister Asquith introduced an Amending Bill which, in his words, was 'to allow the Ulster counties themselves to determine, in the first instance, whether or not they desire to be excluded ... [for] a term of six years'. Support for exclusion had been building in Unionist circles, and Asquith's proposal was a major concession to the UVF's campaign against Home Rule. In Connolly's words, it meant 'that a local majority, in Belfast or Derry, for instance, are to be given the power to wreak their hatred upon Ireland by dismembering her, by cutting Ireland to pieces as a corpse would be cut upon the dissecting table'. The Unionist position was further boosted on 20 March, when 57 British Army officers resigned their postings rather than take party in mooted military action against the Unionist resistance to Home Rule.

Connolly threw himself into opposition to partition. On 14 March, Connolly predicted, famously, that:

Such a scheme as that agreed to by Redmond and Devlin, the betrayal of the national democracy of industrial Ulster would mean a carnival of reaction both North and South, would set back the wheels of progress, would destroy the oncoming unity of the Irish Labour movement and paralyse all advanced movements whilst it endured.[1089]

Though Connolly was a particularly eloquent exponent of this view, he was far from alone. When the ITUC considered the matter at the beginning of June, delegate after delegate lined up to oppose the scheme. The debate, as Emmet O'Connor has argued, 'reflected the common opinion – so often attributed to Connolly alone – that partition would weaken Labour or was a device to that end' and a motion condemning partition was carried by 84 votes to 2.[1090]

Connolly's demand that the labour movement 'should fight even to the death, if necessary, as our fathers fought before us' against the partition plan took on an added significance with the re-organisation of the Citizen Army in early 1914. At O'Casey's persuasion, the ICA adopted a more formal constitution and army council at a conference on 22 March.[1091] As well as holding the organisation together in the wake of the Lockout's defeat, the new structure marked a shift in emphasis from the ICA as a trade union defence force to a military body in the Irish separatist tradition. The first article of the constitution held that 'the first and last principle of the Irish Citizen Army is the avowal that the ownership of Ireland, moral and material, is vested of right in the people of Ireland'.[1092] This slightly ambiguous formula was a blend of socialism with the Lalor-inspired expansion of popular sovereignty into the material realm which characterised Connolly's rooting of Marxism in an Irish soil. With Asquith's partition plan in mind, the second principle of the new ICA constitution stated 'that the Citizen Army shall stand for the absolute unity of Irish nationhood'. This was given an internationalist dimension, in the context of growing diplomatic tension in Europe, with the assertion that the ICA shall 'support the rights and liberties of the democracies of all nations'.[1093] The third principle, more republican than socialist, was that one of the objects of the ICA 'shall be to sink all differences of birth, property and creed under the common name of Irish people'. The specifically working-class and labour movement identity of the ICA, however, was further guaranteed by fifth clause, included at Larkin's insistence, that 'every applicant must, if eligible, be a member of his trade union, such union to be recognised by the Irish Trade Union Congress'.[1094]

Taken together, this blend of republican, internationalist, trade union and socialist principles strongly differentiated the working-class ICA from the bourgeois nationalist Volunteers. Though the ICA had stepped firmly on to the territory of separatist republicanism, this was by no means a new departure, for this rhetoric had long been a staple of the ITGWU and the *Irish Worker*. The ICA hoped to create a pole of attraction for republican-minded workers and was pitched in direct competition with the Volunteers, which Larkin denounced as 'a Castle-controlled organisation' that would 'if given the opportunity, attack, baton, shoot and massacre the organised working class'.[1095] Connolly, it must be pointed out, was not heavily involved in the ICA at this time. However, his views can be gleaned from his address to delegates at the ITUC Congress, which was previewed in the *Irish Worker*. Connolly told the assembled workers that

> there are no real Nationalists in Ireland outside of the Irish Labour movement. All others merely reject one part or another of the British Conquest, the Labour movement alone rejects it in its entirety, and sets itself the Re-conquest of Ireland as its aim.[1096]

Regardless of the hostility from the ITGWU and the Citizen Army, the Irish Volunteers grew rapidly on a purely nationalist basis. As the Home Rule crisis deepened, the Volunteers reached 180,000 members by the summer of 1914.[1097] Though many of the Volunteers were at this stage Home Rulers in their politics, the IRB was well aware of the radicalising potential of the movement. In March 1914, its newspaper *Irish Freedom*, wrote that: 'The young men who stand together ... for Gaelic League and Sinn Féin and Republican principles, who are crowding into the Volunteers, can save Ireland and will.'[1098] IRB activists were instructed to join up and work their way into positions of influence and control.

The growth of the IRB within the Irish Volunteers did not go unnoticed by the more moderate forces of Irish nationalism. Fearing a threat to his dominance in the nationalist movement, Home Rule leader John Redmond moved to bring the Volunteers under his control in June 1914. That month, after protracted negotiations with MacNeil, Redmond forced the Volunteer's leading Provisional Committee to accept the co-option of 25 supporters of the IPP.[1099] With many of the moderate forces on the Committee supporters of Redmond already, the vote was almost a certainty. It provoked a split in the IRB ranks too, however. Bulmer Hobson, one of the IRB Supreme Council members most responsible for the foundation of the Volunteers, voted in favour of the inclusion of Redmond's appointees. Tom Clarke, who bitterly opposed the move, asked Hobson how much Dublin Castle had paid him, insinuating that he was working for the British. The two men never spoke again.

This development seemed to justify that faction of the Citizen Army, including figures such as Larkin, who denounced the Volunteers as an extension of the Hibernians, and as aspirant enforcers of bourgeois order in a Home Rule Ireland. Connolly, drawing on his reading of Irish history, saw in the Volunteers' capitulation to Redmond a repeat of past betrayals. He implored readers of the *Irish Worker* to mark well the words of 'the greatest Irish Revolutionist, Wolfe Tone', that 'when the aristocracy come forward the people fall backward; when the people come forward the aristocracy, fearful of being left behind, insinuate themselves into our ranks and *rise into timid leaders or treacherous auxiliaries*'. Connolly was scathing: 'I have had few more unpleasant experiences in my life than I underwent when listening to the pitiful attempts of some members of the Provisional Committee to explain and justify their votes upon their surrender.' They were, he wrote, 'attempting to do the work of a revolutionary movement by the methods of a ward-canvasser in a Municipal election'.[1100]

Despite its internal convulsions, on 26 July 1914 the Irish Volunteers successfully carried off a gunrunning operation at Howth, a village just north of Dublin. In an operation masterminded by Hobson, the Volunteers landed 1,500 1871 vintage Mauser rifles which had been sourced from Germany by the former British diplomat Sir Roger Casement. The Howth gunrunning was an echo of a UVF operation that had taken place in April, when the loyalists landed 25,000 rifles and three million rounds of ammunition at Larne in County Antrim, with total immunity from the authorities. In the context of partition and the Curragh Mutiny, the two gunrunnings represented a pronounced escalation of tension. Many began to predict the outbreak of civil war in Ireland. So certain was he that conflict in Ireland was inevitable, the Austro-Hungarian commander-in-chief, Field Marshal Franz Conrad von Hötzendorf, even wrote of it as fact, recording in his diary on 3 August the view there was no desire in England for war 'on account of the Ulster crisis and the civil war'.[1101]

The reaction to the Howth gunrunning exposed clear differences in the British authorities' attitudes towards the Irish Volunteers and the UVF. When the DMP were largely unwilling and certainly unable to prevent the guns being landed at Howth, the King's Own Scottish Borderers were ordered to disarm the Volunteers. In the ensuing scuffle, the troops were humiliated, as the Volunteers escaped largely unscathed. Upon their return to Dublin, the soldiers were accosted by an angry, but unarmed, crowd. The troops opened fire on civilians at Bachelor's Walk, Dublin, killing three and injuring almost 40. Connolly reported for the Glasgow-based ILP newspaper, *Forward*:

> The first shots of the threatened civil war have at length been fired, and the streets of an Irish city have run red with the blood of Irishmen. But contrary to all the threats, omens and portents, it was not an Ulster city that witnessed calamity; it was not the blood of Ulstermen that was shed in defence of their rights and liberties. It was only the blood of common ordinary Irishmen who dared to fancy that what was sauce for the Orange goose was also sauce for the Nationalist gander.[1102]

The Bachelor's Walk massacre was particularly resonant for Dublin's working-class population, coming as it did less than a year after the baton charges of the RIC and the DMP during the Lockout. The ICA and the Volunteers took their place in the guard of honour at the funerals for those who had died. O'Casey who, it will be remembered, was a firm critic of the Volunteers, recalled that 'the celebrated episode of the Howth gunrunning had engendered fellow feeling between the rank and file of both movements, which was near akin to comradeship'.[1103]

War

Two days after the Bachelor's Walk massacre, Austria-Hungary declared war on Serbia, soon tipping most of Europe into conflict. Initially, in line with the somewhat fractious relationship between the labour movement and the republicans up until that point, Connolly's view was that 'it would be worse than foolish – it would be a crime against all our hopes and aspirations – to take counsel from any other source' than 'the working-class democracy of Ireland in the face of the present crisis'. In supporting the war effort, Connolly wrote on 8 August, Redmond had in effect told the British Empire that 'the Irish slaves will guarantee to protect the Irish estate of England until their masters come back to take possession'. Looking towards the republicans, his view was that 'the advanced Nationalists have neither a policy nor a leader'. Connolly recalled that during the Russian Revolution of 1905, when Russia was considered an enemy of Britain in international diplomacy, republican

> spokesmen, orators and writers vied with each other in laudation of Russia and vilification of all the Russian enemies of Czardom'. Now that the Russian and British Empire were on the same side against Germany, Connolly wrote, 'surely the childish intellects that conceived of the pro-Russian campaign of nine years ago cannot give us light and leading in any campaign for freedom from the British allies of Russia today?

The following week, however, Connolly detected signs that what he called the 'advanced Nationalists' were coming out from under the Redmondite shadow. On 15 August, in an article in the *Irish Worker,* Connolly wrote how 'last week I said that only from the working-class democracy could a real lead be expected in this crisis. I am happy to be able to state that we are not so isolated in this matter as I at first feared.' He pointed to agreement from the separatists on the need to safeguard foodstuffs: 'The editor of Sinn Féin strikes a perfectly correct and sane note upon the crisis, we are glad to say, as does also Claidheamh Soluis, the Gaelic League weekly. Other newspapers and journals make tentative and truly fearful suggestions along the same lines.' Moreover,

> in many Dublin companies of Volunteers the members have discussed the matter and came to agreement on the right side, and despite the fearful wave of pro-English filth now spread over the country signs are multiplying that in actions upon these lines there will be found the possibility of making a stand for Ireland that will win the adhesion of all that is best in the land.[1104]

Viewing these positive developments, Connolly called for 'the formation of a Committee of all the earnest elements, outside as well as inside the Volunteers, to consider means to take and hold Ireland and the food of Ireland for the people of Ireland'. He added that the ITGWU and there ICA were 'ready for any such co-operation' and could 'bring to it the aid of drilled and trained men' and 'the services of thinkers and organisers who know that different occasions require different policies, that you cannot legalise revolutionary actions, and that audacity alone can command success in a national crisis like this'.

At the same time as Connolly was calling for united action on the issue of foodstuffs, the IRB turned towards a policy of instituting broad and open front organisations to expand its influence on the fast-developing situation. A meeting was held on 9 September in Sean T. O'Kelly's offices in the Gaelic League headquarters in 25 Parnell Square. Connolly was in attendance, alongside William O'Brien, Pearse, Plunkett, MacDonagh, Arthur Griffith and John MacBride. It was decided that a Rising would take place in any of three contingencies: 'a German victory in the war, an attempt by the British to enforce conscription in Ireland, or if the war was coming to an end without the other circumstances having arisen,' so that Ireland could claim belligerent rights at any post-war Peace Conference.[1105] According to William O'Brien, the 9 September meeting 'agreed to appoint two sub-committees, one to endeavour to form contact with Germany, and the other to organise an open organisation to be used for propaganda purposes and as a recruiting ground for the secret movement'. It is unclear what the status of the first committee was, especially given that the IRB had already made contact with Germany in August through its American sister organisation, *Clan na Gael*.[1106] The result of the second decision, however, was the formation of the short-lived Irish Neutrality League , with Connolly as President. Though it did 'useful work', thought O'Brien, the short-lived pressure group 'was an organisation of leaders without members'.[1107]

Events were moving quickly. On 20 September, Redmond, in a speech at Woodenbridge, County Wicklow, went even further in his support for the British war effort than he had done so previously in the House of Commons. Speaking to a parade of Volunteers, Redmond urged them to fight, not just in Ireland, but 'wherever the firing line extends in defence of right, of freedom and religion in this war'. Enraged by this call for Irishmen to join the war effort of the British Empire, republican opponents of Redmond took the opportunity to sese the Volunteer Headquarters on 24 September. An order was signed to expel Redmond's men from the Volunteers, leading to a split in the organisation.

In a sign of the increasing co-operation between the republicans and the radical labour movement, it appears that Connolly and William O'Brien were aware of the moves beforehand. In the *Irish Worker*, Connolly praised 'the Napoleon-like stroke of the old Provisional Committee in resuming control' of the Volunteers.[1108] Connolly then stressed the 'necessity of a "Forward" policy for the Irish Volunteers', to take 'aggressive action' against the Redmondites and their agents, who were attempting to 'betray Ireland into the grasp of British Imperialism'. Rather than waiting to patiently convince those Volunteers 'not yet sufficiently convinced of the treachery of their leaders', Connolly urged the anti-war Provisional Committee to 'attack aggressively, resolutely, openly', and carry a campaign of agitation 'to educate and organise public opinion on its side' around pledges to remain 'in armed service in Ireland for Ireland' and to 'enforce the repeal of all clauses in the Home Rule Act denying to Ireland powers of self-government now enjoyed by South Africa, Australia or Canada'.

Such a campaign, Connolly argued, would push 'the onus of defending things morally and politically indefensible' back on the Redmondites. Either, Connolly argued, they would defend recruiting and 'all the worst iniquities in the Home Rule Act', or else repudiate both and cede ground to their republican and socialist critics. Encouraging the Volunteers to adopt the demand for Commonwealth status (very similar to what was eventually achieved by the Free State in 1922), and outcome far below Connolly's ultimate goal of a Workers' Republic or even full independence, was a tactical ploy, designed to push the Volunteers into confrontation with the British, and further drive a wedge between the moderates and more radical forces.

Connolly's attempts to win influence in the new Volunteers were not limited to literary exercises. One day after the split between the anti-war forces and Redmond, a joint operation was planned between the IRB, the Volunteers and the Citizen Army. Asquith was due to speak at the Mansion House on 25 September alongside Redmond and John Dillon in a rally to promote military recruitment for the war effort. The plan was for 100 volunteers from the three organisations to seize the building on the day of the rally to prevent it from taking place. In the end, the building was heavily guarded by both the RIC and the National Volunteers – a sign of the extent to which the movement had been split – and the operation was called off. Nevertheless, it is of significance as the first joint operation between the forces that would eventually organise the Easter Rising.

Connolly's strategy around this time, then, was to hegemonise those elements of the Irish Volunteers who were disgusted with Redmond's betrayal, by drawing them closer to the ITGWU and the Citizen Army. Developments within the union itself were seen through that lens. Around this time, Larkin planned to sail to America to raise funds, and leave P.T. Daly in charge of the ITGWU in his absence. On 9 October, Connolly wrote to Larkin about his plans for the union. Connolly argued that appointing Daly, after Connolly had been placed in charge previously when Larkin was in jail during the Lockout, 'would be equal to announcing to the public that you had come to the conclusion that I was not fit to be trusted'. More pressingly, however, Connolly argued that appointing Daly (who had been expelled from the IRB in 1910 in a row over funds) would create a barrier to working with the republicans. He wrote:

> We are at present in a very critical stage for the whole of Ireland as well as for the Labour movement. One result of this is that we have an opportunity of taking the lead of the real Nationalist movement, and a certainty of acquiring great prestige among Nationalists outside of the Home Rule gang, provided that our own movement is in the charge of somebody in whom the Nationalists have confidence.[1109]

In order to gain a hearing in the advanced nationalist milieu, there is evidence that Connolly toned down, at least rhetorically, some of the sharper edges of his class-based socialist politics. At the inaugural public meeting of the INL in October 1914, for instance, Connolly found himself in strange company on the platform. There was nothing unusual about Connolly speaking alongside William O'Brien and Constance Markievicz; nor even, in the circumstances, Arthur Griffith and Seán Milroy from Sinn Féin. But they were also joined by representatives of the Ancient Order of Hibernians. In his speech, Connolly noted that he had 'with him on the platform men drawn from all classes' including 'men who by no stretch of the imagination could be called labour men. They had Home Rulers and Republicans, Socialists and Sinn Féiners ...' As Connolly noted, 'All of these represented ideals that were strangely different and ideas of the future that were strangely hostile ...'. All agreed, however, 'that the interests of Ireland were more dear to them than the interests of the British Empire'.[1110]

Connolly's strategy, however, did not come off. 'It was not Redmond who was to be isolated and marginalised,' as Newsinger wrote, 'but the Citizen Army and the breakaway Volunteers. They were swept aside as the overwhelming majority of the Volunteer rank and file rallied to Redmond and the British Empire.'[1111] Redmond's new pro-war National Volunteers took an estimated 90 per cent of the 180,000 members, leaving around 11,000 in Eoin MacNeill's Irish Volunteers.[1112] Connolly still hoped that the Citizen Army could co-operate closely with the anti-war rump. The limitations of this co-operation soon became evident. When MacNeill's Volunteer's held their founding convention on 25 October, Milroy, at Connolly's behest, asked if the Citizen Army could affiliate and be given two seats on its Executive. These overtures were rejected, as it was feared allying with the Citizen Army would drive even more members over to

Redmond.[1113]

A month later, on 24 October 1914, Larkin set sail for the United States. His stated reason was to raise money for the ITGWU and the Dublin labour movement. The truth was, Larkin was depressed and demoralised by defeat of the Lockout and sought other outlets for his talents. To the dismay of many, and the relief of some, he did not return to Ireland until 1923, after a period in the US focused on anti-war and political agitation. His role in the founding of the communist movement in America saw Larkin caught up in the red scare of 1919-20 and sentenced to five to ten years in Sing Sing prison for 'criminal anarchy'.[1114]

Larkin's absence from Ireland paved the way for Connolly to take over as acting general secretary of the ITGWU and commander of the Citizen Army. Connolly soon set about turning the latter organisation into a tightly knit military vanguard. One ICA member, James O'Shea, recalled that 'after a little time it was apparent to us that Jim Connolly meant business; what kind we did not know'. Michael Mallin, a former British army drummer became chief-of-staff and, in O'Shea's words, 'things started to hum'.[1115]

The Citizen Army: Ourselves Alone?

Increasing repression by the British government in late 1914 pushed the IRB to launch a more cautious strategy. Greaves argued that the '"broad" policy was quietly dropped and the committees which had been formed were allowed to lapse'.[1116] Unaware that preparations for the insurrection continued in secret, Connolly took the IRB's shift as a sign that the republicans were stepping back from their commitment to action. His sense that more moderate voices were triumphing was only reinforced by the anti-war Volunteers' rejection on 25 October of the Citizen Army's attempts to affiliate.

Having attempted to forge a united front between the Citizen Army and the anti-war Volunteers throughout autumn 1914, Connolly now adapted a new strategy. From late 1914 to January 1916, he adopted a dual perspective. On the one hand, he continued to make general propaganda for a socialist revolution, while fighting to protect workers' living standards through the ITGWU and the Labour Party; on the other, he became the most prominent public advocate of armed insurrection, using the ICA to put pressure on the wider Irish Volunteer movement to act, while reserving the right to take up arms unilaterally if action from the Volunteers was not forthcoming.

In this period, while agitating for insurrection, Connolly at the same time acted as a model trade union general secretary. As Helga Woggon put it, '[as] the leader of the ITGWU from 1914 to 1916, Connolly did not miss any opportunity to raise the economic demands of workers'.[1117] Under his guidance, Liberty Hall was re-organised, and the union put on a much sounder financial footing than it had been since the beginning of the Dublin Lockout. Branches were re-organised, and other steps included attempts to 'establish a new branch in Limerick, control of indiscipline in Sligo, to establish an accepted national standing committee, and to increase membership fees'.[1118] Connolly stirred up and reported on workers' struggles against the erosion of their rights in the *Workers' Republic*, and conducted a series of important and militant strikes against the Dublin employers. In the winter of 1914-1915, the ITGWU won wage increases for a range of occupations with little trouble. Notably, a strike that winter against the Burns and Laird shipping lines saw the ICA used as an armed picket.

Then, in the autumn of 1915, the union embarked on a new round of negotiations with the shipping companies on Dublin port to gain an increase for the dockers. Connolly's strategy was to isolate the hard-line management of the City of Dublin Steamship Company by sparing them a strike until the other lines had fallen into agreement. Sure enough, with the strike weapon wielded, an agreement was signed with five lines on 23 October 1915, leaving the Dublin company yet to settle. Four days later, amidst heavy policing, a strike began. The dockers received the full support of the Dublin Trades Council, with over 1,000 turning out for a meeting on 14 November, addressed by speakers including William O'Brien, Thomas Farren, P.T. Daly and Connolly.

Even though Connolly was by now concerned with preparations for the Rising, the dispute would last over a year, finally being resolved in December 1916, seven months after Connolly's execution. In its use of sympathetic strike action and in preventing the employers from uniting against the ITGWU as in 1913, the strike, concluded one assessment, 'bore the mark of Connolly's tactical leadership and exemplified some basic lessons in industrial unionism as a science of fighting'. Above all, argued Woggon, the 'Dublin dock dispute had established one thing – that in spite of all its financial problems the ITGWU, far from being moribund, was, within two years of the 1913 Lockout, securing for itself a dynamic place in Irish economic and political life'.[1119]

While dutifully carrying out his role as a trade union general secretary during the day, by night, so to speak, Connolly agitated and organised for insurrection as the commandant of the Citizen Army and editor of the *Workers' Republic*. On this front, Connolly became restless. According to one account, 'by the end of 1915 Connolly was demanding action, threatening that if nobody else took the lead he would strike alone with his tiny Citizen Army'.[1120] In October 1915, for example, he made the threat explicit, announcing that

> [the] Irish Citizen Army will only co-operate in a forward movement. The moment that forward movement ceases it reserves to itself the right to step out of the alignment, and advance by itself if needs be, in an effort to plant the banner of freedom one reach further towards its goal.[1121]

Much of Connolly's agitation was focused on the Volunteers, aiming to goad its leaders into action. 'His strategy,' one account explains, 'was to appeal over their heads to the rank and file in the hope that if the Citizen Army rose then ordinary Volunteers would support it and drag the Volunteer Executive and Headquarters Staff into the struggle.'[1122] Connolly did this in a number of ways, with his articles in the *Workers' Republic* and through public interventions into the Volunteer movement. For example, on 13 November 1915 Connolly published a survey of the Young Ireland movement in 1848, an attempt in rebellion that had ended in unmitigated failure. Connolly drew the lesson, inspired perhaps more by his present needs than by the historical record, that the 'revolutionary position was there, the people were ready, but the leaders were lacking in dash and recklessness'. With a contemporary audience very much in mind, he wrote:

> Revolutionists who shrink from giving blow for blow until the great day has arrived, and they have every shoe string in its place, and every man has got his gun, and the enemy has kindly consented to postpone action in order not to needlessly hurry the revolutionists nor disarrange their plans – such revolutionists only exist in two places – the comic opera stage, and the stage of Irish National politics.[1123]

That same month, Pearse addressed the John Mitchel century commemoration. The event remembered the Dungiven-born Irish nationalist and Young Ireland activist. In his oration, when Pearse argued that 'Irish risings of the past had all come too late rather than early, Connolly, from the audience, immediately interjected: "Will the next one be too late?"'[1124]

On 4 December, Connolly demanded that the Irish Volunteer leadership take the initiative. He defended his paper, writing that it was 'poor quibbling to say that the Workers' Republic stands for reckless fighting and ill-considered action. It does not.' Connolly's preference, still, was for mass action by the Volunteers and the Citizen Army:

The Workers' Republic holds that at any time since the war broke out the British Government could have been halted in its inroads upon public liberties in Ireland by a flat refusal on the part of the majority of its armed citizens to allow their rights as citizens to be interfered with.

It needed no insurrection, no flying to arms, no storming of jails, it only needed that the armed Volunteers who claimed to stand for Ireland should mobilise and speak for Ireland ... Not a troop would have been moved against them, nor a shot fired.

However, Connolly left his readers in no doubt of the sort of action the *Workers' Republic* was agitating for. In a passage underlined by the Detective Department of the Dublin Metropolitan Police, Connolly wrote: 'We believe in constitutional action in normal times; we believe in revolutionary action in exceptional times. These are exceptional times.'[1125]

There were still those in the Volunteers, such as MacNeill, who argued that only a purely defensive strike was morally acceptable. Connolly would have none of this, writing: 'If your leaders who alone have plans are arrested your flying to arms will be that of a leaderless mob in a planless insurrection.' He added: 'Finally: think over this chunk of wisdom. A revolutionist who surrenders the initiative to the enemy is already defeated before a blow is struck. It is a fine day if it wasn't for the rain.'[1126]

Evidence that Connolly seemed willing to go it alone if the Volunteers refused to act is provided by his re-organisation of the ICA. According to ICA veteran Frank Robbins, who fought in the Rising and the subsequent War of Independence, in late 1915 'matters appeared to be tuning up, and Connolly ordered a complete mobilisation he regarded as being of great importance.' Connolly told the members that 'the situation was now becoming dangerous and it might mean that the Citizen Army would have to fight alone', and he summoned each individually into another room in Liberty Hall. In the presence of Connolly, Michael Mallin and Lieutenant Thomas Kain, each ICA member was asked: 'Was the individual prepared to take part in the fight for Ireland's freedom; would he be prepared to fight alongside the Irish Volunteers, and would he be prepared to fight without the aid of the Irish Volunteers or any other military force.' If all three questions were answered in the affirmative, the member was given 'a secret number which would be embossed on a block to be carried round such person's neck for identification purposes. Corresponding numbers and names,' Connolly told the assembled, 'would be handed to a trusted person, who would be able to identify them in the event of complete annihilation.'[1127]

By early 1916, then, Connolly 'through his speeches, calls to arms and parades, was making an impact far beyond the actual resources of his 200-strong Citizen Army'.[1128] Some IRB men, growing aware of Connolly's influence, reacted in horror to his approach. IRB leader Sean McGarry, in a witness statement gathered by the Bureau of Military History, contrasted Connolly's 'method of approach to revolution' from that of the more cautious and secretive Tom Clarke. Connolly, McGarry recounted, wanted 'to shout it from the housetops, did not care how soon it started or with how many men. He believed that once the standard of revolt was raised the people – his people – would rally to it and he was afraid of a sudden collapse of the war.' Another senior IRB man, Diarmuid Lynch, was even blunter: Connolly's position 'was not merely "unorthodox" from the I.R.B. standpoint, it was sheer madness – expressed, it is true, in complete ignorance of I.R.B. decisions and plans conducted through the Military Council.'[1129] This was not just a retrospective judgement; Pearse himself was reported to have said of Connolly in Christmas 1915 that he 'will never be satisfied until he goads us into action and then he will think most us too moderate, and want to guillotine half of us'.[1130]

An important turning point appears to have been a conversation between Connolly and the Limerick-based Volunteer and IRB activist, Eamon O'Dore at the end of 1915. O'Dore recalls that in late November or early December, William O'Brien summoned him to Liberty Hall and told him that 'James Connolly desired to have an earnest talk' with him. The Limerick man was aware of Connolly's writings and his recent *Workers' Republic* editorials 'in which he castigated the Volunteer Executive for its tardiness in setting a Rising going' and it soon became apparent that Connolly was seeking information on whether Volunteers officers had been made aware of plans for a Rising. After O'Brien ushered Dore into Connolly's office, Dore recounts:

> Connolly came the point in his forthright way … He pointed out then that he feared the national leaders, if they intended a rising at all, might put it off until it would be too late. The time to act was whilst England was engaged in this war, and the war cannot last forever. He further said that he was determined to strike and that before long, unless he had some assurance that the Irish Volunteers would strike soon.

Connolly then asked Dore directly if a Rising was projected. Dore replied that 'there appeared to be every certainty that a rising would take place' and warned Connolly 'that if he came out prematurely with the Citizen Army the planning for a rising by the bigger organisation would be gravely injured'. Connolly replied that although 'this was the general opinion of Irish Volunteer members … he could not wait much longer'. With Connolly's agreement, Dore went straight to Parnell Street to inform Tom Clarke of his talk with the Citizen Army commander, and recommended that a meeting take place between the IRB leaders and Connolly. According to Dore, 'Clarke agreed and said that it was vital that this should be done and that my talk with Connolly was very valuable'.[1131]

The road to the Rising

What Connolly did not know, and what accounts for his growing impatience, was that the IRB's planning for an insurrection had gone underground. Indeed, the plans were hidden even from the organisation's own Supreme Council. Hobson later recalled that when the decision to rise was made following the war's outbreak, no firm time was set but a 'small committee, of which MacDermott and Clarke were the effective members, was appointed with instructions to examine the project and report back to the Supreme Council. They never reported back [and the] Supreme Council was, in effect, superseded and ceased to count.'[1132] MacDermott and Clarke effectively controlled the Executive of the IRB, and excluded the third member, the Belfast-based President Denis McCullough, from their plans. The two men then effectively 'subcontracted the actual planning of the Rising to a committee' in May 1915 made up of Joseph Plunkett, Eamon Ceannt and Pearse, whose deliberations in one historian's view 'were characterised by extreme secrecy, unwavering dedication to its objective, and ruthless duplicity'.[1133]

The previous month, Plunkett had set off for Berlin to make contact with the German government. Disguised with a fake moustache and beard, he travelled via Spain, Italy and Switzerland. Once in Berlin, Plunkett met up with Sir Roger Casement, who had been in the city since the beginning of the war seeking German support for Irish independence. The two men submitted a 32-page memorandum, which described the political situation and outlined how a German naval invasion could spark a nationwide rebellion in Ireland. Though the Germans rejected this ambitious, and some would say fanciful, plan, these contacts nevertheless did result in a German attempt to land arms in Kerry on the eve of the Rising.[1134]

In September 1915, Clarke and MacDermott themselves formally joined what they now called the 'Military Council' and began to push forward plans for a Rising. The secretive committee was in an increasingly strong position. Three members of the Military Council, Pearse, Plunkett and Eamonn Ceannt, shared overlapping membership of the Military Council, the Executive of the Volunteers and the Volunteers Headquarter Staff. In addition, the Military Council controlled the four Dublin Volunteer battalions through their IRB commanders. Commandants in Cork, Kerry, Limerick and Galway and most provincial Volunteer organisers were also IRB members. As 1916 began, however, there was a real possibility that the Allies would lose the war. Germany had occupied Belgium, the north-east of France, and much of western Russia. The German U-boat campaign had inflicted serious damage to Allied naval operations, and Clarke and MacDermott were by now convinced of a German victory. Their major fear was that the war would end, and any post-war peace conference would not include Ireland as an independent nation.[1135] These considerations pushed the Military Council to formally set a date for the Rising, fixing it for Easter Sunday 1916.

Connolly's public advocacy of insurrection, however, threatened to derail the carefully laid plans of the Military Council. The conspirators feared that Connolly would precipitate a hasty conflict, dragging the Volunteers with him, or could invite British state repression on the whole movement. On 16 January 1916, Hobson, MacNeill and Pearse attended a meeting at the Irish Volunteer Headquarters. The former pair confronted Connolly about his plans. 'Everyone', it was said, 'was appalled by Connolly's candid admission that he was prepared to use the Citizen Army to ignite a nationwide chain reaction.'[1136] Pearse, who of course had his own plans for insurrection, unknown to both Hobson and MacNeill, raised the alarm with his co-conspirators. Together, they made a plan to neutralise Connolly by bring him into the Military Council's own plans for insurrection.

Alarm spread in Dublin's labour circles when, on Wednesday 19 January, Connolly disappeared. He did not reappear until Saturday 22 January, and had spent the intervening days locked in intense negotiation with the IRB conspirators, Pearse, McDermott and Plunkett. By the time Connolly resurfaced, he had become a member of the IRB and the secret Military Council. Connolly had been convinced that the IRB men meant business and agreed to halt his calls for the ICA to go it alone. Some older accounts allege that the IRB men kidnapped Connolly and only released him when they had convinced them of their plan.[1137] William O'Brien is surely correct, however, that as headstrong a character as Connolly would have resented his kidnapping to such an extent that it would have made future collaboration impossible.[1138] More recent scholarship, too, strongly suggests he went of his own volition.[1139] It appears that the IRB men did make contingency plans to 'arrest Connolly if he did not come voluntarily' but, according to Dore, in the end 'Connolly went of his own accord, had a two-day interview, came away satisfied and everything went almost to plan after'.[1140]

In the account of Plunkett's sister, Geraldine Dillon Plunkett, her brother told her that 'they with difficulty persuaded Connolly to discuss anything' and that he 'was very angry at first, but they had come to a complete agreement …'.[1141] The agreement was, indeed, total. After hearing the Military Council's plans, Connolly is said to have admitted: 'I have been beaten at my own game.'[1142] According to Liam Ó Briain, Irish language scholar and IRB member, once Connolly had been brought into the confidence of the Military Council, he then joined the IRB. 'His name was read out for approval at the various circles in the usual way,' Ó Briain remembered. 'I heard it myself at a meeting of the "Clarence Mangans" in 41 Parnell Square.'[1143]

Connolly was now content that the Military Council shared his sense of urgency. In the subsequent issue of the *Workers' Republic,* the language is, in Lorcan Collins's words, 'more subdued, and a kind of calm sense of the inevitable is evident.' Connolly informs his readers elliptically:

> Our notes this week will be short. The issue is clear and we have done our part to clear it. Nothing we can now say can add point to the arguments we have put before our readers in the past few months; nor shall we continue to labour the point … For the moment and hour of that ripening, that fruitful and blessed Day of Days, we are ready.
>
>   Will it find you ready?

Between late January and April, Connolly tantalised readers of the *Workers' Republic* with indications that action was on the horizon.

The plan Connolly signed up to involved members of the Volunteers seizing a series of strongholds in Dublin 'sufficiently close to one another to form an inner defensive cordon'.[1144] The General Post Office (GPO) on Sackville Street (now O'Connell Street) was to be the headquarters of a new Provisional Government. The large classical Four Courts building was to be captured, protecting the insurgents from the British troops stationed at the Royal Barracks further up the River Liffey. Volunteers were also to occupy the strategic targets of Jacob's biscuit factory to the south, Boland's bakery, and the South Dublin Union. As Foy and Barton have written, the Dublin element of the Rising 'is often depicted as a siege in which encircled defenders endured as long as possible an onslaught of attackers' who held the initiative after overcoming initial surprise. 'Yet enough is known of the Military Council's plans,' they argue, 'to indicate that its strategy was considerably more imaginative, aggressive and optimistic.'[1145] The Dublin

Rising was to be co-ordinated with a Rising in the west of Ireland. The Military Council hoped that a German land of arms, preferably accompanied with an expeditionary force, would inspire popular enthusiasm and electrify the country. Suitably armed, the Volunteers would overwhelm police and troops, and march on the British garrison in Dublin to relieve the insurgents in the capital.

Crucially, this plan was to be kept secret, not only from the wider Volunteer leadership, but also the rest of the Supreme Council of the IRB. The Military Council later hit upon the idea of carrying out the Rising under the cover of routine Volunteer training exercises 'to test mobilisation with equipment', with senior officers of the Volunteers and the Citizen Army only informed of the real plans a few days before in order to prevent leaks to the British or opponents of an insurrection within the movement itself.

Blood sacrifice?

It has become common to present the Rising as a deliberate 'blood sacrifice'. This theory, which has a long pedigree, argues that the Rising was a deliberately hopeless endeavour. Given the depths to which Irish national consciousness had sunk during the war, a mystical embrace of martyrdom was necessary for the cause of national regeneration. The Rising, then, was consciously designed to create martyrs for the Irish cause, with its leaders dying for Ireland as Christ died for human Redemption. While it is not difficult to find numerous examples in the writings of Pearse to evidence a sacrificial mindset,[1146] the problem comes when stretching these to represent the motivations of all the Rising's leaders and to explain the Rising as a whole.

The most straightforward objection is that the extensive preparations outlined above cast doubt on the 'blood sacrifice' theory. As one writer has argued: 'if the main purpose was to play out a redemption drama, there would have been little point in the detailed military planning that preceded it.'[1147] Similarly, for Barton and Foy, Plunkett's detailed memorandum 'casts doubt on the "Blood Sacrifice" theory of the Easter Rising'.[1148]

Secondly, the focus on Pearse inflates his role in the planning. A redemptory 'blood sacrifice' viewpoint may have been expressed by Pearse 'but it was Clarke and MacDermott above all who drove the revolutionary enterprise' since the summer of 1914, and who ranked higher in IRB seniority than the others.[1149] Indeed, as McGarry has argued, there has often been a conflation of the Pearse-ean 'mystical embrace of martyrdom' with the 'much more widespread and perfectly rational belief that it was necessary for separatists to be prepared to fight even if they would probably be defeated'. Thus:

If a single belief united the organisers it was not the blood sacrifice but the conviction that action was preferable to inaction; that the potential advantages of defeat – the reassertion of separatist credibility, the long-term survival of the physical-force tradition, the possibility of inspiring popular support and of destroying Home Rule – outweighed the advantages of inaction.[1150]

More fundamentally, too, when the 'blood sacrifice' is intended to demonise the insurgents, or suggest reckless and bloodthirsty motives, it is vital to bear in mind that it was a Rising *against the imperialist war*. As we have seen, Connolly was horrified when the war broke out, and at the idea of soldiers from one nation turning on their working-class brothers in another army. In January 1915, he insisted that 'there is no such thing as humane or civilized war! War may be forced upon a subject race or subject class to put an end to subjection of race, of class, or sex,' Connolly conceded. 'When so waged it must be waged thoroughly and relentlessly,' he argued, 'but with no delusions as to its elevating nature, or civilizing methods.'

Further evidence of Connolly's perspective is provided by a spat with Pearse at the end of 1915. In December, Pearse, writing anonymously in the journal *The Spark*, had glorified the war still raging on the Western Front. He had written that 'the old heart of the earth needed to be warmed with the red wine of the battlefields,' and welcomed 'the homage of millions of lives given gladly for love of country'. Pearse was apparently hurt when Connolly, in the *Workers' Republic* retorted angrily: 'No! We do not believe that war is glorious, inspiring, or regenerating. We believe it to be hateful, damnable, and damning. Any person,' Connolly wrote, 'whether English, German, or Irish, who sings the praises of war is, in our opinion, a blithering idiot.' While conceding, of course, that when 'a nation has been robbed it should strike back to recover her lost property', Connolly protested: 'do not let us have any more maudlin trash about the "glories of war", or the "regenerative influence of war", or the "sacred mission of the soldier", or the "fertilising of all earth with the heroic blood of her children", etc, etc. We are sick of it, the world is sick of it.' Connolly also very strictly drew the boundaries between tactics justified in wartime and those appropriate for a time of peace. 'We will be no party to leading out Irish patriots to meet the might of an England at peace,' he wrote in January 1916.

Far from being a macabre personal idiosyncrasy, both the idea of being prepared to die for one's ideals or nation and notions about the redemptory potential of warfare were part of the cultural zeitgeist in Europe in 1914. As Pearse's biographer Joost Augusteijn has argued strongly, the glorification of bloodshed was common to imperialist English politicians such as Bonar Law and Churchill. Moreover, the romantic ideal of a shortened life was celebrated by many European writers and poets.[1151]

Finally, what complicates the picture further is the fact that the Rising that took place was not the same, in its scale or execution, as the Rising which had been meticulously planned by the Military Council. As J.J. Lee put it: 'In the event, the Rising had turned into a blood sacrifice. But it had not been planned that way from the outset.'[1152] First, disaster struck the rebels' plans when the German ship, the *SS Libau* (which was masquerading as a neutral Norwegian steamboat, the *Aud)* was sighted off the coast of Cork and cornered by three British destroyers. It had been carrying 20,000 rifles and a million rounds of ammunition for the Rising. The German crew scuttled it to avoid the weapons falling into British hands. Roger Casement, who was to meet the boat on the shore, was arrested on Banna Strand in Tralee Bay, County Kerry. He was executed four months later for treason. As one authoritative account has argued, the capture of the *Aud* was 'a calamity that was to transform the Rising from a planned national insurrection into a predominantly Dublin affair'.[1153]

The plan had been to launch the Rising under the cover of military manoeuvres on Easter Sunday. Volunteers would be mobilised for a routine parade, and only then informed that a Rising was, in fact, on the agenda. The Wednesday before, a forged document, the 'Castle Document', was circulated by the conspirators. Purporting to be from the British authorities, it indicated that the Volunteer leaders were to be interned and the movement suppressed. This was intended to bounce the more conservative faction around MacNeill into action. This element of the plan fell apart when McNeill became aware of the deception and the Military Council's real plans. MacNeill issued a countermanding order cancelling the Sunday manoeuvres, which was published in the national press. This action, which caused delay, demoralisation and confusion, was denounced by Tom Clarke as 'the blackest and greatest treachery,' and ensured that the Rising could not go ahead on Sunday.[1154]

Moreover, the capture of the arms shipment and MacNeill's counter-manding order left the rebels with a dilemma. Either fight and go down to certain defeat with a fraction of the arms and combatants intended in the original plan, or call the Rising off. If the latter, the ringleaders would have inevitably been discovered and arrested, to face almost certain execution for organising a rebellion in wartime in alliance with an enemy. This would have been a devastating and humiliating defeat, made all the worse for not having fought at all. Desmond Ryan understood the problem clearly, as the leaders saw it: 'After all our marchings and speeches what else can we do? Would any one ever listen to our oratory against if we let this chance pass?'[1155]

Pearse cancelled Sunday manoeuvres but then issued an order on Sunday evening calling a mobilisation that next morning. Only 1000 turned out on Easter Monday morning – less than would have done on Sunday. As R.M. Fox described it, when the Rising came, it was 'very largely an improvisation, a mere sketch of what was intended. By Easter Sunday, Connolly realised that all the preparations made so carefully for a great national effort could not be carried out.'[1156] This was the all-important context for Connolly's famous comments on Easter Monday morning. Encountering William O'Brian at Liberty Hall, Connolly told him 'We are going out to be slaughtered'. When O'Brien asked, 'Is there no chance of success,' Connolly responded, 'None whatsoever'.[1157] On Monday morning the leadership and HQ staff met at Liberty Hall and marched to O'Connell Street at 11:50 a.m. with a motley crew of about 150.[1158] The GPO was seized and on the street outside Pearse read the 'Proclamation of the Irish Republic' to those who stopped to listen.

In truth, however, it suits both detractors of the Rising and some of its advocates to play up the Catholic and sacrificial nature of the endeavour. For critics, such as Hobson, there is an obvious value in denouncing Pearse as 'a sentimental egotist, full of curious Old Testament theories about being the scapegoat for the people, [who] become convinced of the necessity for a periodic blood sacrifice to keep the national spirit alive'.[1159] Hobson was opposed to the Rising at the time and the 'blood sacrifice' theory is part of the arsenal in denouncing it as a wholly irrational endeavour. On the other side of the fence, the 'blood sacrifice' provides a powerful origin myth for the post-independence Irish ruling class. In this sense, 'it suited the elite of Catholic Ireland to turn the leaders of the Rising into martyrs so that they could present the insurrection as an event led by almost saintly individuals'.[1160] The memories of the executed heroes provided powerful icons for nationalism and Catholicism; and, in the case of Connolly, the 'blood sacrifice' served to dissolve his revolutionary Marxism in the solvent of a mystical Irish nationalism.

For Connolly, this process happened within a few years of his death. A Catholic priest, Reverend Coffey, wrote a series of articles on Connolly in the *Catholic Bulletin* in 1920. Downplaying Connolly's Marxism, Coffey sought to claim him for the principles of Catholic social teaching, based on the teachings of Pope Leo XIII in his 1891 encyclical *Rerum novarum* (1891) and developed by writers such as G.K. Chesterton and Hilaire Belloc. Viewing property as a fundamental right, these thinkers saw capitalism and socialism as equally flawed; the former's tendency towards monopoly concentrating property ownership in few hands, and the latter because it centralises ownership in the hands of the state. Instead, they favoured co-operatives and small businesses and, in Belloc's case, looked backwards to an idealised view of the guilds of the Middle Ages. This attempt to claim Connolly for Catholicism was further developed in the Rev Lambert McKenna's *The Social Teaching of James Connolly*, published in 1921 by the Catholic Truth Society. In 1924, even Constance Markievicz, by then an abstentionist Sinn Féin TD, conceded that Connolly was a socialist but that this meant only the 'application of the social principle which underlay the Brehon laws of our ancestors'. Though Connolly stood for socialism, she wrote, 'it was the socialism of James Connolly and of nobody else'.[1161]

If Connolly did not join the Rising to sanctify a blood sacrifice, however, why did he think it necessary to give up his life to join an armed insurrection in Easter 1916? We now consider some of the most influential existing interpretations before attempting our own.

Why did Connolly join the Rising?

'Why,' asked Desmond Ryan, one of Connolly's earliest biographers, 'did James Connolly take part in the insurrection of 1916, he whose "Labour in Irish History" is one of the most damaging criticisms of mere insurrection imaginable, whose outlook, until August, 1914, was the orthodox Marxian outlook, notoriously hostile to violent methods [sic], whose temperament was, apparently, cold-blooded and realist?'[1162]

Subsequent biographers, too, have grappled with this question. The debate has raged, in essence, over whether Connolly's involvement in the Rising, 'involved a rupture in his politics or was the logical conclusion of his politics'.[1163] One early view, which could be termed the 'continuity thesis', was perhaps most succinctly expressed by Desmond's father W.P. Ryan, in his early survey of Irish labour movement history, and was quoted in the introduction of this book. For Ryan, Connolly's thought was fixed in 1896, and all that came after were additional 'emphasis, illustration, elucidation, not further discoveries'.[1164] The Rising is thus seen as a logical end point of a lifetime's work.

Another influential explanation is that of Greaves, who as we have seen attempted to claim Connolly for the Stalinist politics of the CPGB. In relation to the Easter Rising, Greaves argued that in the final years of his life, Connolly's views reached maturity, sloughing off his earlier Social-Democratic and syndicalist deviations. It was, argued Greaves, 'Connolly's mature and considered opinion' in 1916 that 'the national revolution takes precedence' and that 'the working class is not the only revolutionary class'.[1165] He recognised that the Irish Revolution would have two distinct stages; first, the 'democratic stage', requiring cross-class alliances with revolutionary nationalists ('the national-bourgeoisie') to win national independence; then, and only then, would the way be cleared for socialist revolution.

Much of this analysis rests on a single phrase, 'the first days of freedom' in an article in the *Workers' Republic* on 15 January 1916 – *before* Connolly's formal alliance with the IRB. In it, Connolly had written how 'as the propertied classes have so shamelessly sold themselves to the enemy, the economic conscription of their property will cause few qualms to whomsoever shall administer the Irish Government in the first days of freedom'. So intent was Greaves on constructing a version of Connolly consistent with the Stalinist theory that revolutions in semi-colonial countries must pass through two separate and distinct 'stages' that he rendered Connolly's phrase as 'the first *stage* of freedom'.[1166]

Other accounts stress the discontinuity in Connolly's thinking and locate the outbreak of war in August 1914 as a crucial rupture point. This view, too, has a long pedigree. In 1919 playwright Sean O'Casey wrote a polemical account of the Citizen's Army, under his Irish-language pseudonym 'P. O Cathasaigh'. O'Casey, who broke bitterly from the ICA in 1914 over its closer relationship with Volunteers, wrote of Connolly that:

> Jim Connolly had stepped from the narrow byway of Irish Socialism on to the broad and crowded highway of Irish Nationalism ... The high creed of Irish Nationalism became his daily rosary, while the higher creed of international humanity that had so long bubbled from his eloquent lips was silent for ever, and Irish Labour lost a Leader.[1167]

This view received more recent treatment with the publication of Austen Morgan's 1988 book *James Connolly: A political biography*, which framed the issue in terms of asking why did 'Connolly, a man who had lived as a socialist, die an Irish nationalist?'. This view presents the two as mutually opposed poles, implicitly downplaying Connolly's longstanding concern with national oppression and the widespread working-class socialist republicanism represented by the ITGWU and the *Irish Worker*. Socialism, in Morgan's view, appears to mean an economistic labourism, accompanied by largely abstract internationalism.

It is not necessary, however, to accept that Connolly ceased to be a socialist in August 1914 to recognise that there was something of a break in his thought and practices in light of the radically transformed political situation. The most fruitful approach is to see Connolly's involvement in the Rising in terms of how the structures of his thought interacted with a very specific set of circumstances – namely the outbreak of the war, the collapse of the Second International, and the weakness of the Irish working-class movement in the wake of the defeat of the Lockout in 1913. Connolly, to paraphrase Marx, made his own history, but he did not make it as he pleased; not 'under self-selected circumstances, but under circumstances existing already, given and transmitted from the past'. As David Howell has argued in his perceptive study of Connolly and nationalism, 'Connolly's actions in 1916 and the debate over the consequences should not be the subject of an historical idealisation, nor of an understandable but misleading presentation as socialist apostasy. Rather,' he argued, 'it was a choice made in what seemed to a long-standing Socialist, an increasingly bleak situation. As such, it raised for Socialists the perennial question of the baffling interplay between creative initiative, and firm, perhaps, dimly perceived constraints.'[1168]

What, then, was the analysis of the situation which lay behind Connolly's creative initiative, and what were the constraints which conditioned his ability to act? The first point to make is that Connolly's pre-1914 politics did not appear to him to apply to the dangers and possibilities posed by the war. In an important article, 'What is Our Programme?' in the 22 January 1916 edition of the *Workers' Republic*, Connolly makes an implicit admission of this point. 'Our programme in time of peace,' Connolly wrote,

> was to gather into Irish hands in Irish trade unions the control of all the forces of production and distribution in Ireland. We never believed that freedom would be realized without fighting for it. From our earliest declaration of policy in Dublin in 1896 the editor of this paper has held to the dictum that our ends should be secured 'peacefully if possible, forcibly if necessary'. Believing so ... we strove to make Labour in Ireland organized – and revolutionary.

That was in peace time. 'What is our programme now?' Connolly asked:

> We believe that in times of peace we should work along the lines of peace to strengthen the nation, and we believe that whatever strengthens and elevates the working class strengthens the nation. But we also believe that in times of war we should act as in war ... While the war lasts and Ireland still is a subject nation we shall continue to urge her to fight for her freedom.

We shall continue, in season and out of season, to teach that the 'far-flung battle line' of England is weakest at the point nearest its heart, that Ireland is in that position of tactical advantage, that a defeat of England in India, Egypt, the Balkans or Flanders would not be so dangerous to the British Empire as any conflict of armed forces in Ireland, that the time for Ireland's battle is NOW, the place for Ireland's battle is HERE. That a strong man may deal lusty blows with his fists against a host of surrounding foes, and conquer, but will succumb if a child sticks a pin in his heart.

What gave added urgency to this injunction to act immediately was the threat, as Connolly and many others perceived it, of conscription. Throughout 1915, Ireland was gripped by rumours that conscription was imminent, and the topic was the subject of regular stories and leader comment in the nationalist press.[1169] The issue of conscription contributed to the ebbing away of support from Redmond as the war dragged on. Though some reacted to the threat by emigrating, for others it meant a greater receptiveness towards anti-war arguments and activity. 'The decline of the Irish Volunteers was halted and then reversed,' according to Fearghal McGarry, 'as new companies evolved from anti-war activity networks.'[1170] With volunteers for the British Army reaching a trickle by late 1915, the Military Service Act was passed in January 1916 introducing conscription in Great Britain. Connolly argued that it was 'inconceivable that the British public should allow conscription to be applied to England and not to Ireland' and that it was 'the duty of all who wish to save Ireland from such shame or such slaughter to strengthen the hand of those of the leaders who are for action as against those who are playing into the hands of the enemy'.[1171]

The conscription issue provided evidence for Connolly that war did not simply represent 'the continuation of politics by other means', as von Clausewitz famously stated. War, rather, had its own more particular rules of political engagement. Connolly argued that 'the first blast of the bugles of war sounds the death knell of the hopes of reform'. He reprinted an American survey, which noted that SPD attempts to lower the voting age in Saxony were repulsed, socialist newspapers had been suppressed in Austria and Italy, and in France 'anti-semitism and monarchism are rampant, and under the specious plea of the Unity of La Patrie it is next to treason to fight those insidious movements'.[1172] Then, in November 1915, he wrote: 'We are now living in an era of ruthless brute force of blood and iron. Whatever effect public opinion may have in times of peace it has little practical effect in time of war.' Opponents of conscription, therefore, 'must not delude themselves into the belief that they are simply embarking upon a new form of political agitation, with no other risks than attend political agitation in times of peace.' If the 'British ruling class has made up its mind that only conscription can save the Empire' then 'it will enforce conscription though every river in Ireland ran red with blood'.[1173] The political implications were clear; now was not the time for the peacetime politics of steadily building the trade unions and the Labour Party.

It was not merely conscription but the increase of the state's wartime powers in general which Connolly saw as representing a potentially existential threat to the labour movement. In an article to mark the new year in January 1916, for example, Connolly 'sketched out the future as it awaits the slave who fears death more than slavery'. His vision anticipated the eradication of 'all the rights and liberties acquired by labour in a century of struggling' with the acquiescence of the labour leaders, and a consequent increase in the division of labour and the rate of exploitation. Peace would mean economic dislocation from the demobilisation of the soldiers, high rates of taxation and intense competition for work, driving down wages. 'The civil rights of the people have gone,' Connolly warned, 'and the ruling class has succeeded in so familiarising the multitude with thoughts of slaughter and bloodshed that the killing of workers on strike will no longer send even a thrill through the nation.' The purpose of this bleak and pessimistic picture was to implore action on the part of his readers. Connolly hoped that those reading were 'rebels in heart, and hence may rebel even at our own picture of the future'. He reminded them that 'opportunities are for those who seize them, and that the coming year may be as bright as we choose to make it'.

Closely related to both conscription and the increase in wartime state power was Connolly's dread that 'the cause of Ireland as a separate nationality' would disappear if Irish men were conscripted by an all-powerful militarist state. Already, argued Emmet O'Connor, Connolly was 'appalled at Irish mass acquiescence to the British war effort in 1914' which 'led him to believe that the nation was on the verge of moral collapse and cultural disintegration'.[1174] In August 1915, he had written that when the war broke out, 'the cause of Ireland as a separate nation, as a nation with a separate life, history, and individuality of its own, was again looked upon as a lost cause, and the fate of Ireland was again accepted as being irrevocably and finally blended with that of the British Empire'.[1175] This fate, Connolly was sure, would be sealed in blood by the conscription of Irishmen to fight in the British Army.

This concern with the moral and spiritual degradation of Ireland is seen most clearly in an article in February 1916 in the *Workers' Republic*. Connolly wrote how he had long pointed out that 'the strings of self-interest bound the capitalist and landlord classes to the Empire' and thus it was 'a waste of time to appeal to those classes in the name of Irish patriotism'. This had not been true, however, for the working class, the 'only class to whom the word "Empire", and the things of which it was the symbol did not appeal'. The war, Connolly regretted, had changed this. Having seen the Irish working class as the repository of the nation's revolutionary energy, Connolly now struck a more pessimistic note. Around half of the ITGWU's membership had signed up to the British Army. This was particularly distressing when we remember that 'Connolly envisaged the ITGWU as an instrument of moral as much as material redemption'. Thus, he reported: 'It is with shame and sorrow we say it but the evil influence upon large sections of the Irish Working Class of the bribes and promises of the enemy cannot be denied.' Pointing to recruitment to the British Army, with serviceman's pay and separation allowances, Connolly despaired that 'For the sake of a few paltry shillings per week thousands of Irish workers have sold their country in the hour of their country's greatest need and greatest hope.'

By February 1916, some of the rhetoric that Connolly had previously criticised in Pearse had crept into Connolly's own vocabulary. He wrote of how a sense of degradation had sunk 'deep in the heart of Ireland', so deep indeed 'that no agency less potent than the red tide of war on Irish soil will ever be able to enable the Irish race to recover its self-respect, or establish its national dignity ...' He closed with the same words uttered by Leo Melliet, the Communard who had been such a pronounced early influence, at the Edinburgh commemoration of the Paris Commune almost a quarter of a century before: 'Without the Shedding of Blood there is no Redemption.'

It was this perspective then – the growth of wartime state powers, the imminent threat of conscription, and the moral degeneration of the Irish nation – that convinced Connolly a pre-emptive strike against British imperialism was necessary. As O'Connor describes it: 'Connolly believed that things were getting worse and only an immediate, desperate act would redeem the spirit of revolution.'

Nine days before the Rising, the situation appeared to be deteriorating, bringing with it a greater resolve to act. Connolly surveyed the situation internationally in the *Workers' Republic*, noting the Australian organ of the IWW had been fined £100 'for publishing statements likely to prejudice recruiting'. Closer to home, in Scotland, events on the Clyde figured in Connolly's calculations. In April 1916, the Clyde Workers' Committee (CWC) was suppressed, its leading members 'seized in the middle of the night' and 'deported without any form of trial'.[1176]

In Ireland, the situation appeared even worse. Connolly reported on 15 April that 'we see prominent organisers of the Irish Volunteers arrested and sentenced to deportation', 'newspapers raided and printing machinery seized by the military' and 'every day arrests of men for passing the most ordinary comments upon the war'. Connolly described the situation in stark terms:

> Free speech and a free press no longer exists. The Rights of Labour have been suppressed; to strike is an offence against the law whenever the authorities choose to declare it so ...
>
> Gradually the authorities have been making successful war upon every public right ... That arbitrary exercise of power which two years ago would have evoked a storm of protest is now accepted with equanimity and even with approval.[1177]

While some socialists, most notably Kautsky, hoped for peace through international arbitration so that the socialist movement could revert to its pre-war strategy of gradual growth within the framework of parliamentary democracy, Connolly knew rightly that normal service would not and could not resume. The war had ripped the international socialist movement apart and a return to pre-1914 'normality' looked unlikely. This put him with the revolutionary left of the Second International. Yet, while the likes of Lenin and Zinoviev predicted that the workers' movement would produce a revolutionary explosion after the war, Connolly's vision was at once both pessimistic and extremely voluntaristic. Revolution was needed *now* to prevent an inevitable slide into barbarism but Connolly's problem was that 'his desire for revolution was not matched by a capacity to bring it about'.[1178] As Connolly admitted himself in January 1916:

> We have succeeded in creating an organization that will willingly do more for Ireland than any trade union in the world has attempted to do for its national government. Had we not been attacked and betrayed by many of our fervent advanced patriots, had they not been so anxious to destroy us ... had they stood by us and pushed our organization all over Ireland it would now be in our power at a word to crumple up and demoralize every offensive move of the enemy against the champions of Irish freedom. Had we been able to carry out all our plans, as such an Irish organization of Labour alone could carry them out, we could at a word have created all the conditions necessary to the striking of a successful blow whenever the military arm of Ireland wished to move.[1179]

In any case, the ITGWU was a trade union, not a revolutionary organisation, the bulk of whose members joined up to improve their wages and material conditions. It is therefore questionable whether, contrary to syndicalist hopes, it would ever have been the appropriate vehicle in itself for such a revolution. Frank Robbins of the ICA reflected that when recruiting to the Citizen Army in 1913 and 1914, Captain Jack White had 'expressed disappointment from time to time at the lack of support by the workers for the army. He could not understand why greater numbers did not participate, particularly in comparison with the Volunteers.' Partly this could be accounted for by the ICA's 'shabby clothing and lack of proper footwear' by comparison with the much larger Volunteers. Added to this was the effect of the defeat of the Lockout, after which, recalled Robbins, 'a deep depression had set in among the workers'. As Greaves has commented on why Connolly did not seek to involve the union more in the Rising, 'when he looked realistically at his union, as he scratched around for strike pay for the City of Dublin Steampacket men, he had to recognise that it was not in a condition to play a major part in the revolution'.[1180]

Perhaps the most important reason, however, 'was the fact that the workers did not understand the ideals behind the creation of a workers' army which were entirely new and most revolutionary in character'. What White had failed to realise, argued Robbins

> was that the workers, while trade unionists, were not by any measure socialists. For the workers to respond rather to the call of the Volunteer Organisation was more likely because of the years of popular agitation for national freedom. The socialistic ideals expressed in the constitution of the Irish Citizen Army, were not understood by the workers and where understood, were not acceptable. The hard core of the Irish Citizen Army who remained loyal to Connolly embraced the ideal of Irish independence as expressed in the very definite terms of the 'Workers' Republic'.

Connolly, as general secretary of the ITGWU, would have been aware of this and it is telling that he did not attempt to more closely reconcile his trade union work with his preparations for revolt. Indeed, as one biographer has argued, 'Connolly's strong anti-war stance in the unions was confined to a propaganda level' and the ICA and the union 'were two discrete areas that hardly overlapped'.[1181] Indeed, as a recent study of the ICA has shown, the union's minutes show that 'no matters regarding the ICA were discussed by Branch No. 1 [based at Liberty Hall] between 29 September 1915 and 12 April 1916,' which 'indicated how separate these activities were'.[1182]

Connolly's dual position as Citizen Army commandant and ITGWU acting general secretary did, however, make possible the use of Liberty Hall in the planning of the revolt. Matthew Connolly of the ICA recalled how in the immediate run-up to the Rising, Liberty Hall was guarded by men who were 'all fully armed and the building resembled a military barracks in all but name'. The union headquarters operated as a munitions and explosives factory, a barracks for the ICA and a storehouse for the armaments of the wider republican movement. Nevertheless, as Lorcan Collins put it: 'in essence, there were two Liberty Halls. One was upstairs, where members came and paid their dues, documents were filed, and an air of respectability reigned. Downstairs and underground, revolution was being planned and stacks of explosives were being stored in preparation for the coming Rising.'[1183]

These illicit basement activities put the union headquarters at substantial risk, and those at Liberty Hall were determined to prevent a police raid, which would have had disastrous consequences. On the 26 March 1916 the Dublin Metropolitan Police (DMP) seized 1,000 copies of the nationalist newspaper the *Gael*, and then turned their sights on the co-operative shop in Liberty Hall run by Jane Shanahan and Helena Molony. Dangerously, as well as stocking a range of seditious materials the shop led directly to the printing room in Liberty Hall, where the *Workers' Republic* was printed. A full mobilisation of the ICA was ordered to protect the building.[1184] According to Christopher Brady, who printed both the *Workers' Republic* and the future Proclamation of the Irish Republic, once Connolly was made aware of the DMP's arrival, he 'came down quickly, walked, quietly to the counter, with drawn gun in his hand', joining Molony who already had her automatic pointed at the police. 'Connolly looked sternly at the police and gave his command to them,' Brady recalled: '"Drop these papers or I will drop you".' Admitting that they did not have a warrant, the police beat a hasty retreat. Within an hour, 'a large contingent of Citizen Army men were mobilised to defend Liberty Hall' and it remained under guard until the Rising.[1185]

A telling incident occurred just weeks before the Rising. On 8 April, the *Workers' Republic* reported that the ICA took a decision that a green flag would be hoisted over Liberty Hall on 26 April 'as the symbol of our faith in freedom, and as a token to all the world that the working class of Dublin stands for the cause of Ireland, and the cause of Ireland is the cause of a separate and distinct nationality'.[1186] It was one thing to prepare explosives secretly in the basement, but this very public act of defiance led to 'murmurs of dissent' from members of the ITGWU. On 12 April, objections were expressed at a meeting of Branch No. 1 and it took Connolly's threat of resignation to ensure that the decision to fly the flag stood. What this revealed, argued Jeffrey Leddin in his recent account of the ICA, 'was that Connolly, who struggled to achieve a majority in favour of his proposal, would not have been able to bring the union into the same political space as the ICA. There was no possibility that the union would take any official part in the revolution.'[1187]

Nor did Connolly have a reliable political organisation to propagate his perspectives for the revolution. As Allen records, the Independent Labour Party of Ireland, the ILP(I), 'virtually collapsed with the crisis posed by the outbreak of war'.[1188] Its leading activists, Tom Johnson and David Campbell, backed the Allies, while Connolly opposed the war and wished Britain's defeat. When Connolly spoke at a public meeting 'on the war and its effects industrially' organised by the Belfast branch of the ILP(I) in August 1914, the *Irish Worker* report of the meeting candidly admitted that 'like all other parties his own was divided in opinion. For that reason he made it clear that his opinions were personal and did not necessarily bind others who spoke from that platform.'[1189] Facing increasingly virulent opposition from the bulk of Belfast workers who supported the war, the ILP eventually decided to discontinue its meetings. Connolly wrote angrily to William O'Brien that 'the interruptions of about a dozen young Orange hooligans were magnified into an awful danger and the majority decided against me'. He bemoaned the weakness of his party colleagues in Belfast, complaining that his efforts 'pushing forward the movement here for past three years' have been 'labelled as a desire for cheap notoriety', and adding that he was 'sick, Bill, of this part of the globe'.[1190]

Connolly was the general secretary of the ITGWU and a founder of the ILP(I); however, in the absence of a proper organisation of co-thinkers, it was simply not possible through strength of will alone, even one as powerful as Connolly's, to transform either into a force that could play a leading role in an insurrection. One analysis of Connolly's participation in the Rising argues, rightly, that though Connolly was centrally involved in the ILP(I) and its predecessor the SPI, the Irish Labour Party, the ITGWU and the ICA, and that all of these organisations embodied 'the propagandistic, political, trade union and military aspects' of Connolly's politics, nevertheless:

these commitments were ostensibly separated from each other, organisationally and ideologically. The SPI was not attached to the Labour Party, nor was the Citizen Army part of the ITGWU; indeed, the ICA was programmatically nearer to the Irish Volunteers than to the union which it is forever associated. The Irish Labour Party had no clear socialist programme, nor did the ITGWU have a revolutionary syndicalist programme.[1191]

While some have argued that these organisations were linked by 'a wider homogenous revolutionary philosophy' and a 'clear symbiosis of principles which suggested the means for complete revolution', this is to overstate the degree to which they could be practically co-ordinated for this purpose.[1192] As Woggon argued:

> It would not be going too far to say that without the uniting link of Connolly's personality, and his role as a socialist and trade union leader in the national uprising, the constituent parts of his ideologically complex, ambivalent and organisationally divergent lifework did not form a cohesive entity.[1193]

This gulf between the urgency of the task, as Connolly saw it, and the forces at his disposal led Connolly into a conception of revolution by an armed minority. It is important to note that he already formed this view *before* he made an alliance with the IRB in January 1916. In preparing the Citizen Army to go it alone in late 1915, Connolly had already embraced the methodology of insurrectionism, and exhibited an increasingly voluntaristic streak. This was noticed at the time by comrades who had long known Connolly in the British socialist movement. 'It was a revelation at first to me,' recalled the SLP's Tom Bell, 'who had known Connolly, the quiet, persuasive propagandist, the editor, the poet, the economist, historian, philosopher and organiser, to hear that now he was to be seen in an irregular military uniform seriously drilling the workers who frequented Liberty Hall.' Bell recalled, too, that his comrade Arthur MacManus asked Connolly, 'Was the time ripe?', questioning the objective basis for a revolution in Ireland. He received the following startling reply: '"The time is never ripe," said Connolly, "until you try. If you fail – then it is not ripe. If you succeed – then it *is* ripe."'[1194] Bulmer Hobson, who led a rival faction in the IRB arguing for a 'defensive strategy' of only launching an attack in response to British efforts to suppress the Volunteers, confirms this sense of Connolly, albeit in a more hostile manner. Hobson recalled later that 'Connolly, towards the end of 1915, decided to have a little insurrection with the Citizen Army', and recalls a row with him in a Dublin restaurant:

> His conversation was full of clichés derived from the earlier days of the socialist movement in Europe. He told me that the working-class was always revolutionary, that Ireland was powder magazine and that what was

necessary was for someone to apply the match. I replied that if he must talk in metaphors, Ireland was a wet bog and the match would fall in the puddle.

In truth, the Military Council's plans merely meant that instead of taking the Citizen Army out alone, 'in exchange for a few months' delay [Connolly] had been promised certain action by a far larger number of men than he could ever hope to put on the field'.[1195] In effect, 'he was getting more or less what he had been looking for: this looked like a serious attempt to strike a blow against British rule, with credible plans and timescales'.[1196]

However, when Connolly did enter into an alliance with the IRB in January 1916, he did so from a position of relative weakness. With no formal political organisation behind him, Connolly's forces comprised of the small but committed ICA and a coterie of close co-thinkers – such as Constance Markievicz, Michael Mallin, Helena Molony and Winifred Carney. The ICA 'represented' or acted as a locum for the wider labour movement but the alliance was an essentially military one, between a section of the Volunteers and the ICA militia.

'Hold on to your rifles'? The Easter Rising and socialism

This balance of forces meant that Connolly felt obliged to make concessions to his more powerful allies. Though he left his mark on the planning of the Rising, the main concession Connolly made was on its political programme. On 15 January, four days before his disappearance, Connolly published an important programmatic article in the *Workers' Republic*. In it, Connolly re-appropriates the term 'economic conscription', which had previously been used to describe 'the policy of forcing men into the army by depriving them of the means of earning a livelihood'.[1197] Instead, Connolly wrote,

> We must also conscript ... All the material of distribution – the railways, the canals, and all their equipment will at once become the national property of the Irish state. All the land stolen from the Irish people in the past, and not since restored in some manner to the actual tillers of the soil, ought at once to be confiscated and made the property of the Irish state ... All factories and workshops owned by people who do not yield allegiance to the Irish Government immediately upon its proclamation should at once be confiscated, and their productive powers applied to the service of the community loyal to Ireland, and to the army in its service.

The Proclamation of the Irish Republic, printed in the basement of Liberty Hall and read out by Pearse on the morning of the Rising was a progressive document, to be sure. Addressed to women and men equally, it 'eschew[ed] a narrow Catholic nationalism … in favour of a more generous social and political vision,' promising 'religious and civil liberty, equal rights and equal opportunities to all' and, alluding to the Protestant minority, rejected the 'differences carefully fostered by an alien government, which have divided a minority from the majority in the recent past'.[1198] Although it bore clear marks of Connolly's influence, both in espousing equal rights for women and in asserting 'the right of the people to the ownership of Ireland', it was clearly, however, a bourgeois-democratic document rather than a socialist one.

This reflected the very nature of the Rising itself. In one sense, the Rising reached back into the nineteenth-century Jacobin tradition. It was, argued Owen McGee, 'a citizens' revolt or the last 1848-style rebellion in European history, when would-be "free citizens" simply "manned the barricades" in defence of a cause of "national" liberty against an unaccountable, monarchical government and virtually waited to be shot to pieces'.[1199] Yet one should not underestimate the scale of the Rising. It involved around 1,300 insurgents and tied down the largest military power in the world for almost a week. As one author put it, the Rising 'blasted the widest breach in the ramparts of the Empire since Yorktown', during the American War of Independence.[1200] In this sense, the Rising anticipated later twentieth century anti-colonial movements and uprisings against the British Empire. It found immediate echo among revolutionary nationalists in Egypt and in India, and triggered a chain of events that culminated in 26 counties of Ireland winning eventual independence from Britain.

Though it was a radical bourgeois-democratic uprising, this does not imply that it was directly *led* by representatives of the Irish bourgeoisie, far less by the capitalist class more narrowly defined. Indeed, outside of Ulster, both the urban and rural Irish bourgeoisie at this time largely supported Redmond and the Irish Parliamentary Party and abhorred the Rising. One account of the Rising has described the 'extremely diverse group' who made up the core conspirators:

They included a headmaster, a university lecturer, a corporation official and a former barman. They ranged from sophisticated cosmopolitans who wrote poems and plays, one the son of a count, to proletarians with an elementary education; men who seemed not so much from different generations as from different worlds.[1201]

It was, then, a Rising led by the radical petite bourgeoisie, supported by sections of the working class.

Debate has raged subsequently about Connolly's participation in the Rising, and whether it is justified from a socialist perspective. In particular dispute has been the question of whether Connolly preserved his political independence from his bourgeois-nationalist allies.

On the morning of the Rising, Connolly is recorded as having told his Citizen Army comrades: 'In the event of victory, hold on to your rifles, as those with whom we are fighting may stop before our goal is reached. We are out for economic as well as political liberty.' Some claim, citing this speech, that Connolly did not collapse his political identity into that of the IRB and the Volunteers. His words are quoted in both Greaves's biography and in R.M. Fox's 1943 *History of the Irish Citizen Army,* and have been read as Connolly's assertion of working-class political independence from the bourgeois republicans.[1202] Others disagree; historian John Newsinger has queried the provenance of the quotation, and argued that 'it is starkly contradicted by just about everything we know for certain [Connolly] did say and write'.[1203] Newsinger's contention that Connolly subsumed his politics into those of the IRB is supported by the fact that Connolly put his name to the Proclamation alongside the IRB men, a document which contained little in the way of a social programme. Further, Connolly released no separate statement of the Citizen Army's position, nor any warning that a further struggle would be necessary to realise the ultimate goal of a Workers' Republic. Moreover, a number of ICA members recollected being told by Connolly that there was no longer an ICA nor the Volunteers but only an army of the Irish Republic. Leddin's work on the ICA quotes one veteran, George Oman, to the effect that 'the Citizen Army ceased to exist on Monday of Easter Week', and another, James O'Neill, recalling that 'when the joint forces were brought together on Easter Sunday there was no distinction between the Volunteers and the Citizen Army'.[1204] In effect, Newsinger argued, Connolly lowered the red flag for the green.

There is evidence, however, to suggest Connolly did give some indication of a coming struggle with his nationalist allies. As Aindras Ó Cathasaigh points out, R.M. Fox's history of the ICA, in which the order appears, 'is reinforced by the fact that his account was read and corrected chapter by chapter by a committee of veterans, many of whom would have been present'.[1205] John O'Keefe, a veteran of both the SPI and the Citizen Army, also says that Connolly warned of a struggle yet to come with his non-socialist allies. O'Keefe recalled in an article in 1932 that:

Connolly's address to the Citizen Army a couple of days before the Rising should never be forgotten by the Irish workers. 'Being the lesser party', he said, 'we join in this fight with our comrades of the Irish Volunteers. But hold your arms. If we succeed, those who are our comrades today we may be compelled to fight tomorrow. And when one of our number raised the question of our strength came the reply: 'The people will help.'[1206]

Recollections of Connolly expressing similar sentiments can also be found. In 1937, the Irish Labour Party held a meeting to mark the 21st anniversary of Connolly's execution. The meeting heard from Cathal O'Shannon, Frank Robbins, and Archie Heron, a trade unionist and Irish Labour politician married to Connolly's daughter Ina. In his contribution to the debate, Robbins said that he 'could personally recall as a member of the I.C.A., Connolly revealed his mind clearly on [the] question of preparing for the fight he ultimately entered with the I.C.A. as a step in the fight for working-class emancipation. Connolly had told them their real fight would begin when the fight for separatism was over.'[1207]

That several almost identical eyewitness accounts of Connolly's call to arms exist strongly suggest he did speak in terms of a coming struggle. Nevertheless, the controversy surrounding this famous quotation may well reflect real ambiguities in Connolly's position.

Connolly had long assumed that a *genuinely* nationalist revolution would simultaneously be a socialist one. He based this assumption on his analysis that British colonialism in Ireland had two aspects, a denial of political independence but also the destruction of a socialistic Gaelic social order in the seventeenth century. According to Connolly, therefore 'the Irish National question was at bottom an economic question' and 'the Irish Socialist was in reality the best Irish patriot …'. Thus, a mere fortnight before the Rising, Connolly wrote in the *Workers' Republic*:

We are out for Ireland for the Irish. But who are the Irish? Not the rack-renting, slum-owning landlord; not the sweating, profit-grinding capitalist; not the sleek and oily lawyer; not the prostitute pressman – the hired liars of the enemy. Not these are the Irish upon whom the future depends. Not these, but the Irish working class, the only secure foundation upon which a free nation can be reared.

The cause of labour is the cause of Ireland, the cause of Ireland is the cause of labour. They cannot be dissevered. Ireland seeks freedom. Labour seeks that an Ireland free should be the sole mistress of her own destiny, supreme owner of all material things within and upon her soil …[1208]

But dissevered they were. The Rising was for political independence but this implied no immediate socialist commitment, nor the goal of carrying out the social 're-conquest of Ireland' that was Connolly's own ultimate aim. The cause of Ireland may have been the cause of labour, given the socialist republican commitment of the ITGWU, but the cause of labour was most definitely not the cause of all those stepping out on Easter Monday morning to fight for Irish freedom. As Connolly's close comrade Helena Molony reflected later, 'Perhaps the time was not ripe for success' as '[the Irish] people had no widespread economic knowledge to cope with social evils'. She added that 'I should have hated to see Padraic Pearse as President of an Irish Republic if the misery and wretchedness of the tenements had still gone on'.[1209]

Connolly wished to strike a blow for Irish independence, and worked with non-socialist forces to do so. Perhaps he believed that the Rising would develop a mass character, and that the rank-and-file Volunteers would be pulled into struggle that fused the national struggle with socialism, a fight for both a political and social 're-conquest of Ireland'. If they would not, however, Connolly believed that a more thoroughgoing social revolution would need to be brought about by the Citizen Army leading the wider working-class movement. This view, it seems, was expressed to his closest followers ahead of the Rising. Yet Connolly chose not to shout it from the rooftops. Mike Milotte is surely correct, then, in the observation that

> Connolly's somewhat cryptic 'hold on to your rifles' speech was no substitute for a clear and precise statement of just how the revolt might *actually* be made permanent. He presented no programme for the working class to follow in the period ahead that might have enabled the most militant sections to cut through the confusion that reigned in the ranks of organised labour after his death so as to achieve a leading position in the ensuing fight for freedom.[1210]

This itself was a sign, perhaps, that the more immediate concern of Irish independence was foremost in Connolly's mind. Much contemporary political confusion around Connolly's legacy and the relationship of socialism to Irish nationalism has its roots in the absence of how he saw the struggle continuing after his death.

Reactions to the Rising

Judged by the yardstick of socialist internationalism, the British labour and socialist movement did not cover itself in glory with its reaction to the Easter Rising. Connolly himself, aware of the long-standing equivocation of the socialist movement with regards to matters of Irish self-determination reportedly told his daughter Nora on the eve of his execution that: 'The socialists will never understand why I am here; they will all forget that I am an Irishman.'[1211] As his old SLP comrade Arthur McManus reflected eight years later, Connolly 'was speaking at a moment when the Socialist movement had not reached an understanding of the significance of struggling subjected ...'.[1212]

The reaction of the various trade union, Labour and socialist organisations to the Rising largely tracked their respective views on the wider war. As Geoff Bell has argued in his study of the British labour movement and the Irish revolution 'the leadership of the labour movement who had enlisted in Britain's war effort and had agreed to a national truce was always highly likely to react critically to those who they saw as taking up arms against the war effort and against that truce'.[1213] Arthur Henderson, who had joined the War Cabinet and therefore arguably bore some political and moral responsibility for the executions, was dogged for years to come by accusations (which he denied) that he had cheered when news of the first three executions was announced in the House of Commons.[1214]

When not expressing outright hostility, the reaction was one of bewildered confusion at Connolly's involvement. Following the first wave of executions, Citizen Army member Maeve Cavanagh, and sister of *Irish Worker* cartoonist Ernest Cavanagh, travelled to London as part of an unsuccessful delegation to prevent the execution of Casement. 'I had a long talk with Ramsay MacDonald,' she recalled, 'who spoke to me in a very low voice, expressing his astonishment that Connolly had acted as he did.'[1215]

Similarly mirroring its attitude to the war was the ILP's response to the Rising. In this case adopting a pacifist perspective, the party, in its weekly *Labour Leader*, proclaimed that 'we are opposed to armed force, whether it under the control of the government or a Labour organisation.'[1216] Tom Johnston, editor of the Glasgow ILP's *Forward*, went even further, in spite, or perhaps because, of Connolly's connection to the paper. Not only was Connolly's participation 'mysterious and astounding' but the paper charged that the Rising was 'a futile insurrection' in which 'the insurrectionists were apparently being used as pawns and tools by the German government'.[1217] A similar view to that of the ILP was echoed by the *Daily Herald*, which declared, 'we are against all wars – civil wars no less than wars between nations'.[1218] A more principled stand came from the Fabian George Bernard Shaw, who argued in a letter to the *Daily News* that those executed 'were shot in cold blood'. Bernard Shaw continued, that 'an Irishman resorting to arms to achieve the independence of his country is only doing what an Englishman would do if it be their misfortunate to be invaded and conquered by the Germans in the course of the present war'.[1219]

The SDF did not speak with one voice on the Rising. Renamed the BSP in 1911, following unity with a number of ILP branches and other socialist organisations and individuals, the party was divided. Hyndman backed the war and 'had become steadily more patriotic, denouncing ever more violently all those who opposed its prosecution in any way'.[1220] Such views led to the formation of an increasingly effective internationalist opposition in the party, grouped in Scotland around John MacLean and in London around figures such as Zelda Kahan (whose brother Boris had provided Connolly with a Yiddish translation of his local election manifesto in 1902) and Peter Petroff.[1221] The internationalist opposition gradually increased its support in the party, and finally triumphed over the Hyndmanite old guard at the BSP conference on 23 and 24 April 1916. At the same time as Connolly stepped out of Liberty Hall on Easter Monday morning and bullets flew in Dublin, delegates in Salford ended Hyndman's thirty-year reign at the top of his organisation and freed the BSP to throw itself into anti-war campaigning activity.[1222]

The anti-war BSP opposition had established its own newspaper, the *Call*, which on 1 June would become the party's official organ. Its first comment stated that 'in the absence of more reliable information concerning the Irish rebellion … we refrain from making any exhaustive comment on this latest phase of the war for liberation'. Nevertheless, the editors had 'no hesitation, however, in fixing full responsibility for the antecedents of the affair on the shoulders of successive British governments'. A fortnight later, the position was more equivocal, calling the decision to rise 'with inadequate force' as 'foolish' and 'doomed'.[1223]

The Hyndmanites, after June calling themselves the National Socialist Party and retaining *Justice,* predictably opposed the Rising. In the front page article on 4 May, Hyndman wrote unsympathetically of the rebels as a 'small body of reckless fanatics', and viewed the Rising as a German plot. To his limited credit, Hyndman counsels 'that no vindictiveness should be shown' to the rebels and writes with some sadness of Connolly who, 'though he had long gone out of our movement … did thorough good service while he was with us, and was unquestionably an honest, determined and capable enthusiast with brains'. He regretted, however, that Connolly 'has given his life for his ill-balanced opinions … on this mad endeavour …'.[1224]

Ironically, given Hyndman's anti-German views, his opinion formed the basis of the obituary which appeared in *Vorwaerts*, the paper of the pro-war SPD leadership on 20 May, drawing heavily on reports in *Justice* and

Forward. The SPD noted that 'Connolly's participation in the outbreak of the Sinn-Fein disturbances was completely inexplicable to English socialists' but hoped 'the Irish proletariat will best honour the memory of those socialists who took part in this movement if they keep in mind the teachings of Connolly and his closest friends, and follow those teachings when their time comes'.[1225]

More poignant was the account of John Leslie, who had been Connolly's mentor in Edinburgh over two decades previously, and whose views on the 'Irish Question' were a profound and formative influence. Asked by the editor of *Justice* to provide an estimate of Connolly and his participation in the Rising, Leslie wrote that the request was 'a most difficult task, perhaps the most difficult I have ever undertaken'. Leslie described the Rising, 'the deplorable Dublin tragedy', as 'sad, mad, and bad' and saw little value in Connolly fighting for national self-determination. He described his republican allies as 'the merest reactionaries' who were 'obsessed with a hopeless medievalism' and saw this evidence of a shift in Connolly's politics – 'Sinn Féin had made its mark on him'. At root, felt Leslie, 'Connolly did not place a very high estimate upon the Labour or Socialist movement here' and was 'determined at all costs to identify or indissolubly link the cause of Irish labour with the most extreme Irish nationalism, and to seal the bond of union with his blood if necessary'. Despite all this, there is no mistaking Leslie's affection for the man he 'had the honour of welcoming ... into the socialist movement now well over 20 years ago'. Despite their political differences, Leslie wrote:

> Of all the men whom I have ever known or could ever 'read of in tale or history' there is not one who brought a cleaner soul, a more disinterested enthusiasm or a courage more undaunted to the service of the working people than did James Connolly.[1226]

Though hostile, the Hyndman at least attempted a political reckoning with the Rising and Connolly's participation within it. The same cannot be said for the SLP, the party which Connolly had founded in 1903, and whose leaders maintained a personal link with him. 'It is rather remarkable therefore,' comments Geoff Bell, 'that the SLP monthly newspaper, the *Socialist*, made no comment whatsoever on the Rising and its aftermath.'[1227] There was a short statement in the June edition, which noted blandly that the capitalist state makes use of the army to enforce its rule, but aside from this left 'the merits or demerits of the revolt aside'.[1228] Shockingly, the SLP did not even print an obituary of its founder until 1919, and the *Socialist* contained no coverage of substance on Ireland in the intervening years. As Bell argues, this suggests that something more than the temporary dislocation of the war was to blame for the SLP's silence on Ireland. In its economism, the party did not appreciate the importance of the right of oppressed nations to fight for self-determination and it was therefore critical of Connolly's participation. At the same time, 'because Connolly had been such a prominent member of the SLP, or perhaps because there were differences within the organisation, it preferred to say nothing'.[1229]

Finally, showing characteristic strength of principle was Sylvia Pankhurst and the Women's Suffrage Federation (WSF) – soon to be the Workers' Suffrage Federation – and its paper the *Woman's Dreadnought*. 'Justice can make but one reply to the Irish Rebellion', wrote Pankhurst, 'and that is the demand that Ireland should be allowed to govern itself.' Though Pankhurst considered the Rising to be 'reckless', it was nevertheless 'animated by high deals'. She blamed the British government above all and concluded that 'We understand why rebellion breaks out in Ireland and we share the sorrow of those who are weeping today for the Rebels whom the government has shot'.[1230]

As well as this, the *Dreadnought* contained the best coverage of the Rising on the British left. Indeed, its on-the-spot reportage put it head and shoulders above the British press as a whole. The eye-witness accounts of the Rising were the responsibility of Patricia Lynch, a young Irish member of Pankhurst's WSF, who would later find fame as a prolific children's author. Lynch's partner, the socialist writer and future Connolly biographer, Richard Fox, remembered that, 'When the Rebellion was announced nothing would satisfy her but to go off to Dublin'. Travelling on 'a train packed with military', she found an Irish-background lieutenant who 'told her how he hated being sent to Ireland on that work, as he was Irish himself' and persuaded him to take her 'right through as his sister, while the other civilians were left stranded at Holyhead'.[1231]

Owing to this brave journey, Lynch was able to interview working-class Dubliners, British socialists and relatives of those killed in the Rising. In her 'Scenes from the Rebellion', she captured 'O'Connell Street and along Eden Quay' while 'the dust was still thick upon the ground, the air was heavy with burning, and dense clouds of smoke obscured the ruins'.[1232]

The Rising also figured in socialist debate internationally. Within the 'Zimmerwald Left', those revolutionary socialists who proclaimed their opposition to the Second International's capitulation on the war, issues of national self-determination were hotly contested.[1233] While there was 'firm agreement' on a general level 'in counterposing revolutionary socialism to opportunism and chauvinism', some socialists 'rejected many immediate demands and tactics that the Bolsheviks had successfully integrated into their revolutionary programme and practice'. Chief amongst these was 'the Bolsheviks' support for the democratic demand for the right of oppressed nations to self-determination, which was rejected by both the Dutch and Polish adherents of the 'Zimmerwald Left'.[1234] The Rising, therefore, became a factor in this debate, with all sides assessing it in light of their own theoretical contentions.

Lenin's argument was that part of the 'internationalist education of the workers of the oppressor countries' must involve laying an emphasis 'on their advocating freedom for the oppressed countries to secede and their fighting for it'.[1235] A 'left' faction in the Bolsheviks emerged in 1915, challenging this perspective and Lenin's advocacy of the 'right of nations to self-determination' on the grounds that in the 'imperialist epoch', the 'absorption of small states by large states' could not be challenged without overthrowing imperialism, and therefore capitalism, as a whole. Thus, 'partial' and 'minimum' demands such as the 'right of nations to self-determination' were '*utopian*' as they 'cannot be realized *within the limits of capitalism*'.[1236]

When the Rising took place, Lenin saw it as evidence that revolts by oppressed nations which constitute a vital component of the imminent revolutionary wave. 'The dialectics of history are such that small nations, powerless as an *independent* factor in the struggle against imperialism,' wrote Lenin, 'play a *part* as one of the ferments, one of the bacilli, which help the *real* anti-imperialist force, the socialist proletariat, to make its appearance on the scene.'[1237] Against Karl Radek, a supporter of the 'left' faction, who dismissed the Rising as a 'putsch', Lenin famously argued:

> Whoever calls such a rebellion a 'putsch' is either a hardened reactionary, or a doctrinaire hopelessly incapable of envisaging a social revolution as a living phenomenon.
>
> To imagine that social revolution is conceivable without revolts by small nations in the colonies and in Europe, without revolutionary outbursts by a section of the petty bourgeoisie with all its prejudices, without a movement of the politically non-conscious proletarian and semi-proletarian masses against oppression by the landowners, the church, and the monarchy, against national oppression, etc. – to imagine all this is to repudiate social revolution ...[1238]

It is crucial to stress, however, that Lenin was not writing about Connolly's involvement in the Rising (of which he was then unaware) or about any specific tactics the Irish socialist movement should have adopted towards it. His article cannot therefore be read as an endorsement of either. Rather, this dispute over the Rising played into the much broader argument in the socialist movement about how revolts for national self-determination would factor in the coming European revolution. Less quoted, too, is Lenin's comment that 'the misfortune of the Irish [is] that they rose prematurely, before the European revolt of the proletariat had *had time* to mature'.[1239]

This run-through of the British and wider European left's attitude to the Rising places Connolly within an international socialist movement reckoning with the catastrophe of an imperialist war. Amidst the confusion, debates, struggles and splits of the wartime period, the socialist movement was teetering over the precipice which separated the Second International from the world of post-war world of communist revolution. The conclusion to the book extends this analysis of the international left, arguing that Connolly, as a rebel within the international socialist movement of his day, can be seen more widely as a bridge between the Second and the Third Internationals.

Conclusion

Between the Second and the Third Internationals?

It has been consistently argued throughout this book that James Connolly is best understood as part of the Second International, the international socialist organisation of his day. This was true even when Connolly was an outlier within the International – in opposing Kautsky's compromise resolution on 'ministerialism' at the 1900 Paris Congress or, later, when Connolly adopted a form of 'Marxist-syndicalism' in the SLP and the IWW in reaction to the International's evolutionary, reformist and parliamentary drift. Indeed, the importance of the Second International to Connolly's development was true even when the International collapsed. Its very failure to effectively oppose the war and its very *absence* as a material force after 1914 was a necessary condition for Connolly's journey on the road to the Easter Rising of 1916.

In another sense, Connolly transcended the limitations of the Second International and anticipated major themes of the future communist movement. As British communist J.T. Murphy put it in 1924, 'Connolly [was] among the few great figures of the international working-class movement which belong to the transition from the epoch of imperialist expansion to the epoch of social revolution'.[1240] His 'place in history,' wrote Murphy, 'is among the heralds of a new epoch'.[1241]

The first sense concerns Connolly's essential *revolutionism*. Once, when a heckler asked at a public meeting, 'How do you know so much about revolution Mr Connolly?,' he famously replied: 'My business is revolution, madam.'[1242] He was not wrong. In April 1919, Arthur McManus published, in the SLP's newspaper the *Socialist*, a letter he received from Connolly which had been written in November 1915. In it, Connolly politely declined McManus's invitation to address an anti-conscription meeting in Glasgow, on the grounds that 'every moment in Dublin is full of tragic possibilities' and Connolly's 'presence is required here in constant watchfulness'.

Introducing the letter, McManus wrote that 'Jim Connolly was the first socialist I had met who actually worked for Revolution, and dream of its immediate possibility. He was continually striving to read into every crisis the potentialities of a Revolutionary situation.'[1243]

In this, Connolly provided a blazing contrast to the approach of the Second International. For many in the Second International, the revolution was not a *practical* event to be prepared for, but something to be postponed into the middle future, when 'objective conditions' were ripe and the quantitative growth of working-class consciousness, reflected in the votes for the party and the numbers enrolled in the trade unions, had reached the sufficient level. As Michael Löwy put it, an 'essential article of faith of unimaginative, reductionist Marxism' found in the Second International (and, later, in Stalinism) was 'the quantitative accumulation of productive forces, of the gains of the labour movement, of the number of party members and voters in a movement of linear, irresistible, "automatic" progress'.[1244] What this meant in practice, as Trotsky wrote some years later, was that the Second International 'divided its program into two parts independent of each other: the *minimum program* which limited itself to reforms within the framework of bourgeois society, and the *maximum program* which promised substitution of socialism for capitalism in the indefinite future. Between the minimum and the maximum program,' however, 'no bridge existed. And indeed Social Democracy has no need of such a bridge, since the word *socialism* is used only for holiday speechifying.'[1245]

Secondly, besides a general revolutionary spirit and elan, Connolly's particular recognition of the importance of national liberation to the socialist revolution marks him as a pioneer.

The Second International had discussed questions of imperialism and colonialism at its congresses. It had, however, largely confined its debates to the relationship of these phenomenon to capitalist development, with an emphasis on the duties of socialists in the metropolitan countries rather than on the agency of the oppressed themselves. The Second International did take an anti-colonial stance at its international congresses in Paris in 1900 and Amsterdam in 1904, facing down a pro-colonial minority. In 1907, however, this minority voice won a temporary victory, until the assertion that the congress 'does not reject in principle every colonial policy' and that 'under a socialist regime, colonization could be a force for civilization' was narrowly overturned by Kautsky.[1246] It was this ambivalence, together with the Second International's metropolitan emphasis, which led the Communist International in 1920 to denounce its predecessor as having 'in reality recognized the existence only of people with white skin'.[1247]

It was not until after the Russian Revolution of October 1917, and the foundation of the Communist International in March 1919, that the problem was discussed with greater depth and seriousness. The Second Congress of the Communist International in 1920 discussed in more detail the strategy and tactics for the participation of proletarian parties in bourgeois-democratic movements for national self-determination in oppressed nations. The 'Theses on the National and Colonial Questions' sought to base communist policy on forging 'a closer union of the proletarians and the working masses of all nations and countries for a joint revolutionary struggle to overthrow the landowners and the bourgeoisie'.[1248] In the west, this involved making it clear that 'all Communist parties should render direct aid to the revolutionary movements among the dependent and underprivileged nations', with the 'form of this alliance ... determined by the degree of development of the communist movement in the proletariat of each country, or of the bourgeois-democratic liberation movement of the workers and peasants in backward countries or among backward nationalities'.[1249] In oppressed colonial countries themselves, the policy contained a strategic prescription:

> the need for a determined struggle against attempts to give a communist colouring to bourgeois-democratic liberation trends in the backward countries; the Communist International should support bourgeois-democratic national movements in colonial and backward countries only on condition that, in these countries, the elements of future proletarian parties, which will be communist not only in name, are brought together and trained to understand their special tasks, i.e., those of the struggle against the bourgeois-democratic movements within their own nations. The Communist International must enter into a temporary alliance with bourgeois democracy in the colonial and backward countries, but should not merge with it, and should under all circumstances uphold the independence of the proletarian movement even if it is in its most embryonic form.[1250]

While Connolly's tactics in relation to the republican movement in 1916 can be criticised for their failure to uphold strict proletarian independence, his intense concern with issues of national oppression and liberation bind him closer in *spirit* to the revolutionary communist movement than the equivocation of the Second International.

Thirdly, although it is obviously impossible to say for certain that Connolly would have aligned himself with the communist movement, we can make a more limited claim. Many of the key *political tendencies* within the Second International which Connolly associated with, influenced and was influenced by, were amongst the main contributors to the development of the policies of the early Communist International.

Some in the Leninist tradition utterly disavow the Second International, given its betrayal of socialist internationalism in 1914 and the responsibility of the SPD-led German government in 1919 for the murders of Rosa Luxemburg and Karl Liebknecht.[1251] A total dismissal, however, would simultaneously be a disavowal of the Marxism which trained Lenin himself, not to mention Trotsky, James Connolly and hundreds of thousands of other socialist militants.[1252] When the Communist International was formed in March 1919, it did so by gathering together a diverse range of dissident revolutionary trends within the existing socialist movement.

> [It] picked up many of the threads of earlier socialism, and wove them into a more or less coherent strategy of working-class struggle for power – the direct action of French, British, Irish and American syndicalists, the political 'syndicalism' of the De Leonites, James Connolly, and Jim Larkin, the revolutionary parliamentarianism of Liebknecht, the sometimes acute criticism by communist-anarchists of the parliamentarians of the pre-1914 Socialist International, the concern with national liberation of such as James Connolly and of the Bolsheviks themselves ...[1253]

In January 1919, amidst the sound and fury of the Russian Civil War, the Bolsheviks issued a letter of invitation to 'the revolutionary left wing' of the Second International, the 'syndicalist elements of the labour movement' and 'all those proletarian groups or organisations which, although they have not openly rallied to the revolutionary current, are nevertheless displaying a trend in that direction in their evolution'.[1254] It then listed 39 groups or currents to be invited to the inaugural Congress of the Communist International, including several communist parties from the old Russian Empire, and currents from across Europe, North America, Australia and Japan. Given the relatively international spread, it is striking that Connolly had been a member of no fewer than 7 of the 39 currents: 'the British socialist parties [including the ILP and the BSP]'; 'Socialist Labour Party (Britain)'; 'the revolutionary elements and workers' organisations of Ireland [i.e. The ITGWU and SPI]'; 'SLP (America)'; 'the Left elements of the SP of America (the tendency represented by Debs and the League for Socialist Propaganda)'; and the 'IWW (America)'.

The BSP was, of course, the inheritor of the propagandist tradition of British Marxism, which Connolly received his political training in as a member of the SDF. As we have seen in the previous chapter, a growing left wing in what was (after 1911) the BSP, opposed the Hyndman leadership over issues of militarism and the First World War. This left wing captured the organisation in Easter 1916, and the resulting anti-war BSP comprised the largest component part of the CPGB when it was formed in 1920.

After Connolly left the SDF in 1903, he became an enthusiastic supporter of De Leon and the SLP. Though the BSP provided the bulk of the CPGB's initial membership, the much-smaller SLP provided a disproportionate number of its leadership.[1255] Of the first provisional Executive Committee of the newly formed CPGB in 1920, the SLP provided Tom Bell, William Paul, J.R. Campbell and Arthur MacManus, with J.T. Murphy also playing a prominent role in the CPGB and the Communist International.

The attraction of the industrial unionist SLP to Bolshevism was part of a more general convergence of revolutionary industrial unionism and syndicalism with communism after the Russian Revolution. What made this potential fusion possible was the widespread enthusiasm for the Russian Revolution among militant sections of the working class. In particular, many revolutionary unionists heralded the Russian Revolution initially as the victory of their own revolutionary project. IWW militant Ralph Chaplin, who it will be remembered designed the cover for the US edition of Connolly's *Socialism Made Easy,* recalled how Bill Haywood told him: 'The Russian revolution is the greatest event in our lives. It represents all that we have been dreaming of and fight for all our lives.'[1256] After Haywood had finished reading a letter to the IWW published by the Communist International in 1918, he called Chaplin over to his desk and said to him: 'Here is what we have been dreaming about; here is the I.W.W. all feathered out!'[1257] The Revolution also spurred enthusiasm in French, Italian and Spanish syndicalist circles, with leaders such as Andreu Nin, visiting Moscow. In Ireland, the ITGWU's newspaper the *Voice of Labour* declared that 'Ireland's best and most effective answer is the immediate establishment of Soviets, the instruments which will bring about the dictatorship of the Irish proletariat'.[1258]

As the *Voice of Labour* article suggests, revolutionary unionists – syndicalists, industrial unionists, De Leonites – were attracted to the idea of a state build on soviets (workers' councils).[1259] As Walter Kendall commented, 'In the Soviet system of government, the SLP saw before their eyes the living incarnation of the "Industrial Republic of Labour" advocated by Connolly and De Leon. The Russian Revolution appeared a triumphant vindication of the whole SLP system of ideas.'[1260]

In America, too, the left-wing of the SPA which Connolly joined in 1908 was one of the main currents later forming American communism. The alliance of Charles H. Kerr's *ISR* with the industrialist unionist left of the SPA, argued historian Jack Ross, was one of 'the first manifestations of an actual revolutionary left wing [which was] emerging in the Socialist Party [and] would hound it at the margins of the next decade before ultimately providing the foundation for the American Communist movement'.[1261] Involved in the moves to win the SPA to communism were Connolly's close collaborators Patrick L. Quinlan and Jim Larkin. In Ireland itself, Larkin was also a founder of the Irish Worker League (IWL), which was recognised by the Communist International as its Irish section after 1923 and replaced the first CPI, led by Connolly's son Roddy.

Connolly, of course, did not live to see the transition from the Second International to the Third, nor the shift from the era of war to one of revolution. Contrary to Connolly's prediction that the war spelled all but doom for the international labour movement, the end of the conflict brought with it the eruption of powerful revolutionary movements. Following in the wake of the Russian Revolution of November 1917, the Soviet government dragged Russia out of the war and demanded an end to the conflict, 'an immediate peace without annexations (i.e., without the seizure of foreign lands, without the forcible incorporation of foreign nations) and without indemnities'.[1262] The war finally came to an end when German sailors mutinied at Kiel, sparking a revolution which overthrew the Kaiser and proclaimed a democratic republic. Soon, Soviet Republics were declared in Hungary and Bavaria, and potentially revolutionary upsurges during the *Biennio Rosso* ('Two Red Years') in Italy in 1919-20.

Closer to home, in Ireland, a mass movement arose in April 1918 against the British government's attempts to introduce conscription. It was met with a one-day general strike on 23 April, which closed docks and shipyards, railways and trams, factories and mills, theatres and cinemas, public services, newspapers, shops, and munitions factories. In December 1918, a revivified Sinn Féin movement, which had benefited most from the Rising, swept the board in the General Election. In January 1919, its MPs boycotted Westminster, and declared an independent Irish national parliament, Dáil Éireann. Almost simultaneously, the first shots were fired in what became the Irish War of Independence, which lasted until December 1921.

In this post-war context, the Irish labour movement grew to an unprecedented size and strength. 'Trade union exploded in all directions', wrote Emmet O'Connor. From a base of 100,000 members in 1916, membership affiliated to the Irish Trade Union Congress grew to 225,000 in 1920.[1263] Ireland saw an unprecedented wave of militancy, including 'soviets' in Monaghan in February 1919, Limerick in April and several other areas between 1919 and 1922. As Conor Kostick has summarised:

> Between 1918 and the conclusion of the Irish War of Independence in 1921 the organised Irish working class made five distinct and powerful interventions. On 23 April 1918 a general strike took place against the threat of conscription; for a month at the beginning of 1919 Belfast was gripped by a strike for a shorter working week; in April that year Limerick workers took over their city and declared soviet rule; in April 1920 a massive general strike forced the release of hungerstrikers; and for most of 1920 transport workers sabotaged the movements of men and material by the British Army. Alongside these set-piece battles was a general spirit of resistance and confidence in the possibility of taking action amongst Irish workers, who were themselves part of a great upsurge of revolutionary enthusiasm that was sweeping through Europe.[1264]

Politically, however, the Irish working class felt the absence of James Connolly. Connolly's energy and drive meant that the labour movement, or a radical section of it at least, had punched considerably above its weight during Easter week. It was largely through Connolly's sheer force of personality, will and political clarity, that the Citizen Army occupied such a central place in the Rising. His outsize influence made his murder all the more grievous a loss. In the aftermath of the Rising, despite heroic and unprecedented levels of industrial struggle, the militancy of the Irish working class was channelled by labour's leaders into providing muscle for the wider independence struggle; missing was Connolly's daring perspective of 'taking and keeping the lead' of the 'true Nationalist side'.[1265]

What a huge and irreplaceable loss Connolly's death was to the Irish working-class movement was noted by many contemporaries. Poet Padraic Colum, who had moved to the United States from Ireland in 1914, penned an obituary for Connolly and Francis Sheehy-Skeffington, which was published in the anarchist Emma Goldman's journal *Mother Earth*. Colum wrote that 'when they shot Connolly to death, it seemed as if they had shot the heart and brain out of the Irish proletariat'.[1266]. Similarly, Sylvia Pankhurst, who had become friendly with Connolly during the Lockout, recalled in a memoir that his death 'was more grievous than any, because his rebellion struck deeper than mere nationalism'. After national independence had been achieved, Pankhurst noted, 'the social problems, which we in England were wrestling, would still be present in Ireland'. While 'the execution of the rebels had irrevocably ensured the ultimate success of their uprising,' she argued, 'Connolly was needed so seriously for the after-building; him at least, it seemed, Fate should have spared'.[1267]

This is one of the central tragedies of Connolly's political life. Ten years before his murder, Connolly wrote:

> the duty of a true Socialist, editor or trusted leader, is to train as many comrades as possible to fill his position, to train and make editors, and writers and propagandists, and to encourage every member to develop the cool-headedness and readiness needed in a revolutionary moment ...[1268]

Despite this, while Connolly's efforts undoubtedly inspired thousands of workers at the time, 'his style of politics had no supporters among the first-rank leaders of the labour movement. Connolly left no prominent and able successor.'[1269] Beyond the 'first rank', it is clear too that there was no wider organisation that survived Connolly's death that consistently upheld his political thinking, his concern with working-class struggle and the importance of fusing class politics with the fight for national self-determination. The SPI was revived in 1917 by William O'Brien, in the wake of the Russian Revolution of March 1917. Though it was, in Emmet O'Connor's words, 'perhaps the best connected, best resourced Marxist party in Irish history,' it remained a party of key trade union officials, journalists and politicians – such as O'Brien, Tom Johnson and Cathal O'Shannon – based in Liberty Hall.[1270] Beyond this, its membership remained small, and it 'did not make any serious attempt to organise branches or step into politics as a force in its own right, its role being primarily educational and propagandist'.[1271] As for O'Brien himself, he willingly assumed the mantle of chief bureaucrat and cautious administrator in the ITGWU; roles to which he was much better suited than that of a revolutionary leader.

Connolly's son Roddy established the CPI in 1921, along with Walter Carpenter and Sean McLoughlin, having expelled O'Brien and O'Shannon from the SPI. The CPI remained small and weak, its leaders brave but young and inexperienced. In practical terms the CPI found itself tailing the more powerful anti-Treaty republicans. Soon, the Comintern put its money (quite literally) on Jim Larkin, who returned to Ireland in 1923. It dissolved the young CPI and urged support for Larkin's new grouping. The experience was an unhappy one, owing to Larkin's unreliability, and the Comintern soon established a new section, the Revolutionary Workers' Groups (RWG), led by graduates of the Lenin School in Moscow.[1272]

Increasingly, the Comintern's main priority after the post-Lenin Fifth Congress in mid-1924 was to urge Communist Parties in the colonial and semi-colonial world to politically adapt themselves to nationalist movements. The old Menshevik idea of discrete 'stages' of the revolution, was resurrected: first the completion of the 'bourgeois-democratic revolution', then only later the fight for distinctly working-class concerns. In the first stage, the political independence of the communists was downgraded in favour of support for bourgeois nationalist and anti-colonial movements. This strategy suited the foreign policy interests of the Soviet leadership in Russia, increasingly isolated internationally, but it sparked disaster for the communist movement in semi-colonial countries, particularly China in 1927.[1273]

In Ireland, this meant that communist politics primarily concerned relating to republicanism. Thus, what had earlier been a symptom of inexperience and confusion in the young CPI was elevated to a position of definite policy by its successors. As an approach, it furthered the conflation of revolutionary working-class politics with the populist wing of Irish republicanism, confining the communists to fight for the 'completion' of the Irish revolution in the form of ending partition, before taking up specifically working-class demands.

This gravitation towards populist Irish republicanism by the communists operated in reverse, too. Sections of the republican movement increasingly turned to socialistic rhetoric. During the Irish Civil War 1922-23, a section of the anti-Treaty republicans looked to harness the reservoir of social anger among agricultural labourers and small farmers in their struggle against the Free State forces, backed by the large landowners, the capitalists and the Catholic Church. Primary among them was Liam Mellows, a principled and consistent anti-imperialist, leader of the Rising in Galway and among those elected to the First Dáil in 1918. Mellows argued that 'the commercial interest, so called, money and gombeen men are on the side of the Treaty. We are back to Tone ... relying on "the men of no property".'[1274]

Connolly's ambiguous slogan that 'the cause of Ireland is the cause of labour; the cause of labour is the cause of Ireland' was meant as a flowing together of national and social questions, leading to the victory of the working class as 'the only secure foundation upon which a free nation can be reared'.[1275] By comparison, for Mellows and the left-republicans, the working-class politics was not the central axis of struggle but an external force to be enlisted as a useful social adjunct for the national struggle.

Connolly's key concern, the working-class leadership of the national revolution, was therefore increasingly lost. It was lost by the moderate and cautious leadership of the Irish Labour Party, who were unconcerned with revolution *tout court*; by the communist movement, led by Stalinism towards an embrace of populist Irish republicanism; and by republicanism itself which, despite an occasional flirtation with socialism (the first Saor Éire in 1931 and the Republican Congress in 1934, for example), remained a quintessentially nationalist movement for which social issues were subordinate to national goals.

We have been speaking, so far, in a narrow programmatic political sense. There is, however, another very important sense in which Connolly's impact has been incalculable. From Edinburgh to Troy, and in Dublin and Belfast, memorials have been erected to commemorate Connolly in the places he lived and influenced for the better. As we noted, most major political forces in Ireland see a benefit in trying to lay claim to his name. If the Irish labour movement was defeated in the immediate aftermath of the Rising, it is likely that the defeat would have been even more severe had it not had the recent benefit of Connolly's political and industrial ideas.

It is in this other sense, perhaps, that Connolly's legacy lives most strongly with us. Joel Emmanuel Hägglund was a Swedish-American union organiser. Like Connolly, Hägglund (more commonly known as Joe Hill) was an IWW organiser, and the author of labour songs and poems. Hill was executed after a controversial murder trial in 1915 and is widely believed to have been framed due to his political activity and his status as an immigrant worker. Hill was afterwards, in 1936, memorialised in a famous song by Alfred Hayes and Earl Robinson. In the final stanza, Hayes writes:

From San Diego up to Maine
In every mine and mill
Where working men defend their rights
It's there you'll find Joe Hill, it's there you'll find Joe Hill.

In the same way, whenever workers fight for their rights or against national or manifold other oppressions, the legacy of James Connolly, lives on.

Or, in the words of Dominic Behan's classic song, 'when workers one and all' rise up and rally to the call 'for a workers' Republic and freedom evermore', then James Connolly, who gave his life for the working class, for socialism and for national freedom, will be there with them.

All of those who wish to carve out such a future should reckon, seriously and critically, with Connolly's life, work and writings.

NOTES

1   *Irish Worker,* 14 March 1914.
2   Robert Sweeney, *The State We Are In: Inequality in Ireland 2020,* Dublin: TASC, 2020; Rory Hearne, *Housing Shock: The Irish Housing Crisis and How to Solve It,* Bristol: Policy Press, 2020.
3   Brian O'Boyle and Kieran Allen, *Tax Haven Ireland,* London: Pluto Press, 2021.
4   Desmond Ryan, *James Connolly: his life and writings,* Dublin: Talbot Press, 1924, p. 101. For a useful thesis on the 'claiming' of James Connolly, with a focus on physical-force and left-republicanism, see Phil Chilton, *'Claiming Connolly': the legacy of James Connolly and Irish republicanism, 1966-2005,* PhD thesis, University of Western Australia, 2014.
5   V. I. Lenin, *State and Revolution,* International Publishers New York, 1943, p. 7.
6   Arthur McManus, 'James Connolly His Life and Work,' in *The Communist Review,* May 1924, Vol. 5, No. 1.
7   Peter Graham, 'Developments on the Left in Dublin' in *Workers' Fight,* No. 7, June 1968, p. 30. *Workers' Fight* was the newspaper of the organisation of the same name led by Sean Matgamna, its successor is the Alliance for Workers' Liberty (AWL). Graham was involved in both Saor Éire and the United Secretariat of the Fourth International (USFI).
8   C. Desmond Greaves, *The Life and Times of James Connolly,* London: Lawrence and Wishart, 1972. For the Connolly Association, see Patrick Smylie, 'The CPGB, the Connolly Association and Irish communism, 1945–1962', *Labor History,* 2017, pp. 6-9.
9   One of the more sophisticated academic criticisms of Connolly was in the Introduction to Paul Bew, Peter Gibbon, Henry Patterson, *The State in Northern Ireland, 1921-72,* Manchester: Manchester University Press, 1979.
10   These include David Howell, *A Lost Left: Three Studies in Socialism and Nationalism,* Manchester: Manchester University Press, 1986 and Kieran Allen, *The Politics of James Connolly,* London: Pluto Press, 1990. Mike Taber has done a service to the socialist movement, and to scholarship, by editing the first complete English-language collection of the resolutions adopted by the nine congresses of the Second International between 1889 and 1912, in Mike Taber (ed.), *Under the Socialist Banner: Resolutions of the Second International 1889-1912,* Chicago: Haymarket, 2021.
11   David Berry and Constance Bantman write that such a focus on the history of institutions and leaders, congresses and debates 'clearly left many areas unexplored, as the main emphasis was on the institutional or organisational level, with little attention paid to individual activism or to informal modes of organisation and action … Classical studies of labour internationalism have thus ignored the networks and informal links underpinning or bypassing many established organisations.' David Berry and Constance Bantman (eds), *New Perspectives on Anarchism, Labour and Syndicalism: The Individual, the National and the Transnational,* Newcastle: Cambridge Scholars, 2010, p. 3. Examples of such studies are G.D.H. Cole, *The Second International, 1889-1914,* London: Macmillan, 1963; Julius Braunthal, *History Of The International – Vol. I: 1864-1914,* New York: Frederick A. Praeger, 1967; and James Joll, *The Second International 1889-1914,* New York: Frederick A. Praeger, 1966.

12   Carl Schorske, *German Social-Democracy, 1905-1917*, Cambridge, Mass.: Harvard University Press, 1955 and Gary P. Steenson, *"Not One Man! Not One Penny!"*: *German Social Democracy, 1863-1914*, Pittsburgh: University of Pittsburg Press, 1981.

13   For example, Stefan Berger, *The British Labour Party and the German Social Democrats, 1900–1931*, Oxford: Oxford University Press, 1994.

14   Kevin J. Callaghan, *Demonstration Culture: European Socialism and the Second International, 1889-1914*, Leicester: Troubadour, 2010, p. xviii.

15   Neville Kirk, *Transnational Radicalism and the Connected Lives of Tom Mann and Robert Samuel Ross*, Liverpool: Liverpool University Press, 2017, p. 4.

16   Philip Bonner, Jonathan Hyslop, and Lucien van der Watt, 'Workers'Movements' in Akira Iriye and Pierre-Yves Saunier (eds), *The Palgrave Dictionary of Transnational History*, Basingstoke: Palgrave Macmillan, 2009, p. 1121

17   Neville Kirk, *Transnational Radicalism and the Connected Lives of Tom Mann and Robert Samuel Ross*, pp. 66-7

18   The description is from Ibid., pp. 67-8. Thistlethwaite's original paper is Frank Thistlethwaite, 'Migration from Europe Overseas in the Nineteenth and Twentieth Centuries', XIe Congre International des Sciences Historiques, *Rapports, V: Historie Contemporaine*, 47, Stockholm 1960, pp. 32-60.

19   Emmet O'Connor, Fig 4a and 4b in 'Larkin, Connolly and the Cause of Labour', in *Atlas of the Irish Revolution*, Cork: Cork University Press, 2018, pp. 188-9.

20   Kevin J. Callaghan, *Demonstration Culture*, p. xv.

21   Constance Bantman, 'Internationalism without an International? Cross-Channel Anarchist Networks, 1880-1914' in *Revue belge de Philologie et d'Histoire 84*, no. 4, pp. 961-81.

22   For the attraction of the Paris Commune to late nineteenth-and early twentieth-century socialists, see Laura C. Forster, 'The Paris Commune in the British socialist imagination, 1871–1914', *History of European Ideas*, 46:5, 2020. The Commune is also discussed by Georges Haupt, *Aspects of International Socialism 1871-1914*, Cambridge: Cambridge University Press, 1986.

23   For a useful overview of the publication history of Connolly's writings, see the introduction to Aindrias Ó Cathasaigh (ed.), *The Lost Writings: James Connolly*, London: Pluto Press, 1997, pp. 1-13.

24   Joseph A. Buttigieg (ed.) *Antonio Gramsci Prison Notebooks: Vol II*, New York: Colombia University Press, 2011, p. 137.

25   W. P. Ryan, *The Irish Labour Movement from the 'Twenties to Our Own Day*, Dublin: Talbot Press, 1919 p. 163.

26   The following biographical sketch draws upon one of the most recent biographies of Connolly, which summarises what is known about his early life: Lorcan Collins, *16Lives: James Connolly*, Dublin: The O'Brien Press, 2012, pp. 17-34.

27   James Grant, *Cassell's Old and New Edinburgh: Its History, its People, and its Places, Vol 2*, London: Cassell and Company, Limited, 1887, p. 238.

28   *Workers' Republic*, 15 July 1889.

29   Donal Nevin, *James Connolly: A Full Life*, Dublin: Gill and Macmillan, 2006, p. 33.

30   William Morris, 'The Manifesto of the Socialist League', https://www.marxists.org/archive/morris/works/18 85/manifst1.htm, (accessed 27 January 2022).

31   Seamus Flaherty, *Marx, Engels and Modern British Socialism: the Social and Political*

Thought of H.M. Hyndman, E.B. Bax and William Morris London: Palgrave Macmillan, 2020, p. 27; on late Victorian 'public moralists', Flaherty is quoting Stefan Collini, *Public Moralists: Political Thought and Intellectual Life in Britain 1850-1930,* Oxford: Oxford University Press, 1991, p. 3. Flaherty argues that Hyndman was influenced by contemporary Liberalism, contrary to his reputation in as a 'Tory radical'. For the latter view, see Mark Bevir, *The Making of British Socialism,* Oxford: Oxford University Press, 2011, Chapter 4. The main biography of Hyndman remains Chushichi Tsuzuki, *H.M. Hyndman and British Socialism,* Oxford: The Clarendon Press, 1961.

32 Seamus Flaherty, *Marx, Engels and Modern British Socialism,* p.78.

33 E. P. Thompson, *William Morris: Romantic to Revolutionary,* New York: Pantheon Books, 1976, pp. 276-7.

34 Ibid., p. 284.

35 Ibid., p. 292.

36 Seamus Flaherty, *Marx, Engels and Modern British Socialism,* p. 57.

37 Friedrich Engels to August Bebel, 30 August 1883, https://www.marxists.org/archive/marx/works/1883/letters/83_08_30.htm (accessed 20 July 2021).

38 Socialist League manifesto 'To Socialists', 13 January 1885, quoted in Yvonne Kapp, *Eleanor Marx, Vol. 2,* London: Virago Press, 1979, pp. 63-4.

39 Chushichi Tsuzuki, *H.M. Hyndman and British Socialism,* pp. 70-71.

40 Stephen Yeo, 'A New Life: The Religion of Socialism in Britain, 1883-1896', in *History Workshop,* 4, 1977, p. 28.

41 'The Socialist Agitation', *Westminster Review,* 133, May 1890; quoted in Kirk Willis, 'The Introduction and Critical Reception of Marxist Thought in Britain,1850-1900', *Historical Journal,* 20, 1977, p. 418.

42 Quoted in Ibid., p. 7.

43 *Commonweal,* 2, 9, 16, 23 and 30 March, 6 and 13 April 1889.

44 *Dundee Weekly News,* 10 October 1891.

45 *Dundee Weekly News,* 24 October 1891.

46 E. P. Thompson, *William Morris,* pp. 390-99.

47 C. Desmond Greaves, *The Life and Times of James Connolly,* pp. 30-31.

48 *Justice,* 12 August 1893.

49 Bernard Ransom, *James Connolly and the Scottish Left 1890-1916,* PhD thesis, University of Edinburgh, 1975, p. 7. For a recent account of Connolly's Edinburgh days from a local socialist activist and historian, see Allan Armstrong, *The Ghost of James Connolly: James Connolly and Edinburgh's New Trade Union, Independent Labour and Socialist Movements (1890-96),* Glasgow 2014.

50 Henry Pelling, *A History of British Trade Unionism,* Middlesex: Penguin, 1971, p. 15-16.

51 Ibid.

52 Yvonne Kapp, *Eleanor Marx, Vol.2,* p. 270.

53 Henry Pelling, *A History of British Trade Unionism,* pp. 97-100.

54 Ibid., p. 100.

55 David Howell, *British Workers and the Independent Labour Party 1888-1906,* Manchester: Manchester University Press, 1983, p. 109.

56 Henry Pelling, *A History of British Trade Unionism,* p.100-101.

57   David Howell, *British Workers and the Independent Labour Party 1888-1906*, p. 109.

58   Ibid., pp. 112-113.

59   James Connolly to Lillie Reynolds, April 1890 in Donal Nevin (ed.), *Between Comrades. James Connolly Letters and Correspondence 1889-1916*, Dublin: Gill and Macmillan, 2007, p.83.

60   *Justice*, 12 August 1893.

61   Maria Daniella-Dick, Kirsty Lusk and Willy Maley, '"The Agitator's Wife" (1894): the story behind James Connolly's lost play?' in *Irish Studies Review*, Volume 27, Issue 1, 2019.

62   Bernard Ransom, *James Connolly and the Scottish Left 1890-1916*, p. 15.

63   Tom Mann, *Tom Mann's memoirs*, London: The Labour Publishing Company, 1923, p. 27.

64   *Justice*, 3 May 1890.

65   Bernard Ransom, *James Connolly and the Scottish Left 1890-1916*, p. 29.

66   Ernest Mandel, *The Formation of the Economic Thought of Karl Marx 1843 to Capital*, London: Verso, 2015, pp. 140, 142.

67   Karl Marx, *Wage-Labour and Capital*, 1847, ch. 9 https://www.marxists.org/archive/marx/works/1847/wage-labour/ch09.htm (accessed 17 July 2021).

68   Friedrich Engels to Adolph Sorge, 7 December 1889, https://www.marxists.org/archive/marx/works/1889/letters/89_12_07.htm (accessed 7 January 2022).

69   Ibid.

70   Bernard Ransom, *James Connolly and the Scottish Left 1890-1916*, p. 14.

71   Ibid., p. 18.

72   John Gilray, 'Early days of the socialist movement in Edinburgh', National Library of Scotland (NLS), Acc 4965, quoted in David Howell, *British Workers and the Independent Labour Party 1888-1906*. p. 151.

73   Henry Pelling, *A History of British Trade Unionism*, p. 102.

74   David Howell, *British Workers and the Independent Labour Party 1888-1906*, p. 110.

75   Ibid., p. 147.

76   Bernard Ransom, *James Connolly and the Scottish Left 1890-1916*, p. 23.

77   Ibid., p. 34.

78   Ibid., pp. 23-4.

79   David Howell, *British Workers and the Independent Labour Party 1888-1906*, pp. 146-7. Howell writes that 'trade unionism was generally weak, a situation which spurred activists to develop political organisation as an alternative. Yet in turn such organisations could not rely on trade unions for a steady base of support.'

80   Bernard Ransom, *James Connolly and the Scottish Left 1890-1916*, p. 24.

81   *Justice*, 6 August 1892.

82   David Howell, *A Lost Left*, p. 21.

83   Engels to Sorge, 18 January 1893, https://www.marxists.org/archive/marx/works/1893/letters/93_01_18.htm (accessed 30 December 2020).

84   Engels to Sorge, 18 March 1893, https://www.marxists.org/archive/marx/works/1893/letters/93_03_18.htm (accessed 30 December 2020).

85   *Leith Burgh Pilot*, 18 April 1891, quoted in Bernard Ransom, *James Connolly and the Scottish Left 1890-1916*, p. 20.

86   *Leith Burghs Pilot*, 13 May 1893, quoted in Ibid., p. 36.

87   Ibid., p. 38.

88   Ibid., p. 45.

89   Ibid., p. 43.

90   Ibid., pp. 48-9.

91   Ibid., p. 50.

92   Ibid., p. 51.

93   David Howell, *British Workers and the Independent Labour Party 1888-1906*, p. 129.

94   Stephen Yeo, 'A New Life: The Religion of Socialism in Britain, 1883-1896', pp. 42-3.

95   *Justice*, 15 July 1893, quoted in Bernard Ransom, *James Connolly and the Scottish Left 1890-1916*, p. 37.

96   Bernard Ransom, *James Connolly and the Scottish Left 1890-1916*, p. 53.

97   Ibid., pp. 53-4.

98   *The Clarion*, 22 September 1894.

99   *The Call*, 6 May 1920.

100 See, for example, Constance Bantman, *The French Anarchists in London, 1880-1914: Exile and Transnationalism in the First Globalisation*, Liverpool: Liverpool University Press, 2013.

101 J. Bruce Glasier, *William Morris and the early days of the socialist movement; being reminiscences of Morris' work as a propagandist, and observations on his character and genius, with some account of the persons and circumstances of the early socialist agitation, together with a series of letters addressed by Morris to the author*, London: Longmans, Green and Company, 1921, p. 99.

102 Ransom, *James Connolly and the Scottish Left 1890-1916*, p. 30.

103 E. P. Thompson, *William Morris*, p. 307.

104 Ernest Belfort Bax, *Reminiscences and reflections of a mid and late Victorian*, New York: J Seltzer, 1920, p. 108

105 Bernard Ransom, *James Connolly and the Scottish Left 1890-1916*, p. 8.

106 *The Morning Post*, 13 and 19 February 1872.

107 *Dundee Evening Post*, 27 May 1901.

108 *Manchester Courier and Lancashire General Advertiser*, 19 March 1894.

109 Georges Haupt, *Aspects of International Socialism 1871-1914*, p. 28.

110 Ibid.

111 *Workers' Republic*, May 1899.

112 James Joll, *The Second International 1889-1914*, pp. 22-3.

113 Ibid., p. 23.

114 Kevin J. Callaghan, *Demonstration Culture: European Socialism and the Second International, 1889-1914*, pp. 3-4.

115 James Joll, *The Second International 1889-1914*, pp. 35.

116 Ibid., p. 55.

117 *Justice*, 22 July 1893.

118 James Joll, *The Second International 1889-1914*, pp. 56-8.

119 *Justice*, 22 July 1893.

120 *Edinburgh Evening News*, 8 November 1894.

121 *Clarion*, 3 November 1894.

122 *Edinburgh Evening News*, 24 October 1894.

123 *Labour Chronicle*, 5 November 1894, quoted in C. Desmond Greaves, *The Life and*

Times of James Connolly, p. 60.

124   *Labour Chronicle*, 5 November 1894, quoted in Bernard Ransom, *James Connolly and the Scottish Left 1890-1916*, p. 59.

125   *Edinburgh Evening News*, 23 October 1894.

126   *Edinburgh Evening News*, 25 October 1894.

127   Ibid., 25 October 1894.

128   Ibid., 26 October 1894.

129   Ibid., 27 October 1894.

130   Bernard Ransom, *James Connolly and the Scottish Left 1890-1916*, p. 59.

131   *Edinburgh Evening News*, 27 October 1894; Ibid., p. 59.

132   *Edinburgh Evening News*, 2 November 1894.

133   Ibid., 3 November 1894.

134   C. Desmond Greaves, *The Life and Times of James Connolly*, p. 61.

135   James Connolly to Lillie Reynolds, 18 April 1889 in Donal Nevin (ed.), *Between Comrades*, p. 78.

136   Ibid., p. 147.

137   *Edinburgh Evening News*, 29 October 1894.

138   *Labour Chronicle*, 1 December 1894, https://www.marxists.org/archive/ connolly/1894/12/partypol.htm (accessed 2 January 2021).

139   C. Desmond Greaves, *The Life and Times of James Connolly*, p. 62.

140   *Labour Chronicle*, 5 November 1894.

141   *The Glasgow Herald*, 7 November 1894.

142   *Edinburgh Evening News*, 7 November 1894.

143   *Edinburgh Evening News*, 6 November 1894.

144   *Labour Chronicle*, 1 December 1894, https://www.marxists.org/archive/ connolly/1894/12/partypol.htm (accessed 2 January 2021).

145   *Labour Chronicle*, 1 March 1895.

146   *Labour Chronicle*, 1 May 1895.

147   *Justice*, 28 December 1895.

148   *Justice*, 22 February 1896.

149   Quoted in Bernard Ransom, *James Connolly and the Scottish Left 1890-1916*, p.63.

150   Ibid.

151   *Justice*, 3 May 1896.

152   James Connolly, 'Labour in Irish History' *in Labour in Ireland: I. Labour in Irish History. II. The Re-Conquest of Ireland*, Dublin: Three Candles, 1940, p. 134.

153   D. A. E. Harkness, 'Irish Emigration', in Walter F. Wilcox (eds), *International Migrations, Volume II: Interpretations*, New York: National Bureau of Economic Research, Inc., 1931, p. 267.

154   Ibid.; Louise, Paul-Dubois, *Contemporary Ireland*, Dublin: Maunsel and Company, 1908, p. 231, cited in David Lynch, *Radical Politics in Modern Ireland: The Irish Socialist Republican Party 1898-1904*, Dublin: Irish Academic Press, 2005, p. 12.

155   Karl Marx, 'On the Irish Question', https://www.marxists.org/archive/marx/iwma/ documents/1867/irish-speech.htm (accessed 21 January 2021).

156   Figures cited in Kieran Allen, *The Politics of James Connolly*, p. 13.

157   James R. Barrett, *The Irish Way: Becoming American in the Multi-ethnic City*, New York: Penguin Press, 2012, p. 1.

158   Adrian Grant, *Irish Socialist Republicanism 1909-36*, Dublin: Four Courts Press, 2012, p. 23.

159   Figures quoted in David Lynch, *Radical Politics in Modern Ireland*, pp. 16-17.

160   Fintan Lane, *The Origins of Modern Irish Socialism, 1881-1896*, Cork: Cork University Press, 1997, p. 3.

161   James Connolly, 'Labour in Irish History' in *Labour in Ireland*, pp. 88-9. For a biography of Thompson, see Richard Pankhurst, *William Thompson, 1775-1833: Pioneer Socialist*, London: Pluto Press, 1991.

162   James Connolly, 'Labour in Irish History' in *Labour in Ireland*, p. 91.

163   For a good survey, see Kevin B. Anderson, *Marx at the Margins: On Nationalism, Ethnicity and Non-Western Societies*, Chicago: University of Chicago Press, 2010, Chapter 4.

164   Quoted in Kevin B. Anderson, *Marx at the Margins*, pp. 126-7.

165   Karl Marx to Sigfrid Meyer and August Vogt in New York, 9 April 1870, https://www.marxists.org/archive/marx/works/1870/letters/70_04_09.htm (accessed 18 August 2021).

166   Interview with Friedrich Engels published in the *New Yorker Volkzeitung*, 20 September 1888, quoted in Karl Marx and Friedrich Engels, *Ireland and the Irish Question*, London 1971, p. 460.

167   *Commonweal*, 8 May 1886.

168   Fintan Lane, *The Origins of Modern Irish Socialism*, p. 119.

169   Ibid, pp. 120-21.

170   Ibid., pp. 145-6.

171   Daniel Budden, *The Political Economy of fin-de-siecle Christian Socialism*, Thesis, Swansea University, 2011, http://cronfa.swan.ac.uk/Record/cronfa42261; *Northern Whig*, Friday 05 May 1939, contains an obituary of Wallace which gives more of an insight into his life, including his upbringing and role in the early Fabian Society.

172   James Connolly, 'Labour in Irish History' in *Labour in Ireland*, p. 113; *Northern Whig*, 18 March 1884.

173   Ibid., p. 273.

174   Ibid., p. 171; more on the Brotherhood Church can be found in Ken Weller's *'Don't be a soldier!' The radical anti-war movement in north London 1914-1918*, London 1985, Chapter 16.

175   Fintan Lane, *The Origins of Modern Irish Socialism*, p. 118.

176   Ibid., pp. 192-5.

177   Ibid., p. 197.

178   Ibid., p. 203.

179   Ibid., p. 215.

180   Ibid.

181   C. Desmond Greaves, *The Life and Times of James Connolly*, p. 73.

182   Sean Cronin, *Young Connolly*, pp. 29-30.

183   C. Desmond Greaves, *The Life and Times of James Connolly*, p. 80; David Lynch, *Radical Politics in Modern Ireland*, p. 23.

184   ISRP Programme, https://www.marxists.org/archive/connolly/1896/xx/isrp.htm (accessed 21 January 2021)

185   Ibid.: this view on political action was set out by H. M Hyndman in 'Social-Democrat or Socialist?' *The Social-Democrat*, October 1897.

186 *Workers' Republic*, 22 July 1899.

187 *Justice*, 31 March 1900.

188 *Workers' Republic*, 10 June 1899.

189 Samuel Levenson, *James Connolly. A Biography*, London: Quartet Books, 1973, p. 57.

190 David Lynch, *Radical Politics in Modern Ireland*, pp. 20-22.

191 Adrian Grant, *Irish Socialist Republicanism 1909-36*, p. 19.

192 James Connolly to John Carstairs Matheson, March 1903, in Donal Nevin (ed.), *Between Comrades*, p. 222.

193 David Lynch, *Radical Politics in Modern Ireland*, p. 29.

194 Ibid.

195 Edward MacLysaght (ed.), *Forth the Banners Go: Reminiscences of William O'Brien*, Dublin: Three Candles, 1969, p. 2.

196 *Workers' Republic*, 27 August 1898.

197 *Workers' Republic*, 16 September 1899.

198 *Workers' Republic*, 10 February 1900.

199 F.S.L. Lyons, *Ireland Since the Famine*, London: Fontana, 1979, pp. 273-4.

200 David Howell, *A Lost Left*, p. 29.

201 Fintan Lane, *The Origins of Modern Irish Socialism*, p. 49.

202 ISRP Programme, https://www.marxists.org/archive/connolly/1896/xx/isrp.htm (accessed 18 July 2021).

203 James Connolly, *Erin's Hope: the ends and means*, 1909, in Owen Dudley Edwards and Bernard Ransom (eds), *James Connolly: Selected Political Writings*, London: Jonathan Cape, 1973, p. 166.

204 Ibid., p. 167.

205 *Labour Leader*, 20 June 1896.

206 James Connolly, *Erin's Hope: the ends and means*, 1909, in Owen Dudley Edwards and Bernard Ransom (eds), *James Connolly: Selected Political Writings*, p. 168.

207 Bernard Ransom, *James Connolly and the Scottish Left 1890-1916*, p. 54.

208 John Leslie, *The Present Condition of the Irish Question* [1895], Cork: Cork Workers Club, 1997, p. 3.

209 Ibid., p. 5.

210 James Fintan Lalor, *The Writings of James Fintan Lalor with an introduction embodying personal recollections by John O'Leary and a brief memoir*, Dublin: T. G. O'Donoghue, 1895, p. 94.

211 James Connolly, 'Labour in Irish History' in *Labour in Ireland*, p. 148; Ibid., p. 49.

212 James Fintan Lalor, *The Writings of James Fintan Lalor*, p. 67.

213 Ibid., p. 66.

214 James Connolly, *Erin's Hope: the ends and means*, 1909, in Owen Dudley Edwards and Bernard Ransom (eds.), *James Connolly: Selected Political Writings*, p. 174.

215 Ibid., p. 175.

216 Ibid., p. 174.

217 Ibid., p. 189.

218 Ibid., p. 176.

219 Ibid., p. 172.

220 Bernard Ransom, *Connolly's Marxism*, London 1980, pp. 6-7. We do not at all follow, however, Ransom's attempt to equate Connolly and Mao Tse-tung on the basis that

both adapted Marxism to their respective national specificities. Connolly's ingrained revolutionary democratic concept of socialism is inimical to Maoism's militarised army-party-state.

221 James Connolly, *Erin's Hope: the ends and means,* 1909, in Owen Dudley Edwards and Bernard Ransom (eds), *James Connolly: Selected Political Writings,* p. 166.

222 W.K. Anderson, *James Connolly and the Irish Left,* Dublin: Irish Academic Press, 1994, pp. 42-3.

223 James Connolly, 'Labour in Irish History' in *Labour in Ireland,* p. 1.

224 Ibid., p. 6.

225 Resolution on 'Political Action' from the 1896 London Congress of the Second International, quoted in Mike Taber (ed.), *Under the Socialist Banner,* p. 52.

226 James Connolly, *Erin's Hope: the ends and means,* 1909, in Owen Dudley Edwards and Bernard Ransom (eds.), *James Connolly: Selected Political Writings,* p. 166.

227 Paul Bew, Peter Gibbon, Henry Patterson, *The State in Northern Ireland, 1921-72,* p. 17.

228 *L'Ireland Libre,* 1897.

229 V. I. Lenin, *State and Revolution,* p. 66.

230 *Shan Van Vocht,* January 1897.

231 Paul Bew, Peter Gibbon, Henry Patterson, *The State in Northern Ireland, 1921-72,* pp. 17-18.

232 Paul Dillon, 'James Connolly and the Kerry Famine of 1898' in *Saothar,* Vol. 25, 2000, p. 42.

233 *Workers' Republic,* 8 July 1899.

234 See Aindrias Ó Cathasaigh, 'James Connolly and the writing of "Labour in Irish History" (1910)' in *Saothar,* Vol. 27, Dublin 2002, pp. 103-108.

235 James Connolly, 'Labour in Irish History' in *Labour in Ireland,* p. 1.

236 *The* Harp, September 1908.

237 James Connolly, *Erin's Hope: the ends and means,* 1909, in Owen Dudley Edwards and Bernard Ransom (eds.), *James Connolly: Selected Political Writings,* p. 173.

238 Ralph Samuel, 'British Marxist Historians 1880-1980 (Part I)' in *New Left Review,* 1/120, March/April 1980, p. 35.

239 Heather Laird, 'Time and the Irish: An Analysis of the Temporal Frameworks Employed by Sir Henry Maine, Eóin MacNeill, and James Connolly in Their Writings on Early Modern Ireland' in *Proceedings of the Harvard Celtic Colloquium,* 2008, Vol. 28, Cambridge 2008, pp. 128-41.

240 Frederick Engels to Karl Kautsky, April 26, 1884, in Karl Marx and Frederick Engels, *Collected Works: Volume 47: Engels, 1883-86,* New York 1995, p. 132.

241 Friedrich Engels, *The Origins of the Family, Private Property and the State,* London: Lawrence and Wishart, 1977, p. 71.

242 Thus, Vincent Geoghegan casts doubt on Greaves's presumption that Connolly had Engels's work, in 'The Golden age and Its Return in the Marxism of the Second International', in *Utopian Studies* 2, 1989, p. 67.

243 *Justice,* 8 November 1884, 7 January 1888.

244 *Justice,* 8 November 1884.

245 Lewis H. Morgan, *Ancient Society, or Researches in the Lines of Human Progress from Savagery, through Barbarism to Civilisation* [1877], New York: World Publishing Company, 1963, pp. 561-2.

246 *Justice,* 9 August 1884, 16 July 1892; *Labour Leader,* 1 May 1897.

247 *Clarion,* 30 July 1892; *Freedom,*1 August 1892.

248 J. W. Burrow, '"The village community" and the uses of history in late nineteenth-century England' in Neil McKendrick (ed.), *Historical Perspectives: Studies in English Thought and Society in Honour of J. H. Plumb,* London: Europa Publications, 1974, p. 255.

249 Ibid., p. 254.

250 Ibid., p. 256.

251 Ibid.

252 Christopher Hill, 'The Norman Yoke' *in Puritanism and Revolution: Studies in Interpretation of the English Revolution of the 17th Century,* New York: St Martin's Press, 1997, p. 46. See also Marjorie Chibnall, *The Debate on the Norman Conquest,* Manchester: Manchester University Press, 1999.

253 Ibid., p. 48.

254 Ibid., p. 52.

255 Ibid., p. 53.

256 James Connolly, *Erin's Hope: the ends and means,* 1909, in Owen Dudley Edwards and Bernard Ransom (eds.), *James Connolly: Selected Political Writings,* p. 191.

257 Christopher Hill, 'The Norman Yoke', pp. 99, 100, 108.

258 Ibid., p.109.

259 Helga Woggon (ed.), *Ellen Grimley (Nellie Gordon) - Reminiscences of Her Work with James Connolly in Belfast,* Dublin: Irish Labour History Society, 2000, p. 20.

260 Michael Löwy and Robert Sayre, *Romanticism Against the Tide of Modernity,* Durham: Duke University Press, 2001, p. 14.

261 Ibid., p. 17.

262 Ibid., p. 21.

263 Ibid., p. 22.

264 Ibid., pp. 73-4.

265 Ibid., p. 24.

266 Eoin MacNeill, 'Communal Ownership in Ancient Ireland. I. The Agrarian System' in *The Irish Monthly,* Vol. 47, No. 554, August 1919, pp. 407-415, Eoin MacNeill, 'Communal Ownership in Ancient Ireland. II: The Family Commune' in *The Irish Monthly,* Vol. 47, No. 555, September 1919, pp. 463-4 and *Celtic Ireland,* Dublin 1921.

267 Aodh be Blacam, 'Tribute to Our Chief Historian', in *The Irish Monthly,* Vol. 65, No. 768, June 1937, p. 417

268 David Howell, *British Workers and the Independent Labour Party 1892-1906,* p. 352.

269 Clive Wilmer (ed.), *William Morris: News from Nowhere and Other Writings,* London: Penguin, 2008, p. 228.

270 John Leslie, *The Present Condition of the Irish Question,* p. 14.

271 James Connolly, *Erin's Hope: the ends and means,* 1909, in Owen Dudley Edwards and Bernard Ransom (eds), *James Connolly: Selected Political Writings,* p. 187

272 Vincent Geoghegan, 'The Golden age and Its Return in the Marxism of the Second International', p. 60.

273 Karl Marx, 'The Eighteenth Brumaire', in David Fernbach (ed.) *Surveys from Exile,* Harmondsworth 1973, p. 149.

274 Vincent Geoghegan, 'The Golden age and Its Return in the Marxism of the Second International', p. 60.

275 Friedrich Engels, *The Origins of the Family, Private Property and the State*, p. 161.

276 Teodor Shanin, *Late Marx and the Russian Road: Marx and the Peripheries of Capitalism*, London: Verso, 1983, p. 6.

277 Kevin Anderson, *Marx at the Margins: On Nationalism, Ethnicity and Non-Western Societies*, p. 198.

278 Ibid., p. 7.

279 Ibid., p. 228.

280 Ibid., pp. 228-9.

281 Karl Marx and Friedrich Engels, 'Preface to the Russian Edition of 1882', in *The Communist Manifesto*, Oxford, 2008, p. 43.

282 Karl Marx and Friedrich Engels, *Collected Works*, Volume 27, London 2010, p. 424.

283 James Connolly, *Erin's Hope: the ends and means*, 1909, in Owen Dudley Edwards and Bernard Ransom (eds.), *James Connolly: Selected Political Writings*, pp. 173-4.

284 *Labour Leader*, 10 October 1896.

285 David Howell, *A Lost Left*, p. 32.

286 *Workers' Republic*, 23 September 1899.

287 José Carlos Mariátegui, *Seven Interpretative Essays on Peruvian Reality*, Austin: University of Texas Press, 1971

288 Desmond Ryan (ed.), *The Workers' Republic: a selection from the writings of James Connolly*, Dublin: Three Candles, 1951, pp. 219-20.

289 Antonio Gramsci, *The Modern Prince and Other Writings*, London: Lawrence and Wishart, 1957, p. 133.

290 Joseph Mali, *Mythistory: The Making of a Modern Historiography*, Chicago: University of Chicago Press, 2003.

291 Letter to Katherine Tynan, 1887, in Allan Wade (ed.) *The Letters of W. B. Yeats*, London: R. Hart-Davis, 1954, pp. 33, 35.

292 Liz Curtis, *The Cause of Ireland. From the United Irishmen to Partition*, Belfast: Beyond the Pale Publications, 1994, p. 163.

293 Joe Cleary, 'Postcolonial Ireland', in Kevin Kenny (ed.), *Ireland and the British Empire*, Oxford: Oxford University Press, 2004, p. 259.

294 *Workers' Republic*, 1 October 1898.

295 Desmond Ryan (ed.), *Socialism and Nationalism. A Selection from the Writings of James Connolly*, Dublin: Three Candles, 1948, p. 475.

296 Maud Gonne McBride, *A servant of the Queen. Reminiscences by Maud Gonne MacBride*, London: Victor Gollancz Ltd., 1974, p. 273.

297 Ibid.

298 Ibid.

299 Ibid., p. 275.

300 Owen McGee, *The IRB: The Irish Republican Brotherhood, from the Land League to Sinn Féin*, Dublin: Four Courts Press, 2005, p. 248; pp. 232-65 gives a full account of the 1798 centenary.

301 Donal Nevin, *James Connolly*, p. 98.

302 Owen McGee, *The IRB*, p. 264.

303 Donal Nevin, *James Connolly*, p. 101.

304   *Workers' Republic*, August 13, 1898.

305   *orkers' Republic*, 22 July 1899.

306   John Newsinger, 'James Connolly and the Easter Rising', *Science & Society*, Vol. 47, No. 2, Summer 1983, p. 158.

307   *Workers' Republic*, 22 July 1899.

308   Owen McGee, *The IRB*, pp. 285-6.

309   *Workers' Republic*, 1 July 1899.

310   *James Connolly, Erin's Hope: the ends and means*, 1909, https://www.marxists.org/archive/connolly/1909/hope/erinhope.htm (accessed 18 July 2021).

311   *Shan Van Vocht*, 6 November 1896.

312   Desmond Ryan (ed.), *Socialism and Nationalism*, pp. 335-8.

313   James Connolly, *Erin's Hope: the ends and means*, 1909, in Owen Dudley Edwards and Bernard Ransom (eds.), *James Connolly: Selected Political Writings*, p. 189.

314   Ibid., p. 179.

315   *Workers' Republic*, 24 September 1898.

316   Richard B. Day and Daniel Gaido (eds), *Witnesses to Permanent Revolution: The Documentary Record*, Chicago: Haymarket, 2011, p. 30.

317   Henry Patterson, *The Politics of Illusion: Republicanism and Socialism in Modern Ireland*, London: Hutchinson Radius, 1989, p. 8.

318   John Hutchinson, *The Dynamics of Cultural Nationalism: The Gaelic Revival and the Creation of the Irish Nation State*, London: Allan and Unwin, 1987, pp. 168-9.

319   Ibid., p. 173.

320   Ibid.

321   *Workers' Republic*, 23 June 1900.

322   *Workers' Republic*, March 1902.

323   David Lynch, *Radical Politics in Modern Ireland*, p. 146.

324   Maud Gonne McBride, *A servant of the Queen*, p. 302.

325   David Lynch, *Radical Politics in Modern Ireland*, p. 146.

326   *The Harp*, September 1909.

327   David Lynch, *Radical Politics in Modern Ireland*, p. 91.

328   *Workers' Republic*, August 13, 1898. C. Desmond Greaves, *The Life and Times of James Connolly*, p. 68.

329   *Justice*, 13 August 1898.

330   David Lynch, *Radical Politics in Modern Ireland*, p. 52.

331   Ibid., p. 55.

332   C. Desmond Greaves, *The Life and Times of James Connolly*, p. 73.

333   Laura C. Forster, 'The Paris Commune in the British socialist imagination, 1871–1914', p. 14.

334   Minutes of the ISRP, March 1899, cited in Ibid. and printed in Donal Nevin, *James Connolly: A Full Life*, p. 71.

335   Laura C. Forster, 'The Paris Commune in the British socialist imagination, 1871–1914', p. 15.

336   R. F. Foster, *Modern Ireland 1600-1972*, London: Allan Lane, 1988, p. 448.

337   Donal Lowry, '"A Fellowship of Disaffection": Irish-South African Relations from the Anglo-Boer War to the Perestroika 1902-1991,' in *Etudes irlandaises*, December 1992 17-2, p. 106.

338   Maud Gonne McBride, *A servant of the Queen*, p. 299.

339   Ibid., p. 302.

340   *Workers' Republic*, 4 November 1899.

341   *Workers' Republic*, 9 December 1899.

342   *Workers' Republic*, 4 November 1899.

343   Ibid.

344   Daniel Gaido and Richard Day, *Discovering Imperialism: Social Democracy to World War 1*, Chicago: Haymarket, 2012, pp. 6-7.

345   *Workers' Republic*, 9 December 1899.

346   Karl Kautsky, 'Germany, England and the World Policy', in *The Social Democrat*, 1900, Vol.4, No.8, August 1900, https://www.marxists.org/archive/kautsky/1900/08/world.htm (accessed 10 June 2021).

347   *Workers' Republic*, 20 August 1898.

348   *Commonweal*, February 1885.

349   *Workers' Republic*, 4 November 1899.

350   Graham Johnson, *Social Democratic Politics in Britain 181-1911*, p. 74.

351   Rosa Luxemburg, *The Accumulation of Capital*, London: Routledge and Kegan Paul Ltd., 1951, p. 412.

352   *Freedom*, 1 April 1900.

353   *Workers' Republic*, 30 December 1899.

354   Karl Marx and Friedrich Engels, *The Communist Manifesto*, p. 11.

355   Ibid., p. 18.

356   Engels, *The Peasant Question in France and Germany, 1894*, https://www.marxists.org/archive/marx/works/1894/peasant-question/ (accessed 18 August 2021).

357   Loren Goldner, *Revolution, Defeat and Theoretical Underdevelopment: Russia, Turkey, Spain, Bolivia*, Leiden: Brill, 2016, p. 20.

358   Jairus Banaji, 'Illusions about the peasantry: Karl Kautsky and the agrarian question,' in *The Journal of Peasant Studies*, 17:2 (1990), p. 294.

359   Paul Dillon, 'James Connolly and the Kerry Famine of 1898', p. 29.

360   James Connolly, *Erin's Hope: the ends and means*, 1909, in Owen Dudley Edwards and Bernard Ransom (eds.), *James Connolly: Selected Political Writings*, p. 181.

361   *Workers' Republic*, 27 August 1898.

362   Ibid.

363   ISRP Programme, https://www.marxists.org/archive/connolly/1896/xx/isrp.htm (accessed 21 January 2021).

364   *Workers' Republic*, 27 August 1898.

365   ISRP Programme, https://www.marxists.org/archive/connolly/1896/xx/isrp.htm (accessed 21 January 2021).

366   *Workers' Republic*, 27 August 1898.

367   *Workers' Republic*, 21 October 1899.

368   Ibid., pp. 31-37.

369   Michael Davitt, *Some Suggestions for a Final Settlement of the Land Question* [1902], in Seamus Deane (ed.), *The Field Day Anthology of Irish Writing, volume 2*, Derry: Field Day Publications, 1991, p. 280.

370   Austen Morgan, *James Connolly: A political biography*, Manchester: Manchester University Press, 1988, pp. 29-31.

371 Edward MacLysaght (ed.), *Forth the Banners Go: Reminiscences of William O'Brien*, p. 27.

372 R.M. Fox, *James Connolly: the Forerunner*, Tralee: The Kerryman Ltd., 1946, p. 51.

373 Edward MacLysaght (ed.), *Forth the Banners Go: Reminiscences of William O'Brien*, p. 27.

374 David Howell, *A Lost Left*, p. 44.

375 Ruth Dudley Edwards, *James Connolly*, Dublin: Gill and Macmillan, 1981, p. 36.

376 T.A. Jackson, *Solo Trumpet: Some Memories of Socialist Agitation and Propaganda*, London: Lawrence and Wishart, 1953, p. 80.

377 William O'Brien Papers, NLI MS 16265. On 2 October, the party minuted that no report was furnished, but that E.W. Stewart 'handed in some matter for WR [the *Workers' Republic*].' As for the ISRP's usual Sunday public meeting on the topic: 'The usual public meeting was held, at Foster Place, Lyng presiding, addresses were delivered by him and J Connolly on the Socialist Congress – the proceedings were dull owing to Stewart the only man who knew anything about the matter not turning up.'

378 *Worker's Republic*, 10 October 1900.

379 William O'Brien Papers, NLI MS 15674/2/5.

380 William O'Brien Papers, NLI MS 15674/2/7.

381 William O'Brien Papers, NLI MS 20762.

382 William O'Brien Papers, NLI MS 13939/1/4.

383 Raymond Challinor, The Origins of British Bolshevism, London: Croom Helm, 1977, p. 9.

384 Ibid.

385 Mike Taber, *Under the Socialist Banner*, p. 77.

386 Raymond Challinor, The Origins of British Bolshevism, p. 10.

387 Tom Bell, *Pioneering Days*, London: Lawrence & Wishart, 1941, p. 36.

388 *Justice*, 13 October 1900.

389 *Justice*, 25 May 1901.

390 Rosa Luxemburg, 'Reform or Revolution,' in *Rosa Luxemburg Speaks*, New York: Pathfinder Press, pp. 77-8.

391 Raymond Challinor, *The Origins of British Bolshevism*, p. 10.

392 For an overview of De Leon's life, see Carl Reeve, *The Life and Times of Daniel de Leon*, New York: Humanities, 1972. For De Leon and the Second International, see James A. Stevenson, 'Daniel de Leon and European Socialism, 1890-1914' in *Science & Society*, Vol. 44, No. 2, Summer 1980, p.p. 199-223.

393 David Lynch, *Radical Politics in Modern Ireland*, pp. 96, 103.

394 Quoted in James A. Stevenson, 'Daniel de Leon and European Socialism, 1890-1914', p. 206.

395 Ibid.

396 Ibid., p. 209.

397 Martin Crick, *The History of the Social-Democratic Federation*, Keele: Ryburn Publishing, 1994, pp. 97-9.

398 Chuschichi Tsuzuki, 'The "Impossibilist Revolt" in Britain: The Origins of the S.L.P. and the S.P.G.B', in *International Review of Social History*, Vol. 1, No. 3, Cambridge 1956, p. 384.

399   Tom Bell, *Pioneering Days*, pp. 37-40.

400   Chuschichi Tsuzkuki, 'The "Impossibilist Revolt" in Britain', p. 390

401   Martin Crick, *The History of the Social-Democratic Federation*, pp. 97-8.

402   *Justice*, 31 March 1900.

403   *Justice*, 10 August 1901.

404   *Justice*, 11 August 1900.

405   *Justice*, 10 August 1901.

406   Martin Crick, *The History of the Social-Democratic Federation*, p. 97.

407   *Justice*, 10 August 1901.

408   Tom Bell, *Pioneering Days*, p. 47.

409   Raymond Challinor, *The Origins of British Bolshevism*, p. 18.

410   *Justice*, 29 September 1900.

411   Chuschichi Tsuzkuki, 'The "Impossibilist Revolt" in Britain', p. 387.

412   *Justice*, 6 April 1901.

413   *Justice*, 1 March 1902.

414   *Justice*, 22 March 1902.

415   *Justice*, 29 March 1902.

416   Raymond Challinor, *The Origins of British Bolshevism*, p. 19.

417   *Justice*, 29 March 1902.

418   Raymond Challinor, *The Origins of British Bolshevism*, p. 19.

419   *Justice*, 5 April 1902.

420   Chuschichi Tsuzkuki, 'The "Impossibilist Revolt" in Britain', p. 390.

421   *Justice*, 12 April 1902.

422   *Justice*, 11 April 1903.

423   Raymond Challinor, *The Origins of British Bolshevism*, p. 22.

424   *Justice*, 18 April 1903.

425   Chuschichi Tsuzkuki, 'The "Impossibilist Revolt" in Britain', p. 393.

426   Ibid., p. 396.

427   *The Socialist*, May 1903.

428   Tom Bell, *Pioneering Days*, pp. 40-41.

429   Daniel De Leon, *Flashlights on Amsterdam*, 2007, pp. 123, 124, http://www.marxistsfr.
       org/archive/deleon/pdf/subject/flashlights.pdf (accessed 10 June 2021).

430   Raymond Challinor, *The Origins of British Bolshevism*, p. 25.

431   Ibid.

432   Chuschichi Tsuzkuki, 'The "Impossibilist Revolt" in Britain', p. 394.

433   *Justice*, 16 May 1903.

434   *The Socialist*, June 1903.

435   See Satnam Virdee, *Racism, Class and the Racialized Outsider*, London: Palgrave
       Macmillan, 2014, pp. 66-71 for an account of Connolly's anti-racism, informed by his
       position as a 'racialised outsider' within a largely Protestant conception of the British
       nation.

436   The phrase is Marxist theorist Moishe Postone's, in Martin Thomas, 'Zionism,
       anti-semitism and the left: An Interview with Moishe Postone' in *Solidarity* 3/166,
       4 February 2010.

437   Manus O'Riordan, 'Connolly, socialism and the Jewish worker', in *Saothar* 13, 1988,
       p. 124.

438   Ibid., p. 120.

439   James Connolly, 'Wood Quay Ward, Election Address, Dublin, January 1903', https://www.marxists.org/archive/connolly/1903/01/woodquay.htm (accessed 10 June 2021).

440   William O'Brien Papers, NLI, Typescript copy of an article by the Irish Socialist Republican Party entitled An Appeal to the Working-Class of Irish America', 15 September 1897.

441   *Weekly People*, November 22 1902.

442   William O'Brien Papers, NLI, Letter from Ernest Aviyone, 446 Central Avenue, West Hoboken, New Jersey, to the manager of the *Workers Republic*, 25 September 1902.

443   William O'Brien Papers, NLI, Letter from Timothy McMahon, 520 Lindley Street, Bridgeport, Connecticut to the ISRP, 25 September 1902.

444   William O'Brien Papers, NLI, Letter from M. Sullivan, 100 Braniard Street, Detroit, Michigan, to the manager of the *Workers Republic*, 20 October 1902.

445   William O'Brien Papers, NLI, Letter from Jeremiah Devine, North Abington, Massachusetts to "Comrade", Manager of the Workers' Republic, 2 October 1902.

446   William O'Brien Papers, NLI, Letter from an unidentified sender in Chicago, 13 November 1902.

447   Carl Reeve, *James Connolly and the United States*, pp. 43-4.

448   James Connolly to John Carstairs Matheson, 9 March 1903, in Donal Nevin (ed.) *Between Comrades*, p. 218.

449   David Lynch, *Radical Politics in Modern Ireland*, p. 89.

450   Ibid., p. 127.

451   Carl Reeve and Ann Barton Reeve, *James Connolly and the United States: The Road to the 1916 Irish Rebellion*, Atlantic Heights 1978, p. 44; Ibid., p. 123.

452   David Lynch, *Radical Politics in Modern Ireland*, p. 132.

453   Ibid., p. 138.

454   Tom Bell, *Pioneering Days*, pp. 48-9.

455   Ibid., p. 48.

456   David Lynch, *Radical Politics in Modern Ireland*, p. 153.

457   James R. Barnett, *The Irish Way*, p. 1.

458   'Denis Foley, 'On tour and exiled: James Connolly 1902-1905' in *Saothar*, Vol. 38, 2013, p. 35.

459   *The Socialist*, June 1903.

460   Ibid.

461   Carl Reeve and Ann Barton Reeve, *James Connolly in the United States*, p. 49.

462   *Weekly People*, 9 April 1904.

463   See, for example, Ernest Mandel, *The Formation of the Economic Thought of Karl Marx 1843 to Capital*, p. 150.

464   Karl Marx and Friedrich Engels, 'Value, Price and Profit' in *Selected Works*, Moscow: Progress Publishers, 1977, p. 75.

465   Karl Marx, *Critique of the Gotha Programme*, Peking: Foreign Languages Press, 1972, p. 1.

466   *Weekly People*, 9 April 1904.

467   Ibid.

468   William O'Brien Papers, NLI. 'Transcript of writings in the "Weekly People" titled "National Convention, SLP Attitudes on Trades Unions"', 16 July 1904.

469 *Daily People*, 26 May 1904.

470 James Connolly to John Carstairs Matheson, 22 July 1904, in Donal Nevin (ed.) *Between Comrades*, p. 261.

471 Ibid., p. 262.

472 James Connolly to John Carstairs Matheson, 10th June 1906, p. 295.

473 Ibid., pp. 296-7.

474 Philip S. Foner, *The Industrial Workers of the World 1905-1917*, New York: International Publishers, 1976, p. 29

475 Verity Burgmann, *Revolutionary Industrial Unionism: the Industrial Workers of the World in Australia*, New York: Cambridge University Press, 1995, p. 12.

476 'Eugene V. Debs' Speech Before the Founding Convention of the I.W.W.', *Proceedings of the First Convention of the Industrial Workers of the World*, New York: New York Labor News Company, 1905, pp. 142-3.

477 Carl Reeve and Ann Barton Reeve, *James Connolly in the United States*, p. 106.

478 Quoted in Paul Buhle and Nicole Schulman (ed.), *Wobblies! A Graphic History of the Industrial Workers of the World*, London: Verso, 2005, p. 8.

479 Ibid.

480 Verity Burgmann, *Revolutionary Industrial Unionism*, p. 12.

481 Ann Huber Trip, *The IWW and the Paterson Strike of 1913*, Urbana: University of Illinois Press, 1987, p. 4.

482 Ralph Darlington, *Radical Unionism: The Rise and Fall of Revolutionary Syndicalism*, Chicago: Haymarket, 2013, p. 97.

483 Paul Frederick Brissenden, *The I. W. W. A Study of American Syndicalism*, New York" Colombia University, 1919, p. 53.

484 Philip S. Foner, *The Industrial Workers of the World 1905-1917*, p. 36.

485 Ibid., pp. 68-9.

486 Bob Holton, *British Syndicalism 1900-1914*, London: Pluto Press, 1976, p. 17.

487 Marcel van der Linden and Wayne Thorpe, 'The Rise and Fall of Revolutionary Syndicalism' in Marcel van der Linden and Wayne Thorpe (eds), *Revolutionary Syndicalism: an international perspective*, Aldershot: Scolar Press, 1990, p. 1.

488 Neville Kirk, *Transnational Radicalism and the Connected Lives of Tom Mann and Robert Samuel Ross*, Liverpool: Liverpool University Press, 2017, pp. 66-8.

489 Ralph Darlington, *Radical Unionism*, p. 90.

490 Neville Kirk, *Transnational Radicalism and the Connected Lives of Tom Mann and Robert Samuel Ross*, p. 6. Kirk speaks here of Tom Mann but his remarks are equally applicable to Connolly and to many other contemporaries.

491 Don K. McKee, 'The Influence of Syndicalism Upon Daniel DeLeon' in *The Historian*, Vol. 20, No. 3, May 1958, p. 284. Philip Foner, too, notes the influence of French syndicalism on the IWW via Trautmann and Father Thomas J. Hagerty, in Philip S. Foner, *The Industrial Workers of the World 1905-1917*, p. 23.

492 Ibid. p. 288.

493 Karl Marx and Friedrich Engels, *The Communist Manifesto*, p. 25.

494 Daniel De Leon, *The Socialist Reconstruction of Society*, https://www.marxists.org/archive/deleon/works/1905/050710.htm (accessed 28 September 2021).

495 Ibid.

496 Ibid.

497 Ibid.

498 Carl Reeve and Ann Barton Reeve, *James Connolly in the United States*, pp. 72-3.

499 Anne Huber Trip, *The IWW and the Paterson Strike of 1913*, Urbana 1987, pp. 84-5.

500 *Proceedings of New Jersey Socialist Unity Conference: including the Manifesto / as adopted and authorized for publication by the Conference; James M. Reilly, Secretary for the Socialist Party; John Hossack, Secretary for Socialist Labor Party*, New Jersey: Publisher unknown, 1906, pp. xiii-xvi.

501 For an account of the events, see Philip S. Foner, *The Industrial Workers of the World 1905-1917*, pp. 40-59.

502 Ibid., p. 43.

503 Ibid., pp. 51-2.

504 John Curtis Kennedy, 'Socialistic Tendencies in American Trade-Unions', in *Journal of Political Economy*, Vol. 15, No. 8, October 1907, p. 474.

505 Philip S. Foner, *The Industrial Workers of the World 1905-1917*, pp. 54, 59.

506 Nunzio Pernicone, *Carlo Tresca: Portrait of a rebel*, New York: Palgrave Macmillan, 2005, p. 22.

507 NLI William O'Brien Papers. MS 13,929/4.

508 Elizabeth Gurley-Flynn, *The Rebel Girl: My First Life 1906-1926*, New York: International Publishers, 1973, p. 74.

509 *Industrial Union Bulletin*, 16 May 1908.

510 C. D. Greaves, *The Life and Times of James Connolly*, p. 197.

511 Ibid., p. 207.

512 Ibid.

513 *Industrial Union Bulletin*, 7 December 1907.

514 Philip S. Foner, *The Industrial Workers of the World 1905-1917*, pp. 64-5, 70.

515 *Industrial Union Bulletin*, 14 December, 1907.

516 *Industrial Union Bulletin*, 28 December, 1907.

517 Donal Nevin, *James Connolly*, p. 257.

518 C. D. Greaves, *The Life and Times of James Connolly*, p. 210.

519 *Industrial Union Bulletin*, 26 October 1907.

520 Donal Nevin, *James Connolly*, p. 258.

521 *Industrial Union Bulletin*, 1 February 1908.

522 Ibid., 1 February 1908.

523 Donal Nevin, *James Connolly*, p. 262.

524 *The Harp*, May 1908.

525 Philip S. Foner, *The Industrial Workers of the World 1905-1917*, p. 100.

526 Ibid., p. 106.

527 Melvyn Dubofsky, *We Shall Be All, a History of the Industrial Workers of the World*, Urbana: University of Illinois Press, 1988, p. 137.

528 Philip S. Foner, *The Industrial Workers of the World 1905-1917*, pp. 108-112.

529 John Carstairs Matheson to James Connolly, 2 April 1908, in Donal Nevin (ed.), *Between Comrades*, p. 353.

530 Raymond Challinor, *The Origins of British Bolshevism*, pp. 46-54.

531 Ibid., p. 90.

532 John Carstairs Matheson to James Connolly, 2 April 1908, in Donal Nevin (ed.), *Between Comrades*, p. 353.

533 Donal Nevin, *James Connolly*, p. 265.
534 'Industrialism and the Trade Unions' in *International Socialist Review* (February 1910).
535 James Connolly to John Carstairs Matheson, April 1908, in Donal Nevin (ed.) *Between Comrades*, p. 355.
536 Carl Reeve and Ann Barton Reeve, *James Connolly in the United States*, p. 170.
537 *The Harp*, January 1908.
538 A. O Cathasaigh (ed.), *The Lost Writings James Connolly*, p. 85.
539 David Howell, *A Lost Left*, p. 74.
540 James R. Barnett, *The Irish Way*, p. 1.
541 *The Harp*, January 1908.
542 *The Harp*, 1 January 1909.
543 James R. Barnett, *The Irish Way*, p. 2.
544 Ibid., p. 4.
545 *The Harp*, April 1908.
546 James R. Barnett, *The Irish Way*, pp. 113-22.
547 Elizabeth Gurley-Flynn, *The Rebel Girl: My First Life 1906-1926*, p. 75.
548 *The Harp*, 1 September 1908.
549 *The Harp*, January 1908.
550 Quoted in David Howell, *A Lost Left,*, p. 77.
551 Carl Reeve and Ann Barton Reeve, *James Connolly and the United States*, p. 166.
552 *The Harp*, 1 July 1908.
553 Carl Reeve and Ann Barton Reeve, *James Connolly and the United States*, p. 166.
554 See James R. Barrett and David R. Roediger, 'The Irish and the "Americanization" of the "New Immigrants" in the Streets and in the Churches of the Urban United States, 1900-1930', in *Journal of American Ethnic History* Vol. 24, No. 4, Summer 2005, pp. 3-33.
555 Carl Reeve and Ann Barton Reeve, *James Connolly and the United States*, p. 166.
556 William P. Jones, 'Review: "Nothing Special to Offer the Negro": Revisiting the "'Debsian View' of the Negro Question'" in *International Labor and Working-Class History*, No. 74 Fall, 2008, pp. 212-224.
557 Eugene V. Debs, 'The Negro In The Class Struggle', *International Socialist Review*, 5 November 1903.
558 See Debs's letter in *International Socialist Review*, Vol. XI, No. 1. July 1910 for his view on immigration controls.
559 William P. Jones, 'Review: "Nothing Special to Offer the Negro"', p. 214.
560 Eugene V. Debs, 'The Negro In The Class Struggle', *International Socialist Review*, 5 November 1903.
561 Ibid.
562 Paul Heidemann, *Class Struggle and the Color Line ; American Socialism and the Race Question, 1900-1930*, Chicago 2018, p. 25.
563 Ira Kipnis, *The American Socialist Movement 1897-1912*, Chicago 2005, p. 134.
564 *The Harp*, 1 June 1908.
565 Carl Reeve and Ann Barton Reeve, *James Connolly in the United States*, p. 85.
566 *Weekly People*, 2 March 1907.
567 *The Harp*, January 1908.

568 James Connolly to John Carstairs Matheson, 30 January 1908, in Donal Nevin (ed.) *Between Comrades*, p. 344.

569 Owen Dudley Edwards and Bernard Ransom (eds.), *James Connolly: Selected Political Writings*, p. 20.

570 Ibid., p. 376.

571 Ibid., p. 264.

572 Ibid., p. 265.

573 Ibid.

574 Ibid., p. 268.

575 Ibid., p. 271.

576 Ibid., p. 272.

577 Karl Marx and Friedrich Engels, *The Communist Manifesto*, p. 25.

578 Karl Marx, *The Civil War in France*, Peking: Foreign Languages Press, 1966, pp. 232-3.

579 'Preface to the German Edition of 1872' in Karl Marx and Friedrich Engels, *The Communist Manifesto*, p. 41. The original quote comes from Karl Marx, *The Civil War In France*, pp. 227-8.

580 Karl Kautsky, *The Class Struggle*, Chicago 1910, p. 11.

581 Ibid., p. 188.

582 Karl Kautsky, *Der Parlamentarismus, die Volksgesetzgebung, und die Sozialdemokratie*, Stuttgart 1893, p. 3, quoted in Massimo Salvadori, *Karl Kautsky and the Socialist Revolution*, London: Verso, 1990, p. 37.

583 Ibid., p. 14.

584 W.K. Anderson, *James Connolly and the Irish Left*, p. 34. While Anderson writes that 'there is no evidence that [Connolly] was aware of French syndicalist theorists' this was not the case for De Leon, who influenced Connolly in turn. This underscores the importance of De Leon as a mediating agent between syndicalist and Marxist ideas.

585 Owen Dudley Edwards and Bernard Ransom (eds), *James Connolly: Selected Political Writings*, p. 272.

586 Ibid., pp. 272-3.

587 Ibid., p. 273.

588 Ibid., p. 284.

589 *The Socialist*, August 1903.

590 Owen Dudley Edwards and Bernard Ransom (eds), *James Connolly: Selected Political Writings*, p. 283.

591 *Workers' Republic*, April 1903.

592 James Connolly to John Carstairs Matheson, 10 June 1909 in Donal Nevin (ed.), *Between Comrades*, pp. 404-405.

593 James Connolly to John Carstairs Matheson, 27 September 1908, in Donal Nevin (ed.), *Between Comrades*, p. 375.

594 Ibid., p. 376.

595 *Owen Dudley Edwards and Bernard Ransom (eds.), James Connolly: Selected Political Writings*, pp. 274-5.

596 Ralph Darlington, *The Political Trajectory of J.T. Murphy*, Liverpool: Liverpool University Press, 1998, pp. 9-10.

597 Owen Dudley Edwards and Bernard Ransom (eds.), *James Connolly: Selected Political Writings*, pp. 288-9.

598 Ibid., p. 288.

599 James Connolly to John Carstairs Matheson, 7 May 1908, in Donal Nevin (ed.), *Between Comrades,* p. 362.

600 John Carstairs Matheson to James Connolly, 8 September 1908, in Ibid., p. 373.

601 James Connolly to John Carstairs Matheson, 7 May 1908, in Ibid., p. 362.

602 Ralph Darlington, *The Political Trajectory of J.T. Murphy,* p. 10.

603 Owen Dudley Edwards and Bernard Ransom (eds), *James Connolly: Selected Political Writings,* p. 275.

604 There is a huge literature on the concept of the 'bourgeois revolution' in Marxist political thought. By far the most comprehensive overview is Neil Davidson, *How Revolutionary Were the Bourgeois Revolutions?,* Chicago: Haymarket, 2012.

605 Daniel De Leon, *Two Pages from Roman History,* New York: New York Labor News Co., 1962, pp. 70-71.

606 Owen Dudley Edwards and Bernard Ransom (eds), *James Connolly: Selected Political Writings,* p. 285.

607 James P. Cannon, 'The IWW: The Great Anticipation [1955]' in James P. Cannon, *The First Ten Years of American Communism: Report of a Participant,* New York: Pathfinder Press, 1980, p. 287.

608 Raymond Challinor, *The Origins of British Bolshevism,* p. 177.

609 Daniel De Leon, *Two Pages from Roman History,* p. 100.

610 Ibid, p. 65.

611 Karl Marx and Friedrich Engels, *The German Ideology,* London: Lawrence and Wishart, 1970, p. 64.

612 Owen Dudley Edwards and Bernard Ransom (eds), *James Connolly: Selected Political Writings,* p. 280.

613 Owen Dudley Edwards and Bernard Ransom (eds), *James Connolly: Selected Political Writings,* p. 243.

614 James Connolly to John Carstairs Matheson, 10 June 1909, in Donal Nevin (ed.), *Between Comrades,* p. 404.

615 J. T. Murphy, *New Horizons,* London: The Bodley Head, 1941, p. 42.

616 Tom Mann, *Tom Mann's Memoirs,* p. 239.

617 Ibid., pp. 240-41.

618 Ibid., p. 241.

619 Allen Ruff, *"We Called Each Other Comrade": Charles H. Kerr & Company, Radical Publishers,* Oakland: PM Press, 2011, p. xxi-xxii.

620 Ibid., pp. 87-8.

621 Ibid., p. x.

622 T. A. Jackson, *Solo Trumpet,* p. 67.

623 Ralph Chaplin, *Wobbly: The Rough-And-Tumble Story Of An American Radical,* Chicago: University of Chicago Press, 1948, p. 105.

624 Allen Ruff, *"We Called Each Other Comrade",* p. 118.

625 Ralph Chaplin, *Wobbly,* p. 105.

626 James Connolly, 'Industrialism and the Trade Unions', *International Socialist Review,* February 1910.

627 The articles were 'Ballots, Bullets, Or –', 'Industrialism and the Trade Unions' and 'Revolutionary Unionism and War' in *International Socialist Review,* October 1909, February 1910 and March 1915.

628   James Connolly, *Socialism Made Easy*, in Owen Dudley Edwards and Bernard Ransom (eds), James Connolly: Selected Political Writings, p. 282.
629   Julie Greene, *Pure and Simple Politics: The American Federation of Labor and political activism, 1881-1917*, Cambridge: Cambridge University Press, 1998, pp. 2-3.
630   Ibid., pp. 107-109.
631   Ibid., p. 221.
632   'Industrialism and the Trade Unions', *International Socialist Review*, February 1910.
633   Ibid.
634   Ibid.
635   David Howell, *A Lost Left*, p. 68.
636   Ralph Darlington, *Radical Unionism*, p. 131.
637   Julie Greene, *Pure and Simple Politics*, pp. 10-11.
638   David Howell, *A Lost Left*, pp. 68-9.
639   E.C. Ford and W.Z. Foster, *Syndicalism*, Chicago 1912, p. 38; quoted in Ralph Darlington, *Radical Unionism*, p. 130.
640   Carl Reeve and Ann Barton Reeve, *James Connolly in the United States*, p. 182.
641   Ibid., p. 185.
642   Ibid., p. 204.
643   George Dangerfield, *The Strange Death of Liberal England*, New York: H. Smith & R. Hass, 1935, p. 214.
644   Bruce K. Murray, 'The Politics of the "People's Budget"', in *The Historical Journal*, Vol. 16, No. 3, September 1973, pp. 555-70.
645   Herbert du Parcq, *Life of David Lloyd George. Vol. 4. Speeches*, London: Caxton Publishing Co., 1912, p. 696
646   W.P. Ryan, *The Irish Labour Movement from the 'Twenties to Our Own Day*, p. 161.
647   Desmond Ryan, *Remembering Sion*, Dublin: A. Barker Ltd., 1934, p. 56.
648   Donal Nevin, *James Connolly*, pp. 279-84.
649   *The Harp*, January 1910.
650   *The Harp*, April 1910.
651   Desmond Ryan (ed.), *Socialism and Nationalism. A Selection from the Writings of James Connolly*, pp. 472-3.
652   Donal Nevin, *James Connolly*, p. 386.
653   Desmond Ryan (ed.), *Socialism and Nationalism. A Selection from the Writings of James Connolly*, pp. 473.
654   William McMullen, 'Introduction' to Desmond Ryan (ed.), *The Workers' Republic: A Selection from the Writings of James Connolly*, p. 200.
655   *Forward*, 11 March 1911.
656   See *Forward*, 3 May 1913, for Connolly's outline of the problem of British Labour support for the Home Rule party.
657   *Forward*, 18 March 1911.
658   Emmet O'Connor, 'Friend or foe? John Redmond and the Irish Labour Movement, 1891-1918', https://pure.ulster.ac.uk/ws/portalfiles/portal/71313099/Friend_or_foe._John_Redmond_and_the_labour_movement.pdf (accessed 18 October 2021).
659   Donal Nevin, *James Connolly*, p. 387.
660   *Forward*, 18 March 1911.
661   *Forward*, 23 August 1913.

662 See John Cunningham, '"Something that is new and strange": the 1911 Irish Trade Union Congress in Galway' in *Journal of the Galway Archaeological and Historical Society*, Vol 64, 2012, pp. 169-82.

663 *Forward*, 1 July 1911.

664 See *The Connolly-Walker controversy on socialist unity in Ireland,* Cork: Cork Workers' Club, 1974 for a collection of the articles by Connolly and Walker.

665 Emmet O'Connor, 'Syndicalism, Industrial Unionism, And Nationalism In Ireland,' in Steven Hirsch and Lucien van der Walt (eds), *Anarchism and Syndicalism in the Colonial and Postcolonial World, 1870-1940: Anarchism and syndicalism in the colonial and postcolonial world, 1870-1940: The praxis of national liberation, internationalism and social revolution,* Leiden: Brill, 2010, p. 197.

666 *Report of the Nineteenth Annual Irish Trades Union Congress,* pp. 12-19.

667 *Forward*, 10 May 1913.

668 Donal Nevin, *James Connolly*, pp. 424-6.

669 *Irish Worker*, 26 August 1911.

670 William McMullen, 'Introduction' to Desmond Ryan (ed.), *The Workers' Republic: A Selection from the Writings of James Connolly,* Dublin: Three Candles, 1951, p. 7.

671 Ironically, several years later, Brathwaite would (as Richard Brannigan) become one of the two treasurers of the Irish Citizen Army (ICA), with Constance Markievicz, and address pro-Home Rule meetings in Belfast alongside Connolly. See Peter Collins, 'The Belfast Labour Movement 1881-1921' in Jürgen Elfer (ed.), *Landlord in Geschichte und Gegenwart,* Stuttgart: Steiner, 1994, p. 90 and Jeffrey Leddin, *The 'Labour Hercules': the Irish Citizen Army and Irish Republicanism 1913-23,* Newbridge: Irish Academic Press, 2019, p. 50.

672 J. W. Boyle, 'The Belfast Protestant Association and the Independent Orange Order, 1901-10', *Irish Historical Studies*, Vol. 13, No. 50, September 1962, pp. 138-9.

673 Henry Patterson, *Class Conflict and Sectarianism,* Belfast: Blackstaff Press, 1980, pp. 60-61.

674 David Howell, *A Lost Left,* p.104; *Forward,* 8 July 1911.

675 *Forward*, 27 May 1911.

676 *Forward*, 8 July 1911.

677 David Howell, *A Lost Left,* p. 104.

678 Resolution on 'Political Action' from the 1896 London Congress of the Second International, quoted in Mike Taber (ed.), *Under the Socialist Banner,* p. 52.

679 *Forward*, 10 June 1911.

680 Julian Wright, *Socialism and the Experience of Time: Idealism and the Present in Modern France,* Oxford 2017, p. 48.

681 Quoted in *Forward,* 1 July 1911; the separation of Norway and Sweden was also famously used by Lenin in his 1914 pamphlet *The Right of Nations to Self-Determination,* to demonstrate that formal political separation, through the advocacy by the workers of the oppressor nation of the right of the oppressed nation to secede, could lead to *closer* ties between workers of both countries.

682 Henry Patterson, *Class Conflict and Sectarianism,* p. 87.

683 Ibid., p. 77.

684 Ibid.

685 William McMullen, 'Introduction' to Desmond Ryan (ed.), *The Workers' Republic: A Selection from the Writings of James Connolly,* p. 3.

686   Donal Nevin, *James Connolly*, p. 429.

687   Henry Patterson, *Class Conflict and Sectarianism*, pp. 77-81.

688   C. D. Greaves, *The Life and Times of James Connolly*, p. 283.

689   A.T.Q. Stewart, *Edward Carson*, Dublin: Gill and Macmillan, 1981, p. 73.

690   Patrick Farrell, *Ireland's England Question*, London: Batsford, 1971, p. 249.

691   Henry Patterson, *Class Conflict and Sectarianism*, p. 88.

692   Ibid.

693   Ibid., p. 89.

694   William McMullen, 'Introduction' to Desmond Ryan (ed.), *The Workers' Republic: A Selection from the Writings of James Connolly*, p. 185.

695   Quoted in David Howell, *A Lost Left*, p. 94.

696   *Forward*, 2 August 1913.

697   Ibid.

698   *Forward*, 23 August 1913.

699   *Forward*, 27 May 1911.

700   David Howell, *A Lost Left*, p. 98.

701   Henry Patterson, *Class Conflict and Sectarianism*, p. 145.

702   *Forward*, 27 May 1911.

703   *Forward*, 5 July 1913.

704   *Forward*, 3 May 1913.

705   *Forward*, 18 April 1914.

706   William McMullen, 'Introduction' to Desmond Ryan (ed.), *The Workers' Republic: A Selection from the Writings of James Connolly*, p. 204.

707   *Forward*, 9 August, 1913; Kieran Allen, *The Politics of James Connolly*, p. 111.

708   *Forward*, 9 August 1913.

709   *Forward*, 12 July 1913.

710   Kieran Allen, *The Politics of James Connolly*, p. 110.

711   C. D. Greaves, *The Life and Times of James Connolly*, p. 292.

712   Quoted in Austen Morgan, *Labour and Partition: the Belfast working class 1905-23*, London: Pluto Press, 1991, p. 166.

713   Ibid.

714   *Forward*, 2 August 1913.

715   Henry Patterson, *Class Conflict and Sectarianism*, p. 144.

716   David Howell, *A Lost Left*, p. 95.

717   *The Harp*, September, 1909.

718   V.I. Lenin, 'Critical Remarks on the National Question', in *Collected Works Vol. 20*, Moscow: Progress Publishers, 1972, pp. 17-51, https://www.marxists.org/archive/lenin/works/1913/crnq/6.htm.

719   Karen Hunt, *Equivocal Feminists*, New York: Cambridge University Press, 1996, p. 37.

720   Ernest Belford Bax, *The Fraud of Feminism*, London: Grant Richards Ltd., 1913, p. 161.

721   Chushichi Tsuzuki, *H.M. Hyndman and British Socialism*, p. 191.

722   Karen Hunt, *Equivocal Feminists*, p. 16.

723   Ibid., p. 81.

724   The following account draws on Ibid., pp. 95-106.

725   *Labour Leader*, 18 January 1896.

726 *Labour Leader,* 15 February 1896.

727 James Connolly, 'Wages, Marriage and the Church', https://www.marxists.org/archive/connolly/1904/condel/conart.htm (accessed 11 June 2021).

728 James Connolly, *Labour, Nationality and Religion,* Dublin: New Books, 1983, p. 16.

729 Ibid., p. 40.

730 Rosemary Cullen Owens, *Smashing Times, a History of the Irish Women's Suffrage Movement 1889-1922,* Dublin: Attic Press, 1984, pp. 20-21.

731 Ibid., pp. 31-2.

732 Ibid., p. 32.

733 Ibid., p. 40.

734 James H. Cousins and Margaret E. Cousins, *We Two Together,* Madras: Ganesh and Co., 1950, p. 164, quoted in Margaret Ward, '"Suffrage First, Above All Else!" An Account of the Irish Suffrage Movement', in *Feminist Review,* No. 10, Spring 1982, p. 24.

735 Quoted in Rosemary Cullen Owens, *Smashing Times,* p. 42.

736 Quoted in James McConnel, 'The Franchise Factor in the Defeat of the Irish Parliamentary Party, 1885-1918', in *The Historical Journal,* Vol. 47, No. 2, June 2004, p. 361.

737 Sylvia Pankhurst, *The Suffragette Movement, an intimate account of persons and ideals,* London: Virago, 1977, p. 382.

738 Rosemary Cullen Owens, *Smashing Times,* pp. 46-7.

739 Margaret Ward, *Unmanageable Revolutionaries: Women and Irish Nationalism,* London: Pluto Press, 1983, p. 67.

740 Senia Pašeta, *Irish Nationalist Women 1900-1917,* Cambridge: Cambridge University Press, 2013, p. 123.

741 R. M. Fox, *Rebel Irishwomen,* Dublin: Talbot Press, 1935, p. 123.

742 Ibid., p. 110.

743 *The Nation,* 26 March 1927.

744 James Connolly to John Carstairs Matheson, 6 June 1913, in Donal Nevin, *Between Comrades,* p. 492.

745 *Irish Citizen,* 15 June 1912.

746 *Irish Citizen,* 3 August 1912.

747 Ibid.

748 Margaret Ward, *Hanna Sheehy-Skeffington: a Life,* Cork: Cork University Press, 1997, p. 115.

749 *Irish Citizen,* 11 January 1913.

750 Desmond Ryan (ed.), *The Workers' Republic,* p. 280.

751 Helga Woggon (ed.), *Ellen Grimley (Nellie Gordon) - Reminiscences of Her Work with James Connolly in Belfast,* p. 24.

752 Quoted in Rosemary Owens, '"Votes for Ladies, Votes for Women": Organised Labour and the Suffrage Movement, 18 76-1922', in *Saothar,* Vol. 9, 1983, pp. 37-8.

753 Mary Davis, *Sylvia Pankhurst: a life in radical politics,* London: Pluto Press, 1999, p. 38.

754 James Connolly, 'The Re-Conquest of Ireland' in *Labour in Ireland,* p. 249.

755 Ibid., p. 228.

756 Ibid., p. 222.

757   See Montefiore's report in *Justice*, 14 December 1907, and also Karen Hunt, *Equivocal Feminists*, pp. 170-73.

758   Ibid., pp. 159-70.

759   Ibid., pp. 182-3.

760   James Connolly, 'The Re-Conquest of Ireland' in *Labour in Ireland*, p. 223 and Dora B. Montefiore, *The Position of Women in the Socialist Movement, 1909*, Marxist Internet Archive, https://www.marxists.org/archive/montefiore/1909/xx/socialist_women.htm (accessed 8 October 2021).

761   *ITUC Report for 1914*, pp. 77-9.

762   Andy Johnston, James Larragy, Edward McWilliams, *Connolly: A Marxist Analysis*, p. 98.

763   *Irish Citizen*, 14 March 1914.

764   See Emmet Larkin, 'Socialism and Catholicism in Ireland' in *Irish Quarterly Review*, Vol. 74, No. 293, Spring 1985, pp. 66-92 for useful background to Kane's lectures.

765   James Connolly to John Carstairs Matheson, 30 January 1908, in Donal Nevin (ed.), *Between Comrades*, p. 344.

766   *Catholic Times*, 8 November 1912 (emphasis added).

767   John Newsinger, '"As Catholic as the Pope:" James Connolly and the Roman Catholic Church in Ireland', in *Saothar*, Vol. 11, 1986, p. 1.

768   James Connolly, *Labour, Nationality and Religion*, p. 16.

769   Ibid., p. 7.

770   John Newsinger, '"As Catholic as the Pope:" James Connolly and the Roman Catholic Church in Ireland', p. 8.

771   Bernard Ransom, 'James Connolly and the Scottish Left 1890-1916', p. 206.

772   Harry McShane and Joan Smith, *No Mean Fighter*, London: Pluto Press, 1978, p. 56.

773   Owen Dudley Edwards and Bernard Ransom (eds.), *James Connolly: Selected Political Writings*, pp. 195-6.

774   V. I. Lenin, 'The Attitude of the Workers' Party to Religion' in *Collected Works*, Moscow 1973, https://www.marxists.org/archive/lenin/works/1909/may/13.htm (accessed 6 June 2021).

775   *Justice*, 14 May 1914.

776   *Manchester Guardian*, 16 January 1911.

777   *Belfast News-Letter*, 1 December 1910.

778   *Justice*, 14 May 1914.

779   See Aindrias Ó Cathasaigh, 'James Connolly and the writing of "Labour in Irish History"', pp. 103-8.

780   Ibid., p. 167.

781   *Justice*, 3 December 1910.

782   James Connolly, 'Labour in Irish History' in *Labour in Ireland*, p. 20.

783   Eric Hobsbawm, 'Karl Marx's Contribution to Historiography' in Robert Blackburn (ed.), *Ideology in Social Science*, London: Fontana, 1972, p. 271.

784   'Peripatetic Professor', in *History Ireland*, Volume 3, Issue 2, Summer 1995.

785   James Connolly, 'Labour in Irish History' in *Labour in Ireland*, p. 11.

786   Karl Marx, *Capital. Volume 3*, Moscow: Progress Publishers, 1971, p. 791. The direct relations of exploitation are, however, not the *only* determinant of a mode of production and the latter cannot therefore be simply reduced to the former. See

Jairus Banaji, *Theory as History*, Chapter 2 'Modes Of Production In A Materialist Conception Of History', Chicago: Haymarket, 2011, pp. 45-101.

787 Karl Marx and Friedrich Engels, *The Communist Manifesto*, p. 3.

788 James Connolly, 'Labour in Irish History' in *Labour in Ireland*, p. 155.

789 Ibid., p. 167.

790 Ibid.

791 A variation of this argument is developed in Andy Johnston, James Larragy, Edward McWilliams, *Connolly: A Marxist Analysis*, Chapters 3 and 4, pp. 37-65.

792 James Connolly, 'Labour in Irish History' in *Labour in Ireland*, p. 7.

793 Ibid., p. 164.

794 Ibid., p. 12.

795 See, for instance, Bernard Ransom, *Connolly's Marxism*, p.118 Kieran Allen, *1916: Ireland's Revolutionary Tradition*, London: Pluto Press, 2016, p. 51, Mike Millotte, *Communism in Modern Ireland: The Pursuit of the Workers' Republic Since 1916*, Dublin: Gill and Macmillan, 1984, p. 10.

796 Quoted in Richard B. Day and Daniel Gaido, *Witnesses to Permanent Revolution*, p. 9.

797 Ibid.

798 Ibid., pp. 32-4, 44-7.

799 Leon Trotsky, *The Permanent Revolution and Results and Prospects*, London: Well Red Books, 2004; Leon Trotsky, *1905* Harmondsworth: Pelican, 1973.

800 Leon Trotsky, *The Permanent Revolution and Results and Prospects*, p. 2

801 Ibid., p. 4.

802 Ibid., p. 152.

803 Ibid., p. 154.

804 Ibid., p. 9.

805 Ibid., p. 152.

806 Austen Morgan, 'Connolly and Connollyism: The Making of a Myth' in *The Irish Review*, No. 5, Autumn 1988, p. 45

807 In the sense meant by Michael Löwy, *Redemption and Utopia: Jewish Libertarian Thought in Central Europe*, Stanford: Stanford University Press, 1988, p. 6, in which when distinct ideas start 'from a certain structural analogy, the relationship consists of a convergence, a mutual attraction, an active confluence, a combination that can go as far as a fusion.'

808 James Connolly, 'Labour in Irish History' in *Labour in Ireland*, p. 9

809 Leon Trotsky, 'Introduction' to Harold Isaacs, *The Tragedy of the Chinese Revolution*, Chicago: Haymarket, 2010, p. xiv

810 Leon Trotsky, *The Permanent Revolution and Results and Prospects*, p. 58.

811 Cynthia E. Smith, 'The Land-Tenure System in Ireland: A Fatal Regime' in *Marquette Law Review*, Volume 76, Issue 2, Winter 1993, p. 476.

812 Fergus Campbell, *Land and Revolution: Nationalist Politics in the West of Ireland 1891-1921*, Oxford: Oxford University Press, 2005, p. 303.

813 *Workers' Republic*, 23 September 1899.

814 Michael Davitt, 'Some Suggestions for a Final Settlement of the Land Question' (1902), in Seamus Deane (ed.), *The Field Day Anthology of Irish Writing*, volume 2, p. 280.

815 *Forward*, 4 October 1913.

816   *The Irish Worker*, 20 December 1913.

817   Margaret Ward, *Hanna Sheehy-Skeffington: A Life*, Dublin: Attic Press, 1997, p. 62.

818   Caroline Nelson, 'Jim Larkin', in *International Socialist Review*, Vol. 14, No. 6, December 1913, p. 335.

819   Emmet Larkin, *James Larkin: Irish labour leader*, London: Pluto Press, 1989, p. xx.

820   John Newsinger, *Rebel City: Larkin, Connolly and the Dublin Labour Movement*, London: Merlin Press, 2004, p. 7

821   *Forward*, 9 May 1914.

822   Adrian Grant, *Irish Socialist Republicanism 1909-36*, Dublin: Four Courts Press, 2012, pp. 28-9.

823   John Newsinger, *Rebel City*, p. 12.

824   *Irish Nation*, 2 January, 1909; quoted in Emmet Larkin, *James Larkin*, p. 62.

825   Donal Nevin, *James Larkin: Lion of the Fold: The Life and Works of the Irish Labour Leader*, Dublin: Gill and Macmillan, 1998, p. 149.

826   Adrian Grant, *Irish Socialist Republicanism 1909-36*, p. 34.

827   John Newsinger, *Rebel City*, p. 15.

828   Emmet O'Connor, *A Labour History of Ireland 1824-1960*, Dublin: Gill and Macmillan, 1992, pp. 68-9.

829   Adrian Grant, *Irish Socialist Republicanism 1909-36*, pp. 13-14.

830   *Irish Worker*, 16 September 1911.

831   Emmet O'Connor, *Syndicalism in Ireland*, Cork: Cork University Press, 1988, p. xiv.

832   *The Irish Worker*, 16 September 1911.

833   Bob Holton, *British Syndicalism, 1900-14: Myths and Realities*, London: Pluto Press, 1976, pp. 207-8; John Newsinger, *Rebel City*, p. 16.

834   *Forward*, 2 February 1914.

835   W.P. Ryan, *The Irish Labour Movement From the 'Twenties to Our Own Day*, p. 195.

836   James Connolly, 'Labour in Dublin', *The Irish Review*, Vol. 3, No. 32, October 1913, pp. 385-9.

837   Emmet O'Connor, 'Syndicalism, Industrial Unionism, and Nationalism in Ireland' in Steven Hirsch and Lucien Van Der Walt (eds.), *Anarchism and syndicalism in the colonial and postcolonial world, 1870-1940*, p. 197.

838   Walter Kendall, *The Revolutionary Movement in Britain, 1900–21*, London: Weidenfeld and Nicolson, 1969, p. 26.

839   Emmet O'Connor, *Syndicalism in Ireland*, p. xiv.

840   *Freeman's Journal*, 14 August and 26 August 1913.

841   Passaged based on figures from John Newsinger, *Rebel City*, p. 3.

842   Quoted in Ibid., pp. 4-5.

843   James Connolly, 'The Re-Conquest of Ireland', in *Labour in Ireland*, p.198.

844   John Newsinger, *Rebel City*, p. 32.

845   *Irish Worker*, 30th August 1913.

846   Emmet Larkin, *James Larkin*, p. 118.

847   *Report of the Dublin Disturbances Commission*, London 1914, [Cd. 7269], p. 2.

848   Emmet Larkin, *James Larkin*, pp. 118-19.

849   Padraig Yeates, *Lockout: Dublin 1913*, Dublin: Gill and Macmillan, 2000, pp. 1, 16.

850   Lorcan Collins, *16Lives: James Connolly*, p. 203.

851   Ibid., p. 204.

852   *Irish Citizen*, 20 September 1913.

853   Irish Workers' Party, *1916 Easter Week 1966*, Dublin 1966, p. 8.

854   *Irish Citizen*, 20 September 1913.

855   *Irish Citizen*, 18 October 1913.

856   *Report of the Dublin Disturbances Commission*, p.6.

857   Emmet Larkin, *James Larkin*, p. 125.

858   John Newsinger, *Rebel City*, p. 49.

859   Ibid., p. 54.

860   *Irish Worker*, 30th August 1913.

861   V. I. Lenin, 'Class War in Dublin', in *Severnaya Pravda*, 5 September 1913, https://www.marxists.org/archive/lenin/works/1913/aug/30.htm (Accessed 17 November 2018).

862   Jimmy Sweeney, 'The Dublin Lock-Out, 1913: The Response of British Labour, in *Saothar*, Vol. 6, 1980, p. 104

863   John Newsinger, *Rebel City*, p. 53.

864   Ibid., p. 107.

865   Fergus A. D'Arcy, 'Larkin and the Dublin Lock-Out' in Donal Nevin (ed.), *James Larkin: Lion of the Fold*, p. 471.

866   John Newsinger, *Rebel City*, p. 89.

867   Huw Richards, *The Bloody Circus: The Daily Herald and the Left by Huw Richards*, London: Pluto Press, 1997, p. 13.

868   Ibid., p. 16.

869   Ibid.

870   Ibid.

871   The phrase is Emmet Larkin's, in Emmet Larkin, *James Larkin*, p. 138.

872   John Newsinger, *Rebel City*, pp. 69-70.

873   Ibid., p. 137.

874   Robert Forrant, Jurg K Siegenthaler, Charles Levenstein and John Wooding (eds), *The Great Lawrence Textile Strike of 1912: New Scholarship on the Bread & Roses Strike*, New York: Baywood Publishing Company, 2014. Marjorie Murphy holds up the tactic as evidence of the 'global transmission of IWW ideas', in 'Jim Larkin, James Connolly, and the Dublin Lockout of 1913: The Transnational Path of Global Syndicalism' in Peter Cole, David Struthers and Kenyon Zimmer (eds), *Wobblies of the World: A Global History of the IWW*, London: Pluto Press, 2017, p. 243.

875   T. R. Sykes, 'Revolutionary Syndicalism in the Italian Labour Movement: The Agrarian Strikes of 1907-1908 in the Province of Parma', *International Review of Social History*, 21, 1976, p. 202.

876   Elizabeth Gurley-Flynn, *The Rebel Girl*, p. 137.

877   Ibid., p. 138.

878   Melvyn Dubofsky, *We Shall Be All*, pp. 146-7.

879   Dora Montefiore, *From a Victorian to a Modern*, 1925, https://www.marxists.org/archive/montefiore/1925/autobiography/13.htm (accessed 22 August 2021).

880   Caroline Nelson, 'Jim Larkin', in *International Socialist Review*, Vol. 14, No. 6, December 1913, p. 335.

881   Dora Montefiore, *From a Victorian to a Modern*.

882   Ibid.

883   Ibid.

884   John Newsinger, *Rebel City,* p. 70.

885   For detailed coverage of the affair, including background to religious fears about proselytism, see Padraig Yeates, *Lockout: Dublin 1913,* p. 247-337.

886   *The Irish Times,* 21st October 1913.

887   Padraig Yeates, *Lockout: Dublin 1913,* p. 266.

888   Ibid.

889   John Newsinger, *Rebel City,* p. 72.

890   *Forward,* 1 November 1913.

891   *Forward,* 1 November 1913.

892   Ibid.

893   *Forward,* 1 November 1913.

894   John Newsinger, *Rebel City,* p. 74.

895   Ibid.

896   *Daily Herald,* 3 November 1913.

897   *The Harp,* September, 1908.

898   *Daily Herald,* 31 October 1913.

899   *Daily Herald,* 30 October 1913.

900   *Irish Citizen,* 8 November 1914.

901   Sylvia Pankhurst, *The Suffragette Movement, an intimate account of persons and ideals,* p. 502.

902   *Daily Herald,* 3 November 1913.

903   Sylvia Pankhurst, *The Suffragette Movement, an intimate account of persons and ideals,* p. 502.

904   *Irish Citizen,* 8 November 1913.

905   Quoted in Les Garner, 'Suffragism and Socialism: Sylvia Pankhurst 1903-1914' in Ian Bullock and Richard Pankhurst (eds), *Sylvia Pankhurst: From Artist to Anti-Fascist,* London: Palgrave Macmillan, 1992, p. 75.

906   Barbara Winslow, *Sylvia Pankhurst: sexual politics and political activism,* London: UCL Press, 1996, p. 64.

907   Les Garner, 'Suffragism and Socialism: Sylvia Pankhurst 1903-1914', p. 75.

908   Ibid., p. 75

909   Æ (George W. Russell), *The Dublin Strike,* Dublin: 'Irish Worker' Press, 1913, p. 2. For the relationship between Russell and Connolly, see Nicholas Allen, 'A Revolutionary Cooperation: George Russell and James Connolly', *New Hibernia Review / Iris Éireannach Nua,* Vol. 4, No. 3, Autumn 2000, pp. 46-64.

910   Ibid., p. 1, John Newsinger, *Rebel City,* p. 76.

911   Ibid., p. 76.

912   *Irish Worker,* 1 November 1913.

913   *Daily Herald,* 10 November 1913.

914   Peter Beresford Ellis, *A History of the Irish Working Class,* London: Pluto Press, 1985, p. 200.

915   Padraig Yeats, *LockOut,* p. 393.

916   Ibid., p. 394.

917   *Daily Herald,* 15 November 1913.

918   *Workers' Republic,* 30 October 1915.

919 Padraig Yeates, *Lockout*, pp. 423-4.

920 Ibid., p. 424.

921 Edward MacLysaght (ed.), *Forth the Banners Go: Reminiscences of William O'Brien*, pp. 118-19.

922 G.D. H. Cole, *The Second International, 1889-1914*, p. 31.

923 Edward MacLysaght (ed.), *Forth the Banners Go: Reminiscences of William O'Brien*, p. 119. To be found among papers relating to the ICA in the O'Brien Papers in the National Library of Ireland, too, is a copy of Harry Quelch's *Social-Democracy and the armed nation: Written for the Social-Democratic Federation*, London 1900.

924 *Irish Worker*, 8 November 1913.

925 John Newsinger, *Rebel City*, p. 55.

926 *Daily Herald*, 17 November 1913.

927 William D. Haywood, 'Jim Larkin's Call for Solidarity', in *International Socialist Review* No. 8, February 1914.

928 Ibid.

929 John Newsinger, *Rebel City*, p. 92.

930 William D. Haywood, 'Jim Larkin's Call for Solidarity', in *International Socialist Review* No. 8, February 1914.

931 Quoted in Donal Nevin ed. *James Larkin: Lion of the Fold*, p. 199.

932 J.T. Murphy, *New Horizons*, p. 38.

933 Ibid., pp. 39-40.

934 Ibid., p. 42.

935 See Edd Mustill, *The Sheffield Workers' Committee: rank and file trade unionism during the First World War*, Nottingham: Spokesman Books, 2018.

936 Ralph Darlington, 'British labour movement solidarity in the 1913-14 Dublin Lockout', *Labor History*, 57:4, 2016, pp. 509-10.

937 Ibid., p. 510.

938 Ibid., p. 511.

939 Bob Holton, *British Syndicalism 1900-1914*, pp. 47-8.

940 For Ablett, see Robert Turnbull, *Climbing Mount Sinai: Noah Ablett 1883-1935*, London: Socialist History Society, 2017.

941 *Daily Herald*, 18 September 1913.

942 Bill Moran, '1913, Jim Larkin and the British Labour Movement' in *Saothar*, Vol. 4, 1978, p. 39.

943 Philip Snowden, *Socialism and syndicalism*, Baltimore 1913, p.243; Bill Moran '1913, Jim Larkin and the British Labour Movement', p. 40.

944 *Daily Herald*, 14 November 1913.

945 *Daily Herald*, 19 November 1913.

946 Bill Moran '1913, Jim Larkin and the British Labour Movement', p. 42.

947 Ibid.

948 *Daily Herald*, 21 November 1913.

949 *Daily Herald*, 20 November 1913.

950 Ibid.

951 *Daily Herald*, 22 November 1913.

952 Bill Moran '1913, Jim Larkin and the British Labour Movement', p. 43.

953 *Daily Herald*, 19 November 1913.

954   *Sheffield Daily Telegraph,* 4 December 1913.

955   G.D.H. Cole and R. Page Arnot, *Trade unionism on the railways, its history and problems,* London: G. Allen and Unwin, 1917, p. 36.

956   *Sheffield Daily Telegraph,* 4 December 1913.

957   Quoted in Ralph Darlington, 'British labour movement solidarity in the 1913-14 Dublin Lockout', *Labor History,* 57:4, p. 516.

958   G.D.H. Cole and R. Page Arnot, *Trade unionism on the railways, its history and problems,* p. 35.

959   Ralph Darlington, 'British labour movement solidarity in the 1913-14 Dublin Lockout', p. 516.

960   R.M. Fox, *The Smoky Crusade,* London: Kimble & Bradford, 1937, p. 172.

961   Bill Moran '1913, Jim Larkin and the British Labour Movement', p. 44.

962   *Daily Herald,* 13 December 1913.

963   Ibid.

964   Bill Moran, '1913, Jim Larkin and the British Labour Movement', pp. 44-5.

965   *Forward,* 9 February 1914.

966   Ibid.

967   *Forward,* 2 February 1914.

968   Ibid.

969   For the syndicalist critique of the trade union bureaucracy in this period, see Ralph Darlington, 'British Syndicalism and Trade-Union Officialdom,' in *Historical Studies in Industrial Relations,* 25/26, Spring/Autumn 2008, pp. 103-40.

970   G.D.H. Cole, *Short History of the British Working Class Movement: 1900-1937,* London: Routledge, 2002, p. 74.

971   *New Age,* 30 April 1914.

972   G.D.H Cole, *Short History of the British Working Class Movement: 1900-1937,* p. 74

973   *New Age,* 30 April 1914.

974   *Workers' Republic,* 12 February 1916.

975   Sidney and Beatrice Webb, *The History of Trade Unionism,* London: Longmans, Green & Co., 1920, pp. 466, 469-70, 586.

976   Ralph Darlington, 'British Syndicalism and Trade-Union Officialdom,' p. 109.

977   *New Age,* 30 April 1914.

978   *Forward,* 2 February 1914.

979   Ibid.

980   *Forward,* 2 February 1914, *Forward,* 23 May 1914.

981   Unofficial Reform Committee, *The Miners' Next Step: Being a Suggested Scheme for the Reorganisation of the Federation [1912],* London: Pluto Press, 1972, p. 15.

982   Ibid., p. 22.

983   George Haupt, *Socialism and the Great War: the collapse of the Second International,* Oxford: The Clarendon Press, 1972, p. 1

984   Second International resolution on 'Militarism and International Conflicts', 1907, in Mike Taber, *Under the Socialist Banner,* p. 105.

985   Marc Mulholland, '"Marxists of Strict Obedience?" The Second International, National Defence, and the Question of War,' in the *Historical Journal,* 58, No. 2, 2015, p. 617.

986   *Forward,* 15 August 1914.

987 George Haupt, *Socialism and the Great War: the collapse of the Second International*, pp. 2-3.

988 Connolly was not alone in his shock at hearing the news that the International's most important sections had fallen in behind their respective government's war efforts. Lenin, upon hearing of the SPD's decision to vote for the Kaiser's war credits, is reported to have said: 'It cannot be … it must be a forged number. Those scoundrels, the German bourgeoisie, have specially published such a number of the *Vorwaerts* in order to compel us also to go against the International.' Grigori Zinoviev, *N. Lenin: his life and work*, Toronto: General Workers Unit of the O.B.U. of Toronto, 1920, p. 32.

989 *Forward*, 15 August 1914.

990 *Forward*, 22 August 1914.

991 *Forward*, 15 August 1914.

992 Quoted in Geoffrey Bell, *Hesitant Comrades: the Irish Revolution and the British Labour Movement*, London: Pluto Press, 2016, p. 3.

993 Ibid., pp. 3-4.

994 *Forward*, 22 August 1914.

995 Quoted in Brian Hanley's Irish Labour History Society (ILHS) lecture, 'Connolly and the war', November 2014, reproduced at https://cedarlounge.wordpress.com/2014/11/06/connolly-and-the-war-brian-hanley-at-the-ilhs-november-2014/ (accessed 9 September 2021).

996 *Irish Worker*, 8 August 1914.

997 *Irish Worker*, 5 September 1914.

998 *Irish Worker*, 8 August 1914.

999 Jeffrey Leddin, *The Labour Hercules*, p. 92.

1000 *Irish Worker*, 8 August 1914.

1001 *Forward*, 15 August 1914.

1002 Kieran Allen, *The Politics of James Connolly*, p. 131.

1003 *International Socialist Review*, March 1915.

1004 Pierre Broué, *The German Revolution 1917-1923*, Leiden: Brill 2005, pp. 14-15.

1005 Kevin J. Callahan, *Demonstration Culture: European Socialism and the Second International, 1889-1914*, p. xviii.

1006 Robert Michels, *Political Parties: A sociological study of the oligarchical tendencies of modern democracy*, Glencoe: Free Press, 1958, p. 406.

1007 Quoted in Marcel Liebman, 'Fifty Years Ago 1914: The Great Schism', in *The Socialist Register*, London: Merlin Press, 1964, p. 283.

1008 Gary Steenson, *Not One Man, Not One Penny*, Pittsburgh: Pittsburg University Press, 1981, p. 96.

1009 Richard B. Day and Daniel Gaido, *Witnesses to Permanent Revolution*, p. 47.

1010 Marc Mulholland, '"Marxists of Strict Obedience?" The Second International, National Defence, and the Question of War,' p. 627.

1011 Pierre Broué, *The German Revolution 1917-1923*, p. 44; H.M. Hyndman & E. Belfort Bax, 'Socialism, Materialism & the War', in *English Review*, XIX, December 1914, p. 69.

1012 *Forward*, 22 August 1914.

1013 V. I. Lenin, 'A Caricature of Marxism and Imperialist Economism', in *Collected Works* Vol 23, Moscow 1964, https://www.marxists.org/archive/lenin/works/1916/carimarx/1.htm#v23pp64h-029 (accessed 28 May 2021).

1014 W. K. Anderson, *James Connolly and the Irish Left*, p. 63; Bernard Ransom, *Connolly's Marxism*, p. 79; Peter Beresford Ellis (ed.), *James Connolly: Selected Writings,* London 1997, p. 25; C. Desmond Greaves, *The Life and Times of James Connolly*, p. 353. For a good discussion of the issue of Connolly and Lenin on the war, see Liam O Ruairc, 'James Connolly, Germany and the First World War: Was Connolly a proto-Lenin?' in *Irish Revolution,* 3 December 2015, https://theirishrevolution.wordpress.com/2015/12/03/james-connolly-germany-and-the-first-world-war-was-connolly-a-proto-lenin/ (accessed 9 September 2021).

1015 The edition was P. J. Musgrove (ed.), *A Socialist and War (1914-1916),* London: Lawrence and Wishart, 1941.

1016 Desmond Ryan (ed.), *Socialism and Nationalism. A Selection from the Writings of James Connolly*, p. 475.

1017 *Irish Worker,* 12 September 1914.

1018 *Irish Worker,* 29 August 1914.

1019 *Irish Worker,* 17 October 1914.

1020 *Forward,* 22 August 1914.

1021 *Irish Worker,* 8 August 1914.

1022 *Workers' Republic,* 18 March 1916.

1023 Ibid.

1024 V. I. Lenin, 'The War and Russian Social-Democracy', 1914, https://www.marxists.org/archive/lenin/works/1914/sep/28.htm (accessed 15 September 2021).

1025 Brian Hanley, '"Look Back in Anger" Ireland and World War One', a paper presented by Brian Hanley at the John Boyle O'Reilly Autumn School, Drogheda, 19 October 2014, https://cedarlounge.wordpress.com/2014/10/27/look-back-in-anger-ireland-and-world-war-one/ (accessed 15 September 2021).

1026 *Workers' Republic,* 18 March 1916.

1027 *Irish Worker,* 17 October 1914.

1028 *Workers' Republic,* 18 September 1915.

1029 *Workers' Republic,* 4th December 1915.

1030 James Connolly, *Socialism Made Easy*, Chicago 1909, in Owen Dudley Edwards and Bernard Ransom (eds), *James Connolly: Selected Political Writings*, p. 273.

1031 Brendan Clifford, *Connolly and German Socialism*, Belfast: Athol Press, 2004, p. 31.

1032 *Workers' Republic,* 9 October 1915.

1033 *Workers' Republic,* 19 February 1916.

1034 James Connolly, 'The Re-Conquest of Ireland' in *Labour in Ireland,* p. 265.

1035 Ibid., p. 266.

1036 Marc Mulholland, 'Irish Labour and the "Co-operative Commonwealth" in the era of the First World War', in Lucy Bland and Richard Carr, *Labour, British radicalism and the First World War,* Manchester 2018, pp. 182-200.

1037 Hillaire Belloc, *The Servile State,* Boston: Le Roy Philips, 1913, Preface, p. xi.

1038 James Hinton, *The First Shop-Stewards Movement,* London: Pluto Press, 1973, p. 46.

1039 Ibid., pp. 29-30.

1040 *Irish Work,* 19 December 1914.

1041 Margaret Skinnider, *Doing My Bit For Ireland,* New York: Century Co., 1917, p. 221.

1042 Francis Sheehy-Skeffington to William O'Brien, 3 August 1914, NLI MS 13,967/7.

1043 Donal Nevin, *James Connolly,* p. 628.

1044 *Forward,* 22 August 1914.

1045 *The Worker,* 16 January 1915.

1046 *Irish Worker,* 22 August 1914.

1047 Sir Basil Thomson, *The Scene Changes,* London: Collins, 1939, p. 284.

1048 Austen Morgan, *James Connolly: a political biography,* p. 234.

1049 Ibid., pp. 139, 199.

1050 For a collection which puts Connolly's writings in the context of wider socialist and anarchist anti-war writings, see A. W. Zurbrugg, (ed.), *Not Our War: Writings Against the First World War,* London: Merlin Press, 2014.

1051 Bernard Ransom, *James Connolly and the Scottish Left 1890-1916,* pp. 312-13.

1052 James Curry, '*The Worker:* James Connolly's "organ of the Irish working-class"' in Mark O'Brien and Felix M. Larkin (eds.), *Periodicals and Journalism in Twentieth-Century Ireland: Writing Against the Grain,* Dublin: Four Courts Press, 2014, pp. 75-6.

1053 *The Worker,* 30 January 1915, https://theworkerhuddersfield.wordpress. com/1915/01/30/six-months-on-the-narrow-road/ (Accessed 23 July 2019). This Huddersfield publication should be distinguished from Connolly's own short-lived 1915 newspaper, also called *The Worker.* For more on anti-war activity in England, see Cyril Pearce, *Comrades in conscience: The Story of an English Community's Opposition to the Great War,* London: Francis Boutle, 2001.

1054 *Forward,* 9 January 1915.

1055 Tom Bell, *Pioneering Days,* p. 49; Bernard Ransom, *James Connolly and the Scottish Left 1890-1916,* p. 311.

1056 *The Worker,* 9 January 1915.

1057 James Curry, '*The Worker:* James Connolly's "organ of the Irish working-class', pp. 84-86.

1058 *Workers' Republic,* 29 May 1915.

1059 David Convery, '"To Increase the Intelligence of the Slave": James Connolly and the Workers' Republic', in *Saothar,* Issue 41, 2016, p. 217.

1060 *Workers' Republic,* 11 September 1915.

1061 John Riddell (ed.), *Lenin's Struggle for a Revolutionary International. Documents: 1907-1916. The Preparatory Years,* New York: Pathfinder Press, 1986, p. 320.

1062 *Workers' Republic,* 25 December 1915.

1063 *Vanguard,* December, 1915.

1064 Leon Trotsky, *My Life,* Middlesex: Penguin Books, 1984, p. 258.

1065 Harry McShane and Joan Smith, *No Mean Fighter,* p. 69.

1066 Bernard Ransom, *James Connolly and the Scottish Left 1890-1916,* p. 314.

1067 *Forward,* 9 January 1915.

1068 *Workers' Republic,* 2 October 1915.

1069 *Workers' Republic,* 31 July 1915.

1070 *Workers' Republic,* 24 July 1915.

1071 John Lovell and B.C. Roberts, A *Short History of the Trades Union Congress,* London: Macmillan, 1968, p. 50.

1072 *Workers' Republic,* 3 July 1915.

1073 *Workers' Republic*, 15 April 1916. Though true of Tillett, this seems a rather unfair characterisation of Mann, who was an opponent of the war.

1074 *Irish Worker*, 8 August 1914.

1075 John Newsinger, 'James Connolly and the Easter Rising' in *Science & Society*, 47, Issue 2, 1983, p. 159.

1076 Desmond Greaves, *The Life and Times of James Connolly*, p. 351.

1077 William O'Brien, 'Introduction' to Desmond Ryan (ed.), *Labour and Easter Week: A Selection from the Writings of James Connolly*, Dublin 1949, p. 1.

1078 Donal Nevin, *James Connolly*, p. 602.

1079 The idea of a wartime break of sorts in Connolly's politics is held by Newsinger, Morgan and Allen, though all in different ways.

1080 Fearghal McGarry, *The Rising: Ireland: Easter 1916*, Oxford: Oxford University Press, 2016, p. 98.

1081 P.H. Pearse, *How does she stand? Three addresses*, Dublin: 'Irish Freedom' Office, 1914, p. 87.

1082 Owen McGee, *The IRB*, p. 353.

1083 Michael Laffan, *The Resurrection Of Ireland: The Sinn Féin Party, 1916-1923*, Cambridge: Cambridge University Press, 1999, p. 13.

1084 Ruth Dudley Edwards, *Patrick Pearse: the Triumph of Failure*, London: Gollancz, 1977, p. 212.

1085 John Newsinger, *Rebel City*, p. 82.

1086 Ibid., p. 83.

1087 Ibid..

1088 Ibid., p. 84.

1089 *Irish Worker*, 14 March 1914.

1090 Emmet O'Connor, 'Taking its natural place: Labour and the third Home Rule crisis, 1912-14' in *Saothar*, Vol. 37, 2012, p. 37.

1091 John Newsinger, *Rebel City*, p. 114.

1092 Quoted in Ibid.

1093 Quoted in Jeffrey Leddin, *Labour Hercules*, p. 57.

1094 John Newsinger, *Rebel City*, p. 114.

1095 Quoted in Jeffrey Leddin, *Labour Hercules*, p. 71.

1096 *Irish Worker*, 30 May 1914.

1097 Charles Townshend, *Easter 1916: The Irish Rebellion*, London: Penguin Books, 2015, p. 52.

1098 *Irish Freedom*, March 1914.

1099 J.J. Lee, *Ireland 1912-1985: Politics and Society*, Cambridge: Cambridge University Press, 1989, p. 20.

1100 *Irish Worker*, 15 August 1914.

1101 Jack Beatty, *The Lost History of 1914: Reconsidering the Year the Great War Began*, New York: Walker and Company, 2012, p. 199.

1102 *Forward*, 1 August 1914.

1103 Jeffrey Leddin, *The Labour Hercules*, p. 73.

1104 *Irish Worker*, 15 August 1914.

1105 Florence O'Donogue, 'Plans for the 1916 Rising' in *University Review*, Vol. 3, No. 1, Spring 1963, p. 8.

1106 Ibid., p. 5.

1107 William O'Brien, 'Introduction' to Desmond Ryan (ed.), *Labour and Easter Week: A Selection from the Writings of James Connolly*, p. 4.

1108 *Irish Worker*, 10 October 1914.

1109 Edward MacLysaght (ed.), *Forth the Banners Go: Reminiscences of William O'Brien*, p. 242.

1110 *Irish Worker*, 17 October 1914.

1111 John Newsinger, *Rebel City*, p. 123.

1112 Michael T. Foy and Brian Barton, *The Easter Rising*, p. 20.

1113 John Newsinger, *Rebel City*, p. 123.

1114 See Emmet O'Connor, 'James Larkin in the United States, 1914-23' in *Journal of Contemporary History*, Vol. 37, No. 2, 2002, pp. 183-96.

1115 Bureau of Military History (BMH), WS 733, p. 8.

1116 C. Desmond Greaves, *The Life and Times of James Connolly*, p. 367.

1117 Helga Woggon, '"Not merely a labour organisation": the ITGWU and the Dublin dock strike, 1915-16', in *Saothar*, Vol. 27, 2002, p. 43.

1118 Jeffrey Leddin, *The Labour Hercules*, p. 102.

1119 Helga Woggon, '"Not merely a labour organisation", pp. 51-2.

1120 Michael T. Foy and Brian Barton, *The Easter Rising*, p. 34.

1121 *Irish Worker*, 30 October 1915.

1122 Michael T. Foy and Brian Barton, *The Easter Rising*, pp. 34-5.

1123 *Workers' Republic*, 13 November 1915.

1124 Michael T. Foy and Brian Barton, *The Easter Rising*, p. 35.

1125 *Workers' Republic*, 4 December, Chief Secretary's Office, Crime Branch: Dublin Metropolitan Police (DMP) Movement of Extremists December 1915, NA CSO/ JD/2/150(1).

1126 *Workers' Republic*, 4 December 1915.

1127 BMH WS 585 pp. 27-8.

1128 Michael T. Foy and Brian Barton, *The Easter Rising*, p. 34.

1129 BMH WS 4.

1130 Donal Nevin, *James Connolly*, p. 628.

1131 BMH WS 1403, pp. 28-9.

1132 Leon Ó Broin, *Revolutionary Underground: the Story of the Irish Republican Brotherhood 1858-1924*, Dublin: Gill and Macmillan, 1976, p. 156.

1133 Feargal McGarry, *The Rising*, p. 105.

1134 See Ibid., pp. 105-6 and Michael T. Foy and Brian Barton, *The Easter Rising*, p. 25.

1135 Michael T. Foy and Brian Barton, *The Easter Rising*, pp. 29, 34.

1136 Ibid., p. 35.

1137 Desmond Ryan, *The Rising: The Complete Story of Easter Week*, Dublin: Golden Eagle Books, 1949, pp. 47-63 and Diarmiud Lynch, *The IRB and the 1916 Insurrection*, Cork: The Mercier Press, 1957, pp. 122-30.

1138 Jeffrey Leddin, *Labour Hercules*, p. 128.

1139 Lorcan Collins, *Connolly*, p. 260 and Jeffrey Leddin, *Labour Hercules*, pp. 127-9.

1140 BMH WS 153, p. 8.

1141 BMH WS 358, p. 8.

1142 Ibid.

1143 WS 6, p. 6. The 'Clarence Mangans' were, presumably, an IRB circle named after the Irish poet James Clarence Mangan.

1144 Michael T. Foy and Brian Barton, *The Easter Rising*, p. 37.

1145 Ibid., pp. 37-8.

1146 See John Newsinger, *Rebel City*, pp. 138-41 for a good overview.

1147 Kieran Allen, *1916,*, p. 34.

1148 Michael T. Foy and Brian Barton, *The Easter Rising*, p. 27.

1149 Ibid.

1150 Fearghal McGarry, *The Rising*, p. 101.

1151 Joost Augusteijn, *Patrick Pearse: The Making of a Revolutionary*, London: Palgrave Macmillan, 2010, p. 294.

1152 J.J. Lee, *Ireland 1912-1985*, p. 25.

1153 Michael T. Foy and Brian Barton, *The Easter Rising*, p. 59.

1154 Ibid., p. 27.

1155 Quoted in Joost Augusteijn, *Patrick Pearse: The Making of a Revolutionary*, p. 305.

1156 R.M. Fox, *History of the Irish Citizen Army*, Dublin 1943, pp. 174-5.

1157 William O'Brien, 'Introduction' to Desmond Ryan (ed.), *Labour and Easter Week: A Selection from the Writings of James Connolly*, p. 21.

1158 Charles Townshend, *Easter 1916*, p. 158.

1159 Quoted in Feargal McGarry, *The Rising*, p. 99.

1160 Kieran Allen, *1916*, p. 37.

1161 Constance Markievicz, *James Connolly's policy and Catholic doctrine*, Dublin: James Adam & Sons Ltd, 1924, pp. 3, 7-9.

1162 Desmond Ryan, *James Connolly: his life and writings*, p. 101.

1163 John Newsinger, *Rebel City*, p. 130.

1164 W. P. Ryan, *The Irish Labour Movement from the 'Twenties to Our Own Day*, p. 163.

1165 C. Desmond Greaves, *The Life and Times of James Connolly*, p. 428.

1166 The emphasis is mine. For a debate between Greaves and John Newsinger on this point, see John Newsinger, 'James Connolly and the Easter Rising,' in *Science and Society*, Vol. XLVII, No.2, Summer 1983, pp. 152-77 and C. Desmond Greaves, 'Connolly and Easter Week: A Rejoinder to John Newsinger' in *Science & Society*, Vol. 48, No. 2, Summer 1984, pp. 220-23.

1167 P. O'Cathasaigh, *The Story of the Irish Citizen Army*, Dublin: Maunsel & Company, Ltd., 1919, p. 52.

1168 David Howell, *A Lost Left*, p. 153-4.

1169 Michael Wheatley, *Nationalism and the Irish Party: Provincial Ireland 1910-1916*, Oxford: Oxford University Press, 2005, p.231.

1170 Fearghal McGarry, *The Rising*, p. 90.

1171 *Workers' Republic*, 22 January 1916.

1172 *Workers' Republic*, 18 September 1915.

1173 *Workers' Republic*, 27 November 1915.

1174 Emmet O'Connor, *Syndicalism in Ireland*, p. 17.

1175 *Workers' Republic*, 7 August 1915.

1176 *Workers' Republic*, 15 April 1916.

1177 Ibid.

1178 Kieran Allen, *1916*, p. 57.

1179 *Workers' Republic*, 22 January 1916.

1180 C. Desmond Greaves, *The Irish Transport and General Workers' Union: the formative years 1909-1923*, Dublin: Gill and Macmillan, 1982, pp. 162-163.

1181 Kieran Allen, *The Politics of James Connolly*, p. 141.

1182 Jeffrey Leddin, *The Labour Hercules*, p. 135.

1183 Lorcan Collins, *16Lives: James Connolly*, p. 263.

1184 Jeffrey Leddin, *The Labour Hercules*, p. 137.

1185 BMH W.S. 705.

1186 *Workers' Republic*, 8 April 1916.

1187 Jeffrey Leddin, *The Labour Hercules*, p. 142.

1188 Kieran Allen, *The Politics of James Connolly*, p. 123.

1189 *Irish Worker*, 22 August 1914.

1190 James Connolly to William O'Brien, 22 August 1914, NLI MS 15698.

1191 Helga Woggon, 'Interpreting James Connolly' in Fintan Lane and Donal O'Drisceoil (eds) *Politics and the Irish Working Class, 1830-1945*, Basingstoke: Palgrave Macmillan, 2005, p. 173.

1192 Jeffrey Leddin, *The Labour Hercules*, p. 101.

1193 Helga Woggon, 'Interpreting James Connolly' in Fintan Lane and Donal O'Drisceoil (eds) *Politics and the Irish Working Class, 1830-1945*, Basingstoke 2005, p. 173.

1194 Tom Bell, *Pioneering Days*, p. 50.

1195 Michael T. Foy and Brian Barton, *The Easter Rising*, p. 36.

1196 'The Citizen Army in Easter Week' by Aindras Ó Cathasaigh, in *1916: James Connolly and the Easter Rising*, Socialist History, 49, 2016, p. 38.

1197 *Workers' Republic*, 18 December 1915.

1198 Fearghal McGarry, *The Rising*, pp. 133-4.

1199 Owen McGee, *The IRB*, p. 355-6.

1200 Kieran Allen, *1916*, p. 31.

1201 Michael T. Foy and Brian Barton, *The Easter Rising*, p. 24.

1202 C. D. Greaves, *The Life and Times of James Connolly*, p. 403 and R.M. Fox, *History of the Irish Citizen Army*, p. 128.

1203 John Newsinger, *Rebel City*, pp. 131-2.

1204 Jeffrey Leddin, *The Labour Hercules*, p. 144-5.

1205 'The Citizen Army in Easter Week' by Aindras Ó Cathasaigh, in *1916: James Connolly and the Easter Rising*, Socialist History, 49, 2016, p. 49.

1206 *Irish Workers' Voice*, 14 May 1932 and republished in *1916 Easter Week 1966*, p. 22.

1207 *Labour News*, 3 April 1937.

1208 *Workers' Republic*, 8 April 1916.

1209 R. M Fox, *Rebel Irishwomen*, p. 127.

1210 Mike Millotte, *Communism in Modern Ireland: the Pursuit of the Workers' Republic since 1916*, pp. 19-20.

1211 W. P. Ryan, *The Irish Labour Movement from the 'Twenties to Our Own Day*, p. 248.

1212 Arthur McManus, 'James Connolly His Life and Work' in *The Communist Review*, May 1924, Vol. 5, No. 1, https://www.marxists.org/history/international/comintern/sections/britain/periodicals/communist_review/1924/01/connolly.htm (Accessed 26 July 2020).

1213 Geoffrey Bell, *Hesitant Comrades*, p. 21.

1214 Ibid., p.15 and see the controversy in *Forward* 4 September and 25 September 1920.

1215 BMH No. WS. 258, p.15. For Ernest Kavanagh's works, see James Curry (ed.), *Ernest Kavanagh, Artist of the Revolution, Introduced and Edited*, Cork: Mercier Press, 2012.

1216 Geoffrey Bell, *Hesitant Comrades*, p. 11.

1217 Ibid.

1218 Ibid.

1219 Ibid., p. 14.

1220 Ibid., p. 94.

1221 Walter Kendall, *The Revolutionary Movement in Britain*, pp. 52-55. For the fascinating story of Peter Petroff, see Kevin Morgan, 'In and out of the swamp: the unpublished autobiography of Peter Petroff' in *Scottish Labour History* 48, 2013, pp. 23-51.

1222 Ibid., pp. 101-104.

1223 Geoffrey Bell, *Hesitant Comrades*, p. 12.

1224 *Justice*, 4 May 1916.

1225 *Vorwaerts*, 20 May 1916 (transl. Edward Maltby).

1226 *Justice*, 18 May 1916.

1227 Geoffrey Bell, *Hesitant Comrades*, p. 19.

1228 Ibid., pp. 19-20.

1229 Ibid., p. 21.

1230 *Woman's Dreadnought*, 6 May 1916, Geoffrey Bell, *Hesitant Comrades*, pp. 12-13.

1231 R. M. Fox, *The Smoky Crusade*, p. 214. For the *Dreadnought's* coverage, also see John Newsinger, *Sylvia Pankhurst, the Easter Rising and the Woman's Dreadnought*, Socialist History Society, 2016.

1232 *Woman's Dreadnought*, 13 May 1916.

1233 For a comprehensive survey of the impact of the Rising on the European left, see Jérôme aan de Wiel, 'The Shots that Reverberated for a Long Time, 1916–1932: The Irish Revolution, the Bolsheviks and the European Left' in *The International History Review*, Vol 44, Issue 1, 2020.

1234 John Riddell (ed.), *Lenin's Struggle for a Revolutionary International*, p. 348.

1235 V. I. Lenin, 'The Discussion On Self-Determination Summed Up', July 1916, in https://www.marxists.org/archive/lenin/works/1916/jul/x01.htm (accessed 6 June 2021).

1236 Yuri Pyatakov, Yevgeniya Bosh, and Nikolai Bukharin, 'These on the Right of Nations to Self-Determination', in John Riddell (ed.), *Lenin's Struggle for a Revolutionary International*, pp. 362-3.

1237 V. I. Lenin, 'The Irish Rebellion of 1916', in John Riddell (ed.), *Lenin's Struggle for a Revolutionary International*, p. 378.

1238 Ibid., p. 377.

1239 Ibid., p. 379.

1240 J.T. Murphy, *Labour Monthly*, Vol. VI, No. 6, June 1924, https://www.marxists.org/archive/murphy-jt/1924/06/x01.htm (accessed 25 August 2020).

1241 Ibid.

1242 Desmond Ryan, *James Connolly, his life, work and writings*, p. 112.

1243 *The Socialist*, April 1919.

1244 Michael Löwy, *Fire Alarm: Reading Walter Benjamin's 'On the Concept of History'*, London: Verso, 2016, pp. 68-70.

1245 Leon Trotsky, *The Transitional Programme: the death agony of capitalism and the tasks for the Fourth International [1938]*, London: New Line Books, 1988, p. 4.

1246 Mike Taber, *Under the Socialist Banner*, pp. 107-109.

1247 Quoted in John Riddell 'Origins of the Anti-Imperialist United Front: The Comintern and Asia, 1919-1925' in Oleksa Drachewych and Ian McKay (eds.) *Left Transnationalism: The Communist International and the National, Colonial, and Racial Questions*, Montreal & Kingston: McGill-Queen's University Press, 2019, p. 100.

1248 'These on the National and Colonial Questions' in John Riddell (ed.), *Workers of the World and Oppressed Peoples, Unite! Proceedings and Documents of the Second Congress, 1920*, New York: Pathfinder Press, 1991, p. 314.

1249 Ibid., p. 315.

1250 Ibid., p. 318.

1251 See, for example, Tony Cliff, *Lenin 1914–1917: All Power to the Soviets*, London 1985.

1252 This point is made recently by Mike Taber in his collection of Second International resolutions, *Under the Socialist Banner*, pp. 7-8. Lars T. Lih, *Lenin Rediscovered: What Is to Be Done? in Context*, Leiden: Brill, 2006, proffers the influential argument that Lenin up until 1914 should be considered an 'Erfurt Socialist', that is to say one upholding the orthodox revolutionary Marxism systematised by Engels, and promoted by Kautsky in the Second International. The Bolsheviks, then, take the revolutionary SPD as their model, contrary to arguments in the Stalinist or Cliffite tradition that see the Bolsheviks has having developed a qualitatively different 'party of a new type'.

1253 Sean Matgamna, *The Left in Disarray*, London: Workers' Liberty Press, 2017, p. 25.

1254 Letter of Invitation to the Congress, 24 January 1919, https://www.marxists.org/history/international/comintern/1st-congress/invitation.htm.

1255 See John McIlroy and Alan Campbell, 'The Socialist Labour Party and the Leadership of Early British Communism', in *Critique*, 48, 4, 2020, pp. 609-59.

1256 Ralph Chaplin, *Wobbly*, p. 298.

1257 William D. Haywood, *The Autobiography of Big Bill Haywood*, New York: International Publishers, 1977, p. 360

1258 Quoted in Ralph Darlington, *Radical Unionism*, p. 186.

1259 For a useful, though critical, account of the allure of the 'soviet ideal' amongst the British left, see Ian Bullock, *Romancing the Revolution: the Myth of Soviet Democracy and the British Left*, Alberta: AU Press, 2011.

1260 Walter Kendall, *The Revolutionary Movement in Britain*, p. 133.

1261 Jack Ross, *The Socialist Party of America: a complete history*, Nebraska: University of Nebraska Press, 2015, p. 100.

1262 V.I. Lenin, 'Decree on Peace', in *Collected Works* XXVI, Moscow, 1964, p. 249.

1263 Emmet O'Connor, *A Labour History of Ireland 1824-1960*, p. 94.

1264 Conor Kostick, 'Labour Militancy during the Irish War of Independence', in Fintan Lane and Donal Ó Drisceoil (eds.), *Politics and the Irish Working Class, 1830–1945*, p. 187.

1265 William O'Brien Papers, NLI MS13908 (i), James Connolly to William O'Brien, 7 October 1914.

1266 Padraic Colum, 'On the Death of James Connolly and Francis Sheehy-Skeffington' in *Mother Earth*, Vol. XI, No. 4, June 1916.

1267 Sylvia Pankhurst, *The Home Front*, London: Hutchinson, 1932, p. 322.

1268 Ibid., pp. 296-7.

1269 Helga Woggon, 'Interpreting James Connolly', pp. 175-6.

1270 Emmet O'Connor, 'True Bolsheviks? The Rise and Fall of the Socialist Party of Ireland, 1917-21' in D. George Boyce and Alan O'Day, *Ireland in Transition, 1867-1921*, London: Routledge, 2004, p. 211.

1271 David Convery, '"As imperialistic as our masters"? Relations between British and Irish communists, 1920–1941,' in *Contemporary British History*, Volume 32, Issue 4, 2018, p. 5.

1272 For the socialist movement after Connolly's death, see W. A. Anderson, *James Connolly and the Irish Left*, Mike Milotte, *Communism in Modern Ireland: the Pursuit of the Workers' Republic since 1916* and Emmet O'Connor, *Reds and the Green: Ireland, Russia and the Communist Internationals, 1919-43*, Dublin: University College Dublin Press, 2004.

1273 On China 1925-27, see Harold Isaacs, *The Tragedy of the Chinese Revolution*.

1274 Henry Patterson, *The Politics of Illusion*, p. 19.

1275 *Workers' Republic*, 8 April 1916.

Index

Ablett, Noah 264

American Federation of Labor (AFL) 118, 142-3, 150, 153-5, 162-3, 181-3

anarchists 15, 22, 26, 40-41, 43-4, 58, 60, 75, 105, 144-5, 270, 350, 353

Ancient Order of Hibernians (AOH) 89, 192, 194, 252, 256, 307, 312

Asquith, Herbert 187, 200, 215-16, 304-6, 311

Aveling, Edward 22, 24, 51, 61

Bakunin, Mikhail 43

Behan, Dominic 356

Belfort Bax, Ernest 22, 24, 32, 103, 128, 207-8

Bell, Tom 119, 120, 123, 130, 136, 335

Bellamy, Edward 79

Belloc, Hilaire 247, 290, 324-5

Bennett, Louie 218

Berger, Victor 118, 164

Bernstein, Eduard 14, 116, 117, 120, 225

Bew, Paul 70-71

Blatchford, Robert 75, 77, 79, 101

Boer War (Second), 99-102, 105, 120, 131, 200, 213, 258

Bolshevism 16, 40, 228, 279, 296, 345, 350-51

Bonar Law, Andrew 200, 323

Burns, John 24, 29, 40, 59, 209

Cannon, James P. 175-6

Carney, Winifred 336

Carpenter, Edward 210

Carpenter, Walter 188, 354

Carson, Edward 200-201, 257-8, 303

Casement, Roger 307, 318, 323, 341

Catholic Church 12, 17-18, 89, 132, 192, 221-3, 250-53, 355

Champion, Henry Hyde 24, 25, 40

Chaplin, Ralph 179-180, 351

Charles H. Kerr Company 17, 19, 74, 179-81, 198, 352

Chartism, Chartists 23-4, 40, 76-7

Chesterton, G. K. 247, 324

Christian Socialism 22, 31, 35, 58, 59, 81, 247

Churchill, Winston 205, 323

Clarion 25, 39, 45, 75, 77, 101, 250, 260

Clarke, Tom 303, 307, 317, 318, 319, 321, 323

Clifford, Brendan 288

Colum, Padraic 353

Commonweal 25, 26, 57, 79

Communist International 16, 348-52

Communist Party of Great Britain (CPGB) 13, 119, 179, 248, 262, 285, 325, 351

Communist Party of Ireland (CPI) 17, 352, 354-5, 48, 52, 54, 135

Confederación Nacional del Trabajo (National Confederation of Labour; CNT) 145, 279

Confédération Générale du Travail (General Confederation of Labor; CGT) 145-6, 183, 260, 282

Connell, Jim 40, 224

Connolly, Lillie (née Reynolds) 21-2, 30

Connolly, Roddy 352, 354

Convery, David 296

Craig, James 200, 303

Daily Herald 186, 241, 247-50, 254-6, 260, 263-7, 269, 341

Daly, P. T. 96-7, 237, 311-12, 314
Dangerfield, George 186, 255
Davitt, Michael 232-3
Debs, Eugene V. 118, 142, 149, 151, 158, 160, 164, 179, 181, 182, 260, 350
De Leon, Daniel 17, 109, 110, 116-20, 124, 127, 129, 130-32, 135, 137, 138-42, 146-148, 150, 156-61, 165, 166, 169-71, 174, 176, 210, 351
De Leonism 19, 118-19, 124, 126, 134, 156, 181, 288, 350-51
Democratic Federation 23-4, 40
Despard, Charlotte 186, 208, 254
Devlin, Joseph 192, 305
Dillon, John 212, 311
Dreyfus, Alfred 114, 132

Engels, Friedrich 19, 23-4, 30, 32-3, 35-6, 56-7, 74, 81-4, 106-9, 116, 139, 147, 179, 207, 223, 225-6
Erin's Hope: the ends and means 66-67, 70, 72-5, 77, 80, 84, 86, 93-4, 107, 112, 132, 224, 226

Fabians 27, 28, 35, 59, 61, 62, 116, 117, 129, 228, 341, 363
Fianna Fáil 17
First World War 15, 20, 187, 206, 234, 247, 276, 285-6, 296, 302, 351
Forward 191, 193, 195, 204, 251, 280, 286, 292, 293, 294, 296, 298, 308, 341, 343
Fox, R. M. 111, 268, 324, 338, 344

Gaelic communism 78, 85-6, 226
Gaelic League 86, 306, 309, 310
Gaelic Revival 69, 86, 95, 225
Galway, Mary 194
German Social Democratic Party (SPD) 14, 43, 98, 106, 110, 116, 139, 168, 197, 207, 259, 282-4, 288, 291-2, 296, 328, 342-3, 350, 389, 397
Glasier, John Bruce 27, 41, 51
Goldman, Emma 353
Gonne, Maud 88, 96, 100, 110, 211, 213, 215
Graham, Peter 13

Gramsci, Antonio 18, 86
The 'Great Unrest' 20, 263, 271, 274
Greaves, C. Desmond 13, 47, 48, 152, 200, 284-5, 313, 325-6, 332, 338
Griffith, Arthur 95-6, 100, 134, 310, 312
Guesde, Jules 44, 116, 119, 198
Gurley Flynn, Elizabeth 151, 160, 249

Hanley, Brian 287
Harp 160-61, 163-7, 170, 172, 177, 184, 189, 214, 224
Haywood, William 'Big Bill' 142, 149-51, 179, 182, 260-61, 266, 351
Hardie, James Keir 33, 34, 37, 48, 59, 66, 79, 90, 97, 98, 173, 246, 277-8, 281, 293, 298
Henderson, Arthur 197, 278, 299, 341
Hobsbawm, Eric 226
Hobson, J. A. 102
Hobson, Bulmer 303, 307, 318, 319, 324, 335
Home Rule 47-8, 55, 57, 59, 63, 69, 78, 87, 89-91, 93, 95, 187, 188, 190-97, 199-203, 205-6, 212, 215-16, 234, 243, 258, 294, 302-5, 307, 311-12, 322
Howell, David 30, 79, 85, 112, 183, 197, 205, 327
Hyndman, Henry Myers 23-4, 31, 32, 35, 43, 51, 65, 74, 80, 112-13, 122, 129, 137-8, 141, 173, 199, 207-8, 278, 284, 297, 342-3, 351

imperialism 15, 19, 97, 99, 102-5, 196, 232, 287, 292, 304, 311, 330, 345, 348
Independent Labour Party (ILP) 30, 34-9, 41, 44-5, 51, 59-61, 79, 81, 120-21, 125-6, 128-9, 138, 190, 191, 193, 195-6, 199, 225, 251, 263, 278, 293, 297, 308, 341-2, 350
Independent Labour Party (Ireland) ILP (I) 200, 204, 215, 302, 334
Industrial unionism 16, 19, 144-6, 149, 152-3, 155, 158-9, 161, 166-7, 169, 172-4, 177-9, 190, 221, 239, 270-71, 282, 288-90, 314, 351
Industrial Workers of the World (IWW) 16, 19, 141-61, 166, 170-71, 173, 175-6, 179, 183, 185, 248-9, 260, 330, 347,

350-51, 356

International Socialist Review (ISR) 160, 179-81, 188, 235, 249, 281, 296, 352

Irish Citizen 212-14, 216, 244, 254, 255

Irish Citizen Army (ICA) 214, 258-9, 303, 304, 305-7, 311-19, 321, 332-6, 338-41, 353

Irish Labour Party 188, 193-4, 200, 238, 334-5, 339, 355

Irish Parliamentary Party (IPP) 187, 191-2, 212, 307, 337

Irish Republican Brotherhood (IRB) 89, 91, 100, 294, 302-4, 306-7, 310-11, 312, 313, 317, 318-21, 326, 335-6, 338

Irish Socialist Federation (ISF) 160-61, 163, 165-6, 185

Irish Socialist Republic Party (ISRP) 19, 42, 53, 60-66, 69-70, 72, 86-93, 96, 97-101, 103-6, 109-14, 116-19, 125-7, 132-6, 140, 160, 170, 188, 189, 223

Irish Trade Union Congress (ITUC) 54-6, 66, 188, 193, 194, 196, 199, 220, 237, 240, 305-6

Irish Transport and General Workers Movement (ITGWU) 17, 145, 184, 185, 188, 193-4, 199, 204, 217, 237-8, 242, 243, 245-6, 248-54, 258, 264-5, 269-70, 274, 293, 296, 302, 303-4, 306, 309, 313-14, 326, 330, 332-5, 340, 350, 351, 354

Irish Women's Franchise League (IWFL) 212, 214-18, 234

Irish Worker 204, 238, 242, 243, 257, 280, 285, 287, 292-4, 301, 306, 307, 309, 310, 326, 334

Jackson, T. A. 112, 179

Jaurès, Jean 114, 198, 277

Johnson, Tom 188, 334, 354

Johnston, Tom 225, 294

Joynes, J. L. 24, 31-2

Justice 24, 25, 31, 35, 39, 40, 44, 51, 52, 58, 59, 66, 75, 97, 116, 122, 123, 124, 125, 126, 127, 128, 130-31, 137, 219, 224, 225, 250, 296, 297, 342-3

Kahan, Boris 132

Kahan, Zelda 342

Kautsky, Karl 14, 74, 102, 104-5, 107, 111, 115-17, 121-2, 133, 168, 179, 225, 228, 283, 331, 347-8

Labour, Nationality and Religion 188, 210, 221, 223

Labour in Irish History 17, 55, 58, 67, 72-3, 86, 221, 223-4

Labriola, Antonio 179

Lalor, James Fintan 66-7, 228, 305

Lanchester, Edith 208-9

Lansbury, George 186, 247, 254-5, 262

Larkin, Delia 218, 250-51, 254

Larkin, Jim 15, 136, 145, 184, 186-7, 193-4, 199, 234-40, 242-6, 249-51, 253, 254, 256-69, 271, 293, 301, 304, 306-7, 311, 313, 350, 352, 354

Lee, H. W. 113, 115, 122

Lehane, Con 62, 112, 126

Lenin, Vladimir 12, 70-72, 104, 115, 117, 206, 223, 246, 275, 284-7, 296, 331, 345-6, 350, 379, 389, 397

Leslie, John 22, 27, 35, 36, 45, 52, 66-9, 72, 80, 95, 127, 343

Liebknecht, Karl 279, 292, 296, 350

Liebknecht, Wilhelm 97

Limavady 58

Lloyd George, David 187, 257

Löwy, Michael 77-8, 348

Luxemburg, Rosa 14, 70-72, 104-5, 111, 116-17, 228, 275, 279, 350

Lynch, Patricia 344

McDermott, Sean 303, 318-19, 320

MacDonald, James Ramsay 159, 278, 341

Maclean, John 297, 342

MacNeill, Eoin 79, 303, 312, 316, 319, 323

McCullough, Denis 303, 318

McManus, Arthur 12, 297-298, 341, 347-8

McMullen, William 190, 195, 199, 201, 203

McShane, Harry 223, 297

Mallin, Michael 293, 313, 316, 336

Mann, Tom 15, 24, 30, 31, 40, 177-8, 183, 263, 270, 273, 300

Mariátegui, José Carlos 85-6

Markievicz, Constance 214, 245, 312, 325, 336

Marx, Eleanor 22, 24, 29, 30, 32, 43, 31, 61, 128, 207-8

Marx, Karl 12, 19, 23, 25, 31-2, 40, 43, 51, 54, 55-7, 66, 72, 74, 81, 82-3, 85, 106, 109, 116, 124, 138-9, 147-8, 156, 168, 177, 179, 180, 197-8, 225-6, 228, 327

Marxist-Leninism, 13, 285

Matheson, John Carstairs 62, 121, 124, 125, 127, 129, 134, 136, 138, 141, 159-60, 166, 171-3, 177, 215, 221, 291

Menshevism 228-9, 275, 279, 296, 355

Melliet, Leo 37, 39, 41-2, 51, 330

Mellows, Liam 355

Millerand, Alexandre 114-17, 119, 121

Milligan, Alice 62

Milligan, Ernest 62, 65, 87, 96

Mitchel, John 228, 315

Molony, Helena 213-215, 293, 333, 336, 340

Montefiore, Dora 186, 207-8, 219-20, 248-51, 254

Morgan, Austen 326

Morgan, Lewis Henry 74-5, 81, 179

Morris, William 22, 24, 33, 41, 43, 57, 78-80, 128, 262

Mulholland, Marc 284, 290

Murphy, J. T. 177, 262-3, 274, 347, 351

Murphy, William Martin 93, 234, 242, 261

neo-romanticism 19, 77-9, 81

Newsinger, John 91, 239, 241, 250, 256, 304, 312, 338

'New Unionism' 19, 27-34

New York Labor News Company 17, 123-4

O'Brien, William 17, 59, 61-2, 63, 111-13, 118, 135-6, 184, 187-8, 201, 237, 259, 291, 302, 310, 312, 314, 317, 319, 324, 334, 354

O'Casey, Sean 303-305, 308, 326

O'Connor, Emmet 15, 193, 237, 240, 305, 329, 352, 354

O'Shannon, Cathal 301, 339, 354

Pankhurst, Sylvia 186, 212, 218-19, 254-6, 296, 344, 353

Paris Commune (1871) 16, 19, 23, 41-3, 58, 114-15, 168, 330, 358, 368

Paris Congress of the Second International (1900) 19, 97, 111, 117-18, 120-21, 124, 198, 347

Parnell, Charles Stewart 48, 89, 99, 222

Parsons, Lucy 40, 144

Partridge, William 237, 251

Patterson, Henry 95, 199, 205

Pearse, Patrick 291, 302, 310, 315, 317, 318-19, 321-2, 324, 330, 336, 340

permanent revolution 228-32

Pethick-Lawrence, Frederick 186, 254

Petroff, Peter 297, 342

Plebs League, 264-5

Plekhanov, Georgi 72, 83

Plunkett, Joseph 310, 318, 319, 320, 321

Plunkett, Geraldine 320

Provisional IRA 13

Quelch, Harry 24, 32, 35, 51, 120, 122, 123, 125-6

Quinlan, Patrick 148, 150-51, 160, 352

Redmond, John 187, 192, 212, 216, 279, 305, 307, 309-13, 328, 337

Ricardo, David 31

Robbins, Frank 332, 339

Rothstein, Theodore 124

Ransom, Bernard 27, 33, 35, 69, 223, 225, 284

Re-Conquest of Ireland, The 219, 289

Russell, George 186, 252, 254, 256

Russian Revolution (1905) 230, 280, 309

Russian Revolution (November 1917) 16

Ryan, Desmond 17, 188, 323, 325

Ryan, W.P 18-19, 188, 239, 247, 325

Sanger, Margaret 210, 248

Scheu, Andreas 24, 41, 128

Scottish Socialist Federation (SSF) 27-8, 33-9, 41, 44-7, 49, 51

Scottish Labour Party 34-5

Second International 13-16, 19-20, 42-4, 69-70, 72, 81, 97-98, 102, 104, 106, 111-17, 119, 146, 168, 176, 180, 197, 201, 206-7, 223, 225, 259, 276, 281-5, 293, 296-7, 301, 327, 331, 344, 346, 347-50
Sexton, James 30, 236-7
Shaw, George Bernard 186, 254, 341
Sheehy Skeffington, Francis 188, 199, 214, 215, 218, 247, 291, 353
Sheehy Skeffington, Hanna 212, 218, 234, 244
Sinn Féin 95-96, 303-4, 306, 312, 325, 343, 352
Social Democratic Federation (SDF) 24, 25, 26-7, 28, 30, 31-2, 35, 40
Socialism Made Easy 19
Socialist Labor Party (SLP) 16, 98, 109, 116, 118-19, 127, 129-30, 132-6, 137-42, 146-8, 150, 152, 156-61, 165-6, 170, 173, 189, 350
Socialist Labour Party (SLP) 114, 122, 173, 189, 207, 263, 264, 273, 278, 290, 293-5, 297, 335, 341, 343-4, 347, 350, 351
Socialist League 22, 25, 26-7, 33
Socialist Party of Great Britain (SPGB) 62, 129-30
Socialist Party of Ireland (SPI) 114, 184, 188, 190-93, 196, 199, 214, 302, 334, 350, 354
Socialist Trades and Labor Alliance (STLA) 118, 139-40, 147, 158, 156
Stalinism, 284-5, 325-6, 348, 355
Stewart, E. W. 62-4, 111, 113, 135, 136, 370
syndicalists, syndicalism 15, 16, 18, 20, 61, 136, 144-6, 148, 158-9, 160, 172, 175, 177, 183-4, 186, 199, 238-41, 247, 260, 262-4, 270, 276, 279, 282, 289, 290, 300, 304,

325, 332, 335, 347, 350-51
Thomas, J. H. 263-4, 267, 268-9, 271
Thompson, William 55-6
Thorne, Will 29-30, 33, 59
Tillett, Ben 29-30, 33, 260, 269, 300
Trade Union Congress (TUC) 28, 29, 59, 183, 246-7, 261, 265-9, 278, 299-300
transnational 14-17, 19-20, 119, 146, 117, 178
Trautmann, William 142, 155, 157, 158, 373
Tresca, Carlo 151, 160
Trotsky, Leon 228-9, 231, 296, 297, 348, 350

Ulster Volunteer Force (UVF) 203, 303, 305, 307-8
Unionists 45, 47-9, 55, 88, 192, 197, 199-206, 224, 303, 305

Walker, William 193-9
Wallace, J. Bruce 58
White, Jack 258, 332
Wolfe Tone, Theobald 90-91, 227, 307
Workers' Republic 63-4, 72, 90, 93, 97-8, 100, 101, 105, 113, 133-4, 135, 177, 224, 285, 288-9, 295-6, 297, 314-17, 320, 322, 326-7, 329, 330, 333, 336, 339

Yates, George 115, 117-22, 124-5, 127-9
Yeats, William Butler 86-7

Zassulich, Vera 83
Zetkin, Clara 208, 248
Zimmerwald Congress 296-7, 344-5